KU-571-158

CATHOLIC HYMNS OLD & NEW

kevin
mayhew

Acknowledgements

The publishers wish to express their gratitude to the copyright holders who have granted permission to include their material in this book.

Every effort has been made to trace the copyright holders of all the songs in this collection and we hope that no copyright has been infringed. Apology is made and pardon sought if the contrary be the case, and a correction will be made in any reprint of this book.

For additional information on the copyright holders please contact the Copyright Department at Kevin Mayhew Ltd (copyright@kevinmayhewltd.com).

Important Copyright Information

We would like to remind users of this hymnal that the reproduction of any hymn texts or music without the permission of the copyright holder is illegal. Details of all copyright holders are clearly indicated.

Most of the song texts and music are covered by a Christian Copyright Licensing (CCL) licence and a Music Reproduction Licence. If you possess a licence, it is essential that you check your instruction manual to ensure that the song you wish to use is covered.

If you are not a member of CCL, or the song you wish to reproduce is not covered by your licence, you must contact the copyright holder direct for their permission.

The reproduction of any music not covered by your licence is both illegal and immoral.

If you are interested in joining CCL they can be contacted at the following address:

Christian Copyright Licensing (Europe) Ltd, Chantry House, 22 Upperton Road, Eastbourne, East Sussex BN21 1BF. Tel: 01323 417711, www.ccli.co.uk

Responsorial psalm texts © The Grail, England. Reprinted by permission HarperCollins Publishers Ltd.

First published in Great Britain in 2008 by
KEVIN MAYHEW LTD
Buxhall, Stowmarket, Suffolk IP14 3BW
Tel: + 44 (0) 1449 737978   Fax: +44 (0) 1449 737834
Email: info@kevinmayhewltd.com

www.kevinmayhew.com

© Copyright 2008 Kevin Mayhew Ltd

Organ/Choir edition
ISBN 978 1 84417 883 4
ISMN M 57024 818 6
Catalogue No: 1414102

Melody edition
ISBN 978 1 84417 884 1
ISMN M 57024 819 3
Catalogue No: 1414101

Words edition (paperback)
ISBN 978 1 84417 993 0
ISMN M 57024 889 6
Catalogue No: 1414103

Words edition
ISBN 978 1 84417 885 8
ISMN M 57024 820 9
Catalogue No: 1414100

Index
ISBN 978 1 84867 075 4
ISMN M57024 935 0
Catalogue No: 1414104

9 8 7 6 5 4 3 2

Cover design by Rob Mortonson
Printed and bound by CPI Group (UK) Ltd, Croydon, CR0 4YY

FOREWORD

Like its predecessors, this new and enlarged edition of *Hymns Old & New* is offered to congregations, clergy and musicians in the sincere hope that it will unite the whole Church community in praise of God.

It contains a wealth of both traditional and modern hymns and we hope that everyone who uses it will find their own favourites here as well as discover new and refreshing material.

Texts have been carefully chosen and edited so that their language is inclusive, and archaic forms have been avoided where possible. An asterisk indicates that a verse may be omitted.

Many tunes appear in a choice of keys so that the requirements of specific congregations, such as older people or children, may be taken into account. Except when unavoidable, no tune goes above E flat or below B flat. Sensitive musicians will know which key to choose.

Full liturgy planning indexes will be found in the melody and organ editions of *Catholic Hymns Old & New* and are also available separately from the publisher.

'Those who sing pray twice' was the oft-quoted encouragement of Saint Augustine.

May *Catholic Hymns Old & New* encourage everyone to 'sing with joy in your hearts to the Lord' (Colossians 3:16).

Kevin Mayhew

1

Carey Landry
© 1979 Carey Landry and North American Liturgy Resources

1. A butterfly, *a butterfly,*
an Easter egg, *an Easter egg,*
a fountain flowing in the park,
a fountain flowing in the park.

   These are signs of new life;
   the life of Jesus the Lord.
   And we sing to him, alleluia!
   We give to him our praise!
   We sing to him alleluia!
   Glory be to him! Glory be to him!
   Glory be to Jesus the Lord!

2. A helping hand, *a helping hand,*
a happy smile, *a happy smile,*
a heart so full of hope and joy,
a heart so full of hope and joy.

3. A cup of wine, *a cup of wine,*
a loaf of bread, *a loaf of bread,*
now blest and broken for us all,
now blest and broken for us all.

2

v. 1 unknown, based on John 13:34-35
vs. 2-4 Aniceto Nazareth, based on John 15 and
1 Corinthians 13. © 1984, 1999 Kevin Mayhew Ltd

A new commandment I give unto you:
that you love one another as I have
    loved you,
that you love one another as I have
    loved you.

1. By this shall all know
   that you are my disciples
   if you have love one for another.
   (Repeat)

*2. You are my friends
   if you do what I command you.
   Without my help you can do nothing.
   (Repeat)

*3. I am the true vine,
   my Father is the gard'ner.
   Abide in me: I will be with you.
   (Repeat)

*4. True love is patient,
   not arrogant nor boastful;
   love bears all things, love is eternal.
   (Repeat)

3

Carey Landry
© 1977 Carey Landry and North American Liturgy Resources

Abba, Abba, Father, you are the potter,
we are the clay, the work of your hands.

1. Mould us, mould us and fashion us
   into the image of Jesus, your Son,
   of Jesus, your Son.

2. Father, may we be one in you,
   as he is in you and you are in him,
   and you are in him.

3. Glory, glory and praise to you,
   glory and praise to you for ever, amen,
   for ever, amen.

4

Damian Lundy (1944-1997)
© 1982 Kevin Mayhew Ltd

1. Abba, Father, from your hands
   the living waters flow.
   In your love you give me joy,
   joy so I may grow.
   Abba, Father, from your hands
   the living waters flow.

2. Jesus, Saviour, from your wounds
   the living waters flow.
   In your love you give me peace,
   peace so I may grow.
   Jesus, Saviour, from your wounds
   the living waters flow.

Continued overleaf

3. Holy Spirit, from your pow'r
   the living waters flow.
   In your love you give me pow'r,
   pow'r so I may grow.
   Holy Spirit, from your pow'r
   the living waters flow.

4. Alleluia! From your life
   the living waters flow.
   In your love you give me joy,
   joy so I may grow.
   Alleluia! From your life
   the living waters flow.

5 Virginia Vissing
© 1974, 1998 Sisters of St Mary of Namur

1. Abba, Father, send your Spirit.
   Glory, Jesus Christ. *(Repeat)*

   Glory, hallelujah, glory, Jesus Christ!
   Glory, hallelujah, glory, Jesus Christ!

2. I will give you living water . . .

3. If you seek me you will find me . . .

4. If you listen you will hear me . . .

5. Come, my children, I will teach
   you . . .

6. I'm your shepherd, I will lead you . . .

7. Peace I leave you, peace I give you . . .

8. I'm your life and resurrection . . .

9. Glory, Father, glory, Spirit . . .

6 Henry Francis Lyte (1793-1847)

1. Abide with me,
   fast falls the eventide;
   the darkness deepens;
   Lord, with me abide:
   when other helpers fail,
   and comforts flee,
   help of the helpless,
   O abide with me.

2. Swift to its close
   ebbs out life's little day;
   earth's joys grow dim,
   its glories pass away;
   change and decay
   in all around I see;
   O thou who changest not,
   abide with me.

3. I need thy presence
   ev'ry passing hour;
   what but thy grace
   can foil the tempter's pow'r?
   Who like thyself
   my guide and stay can be?
   Through cloud and sunshine,
   Lord, abide with me.

4. I fear no foe
   with thee at hand to bless;
   ills have no weight,
   and tears no bitterness.
   Where is death's sting?
   Where, grave, thy victory?
   I triumph still,
   if thou abide with me.

5. Hold thou thy cross
   before my closing eyes;
   shine through the gloom,
   and point me to the skies;
   heav'n's morning breaks,
   and earth's vain shadows flee;
   in life, in death, O Lord,
   abide with me.

7 Denis E. Hurley (1915-2004)
© The Archdiocese of Durban

1. Across the years there echoes still
   the Baptist's bold assertion:
   the call of God to change of heart,
   repentance and conversion.

2. The word that John more boldly spoke
in dying, than in living,
now Christ takes up, as he proclaims
a Father all-forgiving.

3. The erring son he welcomes home
when all is spent and squandered.
He lovingly pursues the sheep
that from the flock has wandered.

4. Forgive us, Lord, all we have done
to you and one another.
So often we have gone our way,
forgetful of each other.

5. Forgetful of the cross they bear
of hunger, want, oppression –
grant, Lord, that we may make amends,
who humbly make confession.

8 John Francis Wade

1. Adeste fideles, læti triumphantes;
venite, venite in Bethlehem;
natum videte regem angelorum:

   venite adoremus, venite adoremus,
   venite adoremus Dominum.

2. Deum de Deo, lumen de lumine,
gestant puellæ viscera:
Deum verum, genitum, non factum:

3. Cantet nunc Io! Chorus angelorum:
cantet nunc aula cælestium;
Gloria in excelsis Deo!

4. Ergo qui natus die hodierna,
Jesu tibi sit gloria:
Patris æterni Verbum caro factum!

9 Taizé Community
© Ateliers et Presses de Taizé

Adoramus te, Domine.
Translation: Lord, we adore you.

The following verses may be sung by a
Cantor:

1. With the angels and archangels:

2. With the patriarchs and prophets:

3. With the Virgin Mary, Mother of God:

4. With the apostles and evangelists:

5. With all the martyrs of Christ:

6. With all who witness to the Gospel
of the Lord:

7. With all your people of the Church
throughout the world.

10 Traditional

Adoramus te, Domine Deus.
Adoramus te, Domine Deus.
Translation: We adore you, O Lord God.

11 Hayward Osborne, based on the Canticle of Daniel
© 1975 Josef Weinberger Ltd

1. All creation, bless the Lord.
Earth and heaven, bless the Lord.
Spirits, powers, bless the Lord.
Praise him for ever.
Sun and moon, bless the Lord.
Stars and planets, bless the Lord.
Dews and showers, bless the Lord.
Praise him for ever.

2. Winds and breezes, bless the Lord.
Spring and autumn, bless the Lord.
Winter, summer, bless the Lord.
Praise him for ever.
Fire and heat, bless the Lord.
Frost and cold, bless the Lord.
Ice and snow, bless the Lord.
Praise him for ever.

3. Night and daytime, bless the Lord.
Light and darkness, bless the Lord.
Clouds and lightning, bless the Lord.
Praise him for ever.
All the earth, bless the Lord.
Hills and mountains, bless the Lord.
Trees and flowers, bless the Lord.
Praise him for ever.

Continued overleaf

4. Springs and rivers, bless the Lord.
Seas and oceans, bless the Lord.
Whales and fishes, bless the Lord.
Praise him for ever.
Birds and insects, bless the Lord.
Beasts and cattle, bless the Lord.
Let all creatures bless the Lord.
Praise him for ever.

5. Let God's people bless the Lord.
Men and women, bless the Lord.
All creation, bless the Lord.
Praise him for ever.
Let God's people bless the Lord.
Men and women, bless the Lord.
All creation, bless the Lord.
Praise him for ever.

12 William Henry Draper (1855-1933) alt.

1. All creatures of our God and King,
lift up your voice and with us sing
alleluia, alleluia!
Thou burning sun with golden beam,
thou silver moon with softer gleam:

*O praise him, O praise him,
alleluia, alleluia, alleluia!*

*2. Thou rushing wind that art so strong,
ye clouds that sail in heav'n along,
O praise him, alleluia!
Thou rising morn, in praise rejoice,
ye lights of evening, find a voice:

*3. Thou flowing water, pure and clear,
make music for thy Lord to hear,
alleluia, alleluia!
Thou fire so masterful and bright,
that givest us both warmth and light:

4. Dear mother earth, who day by day
unfoldest blessings on our way,
O praise him, alleluia!
The flow'rs and fruits that in thee
grow,
let them his glory also show.

5. All you with mercy in your heart,
forgiving others, take your part,
O sing ye, alleluia!
Ye who long pain and sorrow bear,
praise God and on him cast your
care:

*6. And thou, most kind and gentle
death,
waiting to hush our latest breath,
O praise him, alleluia!
Thou leadest home the child of God,
and Christ our Lord the way hath
trod:

7. Let all things their Creator bless,
and worship him in humbleness,
O praise him, alleluia!
Praise, praise the Father, praise the
Son,
and praise the Spirit, Three in One.

13 St Theodulph of Orleans (d. 821)
trans. John Mason Neale (1818-1866)

*All glory, laud and honour,
to thee, Redeemer King,
to whom the lips of children
made sweet hosannas ring.*

1. Thou art the King of Israel,
thou David's royal Son,
who in the Lord's name comest,
the King and blessed one.

*2. The company of angels
 are praising thee on high,
 and mortals, joined with all things
 created, make reply.

*3. The people of the Hebrews
 with palms before thee went:
 our praise and prayer and anthems
 before thee we present.

4. To thee before thy passion
 they sang their hymns of praise:
 to thee now high exalted
 our melody we raise.

5. Thou didst accept their praises,
 accept the prayers we bring,
 who in all good delightest,
 thou good and gracious king.

14 St Theodulph of Orleans (d. 821) trans. John
 Mason Neale (1818-1866) paraphrased Andrew
 Moore (b. 1954). © 2005 Kevin Mayhew Ltd

1. All glory, laud and honour
 to you, redeemer, King,
 to whom the lips of children
 made sweet hosannas ring.

 Sing hosanna! Sing hosanna!
 Sing hosanna to the King of kings!
 Sing hosanna! Sing hosanna!
 Sing hosanna to the King!

2. You are the King of Israel,
 you are David's royal son;
 you came in the name of the Lord,
 the King, the blessèd one.

*3. The company of angels
 are praising you on high;
 and all things that are created,
 with us they make reply:

*4. The people of the Hebrews
 laid palms as before you went:
 our praise and prayers and song
 before you we now present.

5. To you, before you suffered,
 they sang their songs of praise;
 to you, now high exalted,
 our melody we raise:

6. Their praises you did receive,
 take now the prayers we bring,
 who love all that which is good,
 you true and shepherd King.

15 Peter Watcyn-Jones (b. 1944)
 © 1978, 1999 Kevin Mayhew Ltd

1. All God's people, here together,
 worship the King!
 For his love will last for ever,
 worship the King!
 Through life's struggles he'll be with us,
 he'll be guiding, watching o'er us.
 We rejoice, sing hallelujah,
 worship the King!

2. All God's people, pray together,
 peace to the world,
 loving brother, loving sister,
 peace to the world!
 God is love and God is kindness,
 he will guide us through the darkness.
 We rejoice, sing hallelujah,
 peace to the world!

3. All God's people, love each other,
 glory to God!
 Though we die we live for ever,
 glory to God!
 We will enter life eternal,
 chosen, blessed, for every praising.
 We rejoice, sing hallelujah,
 glory to God!

16

Edward Perronet (1726-1792)
adapted by Michael Forster (b. 1946)
© This version 1999 Kevin Mayhew Ltd

1. All hail the pow'r of Jesus' name,
   let angels prostrate fall;
   bring forth the royal diadem

   and crown him, crown him, crown him,
   crown him Lord of all.

2. Crown him, all martyrs of your God,
   who from his altar call;
   praise him whose way of pain you
      trod,

   and crown him . . .

3. O prophets faithful to his word,
   in matters great and small,
   who made his voice of justice heard,
   now crown him . . .

4. All sinners, now redeemed by grace,
   who heard your Saviour's call,
   now robed in light before his face,
   O crown him . . .

*5. Let every tribe and every race
   who heard the freedom call,
   in liberation, see Christ's face,
   and crown him . . .

6. Let every people, every tongue
   to him their heart enthral:
   lift high the universal song
   and crown him . . .

17

Tricia Richards (b. 1960)
© 1987 Thankyou Music.
Administered by worshiptogether.com songs

1. All heav'n declares
   the glory of the risen Lord.
   Who can compare
   with the beauty of the Lord?

For ever he will be
the Lamb upon the throne.
I gladly bow the knee
and worship him alone.

2. I will proclaim
   the glory of the risen Lord.
   Who once was slain
   to reconcile us all to God.
   For ever you will be
   the Lamb upon the throne.
   I gladly bow the knee
   and worship you alone.

18

Based on *Meine Hoffnung stehet feste* by Joachim
Neander (1650-1680). Paraphrased by Robert
Bridges (1844-1930) alt.

1. All my hope on God is founded;
   he doth still my trust renew.
   Me through change and chance he
      guideth,
   only good and only true.
   God unknown, he alone
   calls my heart to be his own.

2. Human pride and earthly glory,
   sword and crown betray his trust;
   what with care and toil he buildeth,
   tow'r and temple, fall to dust.
   But God's pow'r, hour by hour,
   is my temple and my tow'r.

3. God's great goodness aye endureth,
   deep his wisdom, passing thought:
   splendour, light and life attend him,
   beauty springeth out of naught.
   Evermore, from his store,
   new-born worlds rise and adore.

4. Still from earth to God eternal
   sacrifice of praise be done,
   high above all praises praising
   for the gift of Christ his Son.
   Christ doth call one and all:
   ye who follow shall not fall.

19
Roy Turner (b. 1940)
© 1984 Thankyou Music.
Administered by worshiptogether.com songs

1. All over the world the Spirit is moving,
all over the world,
as the prophets said it would be.
All over the world
there's a mighty revelation
of the glory of the Lord,
as the waters cover the sea.

2. All over this land the Spirit is
moving . . .

3. All over the Church the Spirit is
moving . . .

4. All over us all the Spirit is moving . . .

5. Deep down in my heart the Spirit is
moving . . .

20
William Kethe (d. 1594) from *Day's Psalter* (1562) alt.

1. All people that on earth do dwell,
sing to the Lord with cheerful voice;
him serve with fear, his praise forth tell,
come ye before him and rejoice.

2. The Lord, ye know, is God indeed,
without our aid he did us make;
we are his folk, he doth us feed
and for his sheep he doth us take.

3. O enter then his gates with praise,
approach with joy his courts unto;
praise, laud and bless his name always,
for it is seemly so to do.

4. For why? the Lord our God is good:
his mercy is for ever sure;
his truth at all times firmly stood,
and shall from age to age endure.

5. To Father, Son and Holy Ghost,
the God whom heav'n and earth adore,
from us and from the angel-host
be praise and glory evermore.

21
Sebastian Temple (1928-1997)
© 1967 OCP Publications

1. All that I am, all that I do,
all that I'll ever have, I offer now to you.
Take and sanctify these gifts
for your honour, Lord.
Knowing that I love and serve you
is enough reward.
All that I am, all that I do,
all that I'll ever have, I offer now to you.

2. All that I dream, all that I pray,
all that I'll ever make, I give to you
today.
Take and sanctify these gifts
for your honour, Lord.
Knowing that I love and serve you
is enough reward.
All that I am, all that I do,
all that I'll ever have, I offer now to you.

22
Lucien Deiss (b. 1921), based on Psalm 100
© 1966 World Library Publications Inc.

All the earth proclaim the Lord,
sing your praise to God.

1. Serve you the Lord, heart filled with
gladness,
come into his presence, singing for joy.

2. Know that the Lord is our creator,
Yes, he is our Father; we are his own.

3. We are the sheep of his green pasture,
for we are God's people, chosen by
God.

4. Come to the gates bringing
thanksgiving,
O enter the courts while singing in
praise.

5. Our Lord is good, with love enduring,
God's word is abiding now with us all.

Continued overleaf

6. Honour and praise be to the Father,
the Son, and the Spirit, world
without end.

All the earth proclaim the Lord,
sing your praise to God.

23
Michael Cockett (b. 1938)
© McCrimmon Publishing Co Ltd

All the nations of the earth,
praise the Lord who brings to birth
the greatest star, the smallest flow'r.
Alleluia.

1. Let the heavens praise the Lord,
alleluia.
Moon and stars, praise the Lord,
alleluia.

2. Snow-capped mountains, praise the
Lord, alleluia.
Rolling hills, praise the Lord, alleluia.

3. Deep sea water, praise the Lord,
alleluia.
Gentle rain, praise the Lord, alleluia.

4. Roaring lion, praise the Lord, alleluia.
Singing birds, praise the Lord,
alleluia.

5. Earthly monarchs, praise the Lord,
alleluia.
Young and old, praise the Lord,
alleluia.

24
Cecil Frances Alexander (1818-1895)

All things bright and beautiful,
all creatures great and small,
all things wise and wonderful,
the Lord God made them all.

1. Each little flow'r that opens,
each little bird that sings,
he made their glowing colours,
he made their tiny wings.

2. The purple-headed mountain,
the river running by,
the sunset and the morning
that brightens up the sky.

3. The cold wind in the winter,
the pleasant summer sun,
the ripe fruits in the garden,
he made them ev'ry one.

4. The tall trees in the greenwood,
the meadows for our play,
the rushes by the water,
to gather ev'ry day.

5. He gave us eyes to see them,
and lips that we might tell
how great is God Almighty,
who has made all things well.

25
Percy Dearmer (1867-1936)
after John Bunyan (1628-1688) alt.

1. All who would valiant be,
'gainst all disaster,
let them in constancy
follow their Master.
There's no discouragement
shall make them once relent
the first avowed intent
to be a pilgrim.

2. Those who beset them round
with dismal stories,
do but themselves confound –
their strength the more is.
No foe shall stay their might,
though they with giants fight:
they will make good the right
to be a pilgrim.

3. Since, Lord, thou dost defend
   us with thy Spirit,
   we know we at the end
   shall life inherit.
   Then fancies flee away!
   we'll fear not what they say,
   we'll labour night and day
   to be a pilgrim.

26 *Quincunque centum quæritis* (18th century)
   trans. Edward Caswall (1814-1878) alt.
   © *This version 1999 Kevin Mayhew Ltd*

1. All you who seek a comfort sure
   in trouble and distress,
   whatever sorrow vex the mind,
   or guilt the soul oppress.

2. Jesus, who gave himself for you
   upon the cross to die,
   opens to you his sacred heart;
   O, to that heart draw nigh.

3. You hear how kindly he invites;
   you hear his words so blest:
   'All you that labour, come to me,
   and I will give you rest.'

4. What meeker than the Saviour's heart?
   As on the cross he lay,
   it did his murderers forgive,
   and for their pardon pray.

5. Jesus, the joy of saints on high,
   the hope of sinners here,
   attracted by those loving words
   to you I lift my prayer.

6. Wash then my wounds in that dear
        blood
   which forth from you does flow;
   by grace a better hope inspire,
   and risen life bestow.

27 Donald Fishel (b. 1950) alt.
   © *1973 Word of God Music. Administered by CopyCare*

Alleluia, alleluia,
give thanks to the risen Lord,
alleluia, alleluia, give praise to his name.

1. Jesus is Lord of all the earth.
   He is the King of creation.

2. Spread the good news o'er all the earth.
   Jesus has died and is risen.

3. We have been crucified with Christ.
   Now we shall live for ever.

4. God has proclaimed the just reward:
   'Life for us all, alleluia!'

5. Come, let us praise the living God,
   joyfully sing to our Saviour.

28 Michael Cockett (b. 1938), based on Psalm 145
   © *McCrimmon Publishing Co. Ltd*

Alleluia, alleluia!
I will praise the Father for all of my life.
I will sing to my God as long as I live.
Alleluia, alleluia, alleluia!

1. Do not place all your trust in
   a woman or man: they cannot save.
   Their schemes will all perish
   when they yield up their breath
   at the end of their days.

2. But so happy are those who
   will trust in their God: they will find
        help.
   For God is the maker
   of the heavens and earth
   and of all that these hold.

3. All the searchers for justice,
   for freedom, for love, God will fulfil.
   The widow, the orphan,
   and the blind and the lame
   in his love are restored.

29 William Chatterton Dix (1837-1898) alt.
© *This version 1999 Kevin Mayhew Ltd*

1. Alleluia, sing to Jesus,
   his the sceptre, his the throne;
   alleluia, his the triumph,
   his the victory alone:
   hark, the songs of peaceful Sion
   thunder like a mighty flood:
   Jesus, out of ev'ry nation,
   hath redeemed us by his blood.

2. Alleluia, not as orphans
   are we left in sorrow now;
   alleluia, he is near us,
   faith believes, nor questions how;
   though the cloud from sight received
     him
   when the forty days were o'er,
   shall our hearts forget his promise,
   'I am with you evermore'?

3. Alleluia, bread of angels,
   here on earth our food, our stay;
   alleluia, here the sinful
   come to you from day to day.
   Intercessor, friend of sinners,
   earth's redeemer, plead for me,
   where the songs of all the sinless
   sweep across the crystal sea.

4. Alleluia, King eternal,
   he the Lord of lords we own;
   alleluia, born of Mary,
   earth his footstool, heav'n his throne;
   he within the veil has entered
   robed in flesh, our great High Priest;
   he on earth both priest and victim
   in the Eucharistic Feast.

30 Hermann the Lame (d. 1054)

Alma redemptoris mater,
quæ pervia cæli porta manes,
et stella maris, succurre cadenti,
surgere qui curat populo:
tu quæ genuisti, natura mirante,
tuum sanctum Genitorem:
virgo prius ac posterius,
Gabrielis ab ore sumens illud Ave,
peccatorum miserere.

31 Vincent Stuckey Stratton Coles (1845-1929)

1. Almighty Father, Lord most high,
   who madest all, who fillest all,
   thy name we praise and magnify,
   for all our needs on thee we call.

2. We offer to thee of thine own,
   ourselves and all that we can bring,
   in bread and cup before thee shown,
   our universal offering.

3. All that we have we bring to thee,
   yet all is naught when all is done,
   save that in it thy love can see
   the sacrifice of thy dear Son.

4. By this command in bread and cup,
   his body and his blood we plead;
   what on the cross he offered up
   is here our sacrifice indeed.

5. For all thy gifts of life and grace,
   here we thy servants humbly pray
   that thou would'st look upon the face
   of thine anointed Son today.

32 vs. 1-4 John Newton (1725-1807) alt.
v. 5 John Rees (1828-1900)

1. Amazing grace! How sweet the sound
   that saved a wretch like me.
   I once was lost, but now I'm found;
   was blind, but now I see.

*2. 'Twas grace that taught my heart to fear,
and grace my fears relieved.
How precious did that grace appear
the hour I first believed.

3. Through many dangers, toils and snares
I have already come.
'Tis grace that brought me safe thus far,
and grace will lead me home.

4. The Lord has promised good to me,
his word my hope secures;
he will my shield and portion be
as long as life endures.

5. When we've been there a thousand years,
bright shining as the sun,
we've no less days to sing God's praise
than when we first begun.

33 Fred Pratt Green (1903-2000)
© 1974 Stainer & Bell Ltd

1. An upper room did our Lord prepare
for those he loved until the end:
and his disciples still gather there,
to celebrate their risen friend.

2. A lasting gift Jesus gave his own:
to share his bread, his loving cup.
Whatever burdens may bow us down,
he by his cross shall lift us up.

3. And after supper he washed their feet,
for service, too, is sacrament.
In him our joy shall be made complete –
sent out to serve, as he was sent.

4. No end there is! We depart in peace,
he loves beyond our uttermost:
in ev'ry room in our Father's house
he will be there, as Lord and host.

34 William Blake (1757-1827)

1. And did those feet in ancient time
walk upon England's mountains green?
And was the holy Lamb of God
on England's pleasant pastures seen?
And did the countenance divine
shine forth upon our clouded hills?
And was Jerusalem builded here
among those dark satanic mills?

2. Bring me my bow of burning gold!
Bring me my arrows of desire!
Bring me my spear! O clouds unfold!
Bring me my chariot of fire!
I will not cease from mental fight,
nor shall my sword sleep in my hand,
till we have built Jerusalem
in England's green and pleasant land.

35 James Montgomery (1771-1854)

1. Angels from the realms of glory,
wing your flight o'er all the earth;
ye who sang creation's story
now proclaim Messiah's birth:

*Come and worship
Christ, the new-born King;
come and worship,
worship Christ, the new-born King.*

2. Shepherds, in the field abiding,
watching o'er your flocks by night,
God with us is now residing,
yonder shines the infant Light:

3. Sages, leave your contemplations;
brighter visions beam afar:
seek the great Desire of Nations;
ye have seen his natal star:

Continued overleaf

4. Saints before the altar bending,
   watching long in hope and fear,
   suddenly the Lord, descending,
   in his temple shall appear:

   Come and worship
   Christ, the new-born King;
   come and worship,
   worship Christ, the new-born King.

5. Though an infant now we view him,
   he shall fill his Father's throne,
   gather all the nations to him;
   ev'ry knee shall then bow down:

36 James Chadwick (1813-1882)

1. Angels we have heard on high
   sweetly singing o'er our plains,
   and the mountains in reply
   echo still their joyous strains.

   Gloria in excelsis Deo.

2. Shepherds, why this jubilee?
   Why your rapt'rous strain prolong?
   Say, what may your tidings be,
   which inspire your heav'nly song.

3. Come to Bethlehem and see
   him whose birth the angels sing:
   come, adore on bended knee
   th'infant Christ, the new-born King.

4. See within a manger laid,
   Jesus, Lord of heav'n and earth!
   Mary, Joseph, lend your aid
   to celebrate our Saviour's birth.

37 Psalm 99, Grail translation
© 1963, 1986, 1993 The Grail, Harper Collins
Religious. Used by permission.

Arise, come to your God,
sing him your songs of rejoicing!

1. Cry out with joy to the Lord,
      all the earth.
   Serve the Lord with gladness.
   Come before him, singing for joy.

2. Know that he, the Lord, is God.
   He made us, we belong to him,
   we are his people, the sheep of his flock.

3. Go within his gates, giving thanks.
   Enter his courts with songs of praise.
   Give thanks to him and bless his name.

4. Indeed, how good is the Lord,
   eternal his merciful love;
   he is faithful from age to age.

5. Give glory to the Father Almighty,
   to his Son, Jesus Christ, the Lord,
   to the Spirit who dwells in our hearts.

38 Anne Conway (b. 1940), based on Isaiah 55
© 1984 Kevin Mayhew Ltd

1. As earth that is dry
   and parched in the sun
   lies waiting for rain,
   my soul is a desert,
   arid and waste;
   it longs for your word, O Lord.

   Come to the waters, all you who thirst,
   come, now, and eat my bread.

2. Though you have no money,
   come, buy my corn
   and drink my red wine.
   Why spend precious gold
   on what will not last?
   Hear me, and your soul will live.

3. As one on a journey
   strays from the road
   and falls in the dark,
   my mind is a wand'rer,
   choosing wrong paths
   and longing to find a star.

4. The Lord is your light,
   the Lord is your strength,
   turn back to him now,
   for his ways are not
   the ways you would choose,
   and his thoughts are always new.

5. As rain from the mountains
   falls on the land
   and brings forth the seed,
   the word of the Lord
   sinks deep in our hearts,
   creating the flow'r of truth.

39 Maria Parkinson (b. 1956)
© 1978 Kevin Mayhew Ltd

1. As I kneel before you,
   as I bow my head in prayer,
   take this day, make it yours
   and fill me with your love.

   Ave, Maria, gratia plena,
   Dominus tecum, benedicta tu.

2. All I have I give you,
   ev'ry dream and wish are yours;
   mother of Christ, mother of mine,
   present them to my Lord.

3. As I kneel before you,
   and I see your smiling face,
   ev'ry thought, ev'ry word
   is lost in your embrace.

40 Bob Hurd (b. 1950), based on Psalm 41 (42)
© 1988 Bob Hurd. OCP Publications

As the deer longs for running streams,
so I long, so I long,
so I long for you.

1. Athirst my soul for you,
   the God who is my life!
   When shall I see, when shall I see,
   see the face of God?

2. Echoes meet as deep
   is calling unto deep,
   over my head, all your mighty waters,
   sweeping over me.

3. Continually the foe
   delights in taunting me:
   'Where is God, where is your God?'
   Where, O where, are you?

4. Defend me, God, send forth
   your light and your truth,
   they will lead me to your holy
       mountain,
   to your dwelling place.

5. Then I shall go unto
   the altar of my God.
   Praising you, O my joy and gladness,
   I shall praise your name.

41 Martin Nystrom (b. 1956), based on Psalm
41(42):1-2. © 1983 Restoration Music Ltd.
Administered by Sovereign Music UK

1. As the deer pants for the water,
   so my soul longs after you.
   You alone are my heart's desire
   and I long to worship you.

   You alone are my strength, my shield,
   to you alone may my spirit yield.
   You alone are my heart's desire
   and I long to worship you.

Continued overleaf

2. I want you more than gold or silver,
   only you can satisfy.
   You alone are the real joy-giver
   and the apple of my eye.

   You alone are my strength, my shield,
   to you alone may my spirit yield.
   You alone are my heart's desire
   and I long to worship you.

3. You're my friend and you are my
      brother,
   even though you are a king.
   I love you more than any other,
   so much more than anything.

42 William Chatterton Dix (1837-1898) alt.

1. As with gladness men of old
   did the guiding star behold,
   as with joy they hailed its light,
   leading onward, beaming bright;
   so, most gracious Lord, may we
   evermore be led to thee.

2. As with joyful steps they sped,
   to that lowly manger-bed,
   there to bend the knee before
   him whom heav'n and earth adore,
   so may we with willing feet
   ever seek thy mercy-seat.

3. As their precious gifts they laid,
   at thy manger roughly made,
   so may we with holy joy,
   pure, and free from sin's alloy,
   all our costliest treasures bring,
   Christ, to thee our heav'nly King.

4. Holy Jesu, ev'ry day
   keep us in the narrow way;
   and, when earthly things are past,
   bring our ransomed souls at last
   where they need no star to guide,
   where no clouds thy glory hide.

5. In the heav'nly country bright
   need they no created light,
   thou its light, its joy, its crown,
   thou its sun which goes not down;
   there for ever may we sing
   alleluias to our King.

43 Ascribed to Jacopone da Todi (d. 1306)
   trans. Edward Caswall (1814-1878)
   adapted by Michael Forster
   © *This version 2004 Kevin Mayhew Ltd*

1. At the cross she keeps her station,
   treading, in her contemplation,
   ev'ry step his feet have trod.

2. Now she hears the sentence spoken,
   feels her heart by sorrow broken,
   mother of incarnate God.

3. As he lifts his cross, she senses
   all the weight of earth's offences,
   vaunted pride and broken trust.

4. Now she sees his body falling,
   hears his anguished spirit calling,
   God-is-with-us in the dust.

5. On his walk of pain she meets him,
   with a kiss of peace she greets him,
   in the midst of cosmic strife.

6. Then she sees a passing stranger
   share his burden, pain and danger,
   on the road to death and life.

7. One kind face among the rabble,
   one kind act amid the babble,
   sets the image of his face.

8. Once again she sees him stumble,
   watches earth its maker humble,
   sees the majesty of grace.

9. Even now, the Man for Others
   hears the cries of anguished mothers,
   weeping for a world of pain.

10. Mother shares the pains that grieve
him,
feels the stony ground receive him:
earth's Redeemer falls again.

11. Then she sees them strip his body,
wearing still their splendid shoddy,
lest the naked truth be told.

12. Spear-like nails that wound and
gore him
pierce the very wound that bore him
– love so warm, with steel so cold.

13. Yet she stays to see his dying,
hears his voice triumphant crying,
share the agony of grace.

14. Take away the body, slighted,
lest the festival be blighted
by God's ugly, suff'ring face!

15. Then amid his mother's sorrows,
someone else's grave he borrows,
nowhere still to lay his head.

16. All creation waits and wonders,
God the final curtain sunders:
life abundant with the dead!

2. Where the paschal blood is poured,
death's dark angel sheathes his sword;
faithful hosts triumphant go
through the wave that drowns the foe.
Praise we Christ, whose blood was shed,
paschal victim, paschal bread;
with sincerity and love
eat we manna from above.

3. Mighty victim from above,
conqu'ring by the pow'r of love;
thou hast triumphed in the fight,
thou hast brought us life and light.
Now no more can death appal,
now no more the grave enthral:
thou hast opened paradise,
and in thee thy saints shall rise.

4. Easter triumph, Easter joy,
nothing now can this destroy;
from sin's pow'r do thou set free
souls new-born, O Lord, in thee.
Hymns of glory and of praise,
risen Lord, to thee we raise;
holy Father, praise to thee,
with the Spirit, ever be.

44 *Ad regias Agni dapes* (7th century)
trans. Robert Campbell (1814-1868)

1. At the Lamb's high feast we sing
praise to our victorious King,
who hath washed us in the tide
flowing from his piercèd side;
praise we him, whose love divine
gives his sacred blood for wine,
gives his body for the feast,
Christ the victim, Christ the priest.

45 Caroline Maria Noel (1817-1877) alt.

1. At the name of Jesus
ev'ry knee shall bow,
ev'ry tongue confess him
King of glory now;
'tis the Father's pleasure
we should call him Lord,
who, from the beginning,
was the mighty Word.

Continued overleaf

*2. At his voice creation
   sprang at once to sight,
   all the angels' faces,
   all the hosts of light,
   thrones and dominations,
   stars upon their way,
   all the heav'nly orders
   in their great array.

*3. Humbled for a season,
   to receive a name
   from the lips of sinners
   unto whom he came,
   faithfully he bore it,
   spotless to the last,
   brought it back victorious
   when from death he passed.

*4. Bore it up triumphant,
   with its human light,
   through all ranks of creatures
   to the central height,
   to the throne of Godhead,
   to the Father's breast,
   filled it with the glory
   of that perfect rest.

5. In your hearts enthrone him;
   there let him subdue
   all that is not holy,
   all that is not true;
   crown him as your captain
   in temptation's hour;
   let his will enfold you
   in its light and pow'r.

6. Truly, this Lord Jesus
   shall return again,
   with his Father's glory,
   with his angel train;
   for all wreaths of empire
   meet upon his brow,
   and our hearts confess him
   King of glory now.

46 Michael Forster (b. 1946)
© 1992 Kevin Mayhew Ltd

1. At your feet, great God, we offer
   bread, the sign of hope we share;
   all the fullness of creation
   in the feast that you prepare.
   Christ our host, in risen splendour,
   gives us food beyond compare.

2. Now, in humble adoration,
   drawn by grace, we offer here
   wine that speaks of love's oblation,
   life from death and hope from fear.
   Sharing in his cup of sorrow,
   our Redeemer we revere.

3. Here, most holy God, we offer,
   with the saints in full accord,
   hearts and gifts for your acceptance,
   broken dreams to be restored.
   All creation cries for healing;
   you alone such grace afford!

47 Based on Luke 1:28-30

Ave Maria, gratia plena,
Dominus tecum,
benedita tu in mulieribus,
et benedictus fructus ventris tui,
Jesus.

Sancta Maria, Mater Dei,
ora pro nobis peccatoribus
nunc et in hora mortis nostrae.
Amen.

48 'Sister M'

1. Ave Maria, O maiden, O mother,
   fondly thy children are calling on thee;
   thine are the graces unclaimed by
      another,
   sinless and beautiful star of the sea.

Mater amabilis, ora pro nobis,
pray for thy children who call upon thee,
ave sanctissima, ave purissima,
sinless and beautiful star of the sea.

2. Ave Maria, the night shades are falling,
   softly, our voices arise unto thee;
   earth's lonely exiles for succour are
   	calling,
   sinless and beautiful star of the sea.

3. Ave Maria, thy children are kneeling,
   words of endearment are murmured
   	to thee;
   softly thy spirit upon us is stealing,
   sinless and beautiful star of the sea.

49 Unknown (12th century)

Ave, Regina cælorum!
Ave, Domina angelorum!
Salve radix, salve porta,
ex qua mundo lux est orta.
Gaude Virgo gloriosa,
super omnes speciosa:
vale, o valde decora,
et pro nobis Christum exora.

50 Unknown

Ave verum corpus,
natum ex Maria virgine;
vere passum, immolatum in cruce
	pro homine.
Cujus latus perforatum unda fluxit et
	sanguine;
esto nobis praegustatum mortis in
	examine.
O Jesu dulcis! O Jesu pie!
O Jesu fili Mariae.

51 John Raphael Peacey (1896-1971)
based on Ephesians 5:6-20 alt.
© By kind permission of the Revd M. J. Hancock

1. Awake, awake: fling off the night!
   for God has sent his glorious light;
   and we who live in Christ's new day
   must works of darkness put away.

2. Awake and rise, in Christ renewed,
   and with the Spirit's pow'r endued.
   The light of life in us must glow,
   and fruits of truth and goodness show.

3. Let in the light; all sin expose
   to Christ, whose life no darkness
   	knows.
   Before his cross for guidance kneel;
   his light will judge and, judging, heal.

4. Awake, and rise up from the dead,
   and Christ his light on you will shed.
   Its pow'r will wrong desires destroy,
   and your whole nature fill with joy.

5. Then sing for joy, and use each day;
   give thanks for everything alway.
   Lift up your hearts; with one accord
   praise God through Jesus Christ our
   	Lord.

52 Daniel L. Schutte (b. 1947)
© 1981 Daniel L. Schutte and New Dawn Music

1. Awake from your slumber!
   Arise from your sleep!
   A new day is dawning
   for all those who weep.
   The people in darkness
   have seen a great light.
   The Lord of our longing
   has conquered the night.

   Let us build the city of God.
   May our tears be turned into dancing!
   For the Lord, our light and our love,
   has turned the night into day!

Continued overleaf

2. We are sons of the morning;
   we are daughters of day,
   the One who has loved us
   has brightened our way.
   The Lord of all kindness
   has called us to be
   a light for his people
   to set their hearts free.

   Let us build the city of God.
   May our tears be turned into dancing!
   For the Lord, our light and our love,
   has turned the night into day!

3. God is light; in him there is no
      darkness.
   Let us walk in his light,
   his children, one and all.
   O comfort my people;
   make gentle your words,
   proclaim to my city
   the day of her birth.

4. O city of gladness,
   now lift up your voice!
   Proclaim the good tidings
   that all may rejoice!

53 William James Kirkpatrick
Alternative vs. 2 and 3: Michael Forster (b. 1946)
© *Alternative verses 2 and 3 1996 Kevin Mayhew Ltd*

1. Away in a manger,
   no crib for a bed,
   the little Lord Jesus
   laid down his sweet head.
   The stars in the bright sky
   looked down where he lay,
   the little Lord Jesus,
   asleep on the hay.

2. The cattle are lowing,
   the baby awakes,
   but little Lord Jesus,
   no crying he makes.
   I love thee, Lord Jesus!
   Look down from the sky,
   and stay by my side
   until morning is nigh.

3. Be near me, Lord Jesus;
   I ask thee to stay
   close by me for ever,
   and love me, I pray.
   Bless all the dear children
   in thy tender care,
   and fit us for heaven,
   to live with thee there.

Alternative verses 2 and 3

2. The cattle are lowing,
   they also adore
   the little Lord Jesus
   who lies in the straw.
   I love you, Lord Jesus,
   I know you are near
   to love and protect me
   till morning is here.

3. Be near me, Lord Jesus;
   I ask you to stay
   close by me for ever,
   and love me, I pray.
   Bless all the dear children
   in your tender care,
   prepare us for heaven,
   to live with you there.

54 *Finita jam sunt proelia* from *Simphonia Sirenum*
(1695). Trans. Ronald Arbuthnott Knox (1888-1957)
© *Burns & Oates Ltd/Continuum*

1. Battle is o'er, hell's armies flee:
   raise we the cry of victory
   with abounding joy resounding,
   alleluia, alleluia.

2. Christ who endured the shameful tree,
o'er death triumphant welcome we,
our adoring praise outpouring,
alleluia, alleluia.

3. On the third morn from death rose he,
clothed with what light in heav'n
   shall be,
our unswerving faith deserving,
alleluia, alleluia.

4. Hell's gloomy gates yield up their key,
paradise door thrown wide we see;
never-tiring be our choiring,
alleluia, alleluia.

5. Lord, by the stripes men laid on thee,
grant us to live from death set free,
this our greeting still repeating,
alleluia, alleluia.

55 John L. Bell (b. 1949) and Graham Maule (b. 1958)
© 1988 WGRG

1. Be still and know that I am God
and there is none beside me. *(x2)*

2. I am the one who calls you my friends
and there is none beside me.

3. I am the one who never fails
and there is none beside me.

4. I am the one who says 'follow me'
and there is none beside me.

5. Be still and know that I am God
and there is none beside me.

56 Anne Conway (b. 1940)
© Anne Scott (Conway). Used by permission.

1. Be still and know I am with you,
be still, I am the Lord.
I will not leave you orphans,
I leave with you my world. Be one.

2. You fear the light may be fading,
you fear to lose your way.
Be still, and know I am near you.
I'll lead you to the day and the sun.

3. Be glad the day you have sorrow,
be glad, for then you live.
The stars shine only in darkness,
and in your need I give my peace.

57 Unknown, based on Psalm 46

1. Be still and know that I am God. *(x3)*

2. I am the Lord that healeth thee. *(x3)*

3. In thee, O Lord, I put my trust. *(x3)*

58 David J. Evans (b. 1957)
© 1986 Thankyou Music.
Administered by worshiptogether.com songs.

1. Be still, for the presence of the Lord,
the Holy One, is here.
Come, bow before him now,
with reverence and fear.
In him no sin is found,
we stand on holy ground.
Be still, for the presence of the Lord,
the Holy One, is here.

2. Be still, for the glory of the Lord
is shining all around;
he burns with holy fire,
with splendour he is crowned.
How awesome is the sight,
our radiant King of light!
Be still, for the glory of the Lord
is shining all around.

3. Be still, for the power of the Lord
is moving in this place;
he comes to cleanse and heal,
to minister his grace.
No work too hard for him,
in faith receive from him.
Be still, for the power of the Lord
is moving in this place.

59 Katherina von Schlegel (b. 1697)
trans. Jane L. Borthwick, alt.

1. Be still, my soul: the Lord is at your
   side;
   bear patiently the cross of grief and
   pain;
   leave to your God to order and provide;
   in ev'ry change he faithful will remain.
   Be still, my soul: your best, your
   heav'nly friend,
   through thorny ways, leads to a joyful
   end.

2. Be still, my soul: your God will
   undertake
   to guide the future as he has the past.
   Your hope, your confidence let
   nothing shake,
   all now mysterious shall be clear at last.
   Be still, my soul: the tempests still
   obey
   his voice, who ruled them once on
   Galilee.

3. Be still, my soul: the hour is
   hastening on
   when we shall be for ever with the
   Lord,
   when disappointment, grief and fear
   are gone,
   sorrow forgotten, love's pure joy
   restored.
   Be still, my soul: when change and
   tears are past,
   all safe and blessèd we shall meet at
   last.

60 Irish (c. 8th century), trans. Mary Byrne (1880-
1931) and Eleanor Hull (1860-1935)

1. Be thou my vision, O Lord of my
   heart,
   naught be all else to me save that
   thou art;
   thou my best thought in the day and
   the night,
   waking or sleeping, thy presence my
   light.

2. Be thou my wisdom, be thou my
   true word,
   I ever with thee and thou with me,
   Lord;
   thou my great Father, and I thy true
   heir;
   thou in me dwelling, and I in thy care.

3. Be thou my breastplate, my sword for
   the fight,
   be thou my armour, and be thou my
   might,
   thou my soul's shelter, and thou my
   high tow'r,
   raise thou me heav'nward, O Pow'r of
   my pow'r.

4. Riches I need not, nor all the world's
   praise,
   thou mine inheritance through all
   my days;
   thou, and thou only, the first in my
   heart,
   High King of heaven, my treasure
   thou art!

5. High King of heaven, when battle is
   done,
   grant heaven's joy to me, O bright
   heav'n's sun;
   Christ of my own heart, whatever
   befall,
   still be my vision, O Ruler of all.

61 Christopher Walker (b. 1947), based on Psalm 23
© 1985 Christopher Walker. OCP Publications

1. Because the Lord is my shepherd,
   I have ev'rything I need.
   He lets me rest in the meadow
   and leads me to the quiet streams.
   He restores my soul and he leads me
   in the paths that are right:

   Lord, you are my shepherd,
   you are my friend.
   I want to follow you always
   just to follow my friend.

2. And when the road leads to darkness,
   I shall walk there unafraid.
   Even when death is close I have courage
   for your help is there.
   You are close beside me with comfort,
   you are guiding my way:

3. In love you make me a banquet
   for my enemies to see.
   You make me welcome, pouring down
   honour from your mighty hand;
   and this joy fills me with gladness,
   it is too much to bear:

4. Your goodness always is with me
   and your mercy I know.
   Your loving kindness strengthens me
   always as I go through life.
   I shall dwell in your presence for ever,
   giving praise to your name:

62 Damian Lundy (1944-1997), based on Psalm 50
© 1982 Kevin Mayhew Ltd

Behold, the Lamb of God, the Holy One!
Behold, the Lord who died to take our
*   sin.*

1. In your great tenderness forgive my sin.
   My guilt is known to you, my Lord!

2. My sin is constantly before my eyes,
   so wash me whiter than the snow.

3. Give me your joy and take away my
   shame,
   and fill my body with new life.

4. Create in me, O Lord, a heart renewed,
   and keep me always pure and clean.

5. Do not deprive me of your spirit, Lord,
   open my lips to sing your praise!

6. I come to offer you a sacrifice:
   the broken heart you have made new.

63 From the Roman Missal

Benedictus qui venit in nomine
   Domini.
Benedictus qui venit in nomine
   Domini.
Hosanna, hosanna, hosanna in
   excelsis.

Translation:
Blessed is he who comes in the name of
*   the Lord.*
Hosanna in the highest.

64 *O sola magnarum urbium* by Aurelius Clemens
Prudentius (348-413), trans. Edward Caswall
(1814-1878), alt. Michael Forster (b. 1946)
© *This version 1999 Kevin Mayhew Ltd*

1. Bethlehem, of noblest cities
   none can once with you compare;
   you alone the Lord from heaven
   did for us incarnate bear.

2. Fairer than the sun at morning
   was the star that told his birth,
   to the lands their God announcing,
   veiled in human form on earth.

3. Guided by its shining glory
   did the eastern kings appear;
   see them bend, their gifts to offer,
   for a greater King is here.

Continued overleaf

4. Solemn things of mystic meaning!
   incense shows God's presence here,
   gold proclaims his sovereign kingship,
   myrrh foreshadows death and tears.

5. Holy Jesus, in your brightness
   to the gentile world displayed,
   with the Father and the Spirit
   endless praise to you be paid.

65
Bob Gillman (b. 1946)
© 1977 Thankyou Music.
Administered by worshiptogether.com songs

Bind us together, Lord,
bind us together with cords
that cannot be broken.
Bind us together, Lord,
bind us together, Lord,
bind us together in love.

1. There is only one God,
   there is only one King.
   There is only one Body,
   that is why we sing:

2. Fit for the glory of God,
   purchased by his precious Blood,
   born with the right to be free:
   Jesus the vict'ry has won.

3. We are the fam'ly of God,
   we are his promise divine,
   we are his chosen desire,
   we are the glorious new wine.

66
Taizé Community, from Psalm 102
© Ateliers et Presses de Taizé

Bless the Lord, my soul,
and bless God's holy name.
Bless the Lord, my soul,
who leads me into life.

1. It is God who forgives all your guilt,
   who heals ev'ry one of your ills,
   who redeems your life from the grave,
   who crowns you with love and
   compassion.

2. The Lord is compassion and love,
   the Lord is patient and rich in mercy.
   God does not treat us according to
   our sins,
   nor repay us according to our faults.

3. As a father has compassion on his
   children,
   the Lord has mercy on those who
   revere him;
   for God knows of what we are made,
   and remembers that we are dust.

67
v. 1: Unknown. vs. 2 and 3: John Ballantine (b. 1942)
© Vs. 2 and 3 1976 Kevin Mayhew Ltd

1. Bless the Lord, O my soul,
   bless the Lord, O my soul,
   and all that is within me,
   bless his holy name.

2. Praise the Lord . . .

3. Love the Lord . . .

68
vs. 1 and 3 John Keble (1792-1866)
vs. 2 and 4 William John Hall *Psalms and Hymns*
(1836) alt.

1. Blest are the pure in heart,
   for they shall see our God;
   the secret of the Lord is theirs,
   their soul is Christ's abode.

2. The Lord who left the heav'ns
   our life and peace to bring,
   to dwell in lowliness with us,
   our pattern and our King.

3. Still to the lowly soul
   he doth himself impart,
   and for his dwelling and his throne
   chooseth the pure in heart.

4. Lord, we thy presence seek;
   may ours this blessing be:
   give us a pure and lowly heart,
   a temple meet for thee.

69 Aniceto Nazareth, based on the Roman Missal
© 1984 Kevin Mayhew Ltd

1. Blest are you, Lord, God of all creation,
   thanks to your goodness
   this bread we offer:
   fruit of the earth, work of our hands,
   it will become the bread of life.

   Blessed be God! Blessed be God!
   Blessed be God for ever! Amen!
   (Repeat)

2. Blest are you, Lord, God of all creation,
   thanks to your goodness
   this wine we offer:
   fruit of the earth, work of our hands,
   it will become the cup of life.

70 Daniel L. Schutte (b. 1947), based on Psalm 91
© 1976 Daniel L. Schutte and New Dawn Music

Blest be the Lord; blest be the Lord,
the God of mercy, the God who saves.
I shall not fear the dark of night,
nor the arrow that flies by day.

1. He will release me from
   the nets of all my foes.
   He will protect me from their wicked
      hands.
   Beneath the shadow of his wings
   I will rejoice
   to find a dwelling-place secure.

2. I need not shrink before
   the terrors of the night,
   nor stand alone before the light of day.
   No harm shall come to me,
   no arrow strike me down,
   no evil settle in my soul.

3. Although a thousand strong
   have fallen at my side,
   I'll not be shaken with the Lord at
      hand.
   His faithful love is all
   the armour that I need
   to wage my battle with the foe.

71 Edwin Hatch (1835-1889) alt.
© This version 1999 Kevin Mayhew Ltd

1. Breathe on me, Breath of God,
   fill me with life anew,
   that as you love, so may I love,
   and do what you would do.

2. Breathe on me, Breath of God,
   until my heart is pure:
   until my will is one with yours
   to do and to endure.

3. Breathe on me, Breath of God,
   fulfil my heart's desire,
   until this earthly part of me
   glows with your heav'nly fire.

4. Breathe on me, Breath of God,
   so shall I never die,
   but live with you the perfect life
   of your eternity.

72 *Victimae Paschali Laudes* attributed to Wipo of
Burgundy (11th century) trans. Walter Kirkham
Blount (d. 1717)

1. Bring, all ye dear-bought nations,
      bring,
   your richest praises to your King,
   alleluia, alleluia,
   that spotless Lamb, who more than
      due,
   paid for his sheep, and those sheep
      you,

   alleluia!

Continued overleaf

2. That guiltless Son, who bought your
      peace,
   and made his Father's anger cease,
   alleluia, alleluia,
   then, life and death together fought,
   each to a strange extreme were brought.

   alleluia!

3. Life died, but soon revived again,
   and even death by it was slain,
   alleluia, alleluia.
   Say, happy Magdalen, O, say,
   what didst thou see there by the way?

4. 'I saw the tomb of my dear Lord,
   I saw himself, and him adored,
   alleluia, alleluia,
   I saw the napkin and the sheet,
   that bound his head and wrapped his
      feet.'

5. 'I heard the angels witness bear,
   Jesus is ris'n; he is not here,
   alleluia, alleluia;
   go, tell his foll'wers they shall see
   thine and their hope in Galilee.'

6. We, Lord, with faithful hearts and voice,
   on this thy rising day rejoice,
   alleluia, alleluia.
   O thou, whose power o'ercame the
      grave,
   by grace and love us sinners save.

73 A Sister of Notre Dame

1. Bring flow'rs of the rarest,
   bring blossoms the fairest,
   from garden and woodland and
      hillside and dale;
   our full hearts are swelling,
   our glad voices telling
   the praise of the lovelist flow'r of the vale.

*O Mary, we crown thee with blossoms
   today,
Queen of the angels and Queen of the
   May.
O Mary, we crown thee with blossoms
   today,
Queen of the angels and Queen of the
   May.*

2. Their lady they name thee,
   their mistress proclaim thee.
   O, grant that thy children on earth
      be as true,
   as long as the bowers
   are radiant with flowers
   as long as the azure shall keep its
      bright hue.

3. Sing gaily in chorus,
   the bright angels o'er us
   re-echo the strains we begin upon earth;
   their harps are repeating
   the notes of our greeting,
   for Mary herself is the cause of our
      mirth.

74 Janet Lunt (b. 1954)
© 1978 Sovereign Music UK

*Broken for me, broken for you,
the body of Jesus, broken for you.*

1. He offered his body, he poured out
      his soul;
   Jesus was broken, that we might be
      whole.

2. Come to my table and with me dine;
   eat of my bread and drink of my
      wine.

3. This is my body given for you;
   eat it remembering I died for you.

4. This is my blood I shed for you,
   for your forgiveness, making you new.

75

Richard Gillard (b. 1953)
© 1977 Scripture in Song/Marantha! Music.
Administered by CopyCare

1. Brother, sister, let me serve you,
   let me be as Christ to you;
   pray that I may have the grace to
   let you be my servant, too.

2. We are pilgrims on a journey,
   fellow trav'llers on the road;
   we are here to help each other
   walk the mile and bear the load.

3. I will hold the Christlight for you
   in the night-time of your fear;
   I will hold my hand out to you,
   speak the peace you long to hear.

4. I will weep when you are weeping;
   when you laugh, I'll laugh with you.
   I will share your joy and sorrow
   till we've seen this journey through.

5. When we sing to God in heaven,
   we shall find such harmony,
   born of all we've known together
   of Christ's love and agony.

6. Brother, sister, let me serve you,
   let me be as Christ to you;
   pray that I may have the grace to
   let you be my servant, too.

76

Frederick William Faber (1814-1863)

1. By the blood that flowed from thee
   in thy grievous agony;
   by the traitor's guileful kiss,
   filling up thy bitterness;

   Jesus, Saviour, hear our cry;
   thou wert suff'ring once as we:
   now enthroned in majesty
   countless angels sing to thee.

2. By the cords that, round thee cast,
   bound thee to the pillar fast,
   by the scourge so meekly borne,
   by the purple robe of scorn.

3. By the thorns that crowned thy head;
   by the sceptre of a reed;
   by thy foes on bended knee,
   mocking at thy royalty.

4. By the people's cruel jeers;
   by the holy women's tears;
   by thy footsteps, faint and slow,
   weighed beneath thy cross of woe.

5. By thy weeping mother's woe;
   by the sword that pierced her through,
   when in anguish standing by,
   on the cross she saw thee die.

77

From Psalm 137
© Copyright Control

1. By the waters, the waters of Babylon,
   we sat down and wept,
   and wept for thee, Zion;
   we remember thee, remember thee,
   remember thee, Zion.

2. On the willows, the willows of
   Babylon,
   we hung up our harps, our harps, for
   thee, Zion;
   how can we sing, can we sing, sing of
   thee, Zion?

3. There our captors, our captors from
   Babylon,
   tried to make us sing, to sing of thee,
   Zion;
   but we could not sing, we could not
   sing, we could not sing, Zion.

78 Nick Fawcett (b. 1957)
© 2000 Kevin Mayhew Ltd

1. Called to shed light where life is dark,
   where faith has died, rekindling a
     spark;
   hope for the poor and strength for
     the weak,
   joy to a world where all seems bleak.

2. Called to be salt here on the earth,
   giving to all a sense of their worth;
   seeing the best though knowing the
     worst,
   putting self last, our neighbour first.

3. Called to show love in all we do,
   making the words of Jesus ring true;
   dying to self that others may live,
   eager to serve, and glad to give.

4. Called to bring joy where there are
     tears,
   courage and strength to overcome fears,
   purpose to lives destroyed by despair,
   comfort to hearts oppressed by care.

5. Called to make peace where there is
     war,
   healing of wounds still weeping and
     raw;
   cancelling debt and wiping the slate,
   bringing at last an end to hate.

6. Called to share life with all we meet,
   until, O Lord, your will is complete.
   Open our eyes and help us to see
   this is the Church we ought to be.

79 David Adam (b. 1936)
© SPCK

Calm me, Lord, as you calmed the
  storm;
still me, Lord, keep me from harm.
Let all the tumult within me cease;
enfold me, Lord, in your peace.

80 Mary MacDonald (1817-1890)
trans. Lachlan MacBean (1853-1931)

1. Child in the manger, infant of Mary;
   outcast and stranger, Lord of all;
   child who inherits all our
     transgressions,
   all our demerits on him fall.

2. Once the most holy child of salvation
   gently and lowly lived below;
   now as our glorious mighty Redeemer,
   see him victorious o'er each foe.

3. Prophets foretold him, infant of
     wonder;
   angels behold him on his throne;
   worthy our Saviour of all their praises;
   happy for ever are his own.

81 Mike Anderson (b. 1956)
© 2004 Kevin Mayhew Ltd

1. Children of Jerusalem
   welcome Christ the King!
   Wave your olive branches
   and loud 'hosannas' sing!
   Save us! Save us!
   Save us King of kings!
   Children of Jerusalem sing out!
   Sing out! Here comes your King!

2. Children of Jerusalem
   welcome Christ the King!
   Lay your cloaks before him
   and loud 'hosannas' sing!
   Save us! Save us!
   Save us King of kings!
   Children of Jerusalem sing out!
   Sing out! Here comes your King!
   Blessèd is the Son of David!
   Blessèd is the One who comes
   in the name of the Lord!

3. Children of Jerusalem
welcome Christ the King!
Shout against oppression
and loud 'hosannas' sing!
Save us! Save us!
Save us King of kings!
Children of Jerusalem sing out!
Sing out! Here comes your King!
Blessed is the Son of David!
Blessed is the One who comes
in the name of the Lord!

4. Children of Jerusalem
welcome Christ the King!
Raise your voice for freedom
and loud 'hosannas' sing!
Save us! Save us!
Save us King of kings!
Children of Jerusalem sing out!
Sing out! Here comes your King!
Sing out! Sing out!
Here comes your King!

82 Adapted from *St Patrick's Breastplate* by James Quinn (b. 1919)
© *1969 Geoffrey Chapman, an imprint of Continuum*

1. Christ be beside me,
    Christ be before me,
Christ be behind me,
    King of my heart.
Christ be within me,
    Christ be below me,
Christ be above me, never to part.

2. Christ on my right hand,
    Christ on my left hand,
Christ all around me,
    shield in the strife.
Christ in my sleeping,
    Christ in my sitting,
Christ in my rising, light of my life.

3. Christ be in all hearts thinking
    about me.
Christ be in all tongues telling of me.
Christ be the vision in eyes that see me,
in ears that hear me, Christ ever be.

83 Ascribed to St Patrick
trans. Cecil Frances Alexander (1818-1895)

1. Christ be with me, Christ within me,
Christ behind me, Christ before me,
Christ beside me, Christ to guide me,
Christ to comfort and restore me.

2. Christ beneath me, Christ above me,
Christ in quiet, Christ in danger,
Christ in hearts of all that love me,
Christ in care of friend and stranger.

84 Ivor J. E. Daniel (1883-1967)
© *Burns & Oates Ltd*

1. Christ is King of earth and heaven!
Let his subjects all proclaim,
in the splendour of his temple,
honour to his holy name.

2. Christ is King! No soul created
can refuse to bend the knee
to the God made man who reigneth,
as 'twas promised, from the tree.

3. Christ is King! Let humble sorrow
for our past neglect atone,
for the lack of faithful service
to the Master whom we own.

4. Christ is King! Let joy and gladness
greet him; let his courts resound
with the praise of faithful subjects
to his love in honour bound.

5. Christ is King! In health and sickness,
till we breathe our latest breath,
till we greet in highest heaven,
Christ the victor over death.

85 *Urbs beata Jerusalem* (c.7th century)
trans. John Mason Neale (1818-1866) alt.

1. Christ is made the sure foundation,
Christ the head and cornerstone,
chosen of the Lord, and precious,
binding all the Church in one,
holy Zion's help for ever,
and her confidence alone.

2. To this temple, where we call you,
come, O Lord of hosts, today;
you have promised loving kindness,
hear your servants as we pray,
bless your people now before you,
turn our darkness into day.

3. Hear the cry of all your people,
what they ask and hope to gain;
what they gain from you, for ever
with your chosen to retain,
and hereafter in your glory
evermore with you to reign.

4. Praise and honour to the Father,
praise and honour to the Son,
praise and honour to the Spirit,
ever Three and ever One,
One in might and One in glory,
while unending ages run.

86 Estelle White (b. 1925)
© 1976 Kevin Mayhew Ltd

Christ is our King,
let the whole world rejoice!
May all the nations sing out with one
voice!
Light of the world,
you have helped us to see that
we are one people and
one day we all shall be free!

1. He came to open the eyes of the blind,
letting the sunlight pour into their
minds.
Vision is waiting for those who have
hope.
He is the light of the world.

2. He came to speak tender words to
the poor,
he is the gateway and he is the door.
Riches are waiting for all those who
hope.
He is the light of the world.

3. He came to open the doors of the jail;
he came to help the downtrodden
and frail.
Freedom is waiting for all those who
hope.
He is the light of the world.

4. He came to open the lips of the mute,
letting them speak out with courage
and truth.
His words are uttered by all those
who hope.
He is the light of the world.

5. He came to heal all the crippled and
lame,
sickness took flight at the sound of
his name.
Vigour is waiting for all those who
hope.
He is the light of the world.

6. He came to love ev'ryone on this earth
and through his Spirit he promised
rebirth.
New life is waiting for all those who
hope.
He is the light of the world.

87 Charles Wesley (1707-1788)

1. Christ the Lord is ris'n today; *alleluia!*
we on earth and angels say:
raise your joys and triumphs high;
sing, ye heav'ns; thou earth, reply:

2. Love's redeeming work is done,
fought the fight, the battle won;
vain the stone, the watch, the seal;
Christ hath burst the gates of hell:

3. Lives again our glorious King;
where, O death, is now thy sting?
Once he died our souls to save;
where's thy vict'ry, boasting grave?

4. Soar we now where Christ hath led,
foll'wing our exalted Head;
made like him, like him we rise;
ours the cross, the grave, the skies:

5. King of Glory! Soul of bliss!
Everlasting life is this,
thee to know, thy pow'r to prove,
thus to sing, and thus to love:

88 Michael Saward
© *Michael Saward/Jubilate Hymns. Used by permission*

1. Christ triumphant, ever reigning,
Saviour, Master, King.
Lord of heav'n, our lives sustaining,
hear us as we sing:

   Yours the glory and the crown,
   the high renown, th'eternal name.

2. Word incarnate, truth revealing,
Son of Man on earth!
Pow'r and majesty concealing
by your humble birth:

3. Suff'ring servant, scorned, ill-treated,
victim crucified!
Death is through the cross defeated,
sinners justified:

4. Priestly King, enthroned for ever
high in heav'n above!
Sin and death and hell shall never
stifle hymns of love:

5. So, our hearts and voices raising
through the ages long,
ceaselessly upon you gazing,
this shall be our song:

89 John Byrom (1692-1763) alt.

1. Christians, awake! salute the happy
morn,
whereon the Saviour of the world
was born;
rise to adore the mystery of love,
which hosts of angels chanted from
above:
with them the joyful tidings first
begun
of God incarnate and the Virgin's
Son.

*2. Then to the watchful shepherds it
was told,
who heard th'angelic herald's voice,
'Behold,
I bring good tidings of a Saviour's
birth
to you and all the nations on the
earth:
this day hath God fulfilled his
promised word,
this day is born a Saviour, Christ the
Lord.'

Continued overleaf

*3. He spake; and straightway the
celestial choir
in hymns of joy, unknown before,
conspire;
the praises of redeeming love they
sang,
and heav'n's whole orb with alleluias
rang:
God's highest glory was their
anthem still,
peace on the earth, in ev'ry heart
goodwill.

*4. To Bethl'em straight th'enlightened
shepherds ran,
to see, unfolding, God's eternal plan,
and found, with Joseph and the
blessèd maid,
her Son, the Saviour, in a manger
laid:
then to their flocks, still praising
God, return,
and their glad hearts with holy
rapture burn.

5. O may we keep and ponder in our
mind
God's wondrous love in saving lost
mankind;
trace we the babe, who hath
retrieved our loss,
from his poor manger to his bitter
cross;
tread in his steps, assisted by his grace,
till our first heav'nly state again takes
place.

6. Then may we hope, th'angelic hosts
among,
to sing, redeemed, a glad triumphal
song:
he that was born upon this joyful day

around us all his glory shall display;
saved by his love, incessant we shall
sing
eternal praise to heav'n's almighty
King.

90 John L. Bell (b. 1949)
© 1993 WGRG, Iona Community

*Christmas is coming,
the Church is glad to sing,
and let the Advent candles
brightly burn in a ring.*

1. The first is for God's promise
to put the wrong things right,
and bring to earth's darkness
the hope of love and light.

2. The second for the prophets,
who said that Christ would come
with good news for many
and angry words for some.

3. The third is for the Baptist,
who cried, 'Prepare the way.
Be ready for Jesus,
both this and ev'ry day.'

4. The fourth is for the Virgin,
who mothered God's own son
and sang how God's justice
was meant for ev'ryone.

5. At last we light the candle
kept new for Christmas Day,
this shines bright for Jesus,
new-born, and here to stay.

*Christ is among us.
The candles in the ring
remind us that our Saviour
will light up ev'rything.*

91

John L. Bell (b. 1949) and Graham Maule (b. 1958)
© 1989 WGRG, Iona Community

1. Christ's is the world in which we move,
   Christ's are the folk we're summoned
     to love,
   Christ's is the voice which calls us to
     care,
   and Christ is the one who calls us here.

   To the lost Christ shows his face;
   to the unloved he gives his embrace;
   to those who cry in pain or disgrace,
   Christ makes with his friends a
     touching place.

2. Feel for the people we most avoid,
   strange or bereaved or never employed;
   feel for the women, and feel for the
     men
   who fear that their living is all in vain.

3. Feel for the parents who've lost their
     child,
   feel for the women whom men have
     defiled,
   feel for the baby for whom there's no
     breast,
   and feel for the weary who find no rest.

4. Feel for the lives by life confused,
   riddled with doubt, in loving abused;
   feel for the lonely heart, conscious of
     sin,
   which longs to be pure but fears to
     begin.

92

Colossians 1:13-20 adpt. by Robert B. Kelly (b. 1948)
© 1999 Kevin Mayhew Ltd.

   Christus vincit, Christus regnat,
   Christus imperat.

1. God has delivered us from the
     dominion of darkness
   and transferred us to the kingdom
     of his beloved Son:
   in Christ, we gain our freedom,
   in him, the forgiveness of our sins.

*2. Christ is the image of the unseen
     God,
   he is the first-born of all creation:
   in Christ, all things were created, in
     heaven and on earth,
   all things, visible and invisible.

3. In Christ, all things were created,
   through him and for him.
   Christ is, and was before all things,
   all things were held in unity by
     Christ.

*4. The Church is the Body of Christ,
   he is its head:
   he is the beginning,
   the first-born from the dead.

5. In Christ all the fullness of God was
     pleased to dwell,
   and through Christ to reconcile all
     things to himself;
   to reconcile everything in heaven or
     on earth,
   making peace by the blood of the
     cross.

93

Sue McClellan (b. 1951), John Paculabo (b. 1946)
and Keith Ryecroft (b. 1949). © 1974 Thankyou
Music. Administered by worshiptogether.com songs

1. Colours of day dawn into the mind,
   the sun has come up, the night is
     behind.
   Go down in the city, into the street,
   and let's give the message to the
     people we meet.

Continued overleaf

So light up the fire and let the flame burn,
open the door, let Jesus return,
take seeds of his Spirit, let the fruit grow,
tell the people of Jesus, let his love show.

2. Go through the park, on into the town;
   the sun still shines on; it never goes
      down.
   The light of the world is risen again;
   the people of darkness are needing
      our friend.

3. Open your eyes, look into the sky,
   the darkness has come, the sun came
      to die.
   The evening draws on, the sun
      disappears,
   but Jesus is living, and his Spirit is near.

94 Nick Fawcett (b. 1957)
© 2004 Kevin Mayhew Ltd

1. Come and celebrate, my friends,
   sing of love that never ends.
   Let go of all that holds you back,
   receive the joy and peace you lack,
   live the life your Father sends.

2. Come and celebrate today,
   put your cares and fears away.
   Give thanks, rejoice in all you do,
   God's love is watching over you,
   light and life are here to stay!

3. Come and celebrate with me,
   Christ the Lord has set me free.
   He tore the chains of doubt apart,
   put living hope within my heart.
   Trust in him and you will see.

4. Come and celebrate his call,
   bring your talents, great and small.
   In faith commit to him your days,
   entrust your lives in grateful praise.
   Love like this demands our all.

95 Shirley Erena Murray (b. 1931)
© 1992 Hope Publishing Company
Administered by CopyCare

1. Come and find the quiet centre
   in the crowded life we lead,
   find the room for hope to enter,
   find the frame where we are freed:
   clear the chaos and the clutter,
   clear our eyes, that we can see
   all the things that really matter,
   be at peace, and simply be.

2. Silence is a friend who calms us,
   cools the heat and slows the pace,
   God it is who speaks and names us,
   knows our being, touches base,
   making space within our thinking,
   lifting shades to show the sun,
   raising courage when we're shrinking,
   finding scope for faith begun.

3. In the Spirit let us travel,
   open to each other's pain,
   let our loves and fears unravel,
   celebrate the space we gain:
   there's a place for deepest dreaming,
   there's a time for heart to care,
   in the Spirit's lively scheming
   there is always room to spare!

96 Valerie Collinson (b. 1933)
© 1972 High-Fye Music Ltd

Come and join the celebration.
It's a very special day.
Come and share our jubilation;
there's a new King born today!

1. See the shepherds
   hurry down to Bethlehem,
   gaze in wonder
   at the Son of God who lay before them.

2. Wise men journey,
   led to worship by a star,
   kneel in homage,
   bringing precious gifts from lands
   afar. So:

3. 'God is with us,'
   round the world the message bring.
   He is with us,
   'Welcome,' all the bells on earth are
   pealing.

97 Andy Carter (b. 1951)
© 1977 Thankyou Music.
Administered by worshiptogether.com songs

Come and praise him, royal priesthood.
Come and worship, holy nation.
Worship Jesus, our Redeemer.
He is risen, King of glory.

98 Gregory Norbert O.S.B, based on Hosea
© 1972 The Benedictine Foundation of the State of
Vermont, Inc.

1. Come back to me with all your heart,
   don't let fear keep us apart.
   Trees do bend, though straight and
   tall;
   so must we to others' call.

   *Long have I waited for your
   coming home to me
   and living deeply our new life.*

2. The wilderness will lead you
   to your heart where I will speak.
   Integrity and justice with
   tenderness you shall know.

3. You shall sleep secure with peace;
   faithfulness will be your joy.

99 Unknown, alt.

*Come, come, come to the manger,
children, come to the children's King;
sing, sing, chorus of angels,
star of morning o'er Bethlehem sing.*

1. He lies 'mid the beasts of the stall,
   who is Maker and Lord of us all;
   the wintry wind blows cold and dreary,
   see, he weeps, the world is weary;
   Lord, have pity and mercy on me!

2. He leaves all his glory behind,
   to be Saviour of all humankind,
   with grateful beasts his cradle chooses,
   thankless world his love refuses;
   Lord, have pity and mercy on me!

3. To the manger of Bethlehem come,
   to the Saviour Emmanuel's home;
   the heav'nly hosts above are singing,
   set the Christmas bells a-ringing;
   Lord, have pity and mercy on me!

100 Discendi, amor santo by Bianco da Siena (d. 1434)
trans. Richard F. Littledale (1833-1890) alt.

1. Come down, O Love divine,
   seek thou this soul of mine,
   and visit it with thine own ardour
   glowing;
   O Comforter, draw near,
   within my heart appear,
   and kindle it, thy holy flame
   bestowing.

2. O let it freely burn,
   till earthly passions turn
   to dust and ashes in its heat consuming;
   and let thy glorious light
   shine ever on my sight,
   and clothe me round, the while my
   path illuming.

Continued overleaf

3. Let holy charity
mine outward vesture be,
and lowliness become mine inner
clothing;
true lowliness of heart,
which takes the humbler part,
and o'er its own shortcomings weeps
with loathing.

4. And so the yearning strong,
with which the soul will long,
shall far outpass the pow'r of human
telling;
nor can we guess its grace,
till we become the place
wherein the Holy Spirit makes his
dwelling.

101 *Veni, Creator Spiritus* ascribed to Rabanus Maurus (776-856). Trans. unknown

1. Come, Holy Ghost, Creator, come
from thy bright heav'nly throne,
come, take possession of our souls,
and make them all thine own.

2. Thou who art called the Paraclete,
best gift of God above,
the living spring, the living fire,
sweet unction and true love.

3. Thou who art sev'nfold in thy grace,
finger of God's right hand;
his promise, teaching little ones
to speak and understand.

4. O guide our minds with thy blest light,
with love our hearts inflame;
and with thy strength, which ne'er
decays,
confirm our mortal frame.

5. Far from us drive our deadly foe;
true peace unto us bring;
and through all perils lead us safe
beneath thy sacred wing.

6. Through thee may we the Father know,
through thee th'eternal Son,
and thee the Spirit of them both,
thrice-blessèd Three in One.

7. All glory to the Father be,
with his co-equal Son:
the same to thee, great Paraclete,
while endless ages run.

102 Unknown

1. Come into his presence, singing,
'Alleluia.' *(x3)*

2. Come into his presence, singing,
'Jesus is Lord.' *(x3)*

3. Come into his presence, singing,
'Glory to God.' *(x3)*

103 Damian Lundy (1944-1997) © 1986 Kevin Mayhew Ltd

1. Come, Lord Jesus, come, Lord Jesus,
come, Lord Jesus, come again.

Come, Lord Jesus, come again.

2. Born of Mary, *(x3)*
come again.

3. Slain to save us, *(x3)*
come again.

4. Raised to new life, *(x3)*
come again.

5. At God's right hand, *(x3)*
come again.

6. Send your Spirit, *(x3)*
come again.

7. Come in glory, *(x3)*
come again.

104
Kevin Mayhew (b. 1942)
© 1974, 1976 Kevin Mayhew Ltd

1. Come, Lord Jesus, come.
   Come, take my hands,
   take them for your work.
   Take them for your service, Lord.
   Take them for your glory, Lord.
   Come, Lord Jesus, come.
   Come, Lord Jesus, take my hands.

2. Come, Lord Jesus, come.
   Come, take my eyes,
   may they shine with joy.
   Take them for your service, Lord.
   Take them for your glory, Lord.
   Come, Lord Jesus, come.
   Come, Lord Jesus, take my eyes.

3. Come, Lord Jesus, come.
   Come, take my lips,
   may they speak your truth.
   Take them for your service, Lord.
   Take them for your glory, Lord.
   Come, Lord Jesus, come.
   Come, Lord Jesus, take my lips.

4. Come, Lord Jesus, come.
   Come, take my feet,
   may they walk your path.
   Take them for your service, Lord.
   Take them for your glory, Lord.
   Come, Lord Jesus, come.
   Come, Lord Jesus, take my feet.

5. Come, Lord Jesus, come.
   Come, take my heart,
   fill it with your love.
   Take it for your service, Lord.
   Take it for your glory, Lord.
   Come, Lord Jesus, come.
   Come, Lord Jesus, take my heart.

6. Come, Lord Jesus, come.
   Come take my life,
   take it for your own.
   Take it for your service, Lord.
   Take it for your glory, Lord.
   Come, Lord Jesus, come.
   Come, Lord Jesus, take my life.

105
George Herbert (1593-1633)

1. Come, my Way, my Truth, my Life:
   such a way as gives us breath;
   such a truth as ends all strife;
   such a life as killeth death.

2. Come, my Light, my Feast, my
       Strength:
   such a light as shows a feast;
   such a feast as mends in length;
   such a strength as makes his guest.

3. Come, my Joy, my Love, my Heart:
   such a joy as none can move;
   such a love as none can part;
   such a heart as joys in love.

106
Marty Haugen (b. 1952)
© 1999 GIA Publications Inc.

1. Come now, the table's spread,
   in Jesus' name we break the bread,
   here shall we all be fed
   within the reign of God.
   Come, take this holy food,
   receive the body and the blood,
   grace is a mighty flood
   within the reign of God.

   *Blessed are they who will feast in the
       reign of God!*
   *Blessed are they who will share the
       bread of life!*
   *Blessed are they who are least in the
       reign of God!*
   They shall rejoice at the feast of life!

Continued overleaf

2. Stand up and do not fear
for Christ is truly present here,
sing out, and cease your tears
within the reign of God.
Welcome the weak and poor,
the sinner finds an open door,
none judged, and none ignored
within the reign of God.

*Blessed are they who will feast in the
reign of God!*
*Blessed are they who will share the
bread of life!*
*Blessed are they who are least in the
reign of God!*
They shall rejoice at the feast of life!

3. Here shall the weary rest,
the stranger be a welcome guest,
so shall we all be blest
within the reign of God.
Now at this wedding feast,
the greatest here shall be the least,
all bonds shall be released
within the reign of God.

107 Sister Mary of St Philip

1. Come, O divine Messiah!
The world in silence waits the day
when hope shall sing its triumph,
and sadness flee away.

*Sweet Saviour, haste: come, come to
earth:*
dispel the night, and show thy face,
and bid us hail the dawn of grace.
Come, O divine Messiah!
The world in silence waits the day
when hope shall sing its triumph,
and sadness flee away.

2. O thou, whom nations sighed for,
whom priests and prophets long
foretold,
wilt break the captive fetters,
redeem the long-lost fold.

3. Shalt come in peace and meekness,
and lowly will thy cradle be:
all clothed in human weakness
shall we thy Godhead see.

108
Patricia Morgan and Dave Bankhead
© 1984 Thankyou Music.
Administered by worshiptogether.com songs

Come on and celebrate
his gift of love, we will celebrate
the Son of God who loved us
and gave us life.

We'll shout your praise, O King,
you give us joy nothing else can bring;
we'll give to you our offering
in celebration praise.

Come on and celebrate, celebrate,
celebrate and sing,
celebrate and sing to the King!
(Repeat)

109
Psalm 116 versified by James Quinn (b. 1919)
© 1969 Geoffrey Chapman, an imprint of
Continuum Int. Publishing Group

1. Come, praise the Lord, the almighty,
the King of all nations!
Tell forth his fame, O ye peoples,
with loud acclamations!
His love is sure,
faithful his word shall endure,
steadfast through all generations!

2. Praise to the Father most gracious,
the Lord of creation!
Praise to his Son, the Redeemer,
who wrought our salvation!
O heav'nly Dove,
praise to thee, fruit of their love,
giver of all consolation!

110

Katherine K. Davis, Henry V. Onorati and Harry Simeone.
© 1941 EMI Mills Music Inc./Delaware Music Corp.

1. Come, they told me,
   pah-rum-pum-pum-pum!
   our new-born King to see,
   pah-rum-pum-pum-pum!
   Our finest gifts we bring,
   pah-rum-pum-pum-pum!
   to lay before the King,
   pah-rum-pum-pum-pum!
   Rum-pum-pum-pum!
   Rum-pum-pum-pum!
   So, to honour him,
   pah-rum-pum-pum-pum!
   when we come.

2. Baby Jesus,
   pah-rum-pum-pum-pum!
   I am a poor child too,
   pah-rum-pum-pum-pum!
   I have no gift to bring,
   pah-rum-pum-pum-pum!
   that's fit to give a King,
   pah-rum-pum-pum-pum!
   Rum-pum-pum-pum!
   Rum-pum-pum-pum!
   Shall I play for you,
   pah-rum-pum-pum-pum!
   on my drum?

3. Mary nodded,
   pah-rum-pum-pum-pum!
   The ox and lamb kept time,
   pah-rum-pum-pum-pum!
   I played my drum for him,
   pah-rum-pum-pum-pum!
   I played my best for him,
   pah-rum-pum-pum-pum!
   Rum-pum-pum-pum!
   Rum-pum-pum-pum!
   Then he smiled at me,
   pah-rum-pum-pum-pum!
   me and my drum.

111

Charles Wesley (1707-1788)

1. Come, thou long-expected Jesus,
   born to set thy people free;
   from our fears and sins release us;
   let us find our rest in thee.

2. Israel's strength and consolation,
   hope of all the earth thou art;
   dear desire of ev'ry nation,
   joy of ev'ry longing heart.

3. Born thy people to deliver;
   born a child and yet a king;
   born to reign in us for ever;
   now thy gracious kingdom bring.

4. By thine own eternal Spirit,
   rule in all our hearts alone:
   by thine all-sufficient merit,
   raise us to thy glorious throne.

112

Gerard Markland (b. 1953)
© 1998 Kevin Mayhew Ltd

1. Come to me, come, my people;
   learn from me, be humble of heart.

2. I your Lord, I your master;
   learn from me, be humble of heart.

3. Follow me to my Father;
   learn from me, be humble of heart.

4. In my death, in my rising;
   learn from me, be humble of heart.

5. Be transformed by my Spirit;
   learn from me, be humble of heart.

6. Glory be to my Father;
   learn from me, be humble of heart.

113

Bernadette Farrell (b. 1957)
© 1982, 2000 Bernadette Farrell.
Published by OCP Publications

Come to set us free,
come to make us your own.
Come to show the way
to your people, your chosen.
Open our lives to the light of your promise.
Come to our hearts with healing,
come to our minds with power,
come to us and bring us your life.

1. You are light which shines in darkness,
   Morning Star which never sets.
   Open our eyes which only dimly see
   the truth which sets us free.

2. You are hope which brings us courage,
   you are strength which never fails.
   Open our minds to ways we do not
   know,
   but where your Spirit grows.

3. You are promise of salvation,
   you are God in human form.
   Bring to our world of emptiness and
   fear
   the word we long to hear.

114

Michael Forster (b. 1946)
© 1999 Kevin Mayhew Ltd

Come to the table of the Lord,
sinners by faith and grace restored;
taste here what earth cannot afford,
alleluia!

1. How I rejoiced when Jesus said,
   'Come to my table, share my bread,
   where souls and bodies both are fed.'

2. 'This is my body, giv'n to be
   broken for you eternally:
   do this when you remember me.'

3. 'This is my lifeblood, flowing free,
   shed for the world eternally:
   do this when you remember me.'

115

Henry Alford (1810-1871) alt.

1. Come, ye thankful people, come,
   raise the song of harvest-home!
   All is safely gathered in,
   ere the winter storms begin;
   God, our maker, doth provide
   for our wants to be supplied;
   come to God's own temple, come;
   raise the song of harvest-home!

2. We ourselves are God's own field,
   fruit unto his praise to yield;
   wheat and tares together sown,
   unto joy or sorrow grown;
   first the blade and then the ear,
   then the full corn shall appear:
   grant, O harvest Lord, that we
   wholesome grain and pure may be.

3. For the Lord our God shall come,
   and shall take his harvest home,
   from his field shall purge away
   all that doth offend, that day;
   give his angels charge at last
   in the fire the tares to cast,
   but the fruitful ears to store
   in his garner evermore.

4. Then, thou Church triumphant, come,
   raise the song of harvest-home;
   all be safely gathered in,
   free from sorrow, free from sin,
   there for ever purified
   in God's garner to abide:
   come, ten thousand angels, come,
   raise the glorious harvest-home!

116

Psalm 117
© Ateliers et Presses de Taizé

Confitemini Domino quoniam bonus.
Confitemini Domino. Alleluia!

Translation: Give thanks to the Lord
for he is good.

117
Michael Hodgetts (b. 1936)
© *Michael Hodgetts. Used by permission*

1. Creator of the day and night,
who turned the darkness into light
and charged us to proclaim the Word,
whom we have touched and seen and
heard.

   The glory that you gave the Son,
   he gives to us, to make us one.

2. Your kingdom in a mystery,
began with twelve in Galilee,
through whom the Son would teach
and cure;
whose fruit would ripen and endure.

3. At Pentecost, with wind and flame,
you sent the Spirit in his name,
to make the Church a present Christ;
anointed Prophet, King and Priest.

4. And when your purpose is complete,
the Son of Man will take his seat;
and Christ will be identified
with these, the least, for whom he died.

118
7th century trans. Irwin Udulutsch
© *1959 The Order of St Benedict*

1. Creator of the stars of night,
the people's everlasting light,
Redeemer, Saviour of us all,
O hear your servants when they call.

2. As once through Mary's flesh you came
to save us from our sin and shame,
so now, Redeemer, by your grace,
come heal again our fallen race.

3. And when on that last judgement day
we rise to glory from decay,
then come again, O Saviour blest,
and bring us to eternal rest.

4. To God the Father, God the Son
and God the Spirit, three in one,
praise, honour, might and glory be
from age to age eternally.

119
Matthew Bridges (1800-1894)

1. Crown him with many crowns,
the Lamb upon his throne;
hark, how the heav'nly anthem drowns
all music but its own:
awake, my soul, and sing
of him who died for thee,
and hail him as thy matchless King
through all eternity.

2. Crown him the Virgin's Son,
the God incarnate born,
whose arm those crimson trophies won
which now his brow adorn;
fruit of the mystic Rose,
as of that Rose the Stem,
the Root, whence mercy ever flows,
the Babe of Bethlehem.

3. Crown him the Lord of love;
behold his hands and side,
rich wounds, yet visible above,
in beauty glorified:
no angel in the sky
can fully bear that sight,
but downward bends each burning eye
at mysteries so bright.

4. Crown him the Lord of peace,
whose pow'r a sceptre sways
from pole to pole, that wars may cease,
absorbed in prayer and praise:
his reign shall know no end,
and round his piercèd feet
fair flow'rs of paradise extend
their fragrance ever sweet.

Continued overleaf

5. Crown him the Lord of years,
   the Potentate of time,
   Creator of the rolling spheres,
   ineffably sublime.
   All hail, Redeemer, hail!
   for thou hast died for me;
   thy praise shall never, never fail
   throughout eternity.

120 *Omni die dic Mariae* ascribed to St Bernard of Cluny (12th century) trans. Henry Bittleston (1818-1886)

1. Daily, daily, sing to Mary,
   sing, my soul, her praises due;
   all her feasts, her actions worship,
   with her heart's devotion true.
   Lost in wond'ring contemplation
   be her majesty confessed:
   call her mother, call her virgin,
   happy mother, virgin blest.

2. She is mighty to deliver;
   call her, trust her lovingly.
   When the tempest rages round thee,
   she will calm the troubled sea.
   Gifts of heaven she has given,
   noble lady, to our race:
   she, the queen, who decks her subjects,
   with the light of God's own grace.

3. Sing, my tongue, the virgin's trophies,
   who for us her Maker bore;
   for the curse of old inflicted,
   peace and blessings to restore.
   Sing in songs of praise unending,
   sing the world's majestic queen;
   weary not, nor faint in telling
   all the gifts she gives to men.

4. All my senses, heart, affections,
   strive to sound her glory forth;
   spread abroad, the sweet memorials,
   of the virgin's priceless worth.
   Where the voice of music thrilling,
   where the tongues of eloquence,
   that can utter hymns beseeming
   all her matchless excellence?

5. All our joys do flow from Mary,
   all then join her praise to sing;
   trembling, sing the virgin mother,
   mother of our Lord and King,
   while we sing her awful glory,
   far above our fancy's reach,
   let our hearts be quick to offer
   love the heart alone can teach.

121 Mike Anderson (b. 1956)
© *1999 Kevin Mayhew Ltd*

Dance in your Spirit,
we dance in your Spirit,
we dance in your Spirit of joy! (Repeat)

1. Jesus, you showed us the way to live,
   and your Spirit sets us free,
   free now to sing, free to dance and
      shout,
   'Glory, glory' to your name.

2. Jesus, you opened your arms for us,
   but we nailed them to a cross;
   but you are risen and now we live,
   free from, free from ev'ry fear.

3. Your Spirit brings peace and gentleness,
   kindness, self-control and love,
   patience and goodness and faith and
      joy,
   Spirit, Spirit fill us now.

122

James Quinn (b. 1919)
© Geoffrey Chapman, an imprint of Continuum
Int. Publishing Group

1. Day is done, but love unfailing
   dwells ever here;
   shadows fall, but hope prevailing
   calms ev'ry fear;
   Loving Father, none forsaking,
   take our hearts, of love's own making,
   watch our sleeping, guard our waking,
   be always near!

2. Dark descends, but light unending
   shines through our night;
   you are with us, ever lending
   new strength to sight;
   one in love, your truth confessing,
   one in hope of heaven's blessing,
   may we see, in love's possessing,
   love's endless light!

3. Eyes will close, but you, unsleeping,
   watch by our side;
   death may come: in love's safe keeping
   still we abide.
   God of love, all evil quelling,
   sin forgiving, fear dispelling,
   stay with us, our hearts indwelling,
   this eventide!

123

John Greenleaf Whittier (1807-1892)

1. Dear Lord and Father of mankind,
   forgive our foolish ways!
   Re-clothe us in our rightful mind,
   in purer lives thy service find,
   in deeper rev'rence praise,
   in deeper rev'rence praise.

2. In simple trust like theirs who heard,
   beside the Syrian sea,
   the gracious calling of the Lord,
   let us, like them, without a word,
   rise up and follow thee,
   rise up and follow thee.

3. O Sabbath rest by Galilee!
   O calm of hills above,
   where Jesus knelt to share with thee
   the silence of eternity,
   interpreted by love!
   Interpreted by love!

4. Drop thy still dews of quietness,
   till all our strivings cease;
   take from our souls the strain and
   stress,
   and let our ordered lives confess
   the beauty of thy peace,
   the beauty of thy peace.

5. Breathe through the heats of our
   desire
   thy coolness and thy balm;
   let sense be dumb, let flesh retire;
   speak through the earthquake, wind
   and fire,
   O still small voice of calm!
   O still small voice of calm!

124

George Ratcliffe Woodward (1848-1934)

1. Ding dong, merrily on high!
   In heav'n the bells are ringing;
   ding dong, verily the sky
   is riv'n with angel singing.

   Gloria, hosanna in excelsis!
   Gloria, hosanna in excelsis!

2. E'en so here below, below,
   let steeple bells be swungen,
   and io, io, io,
   by priest and people sungen.

3. Pray you, dutifully prime
   your matin chime, ye ringers;
   may you beautifully rhyme
   your evetime song, ye singers.

125 Gerard Markland (b. 1953), based on Isaiah 43:1-4. © 1978 Kevin Mayhew Ltd

Do not be afraid, for I have redeemed you.
I have called you by your name;
you are mine.

1. When you walk through the waters,
   I'll be with you.
   You will never sink beneath the
   waves.

2. When the fire is burning all around
   you,
   you will never be consumed by the
   flames.

3. When the fear of loneliness is
   looming,
   then remember I am at your side.

4. When you dwell in the exile of the
   stranger,
   remember you are precious in my eyes.

5. You are mine, O my child, I am your
   Father,
   and I love you with a perfect love.

126 Traditional

Dona nobis, nobis pacem,
dona nobis pacem.

Translation: Give us peace.

127 Karen Lafferty (b. 1948)
© 1981 Maranatha! Music.
Administered by CopyCare

Don't build your house on the sandy
   land,
don't build it too near the shore.
Well, it might look kind of nice,
but you'll have to build it twice,
oh, you'll have to build your house
   once more.

You'd better build your house upon a
   rock,
make a good foundation on a solid
   spot.
Oh, the storms may come and go
but the peace of God you will know.

128 Taizé Community, based on Scripture
© Ateliers et Presses de Taizé

Eat this bread, drink this cup,
come to him and never be hungry.
Eat this bread, drink this cup,
trust in him and you will not thirst.

The following verses may be sung by a
Cantor:

1. Christ is the Bread of Life,
   the true bread sent from the Father.

2. Your ancestors ate manna in the desert,
   but this is the bread come down from
   heaven.

3. Eat his flesh, and drink his blood,
   and Christ will raise you up on the
   last day.

4. Anyone who eats this bread
   will live for ever.

5. If we believe and eat this bread
   we will have eternal life.

129 June Boyce-Tillman (b. 1943)
© Stainer & Bell Ltd

1. Embrace the universe with love,
   and shine with God in splendour.
   Embrace the earth, embrace the sky
   and find God, our defender.

2. Find wisdom hidden in the stars
   and faith within the rainbow.
   Find righteousness in flowing streams
   and hope in moon and meadow.

3. Embrace your friend, embrace your foe,
and find the Christ within them,
embrace your body and your mind;
these also are God-given.

4. For mercy dwells in human hearts
and needs our love to shape it.
Put out a hand and touch a heart
and help to consecrate it.

5. Share all you have with all you meet
and find the strength of Scripture;
prepare the heart, prepare the mind
and leave to God the future.

130 William Whiting (1825-1878) alt.

1. Eternal Father, strong to save,
whose arm doth bind the restless wave,
who bidd'st the mighty ocean deep
its own appointed limits keep:
O hear us when we cry to thee
for those in peril on the sea.

2. O Saviour, whose almighty word
the winds and waves submissive heard,
who walkedst on the foaming deep,
and calm, amid its rage, didst sleep:
O hear us when we cry to thee
for those in peril on the sea.

3. O sacred Spirit, who didst brood
upon the waters dark and rude,
and bid their angry tumult cease,
and give, for wild confusion, peace:
O hear us when we cry to thee
for those in peril on the sea.

4. O Trinity of love and pow'r,
our brethren shield in danger's hour.
From rock and tempest, fire and foe,
protect them whereso'er they go,
and ever let there rise to thee
glad hymns of praise from land and sea.

131 Traditional

Exaudi nos, Domine,
dona nobis pacem tuam.

*Translation: Hear us, O Lord, give us
your peace.*

132 Frederick William Faber (1814-1863)

1. Faith of our fathers, living still
in spite of dungeon, fire and sword;
O, how our hearts beat high with joy
whene'er we hear that glorious word!

*Faith of our fathers! Holy faith!
We will be true to thee till death,
we will be true to thee till death.*

2. Our fathers, chained in prisons dark,
were still in heart and conscience free;
how sweet would be their children's fate,
if they, like them, could die for thee!

3. Faith of our fathers, Mary's prayers
shall win our country back to thee;
and through the truth that comes
from God
this land shall then indeed be free.

4. Faith of our fathers, we will love
both friend and foe in all our strife,
and preach thee too, as love knows how,
by kindly words and virtuous life.

133 A. J. Newman

1. Father and life-giver,
grace of Christ impart;
he, the Word incarnate,
food for mind and heart.
Children of the promise,
homage now we pay;
sacrificial banquet
cheers the desert way.

Continued overleaf

2. Wine and bread the symbols,
   love and life convey,
   offered by your people,
   work and joy portray.
   All we own consigning,
   nothing is retained;
   tokens of our service,
   gifts and song contain.

3. Transformation wondrous,
   water into wine;
   mingled in the Godhead
   we are made divine.
   Birth into his body
   brought us life anew,
   total consecration,
   fruit from grafting true.

4. Christ, the head, and members
   living now as one,
   offered to the Father
   by this holy Son;
   and our adoration
   purified we find,
   through the Holy Spirit
   breathing in mankind.

134 Jenny Hewer (b. 1945)
© 1975 Thankyou Music.
Administered by worshiptogether.com songs

1. Father, I place into your hands
   the things I cannot do.
   Father, I place into your hands
   the things that I've been through.
   Father, I place into your hands
   the way that I should go,
   for I know I always can trust you.

2. Father, I place into your hands
   my friends and family.
   Father, I place into your hands
   the things that trouble me.
   Father, I place into your hands
   the person I would be,
   for I know I always can trust you.

3. Father, we love to see your face,
   we love to hear your voice,
   Father, we love to sing your praise
   and in your name rejoice.
   Father, we love to walk with you
   and in your presence rest,
   for we know we always can trust you.

4. Father, I want to be with you
   and do the things you do.
   Father, I want to speak the words
   that you are speaking too.
   Father, I want to love the ones
   that you will draw to you,
   for I know that I am one with you.

135 Frank Anderson
© Frank Anderson. Used by permission

1. Father, in my life I see,
   you are God who walks with me.
   You hold my life in your hands;
   close beside you I will stand.
   I give all my life to you:
   help me, Father, to be true.

2. Jesus, in my life I see,
   you are God who walks with me.
   You hold my life in your hands;
   close beside you I will stand.
   I give all my life to you:
   help me, Jesus, to be true.

3. Spirit, in my life I see,
   you are God who walks with me.
   You hold my life in your hands;
   close beside you I will stand.
   I give all my life to you:
   help me, Spirit, to be true.

136 Terrye Coelho (b. 1952)
© 1972 CCCM Music/Maranatha! Music
Administered by CopyCare

1. Father, we adore you,
   lay our lives before you.
   How we love you!

2. Jesus, we adore you . . .

3. Spirit, we adore you . . .

137 Donna Adkins (b. 1940)
© 1976 Maranatha! Music
Administered by CopyCare

1. Father, we love you,
   we worship and adore you,
   glorify your name in all the earth.
   Glorify your name, glorify your name,
   glorify your name in all the earth.

2. Jesus, we love you . . .

3. Spirit, we love you . . .

138 Robin Mann (b. 1949)
© 1986 Kevin Mayhew Ltd

Father welcomes all his children
to his fam'ly through his Son.
Father giving his salvation,
life for ever has been won.

1. Little children, come to me,
   for my kingdom is of these.
   Love and new life have I to give,
   pardon for your sin.

2. In the water, in the word,
   in his promise, be assured:
   all who believe and are baptised
   shall be born again.

3. Let us daily die to sin;
   let us daily rise with him –
   walk in the love of Christ our Lord,
   live in the peace of God.

139 Nick Fawcett (b. 1957)
© 2005 Kevin Mayhew Ltd

1. Fearful, uncertain, troubled, confused,
   Mary, you listened, prepared to be used,
   ready to give yourself, body and soul,
   bearing the one who would make the
     world whole.

2. Innocent, humble, honest, sincere,
   Mary, you trusted, though much was
     unclear,
   willing to follow as God chose to lead,
   wanting to serve him in thought,
     word and deed.

3. Jubilant, grateful, spirit alight,
   Mary, you worshipped, sang out in
     delight:
   hope for the broken and strength for
     the weak,
   food for the hungry, esteem for the
     meek.

4. Pondering, pensive, wrapped up in
     thought,
   Mary, you marvelled at all God had
     brought,
   eagerly searching to understand more,
   hungry to fathom what else lay in
     store.

5. Lord born of Mary, hear us today:
   we, like your mother, would trust
     and obey.
   Take all we are and, in all that we do,
   help us to give ourselves wholly to you.

140 John Samuel Bewley Monsell (1811-1875) alt.

1. Fight the good fight with all thy might;
   Christ is thy strength, and Christ thy
     right;
   lay hold on life, and it shall be
   thy joy and crown eternally.

Continued overleaf

2. Run the straight race through God's
      good grace,
   lift up thine eyes and seek his face;
   life with its way before us lies;
   Christ is the path, and Christ the prize.

3. Cast care aside, lean on thy guide;
   his boundless mercy will provide;
   trust, and thy trusting soul shall prove
   Christ is its life, and Christ its love.

4. Faint not nor fear, his arms are near;
   he changeth not, and thou art dear;
   only believe, and thou shalt see
   that Christ is all in all to thee.

141 Peter Kearney
*© 1971 B. Feldman & Co. Ltd./
EMI Music Publishing Ltd.*

1. Fill my house unto the fullest,
   eat my bread and drink my wine.
   The love I bear is held from no one.

   All I own and all I do I give to you.

2. Take my time unto the fullest,
   find in me the trust you seek,
   and take my hands to you outreaching.

3. Christ our Lord with love enormous
   from the cross his lesson taught:
   'Show love to all, as I have loved you.'

4. Join with me as one in Christ-love,
   may our hearts all beat as one,
   and may we give ourselves completely.

142 Timothy Dudley-Smith (b. 1926)
© Timothy Dudley-Smith

1. Fill your hearts with joy and gladness,
   sing and praise your God and mine!
   Great the Lord in love and wisdom,
   might and majesty divine!
   He who framed the starry heavens
   knows and names them as they shine!
   Fill your hearts with joy and gladness,
   sing and praise your God and mine!

2. Praise the Lord, his people, praise him!
   Wounded souls his comfort know;
   those who fear him find his mercies,
   peace for pain and joy for woe;
   humble hearts are high exalted,
   human pride and pow'r laid low.
   Praise the Lord, his people, praise him!
   Wounded souls his comfort know.

3. Praise the Lord for times and seasons,
   cloud and sunshine, wind and rain;
   spring to melt the snows of winter
   till the waters flow again;
   grass upon the mountain pastures,
   golden valleys thick with grain.
   Praise the Lord for times and seasons,
   cloud and sunshine, wind and rain.

4. Fill your hearts with joy and gladness,
   peace and plenty crown your days;
   love his laws, declare his judgements,
   walk in all his words and ways;
   he the Lord and we his children:
   praise the Lord, all people, praise!
   Fill your hearts with joy and gladness,
   peace and plenty crown your days!

143 John Henry Newman (1801-1890) alt.

1. Firmly I believe and truly
   God is Three and God is One;
   and I next acknowledge duly
   manhood taken by the Son.

2. And I trust and hope most fully
   in the Saviour crucified;
   and each thought and deed unruly
   do to death as he has died.

3. Simply to his grace and wholly
   light and life and strength belong,
   and I love supremely, solely,
   him the holy, him the strong.

4. And I hold in veneration,
   for the love of him alone,
   holy Church as his creation,
   and her teachings as his own.

5. Adoration ay be given,
   with and thro' th'angelic host,
   to the God of earth and heaven,
   Father, Son and Holy Ghost.

144

Michael Cockett (b. 1938)
© 1978 Kevin Mayhew Ltd

Follow me, follow me,
leave your home and family,
leave your fishing nets and boats
  upon the shore.
Leave the seed you have sown,
leave the crops that you've grown,
leave the people you have known
  and follow me.

1. The foxes have their holes
   and the swallows have their nests,
   but the Son of Man
   has no place to lie down.
   I do not offer comfort,
   I do not offer wealth,
   but in me will all happiness be found.

2. If you would follow me,
   you must leave old ways behind.
   You must take my cross and
   follow on my path.
   You may be far from loved ones,
   you may be far from home,
   but my Father will welcome you at last.

3. Although I go away
   you will never be alone,
   for the Spirit will be
   there to comfort you.
   Though all of you may scatter,
   each follow his own path,
   still the Spirit of love will lead you
     home.

145

William Walsham How (1823-1897)
Adapted by Michael Forster (b. 1946)
© 2000 Kevin Mayhew Ltd

1. For all the saints who from their
     labours rest,
   who thee by faith before the world
     confessed,
   thy name, O Jesus, be forever blest:
   Alleluia!

2. Thou wast their rock, their refuge
     and their might,
   thou, Lord, the vision ever in their
     sight,
   thou in the darkness drear their one
     true light.
   Alleluia!

3. O may thy servants, faithful, true
     and bold,
   strive for thy kingdom as the saints
     of old,
   and win with them the glorious
     crown of gold:
   Alleluia!

4. O blest communion, fellowship
     divine!
   We feebly struggle, they in glory shine,
   yet all are one in thee, for all are thine:
   Alleluia!

*5. And when the road is steep, the
     journey long,
   steals on the ear the distant
     welcome song,
   and hope is bright again, and faith
     is strong:
   Alleluia!

*6. The golden evening brightens in the
     west,
   soon, soon to faithful pilgrims
     cometh rest:
   sweet is the calm of Paradise the blest.
   Alleluia!

Continued overleaf

*7. But lo! There breaks a yet more
    glorious day;
  the saints triumphant rise in bright
    array:
  the King of glory passes on his way:
  Alleluia!

*8. From earth's wide bounds, from
    ocean's farthest coast,
  through gates of pearl streams in the
    countless host,
  singing to Father, Son and Holy
    Ghost.
  Alleluia!

For all saints days and those celebrated between January and June (see overleaf for July to December)

146 Horatio Bolton Nelson (1823-1913), adapted by Stuart Thomas (b. 1954), except Holy Innocents: Susan Sayers (b. 1946)
© 2004 Kevin Mayhew Ltd

1. For all your saints still active,
  for those whose work is done;
  for saints with you in glory whose
    earthly race is run.
  You rose as King and Sov'reign,
  that they the crown might wear,
  reserved for those who humbly
  your earthly pathway share.

Verse 2 may be replaced with any feast day verse that follows.

2. Apostles, prophets, martyrs,
  who served you here on earth,
  now reign with you in heaven,
  singing your praise and worth.
  With them, and all whose witness
  is known to you alone,
  we share our earthly journey
  towards your heav'nly throne.

3. We praise you, God our Father,
  we worship Christ, your Son,
  we glorify your Spirit,
  forever three, yet one.
  On earth we see you dimly,
  in heaven face to face;
  and then with all who've served you,
  we'll praise you, God of grace.

25th January *Conversion of St Paul*
Blinded by light from heaven
which blazed down from above,
fired by the glorious vision
Paul chose your way of love.
So Lord, like Paul, convert us,
transform our night to day;
empow'r us with your Spirit,
and guide us in your way.

1st March *St David*
We praise you, Lord, for David,
called to proclaim your law;
compassionate and holy,
he cared for sick and poor.
Through prayer and meditation,
his life displayed your grace;
may we, too, bring Christ's healing
in ev'ry time and place.

17th March *St Patrick*
Saint Patrick, Lord, we honour,
whose life obeyed your call;
accepting pain and hardship
he spoke of Christ to all.
In fellowship and witness
your name he spread abroad;
we too would share this message,
proclaiming Christ as Lord.

19th March *St Joseph of Nazareth*
We praise you, Lord, for Joseph,
true carer for your Son;
Jesus he did take to Egypt
till Herod's rage was done.

A carpenter by training,
he made for Christ a home;
through Joseph's care and nurture
our Father's love is known.

25th March *The Annunciation of
our Lord to the Blessed Virgin Mary*
With joy we sing of Mary,
whose heart with love was stirred,
when young and inexperienced,
the angel's voice she heard.
We sing with her your praises,
your mighty works proclaim;
through Mary's glad obedience
your great salvation came.

25th April *St Mark*
For Mark, the first Evangelist,
we offer you our praise;
the witness of his gospel
reveals to us your ways.
The story of Christ's mission
Mark tells, that we might know
the Saviour who redeemed us;
to share his love we go.

3rd May *Ss Philip and James*
We thank you, Lord, for Philip,
who spoke with Greek and Jew
to tell them of your mercy,
that they might follow you.
For James, the young and faithful,
we praise and bless your name;
called like them, may we follow,
your glory to proclaim.

14th May *St Matthias*
To take the place of Judas,
disciples sought God's will;
the lot fell to Matthias
that needed space to fill.
We follow his example
with you, Lord, as our friend;
may we, with you beside us,
continue to the end.

9th June *St Columba*
Columba, saint and pilgrim,
is worthy of all praise;
he journeyed far, and boldly
declared your mighty ways.
Loving your Word, he brought it
alike to high and low;
his pattern may we follow,
your Spirit's presence show.

11th June *St Barnabas*
For Barnabas we praise you,
who journeyed far with Paul;
encouraging and hopeful,
your love he shared with all;
in ministry and caring
may we bring hope and cheer,
to banish doubt and darkness,
and drive away all fear.

24th June *Birth of St John the Baptist*
Give thanks for John the Baptist,
forerunner of the Word,
who went ahead preparing
the way for Christ our Lord.
Greatest among the prophets,
he saw in Christ the One
whom God had sent to save us,
Jesus, his only Son.

29th June *Ss Peter and Paul*
We offer thanks and praises
for Peter and for Paul;
they heard your voice and followed,
responding to your call.
To Jew or Gentile preaching,
your gospel they proclaimed.
To all without distinction
may we declare your name.

Continued overleaf

For saints days celebrated between July and December (see previous page for January to June)

1. For all your saints still active,
   for those whose work is done;
   for saints with you in glory whose
      earthly race is run.
   You rose as King and Sov'reign,
   that they the crown might wear,
   reserved for those who humbly
   your earthly pathway share.

2. *Choose the appropriate saint*

3. We praise you, God our Father,
   we worship Christ, your Son,
   we glorify your Spirit,
   forever three, yet one.
   On earth we see you dimly,
   in heaven face to face;
   and then with all who've served you,
   we'll praise you, God of grace.

3rd July *St Thomas*
For Thomas we now thank you,
who wanted you to prove
that you indeed were risen,
the Lord of life and love.
In all our human searching,
inspire us with your grace,
and even when we're doubting,
help us to see your face.

11th July *St Benedict*
For Benedict, our brother,
we offer praise, and bless
his Rule, which shows weak humans
the life of holiness.
Such wisdom and instruction
enable us to see
how, serving you together,
we live in unity.

22nd July *St Mary Magdalene*
We praise you now for Mary,
whose life was changed and turned
by you, her friend and master;
for you she longed and yearned.
In tears, she sensed you call her
and as your voice she heard,
the woman once rejected
saw first the Risen Lord.

25th July *St James*
We praise you for the witness
of James, the one who died
in telling of his Saviour,
Jesus the Crucified.
Lord, help us not to treasure
our worldly goods or fame,
but may we, trials enduring,
bring glory to your name.

11th August *St Clare*
For Clare, who built your people
into community,
we thank you, Lord, and treasure
her holy legacy.
Devoted to our Saviour,
we contemplate, and pray
that all may be included,
and welcomed in your way.

24th August *St Bartholomew*
Bartholomew th'apostle,
least known among your friends,
remained a faithful foll'wer
and served you to the end.
His deeds may not be noted,
but he to Christ stayed true;
may we too seek your glory,
and only honour you.

21st September *St Matthew*
Matthew the tax-collector,
left all his worldly gain,
to rise and follow Jesus;
he tells us: 'Do the same!'
The good news of our Saviour
his gospel words declare;
may we forsake what's passing,
his risen life to share.

4th October *St Francis of Assisi*
For Francis, meek and humble,
our thanks and praise are due;
denying wealth and comfort,
he turned and followed you.
Embracing poor and suff'ring,
the mark of Christ he bore;
inspire us with his passion
to love and serve you more.

18th October *St Luke*
For Luke, the faithful doctor,
we thank you; for he shows
the healing Christ, who reaches
to share our pains and woes.
Stretch out your hand to save us,
to cleanse us deep within,
and make us whole to serve you,
to heal this world of sin.

28th October *Ss Simon and Jude*
For Jude and Simon, praise, Lord,
who walked the pilgrim way;
the call of Christ compelled them
to serve him, come what may.
Like them, with hearts enlivened,
may we that hope retain,
and walk the rugged pathway
eternal life to gain.

30th November *St Andrew*
We thank you, Lord, for Andrew,
who, answering your call,
went straight to tell his brother
he'd met the Lord of All.
At once he left his fishing,
and home beside the sea.
May we take up your challenge:
'Get up! Come, follow me!'

26th December *St Stephen*
For Stephen, true and righteous,
we praise you, Lord, and bless;
he stood to challenge evil,
and your great name confess.

Like him, may we be willing
your Lordship to proclaim;
that, faced with opposition,
we may uphold your Name.

27th December *St John the Evangelist*
John, your belov'd disciple,
wrote down all that he knew
of Christ, our Lord and Saviour,
that we might know him too.
We praise you for his record
of peace and love and grace;
through Christ we see the Father,
and meet him in this place.

28th December *Holy Innocents*
With aching hearts we honour
those infants killed in hate
by Herod's jealous fury
faced with a Prince so great.
Such innocents as martyrs
unnerve us with their pain;
yet safe in Jesus' keeping
they shall not die again.

Mother Theresa
With mercy and devotion,
Theresa showed your care
in tending poor and dying,
that they your love might share.
Her life of selfless mercy
brought healing and release;
give us her deep compassion
to spread your holy peace.

Pope John XXIII
Pope John, filled with your Spirit,
challenged the church to be
one people, called to worship
and serve in unity.
Help us to break down barriers,
to end past fear and strife;
in Christ may we go forward,
living your risen life.

147

John Raphael Peacey (1896-1971)
© By kind permission of the Revd M. J. Hancock

1. For Mary, mother of our Lord,
   God's holy name be praised,
   who first the Son of God adored,
   as on her child she gazed.

2. The angel Gabriel brought the word
   she should Christ's mother be;
   Our Lady, handmaid of the Lord,
   made answer willingly.

3. The heav'nly call she thus obeyed,
   and so God's will was done;
   the second Eve love's answer made
   which our redemption won.

4. She gave her body for God's shrine,
   her heart to piercing pain,
   and knew the cost of love divine
   when Jesus Christ was slain.

5. Dear Mary, from your lowliness
   and home in Galilee,
   there comes a joy and holiness
   to ev'ry family.

6. Hail, Mary, you are full of grace,
   above all women blest;
   and blest your Son, whom your
      embrace
   in birth and death confessed.

148

Nick Fawcett (b. 1957)
© 2004 Kevin Mayhew Ltd

1. For the days when you feel near,
   for the times when all is clear;
   when your presence seems so real,
   that it colours all we feel –
   for the blessing of such days,
   Lord, accept our grateful praise.

2. For the times when you feel far,
   when we wonder where you are;
   when we call and call again,
   but our pray'rs appear in vain –
   when it seems you just don't care,
   Lord, assure us you're still there.

3. For the truth that day by day
   you are present, come what may:
   when we see you, when we don't,
   when we trust you, when we won't.
   For the peace such love imparts,
   Lord, we come with grateful hearts.

149

Fred Pratt Green (1903-2000)
© 1970 Stainer & Bell Ltd

1. For the fruits of his creation,
   thanks be to God;
   for his gifts to ev'ry nation,
   thanks be to God;
   for the ploughing, sowing, reaping,
   silent growth while we are sleeping,
   future needs in earth's safekeeping,
   thanks be to God.

2. In the just reward of labour,
   God's will is done;
   in the help we give our neighbour,
   God's will is done;
   in our world-wide task of caring
   for the hungry and despairing,
   in the harvests we are sharing,
   God's will is done.

3. For the harvests of his Spirit,
   thanks be to God;
   for the good we all inherit,
   thanks be to God;
   for the wonders that astound us,
   for the truths that still confound us,
   most of all, that love has found us,
   thanks be to God.

150

Fred Kaan (b. 1929)
© 1968 Stainer & Bell Ltd

1. For the healing of the nations,
   Lord, we pray with one accord;
   for a just and equal sharing
   of the things that earth affords.
   To a life of love in action
   help us rise and pledge our word.

2. Lead us, Father, into freedom,
   from despair your world release;
   that, redeemed from war and hatred,
   all may come and go in peace.
   Show us how through care and
     goodness
   fear will die and hope increase.

3. All that kills abundant living,
   let it from the earth be banned;
   pride of status, race or schooling
   dogmas that obscure your plan.
   In our common quest for justice
   may we hallow life's brief span.

4. You, creator-God, have written
   your great name on humankind;
   for our growing in your likeness
   bring the life of Christ to mind;
   that by our response and service
   earth its destiny may find.

151

Rosamond E. Herklots (1905-1987) alt.
© Oxford University Press

1. 'Forgive our sins as we forgive',
   you taught us, Lord, to pray;
   but you alone can grant us grace
   to live the words we say.

2. How can your pardon reach and bless
   the unforgiving heart
   that broods on wrongs, and will not let
   old bitterness depart?

3. In blazing light your Cross reveals
   the truth we dimly knew:
   what trivial debts are owed to us,
   how great our debt to you!

4. Lord, cleanse the depths within our
     souls,
   and bid resentment cease.
   Then, bound to all in bonds of love,
   our lives will spread your peace.

152

James Quinn (b. 1919)
© 1969 Geoffrey Chapman, London. An imprint
of Continuum Int. Publishing Group

1. Forth in the peace of Christ we go;
   Christ to the world with joy we bring;
   Christ in our minds, Christ on our lips,
   Christ in our hearts, the world's true
     King.

2. King of our hearts, Christ makes us
     kings;
   kingship with him his servants gain;
   with Christ, the Servant-Lord of all,
   Christ's world we serve to share
     Christ's reign.

3. Priests of the world, Christ sends us
     forth
   this world of time to consecrate,
   our world of sin by grace to heal,
   Christ's world in Christ to re-create.

4. Prophets of Christ, we hear his Word:
   he claims our minds to search his ways;
   he claims our lips to speak his truth;
   he claims our hearts to sing his praise.

5. We are his Church, he makes us one:
   here is one hearth for all to find;
   here is one flock, one Shepherd-King;
   here is one faith, one heart, one mind.

153

Charles Wesley (1707-1788) alt.

1. Forth in thy name, O Lord, I go,
   my daily labour to pursue;
   thee, only thee, resolved to know,
   in all I think or speak or do.

2. The task thy wisdom hath assigned
   O let me cheerfully fulfil;
   in all my works thy presence find,
   and prove thy good and perfect will.

3. Thee may I set at my right hand,
   whose eyes my inmost substance see,
   and labour on at thy command,
   and offer all my works to thee.

4. Give me to bear thy easy yoke,
   and ev'ry moment watch and pray,
   and still to things eternal look,
   and hasten to thy glorious day.

5. For thee delightfully employ
   whate'er thy bounteous grace hath
       giv'n,
   and run my course with even joy,
   and closely walk with thee to heav'n.

154

George Hunt Smyttan (1822-1870)
adapted by Michael Forster (b. 1946)
© 1999 Kevin Mayhew Ltd

1. Forty days and forty nights
   you were fasting in the wild;
   forty days and forty nights,
   tempted still, yet unbeguiled.

2. Sunbeams scorching all the day,
   chilly dew-drops nightly shed,
   prowling beasts about your way,
   stones your pillow, earth your bed.

3. Let us your endurance share,
   and from earthly greed abstain,
   with you vigilant in prayer,
   with you strong to suffer pain.

4. Then if evil on us press,
   flesh or spirit to assail,
   Victor in the wilderness,
   help us not to swerve or fail.

5. So shall peace divine be ours;
   holy gladness, pure and true:
   come to us, angelic powers,
   such as ministered to you.

6. Keep, O keep us, Saviour dear,
   ever constant by your side,
   that with you we may appear
   at th'eternal Eastertide.

155

Graham Kendrick (b. 1950)
© 1983 Thankyou Music.
Administered by worshiptogether.com songs

1. From heav'n you came, helpless babe,
   entered our world, your glory veiled;
   not to be served but to serve,
   and give your life that we might live.

   This is our God, the Servant King,
   he calls us now to follow him,
   to bring our lives as a daily offering
   of worship to the Servant King.

2. There in the garden of tears,
   my heavy load he chose to bear;
   his heart with sorrow was torn.
   'Yet not my will but yours,' he said.

3. Come see his hands and his feet,
   the scars that speak of sacrifice,
   hands that flung stars into space,
   to cruel nails surrendered.

4. So let us learn how to serve,
   and in our lives enthrone him;
   each other's needs to prefer,
   for it is Christ we're serving.

156 Sister M. Teresine, based on Psalm 129

1. From the depths we cry to thee,
   God of sov'reign majesty!
   Hear our chants and hymns of praise;
   bless our Lent of forty days.

2. Though our consciences proclaim
   our transgressions and our shame,
   cleanse us, Lord, we humbly plead,
   from our sins of thought and deed.

3. Lord, accept our Lenten fast
   and forgive our sinful past,
   that we may partake with thee
   in the Easter mystery.

157 Michael Forster (b. 1946)
© 1992, 1994 Kevin Mayhew Ltd

1. From the very depths of darkness
   springs a bright and living light;
   out of falsehood and deceit
   a greater truth is brought to sight;
   in the halls of death, defiant,
   life is dancing with delight!
   The Lord is risen indeed!

   Christ is risen! Hallelujah! (x3)
   The Lord is risen indeed!

*2. Jesus meets us at the dawning
   of the resurrection day;
   speaks our name with love, and gently
   says that here we may not stay:
   'Do not cling to me, but go to
   all the fearful ones and say,
   "The Lord is risen indeed!"'

*3. So proclaim it in the high-rise,
   in the hostel let it ring;
   make it known in Cardboard City,
   let the homeless rise and sing:
   'He is Lord of life abundant,
   and he changes ev'rything;
   the Lord is risen indeed!'

4. In the heartlands of oppression,
   sound the cry of liberty;
   where the poor are crucified,
   behold the Lord of Calvary;
   from the fear of death and dying,
   Christ has set his people free;
   the Lord is risen indeed!

5. To the tyrant, tell the gospel
   of a love that can't be known
   in a guarded palace-tomb,
   condemned to live and die alone:
   'Take the risk of love and freedom;
   Christ has rolled away the stone!
   The Lord is risen indeed!'

6. When our spirits are entombed
   in mortal prejudice and pride;
   when the gates of hell itself
   are firmly bolted from inside;
   at the bidding of his Spirit,
   we may fling them open wide;
   the Lord is risen indeed!

158
Jean Holloway (b. 1939)
© 1994, 1999 Kevin Mayhew Ltd

Gather around, for the table is spread,
welcome the food and rest!
Wide is our circle, with Christ at the
    head,
he is the honoured guest.
Learn of his love, grow in his grace,
pray for the peace he gives;
here at this meal, here in this place,
know that his Spirit lives!
Once he was known
    in the breaking of bread,
shared with a chosen few;
multitudes gathered
    and by him were fed,
so will he feed us too.

159
Christine McCann (b. 1951)
© 1978 Kevin Mayhew Ltd

1. Gifts of bread and wine, gifts we've
        offered,
    fruits of labour, fruits of love, taken,
    offered, sanctified, blessed and broken;
    words of one who died;

    'Take my body, take my saving blood.'
    Gifts of bread and wine: Christ our Lord.

2. Christ our Saviour, living presence
        here,
    as he promised while on earth:
    'I am with you for all time,
    I am with you in this bread and wine.'

3. To the Father, with the Spirit,
    one in union with the Son,
    for God's people, joined in prayer,
    faith is strengthened by the food we
        share.

160
Psalm 50(51) adapted by Christopher Walker
(b. 1947). © 1988, 1989 Christopher Walker.
OCP Publications

Give me a new heart, O God.
Put your Spirit in me.
Keep me with you, give me joy.
Give me a new heart, O God.

1. God, in your love, have mercy on me.
    In your compassion cleanse me.
    All of my guilt, wash it away.
    Lord, make me clean from my sin.

2. All of my faults, I know them so well.
    All of my sins, I know them.
    For against you alone have I sinned.
    Evil in your sight have I done.

3. Truth in the heart you love most of all.
    Now fill my mind with wisdom.
    Wash me from sin and I shall be clean;
    I shall be as pure as the snow.

4. Give me again the joy of your help.
    Put a new spirit in me,
    that I may teach sinners your ways,
    that they will turn back to you.

5. You do not want a sacrifice made.
    You would refuse burnt off'rings.
    My spirit is humble, offered to you.
    You will not spurn my humble heart.

6. O spare my life and save me, O God.
    I will proclaim your goodness.
    Open my lips and help me to speak
    and I will praise you with joy.

161 Traditional

1. Give me joy in my heart, keep me
        praising,
    give me joy in my heart, I pray.
    Give me joy in my heart, keep me
        praising,
    keep me praising till the end of day.

Sing hosanna! Sing hosanna!
Sing hosanna to the King of kings!
Sing hosanna! Sing hosanna!
Sing hosanna to the King!

2. Give me peace in my heart,
keep me resting . . .

3. Give me love in my heart,
keep me serving . . .

4. Give me light in my heart,
keep me shining . . .

162 Estelle White (b. 1925)
© 1976 Kevin Mayhew Ltd

1. Give me peace, O Lord, I pray,
in my work and in my play;
and inside my heart and mind,
Lord, give me peace.

2. Give peace to the world, I pray,
let all quarrels cease today.
May we spread your light and love:
Lord, give us peace.

163 Martin E. Leckebusch (b. 1962)
© 2004 Kevin Mayhew Ltd

1. Give thanks for those whose faith is
firm
when all around seems bleak:
on God's good promise they rely,
so while they live and when they die
how forcefully they speak –
the strong who once were weak!

2. Give thanks for those whose hope is
clear,
beyond mere mortal sight:
who seek the city God has planned,
the true, eternal promised land,
and steer towards that light,
a beacon ever bright.

3. Give thanks for those whose love is
pure,
a sparkling, precious stone:
they show by what they say and do
an inward beauty, warm and true,
for God's concerns they own –
his love through them is known.

4. Give thanks for saints of ages past
and saints alive today:
though often by this world despised,
their hearts by God are richly prized –
give thanks that we may say
we share their pilgrim way.

164 Henry Smith (1857-1939)
© 1978 Integrity's Hosanna! Music
Administered by Sovereign Music UK

Give thanks with a grateful heart,
give thanks to the Holy One,
give thanks because he's given
Jesus Christ, his Son.
And now let the weak say, 'I am strong',
let the poor say, 'I am rich',
because of what the Lord has done
    for us.
And now let the weak say, 'I am strong',
let the poor say, 'I am rich',
because of what the Lord has done
    for us.

165 John Newton (1725-1807)
based on Isaiah 33:20-21, alt.

1. Glorious things of you are spoken,
Sion, city of our God:
he whose word cannot be broken
formed you for his own abode.
On the Rock of Ages founded,
what can shake your sure repose?
With salvation's walls surrounded,
you may smile at all your foes.

Continued overleaf

2. See, the streams of living waters,
   springing from eternal love,
   well supply your sons and daughters,
   and all fear of want remove.
   Who can faint while such a river
   ever flows their thirst to assuage?
   Grace which, like the Lord, the giver,
   never fails from age to age.

3. Blest inhabitants of Sion,
   washed in their Redeemer's blood:
   Jesus, whom their souls rely on,
   makes them kings and priests to God.
   'Tis his love his people raises
   over self to reign as kings,
   and, as priests, his solemn praises
   each for a thank-off'ring brings.

4. Saviour, since of Sion's city
   I, through grace, a member am,
   let the world deride or pity,
   I will glory in your name:
   fading is the worldling's pleasure,
   all his boasted pomp and show;
   solid joys and lasting treasure
   none but Sion's children know.

166 Daniel L. Schutte (b. 1947),
based on Psalms 64, 65
© 1976 Daniel L. Schutte and New Dawn Music

Glory and praise to our God,
who alone gives light to our days.
Many are the blessings he bears
to those who trust in his ways.

1. We, the daughters and sons of him
   who built the valleys and plains,
   praise the wonders our God has done
   in ev'ry heart that sings.

2. In his wisdom he strengthens us,
   like gold that's tested in fire.
   Though the power of sin prevails,
   our God is there to save.

3. Ev'ry moment of ev'ry day
   our God is waiting to save,
   always ready to seek the lost,
   to answer those who pray.

4. God has watered our barren land
   and sent his merciful rain.
   Now the rivers of life run full
   for anyone to drink.

167 *Viva, viva, Gesù,* 18th century,
trans. Edward Caswall (1814-1878) alt.

1. Glory be to Jesus
   who, in bitter pains,
   poured for me the lifeblood
   from his sacred veins.

2. Grace and life eternal
   in that blood I find:
   blest be his compassion,
   infinitely kind.

3. Blest, through endless ages,
   be the precious stream
   which, from endless torment,
   did the world redeem.

*4. There the fainting spirit
   drinks of life her fill;
   there, as in a fountain,
   laves herself at will.

*5. Abel's blood for vengeance
   pleaded to the skies,
   but the blood of Jesus
   for our pardon cries.

6. Oft as it is sprinkled
   on our guilty hearts
   Satan in confusion
   terror-struck departs.

7. Oft as earth exulting
   wafts its praise on high
   angel hosts rejoicing,
   make their glad reply.

8. Lift, then, all your voices,
   swell the mighty flood;
   louder still and louder,
   praise the precious blood.

168
John Greally (b. 1934)
© Trustees for Roman Catholic Purposes Registered

1. Glory to thee, Lord God!
   In faith and hope we sing.
   Through this completed sacifice
   our love and praise we bring.
   We give thee for our sins
   a price beyond all worth,
   which none could ever fitly pay
   but this thy Son on earth.

2. Here is the Lord of all,
   to thee in glory slain;
   of worthless givers, worthy gift,
   a victim without stain.
   Through him we give thee thanks,
   with him we bend the knee,
   in him be all our life, who is
   our one true way to thee.

3. So may this sacrifice
   we offer here this day,
   be joined with our poor lives in all
   we think and do and say.
   By living true to grace,
   for thee and thee alone,
   our sorrows, labours,and our joys
   will be his very own.

169
Thomas Ken (1637-1710)

1. Glory to thee, my God, this night
   for all the blessings of the light;
   keep me, O keep me, King of kings,
   beneath thine own almighty wings.

2. Forgive me, Lord, for thy dear Son,
   the ill that I this day have done,
   that with the world, myself and thee,
   I, ere I sleep, at peace may be.

3. Teach me to live, that I may dread
   the grave as little as my bed;
   teach me to die, that so I may
   rise glorious at the aweful day.

4. O may my soul on thee repose,
   and with sweet sleep mine eyelids
      close;
   sleep that may me more vig'rous make
   to serve my God when I awake.

5. Praise God, from whom all blessings
      flow;
   praise him, all creatures here below;
   praise him above, ye heav'nly host;
   praise Father, Son and Holy Ghost.

170
Michael Forster (b. 1946)
© 2004 Kevin Mayhew Ltd

1. Go back, go back to Galilee,
   go with the one who died,
   and witness there to risen life
   among the crucified.
   Where human folk are living still
   in fear of worldly pow'r,
   their Christ, with wounds still open,
   stands and shares their finest hour.

2. Go back, go back to Galilee,
   Christ meets us on the way,
   and calls us all to follow truth
   where evil still holds sway.
   There in the face of hate and fear,
   the Spirit gives us breath;
   his song is life and liberty
   which puts an end to death.

Continued overleaf

3. 'Go back, go back to Galilee,'
the centuries repeat,
'where evil, faced with deathless hope,
still struggles in defeat.'
So when we find the empty tomb
a safer place to be,
the angel prompts us yet again,
'Go back to Galilee.'

4. Go forth and tell!
the doors are open wide:
share God's good gifts –
let no one be denied;
live out your life
as Christ your Lord shall choose,
your ransomed pow'rs
for his sole glory use.

5. Go forth and tell!
O Church of God, arise!
Go in the strength
which Christ your Lord supplies;
go till all nations
his great name adore
and serve him, Lord and King,
for evermore.

171 James Edward Seddon (1915-1983)
© *The representatives of the late James Edward Seddon/ Jubilate Hymns. Used by permission*

1. Go forth and tell!
O Church of God, awake!
God's saving news
to all the nations take:
proclaim Christ Jesus,
Saviour, Lord and King,
that all the world
his worthy praise may sing.

2. Go forth and tell!
God's love embraces all;
he will in grace
respond to all who call:
how shall they call
if they have never heard
the gracious invitation
of his word?

3. Go forth and tell!
where still the darkness lies;
in wealth or want,
the sinner surely dies:
give us, O Lord,
concern of heart and mind,
a love like yours
which cares for all mankind.

172 Susan Sayers (b. 1946)
© *2004 Kevin Mayhew Ltd*

Go forward, people of God today,
be a people of God who pray the
moments one by one,
till God's kingdom comes.

1. Take courage people of God, be bold,
jars of clay that inside will hold
the shining love of Jesus bright as gold.

2. Keep faithful people of God and be
healing salt in community
through your compassion and
humility.

3. In friendship people of God unite
let the flame of your love stay bright
till darkness melts in heaven's glorious
light.

173
Aniceto Nazareth
© 1984 Kevin Mayhew Ltd.

Go in peace to be Christ's body.
Go in peace, proclaim his Word.
You have shared his dying and his rising.
Go in peace, Christ lives in you.

1. But our treasure is in earthen vessels,
   proving we are weak and need God's
   strength.
   Bearing in our flesh the death of Jesus,
   we must show his life at work in us.

2. Though our outer nature may seem
   wasted,
   daily is the inner self renewed.
   For the love of Jesus Christ controls us,
   since we know that one man died for
   all.

174
Traditional

Go, tell it on the mountain,
over the hills and ev'rywhere.
Go, tell it on the mountain
that Jesus Christ is born.

1. While shepherds kept their watching
   o'er wand'ring flocks by night,
   behold, from out of heaven,
   there shone a holy light.

2. And lo, when they had seen it,
   they all bowed down and prayed;
   they travelled on together
   to where the babe was laid.

3. When I was a seeker,
   I sought both night and day:
   I asked my Lord to help me
   and he showed me the way.

4. He made me a watchman
   upon the city wall,
   and, if I am a Christian,
   I am the least of all.

175
Marie Lydia Pereira (b. 1920)
© 1976 Kevin Mayhew Ltd

1. Go, the Mass is ended,
   children of the Lord.
   Take his Word to others
   as you've heard it spoken to you.
   Go, the Mass is ended,
   go and tell the world
   the Lord is good, the Lord is kind,
   and he loves ev'ryone.

2. Go, the Mass is ended,
   take his love to all.
   Gladden all who meet you,
   fill their hearts with hope and courage.
   Go, the Mass is ended,
   fill the world with love,
   and give to all what you've received –
   the peace and joy of Christ.

3. Go, the Mass is ended,
   strengthened in the Lord,
   lighten ev'ry burden,
   spread the joy of Christ around you.
   Go, the Mass is ended,
   take his peace to all.
   This day is yours to change the world –
   to make God known and loved.

176
Book of Hours (1514)

God be in my head,
and in my understanding;
God be in mine eyes,
and in my looking;
God be in my mouth,
and in my speaking;
God be in my heart,
and in my thinking;
God be at mine end,
and at my departing.

177

Donald Hughes (1911-1967)
Based on J. E. Rankin (1828-1904)
© Paul Hughes

1. God be with you till we meet again;
   may he through the days direct you;
   may he in life's storms protect you;
   God be with you till we meet again.

   Till we meet! Till we meet!
   Till we meet at Jesus' feet;
   till we meet! Till we meet!
   God be with you till we meet again!

2. God be with you till we meet again;
   and when doubts and fears oppress you,
   may his holy peace possess you;
   God be with you till we meet again.

3. God be with you till we meet again;
   in distress his grace sustain you;
   in success from pride restrain you;
   God be with you till we meet again.

4. God be with you till we meet again;
   may he go through life beside you,
   and through death in safety guide you;
   God be with you till we meet again.

178

Bernadette Farrell (b. 1957)
© 1990 Bernadette Farrell/OCP Publications

1. God, beyond our dreams,
   you have stirred in us a mem'ry;
   you have placed your pow'rful Spirit
   in the hearts of humankind.

   All around us we have known you,
   all creation lives to hold you,
   in our living and our dying
   we are bringing you to birth.

2. God, beyond all names,
   you have made us in your image;
   we are like you, we reflect you;
   we are woman, we are man.

3. God, beyond all words,
   all creation tells your story;
   you have shaken with our laughter,
   you have trembled with our tears.

4. God, beyond all time,
   you are labouring within us;
   we are moving, we are changing
   in your Spirit ever new.

5. God of tender care,
   you have cradled us in goodness,
   you have mothered us in wholeness,
   you have loved us into birth.

179 Harold Riley

1. God everlasting, wonderful and holy,
   Father most gracious, we who stand
     before thee
   here at thine altar, as thy Son has
     taught us,
   come to adore thee.

2. Countless the mercies thou has
     lavished on us,
   source of all blessing to all creatures
     living;
   to thee we render, for thy love
     o'erflowing,
   humble thanksgiving.

3. Now in remembrance of our great
     Redeemer,
   dying on Calv'ry, rising and ascending,
   through him we offer what he ever
     offers,
   sinners befriending.

4. Strength to the living, rest to the
     departed,
   grant, Holy Father, through this pure
     oblation:
   may the life-giving bread for ever
     bring us
   health and salvation.

180 Jean-Paul Lécot (b. 1942), based on Luke 1:46-55, trans. Michael Hodgetts (b. 1936) © 1974 Michael Hodgetts

God fills me with joy, alleluia.
His holy presence is my robe, alleluia.

1. My soul, now glorify the Lord
   who is my Saviour.
   Rejoice, for who am I,
   that God has shown me favour?

2. The world shall call me blest
   and ponder on my story.
   In me is manifest
   God's greatness and his glory.

3. For those who are his friends,
   and keep his laws as holy,
   his mercy never ends,
   and he exalts the lowly.

4. But by his pow'r the great,
   the proud, the self-conceited,
   the kings who sit in state,
   are humbled and defeated.

5. He feeds the starving poor,
   he guards his holy nation,
   fulfilling what he swore
   long since in revelation.

6. Then glorify with me
   the Lord who is my Saviour:
   one holy Trinity
   for ever and for ever.

181 Carol Owens (b. 1931) © 1972 Bud John Songs/EMI Christian Music Publishing. Administered by Kevin Mayhew Ltd

1. God forgave my sin in Jesus' name.
   I've been born again in Jesus' name.
   And in Jesus' name I come to you
   to share his love as he told me to.

He said: 'Freely, freely you have received;
freely, freely give.
Go in my name, and because you believe,
others will know that I live.'

2. All pow'r is giv'n in Jesus' name,
   in earth and heav'n in Jesus' name.
   And in Jesus' name I come to you
   to share his pow'r as he told me to.

3. God gives us life in Jesus' name,
   he lives in us in Jesus' name.
   And in Jesus' name I come to you
   to share his peace as he told me to.

182 Jean-Paul Lécot (b.1942) based on Luke 1:46-55, trans. W. R. Lawrence © 1988 Kevin Mayhew Ltd

God has filled me with endless joy,
   alleluia!
He has vested me with holiness,
   alleluia!

1. My soul praises the glory of the Lord,
   and my spirit exults in God my
   Saviour.

2. He has looked on his handmaid's
   lowliness;
   from now on ev'ryone shall call me
   blessèd.

3. The Almighty has done great things
   for me,
   and his mercy is shown to all who
   fear him.

4. He has put down the mighty from
   their thrones,
   and has raised up on high the poor
   and lowly.

5. He has filled those who hunger with
   good things,
   but the rich he has sent away quite
   empty.

Continued overleaf

6. He protected his servant Israel,
   as he promised to Abraham for ever.

   God has filled me with endless joy,
   alleluia!
   He has vested me with holiness,
   alleluia!

7. God the Father, the Son and Spirit
   praise,
   as it was, and is now, and ever shall be.

183 John L. Bell (b. 1949) and Graham Maule
(b. 1958). © *1989 WGRG, Iona Community*

1. God, in the planning and purpose of
   life,
   hallowed the union of husband and
   wife:
   this we embody where love is
   displayed,
   rings are presented and promises
   made.

2. Jesus was found, at a similar feast,
   taking the roles of both waiter and
   priest,
   turning the worldly towards the
   divine,
   tears into laughter and water to wine.

3. Therefore we pray that his Spirit
   preside
   over the wedding of bridegroom and
   bride,
   fulfilling all that they've hoped will
   come true,
   lighting with love all they dream of
   and do.

4. Praise then the Maker, the Spirit, the
   Son,
   source of the love through which two
   are made one.
   God's is the glory, the goodness and
   grace
   seen in this marriage and known in
   this place.

184 Traditional

1. God is love, and the one who lives in
   love
   lives in God, and God lives in him.
   God is love, and the one who lives in
   love
   lives in God, and God lives in her.
   And we have come to know and have
   believed
   the love which God has for us.
   God is love, and all those who live in
   love
   live in God, and God lives in them.

2. God is hope . . .

3. God is peace . . .

4. God is joy . . .

185 Percy Dearmer (1867-1936) alt.

1. God is love: his the care,
   tending each, ev'rywhere.
   God is love, all is there!
   Jesus came to show him,
   that we all might know him!

   Sing aloud, loud, loud!
   Sing aloud, loud, loud!
   God is good! God is truth!
   God is beauty! Praise him!

2. None can see God above;
   we can share life and love;
   thus may we Godward move,
   seek him in creation,
   holding ev'ry nation.

3. Jesus lived on the earth,
   hope and life brought to birth
   and affirmed human worth,
   for he came to save us
   by the truth he gave us.

4. To our Lord praise we sing,
   light and life, friend and King,
   coming down, love to bring,
   pattern for our duty,
   showing God in beauty.

186 Arthur Campbell Ainger (1841-1919)
adapted by Michael Forster (b. 1946)
© *This version 1996 Kevin Mayhew Ltd*

1. God is working his purpose out
   as year succeeds to year.
   God is working his purpose out,
   and the time is drawing near.
   Nearer and nearer draws the time,
   the time that shall surely be,
   when the earth shall be filled
   with the glory of God
   as the waters cover the sea.

*2. From the east to the utmost west
    wherever foot has trod,
    through the mouths of his messengers
    echoes forth the voice of God:
    'Listen to me, ye continents,
    ye islands, give ear to me,
    that the earth shall be filled
    with the glory of God
    as the waters cover the sea.'

3. How can we do the work of God,
   how prosper and increase
   harmony in the human race,
   and the reign of perfect peace?
   What can we do to urge the time,
   the time that shall surely be,
   when the earth shall be filled
   with the glory of God
   as the waters cover the sea?

*4. March we forth in the strength of
    God,
    his banner is unfurled;
    let the light of the gospel shine
    in the darkness of the world:
    strengthen the weary, heal the sick
    and set ev'ry captive free,
    that the earth shall be filled
    with the glory of God
    as the waters cover the sea.

5. All our efforts are nothing worth
   unless God bless the deed;
   vain our hopes for the harvest tide
   till he brings to life the seed.
   Yet ever nearer draws the time,
   the time that shall surely be,
   when the earth shall be filled
   with the glory of God
   as the waters cover the sea.

187 Nick Fawcett (b. 1957)
© *1997 Kevin Mayhew Ltd*

1. God of life, God of love,
   all around we glimpse your greatness,
   here on earth and far above.
   We would worship all our days
   even though no words can ever
   give to you sufficient praise.

Continued overleaf

2. God of life, God of truth,
we rejoice that you are with us,
never distant or aloof.
Like a father, you are there,
reaching out your arms to hold us,
speaking words that show you care.

3. God of life, God of grace,
you have walked this earth before us,
giving truth a human face.
Knowing sorrow, knowing pain,
you were beaten, bruised and broken,
but in triumph rose again.

4. God of life, God of love –
felt as wind and tongues of fire
yet as gentle as a dove –
ev'ry moment, ev'ry hour,
you are working deep within us
through your sov'reign selfless pow'r.

5. God of life, God on high,
we can barely grasp your goodness,
language fails us when we try.
As a father, through your Son,
by the Spirit you are with us,
somehow three, yet also one.

188 Nick Fawcett (b. 1957)
© 1997 Kevin Mayhew Ltd.

1. God of life, we come in worship,
lost in wonder, filled with awe,
at your feet we kneel in homage,
here to marvel and adore.
Words cannot express your greatness,
awesome is your majesty.
Higher than the highest mountain,
deeper than the deepest sea.

2. God of love, we come rejoicing,
here to celebrate your grace.
Consecrate this sacred moment,
help us meet you face to face.
In the name of Christ we gather,
by his touch our lives made new,
cleansed, renewed, restored,
    refashioned,
all we are and all we do.

3. God of light, we come in gladness,
souls on fire and hearts ablaze,
reaching out in adoration,
songs resounding to your praise.
Take the hope that flames within us,
take the joy that burns so bright;
may our lives reflect your glory
and find favour in your sight.

189 Edmund Vaughan (1827-1908), alt.

1. God of mercy and compassion,
look with pity upon me;
Father, let me call thee Father,
'tis thy child returns to thee.

Jesus, Lord, I ask for mercy,
knowing it is not in vain:
all my sins I now detest them,
help me not to sin again.

2. Only by thy grace and mercy
may I hope for heav'n above,
where the Saints rejoice for ever
in a sea of boundless love.

3. See our Saviour, bleeding, dying
on the cross of Calvary;
to that cross my sins have nailed him,
yet he bleeds and dies for me.

190

Michael Forster (b. 1946)
© 1993 Kevin Mayhew Ltd

1. God of the Passover,
   Author and Lord of salvation,
   gladly we gather to bring
   you our heart's adoration;
   ransomed and free,
   called and commissioned to be
   signs of your love for creation.

2. Here we remember that evening
   of wonder enthralling,
   myst'ry of passion divine,
   and betrayal appalling.
   Breaking the bread,
   'This is my body,' he said,
   'do this, my passion recalling.'

3. God of the Eucharist,
   humbly we gather before you
   and, at your table,
   for pardon and grace we implore you.
   Under the cross,
   counting as profit our loss,
   safe in its shade, we adore you.

191

Stephen Eric Smyth
© Stephen Eric Smyth

1. God, our Creator, hear us sing in
   praise.
   God, always tender, God who knows
   our ways.
   God, always present, God who really
   cares.
   We offer thanks for all the love you
   share.
   We sing in praise for the great gifts
   you give:
   all of creation, ev'rything that lives,
   glories of nature, our own time on
   earth,
   sending your Son among us proves
   our worth.

Loud is our praise as we sing of you,
one with people of faith, ancient and new.
Bless us afresh with your grace, we pray.
Help us witness your love today.

2. Thanks for the blessings of the
   talents, skills,
   fam'lies and friendships by which
   lives are filled.
   Thanks for the graces, gifts you
   spread so wide:
   those that the world sees and those
   deep inside.
   Even in hard times we can praise
   your name.
   You're always with us, loving just the
   same.
   Sickness or sorrow, loneliness or doubt,
   help us remember your hand reaches
   out.

3. Gathered together, sisters, brothers all,
   baptised in Jesus, faithful to your call,
   we are one fam'ly. May your will be
   done
   and, for all people, may your
   Kingdom come.
   'God who is love', you are our Father
   true;
   Jesus, our brother, fully human too;
   Spirit, your presence, with us ev'ry day;
   love is your essence, love our truest way.

Repeat verse 1

192

Traditional, alt.

1. God rest you merry, gentlefolk,
   let nothing you dismay,
   for Jesus Christ our Saviour
   was born on Christmas Day,
   to save us all from Satan's pow'r
   when we were gone astray:

Continued overleaf

O tidings of comfort and joy,
comfort and joy,
O tidings of comfort and joy.

2. In Bethlehem, in Jewry,
   this blessèd babe was born,
   and laid within a manger,
   upon this blessèd morn;
   at which his mother Mary
   did nothing take in scorn:

3. From God, our heav'nly Father,
   a blessèd angel came,
   and unto certain shepherds,
   brought tidings of the same,
   how that in Bethlehem was born
   the Son of God by name:

4. 'Fear not,' then said the angel,
   'let nothing you affright,
   this day is born a Saviour,
   of virtue, pow'r and might;
   by him the world is overcome
   and Satan put to flight.'

5. The shepherds at those tidings
   rejoicèd much in mind,
   and left their flocks a-feeding,
   in tempest, storm and wind,
   and went to Bethlehem straightway
   this blessèd babe to find:

6. But when to Bethlehem they came,
   whereat this infant lay,
   they found him in a manger,
   where oxen feed on hay;
   his mother Mary kneeling,
   unto the Lord did pray:

7. Now to the Lord sing praises,
   all you within this place,
   and with true love and fellowship
   each other now embrace;
   this holy tide of Christmas
   all others doth deface:

193 John L. Bell (b. 1949) and Graham Maule (b. 1958). © 1997 WGRG, Iona Community

God to enfold you, Christ to uphold
   you,
Spirit to keep you in heaven's sight;
so may God grace you, heal and
   embrace you,
lead you through darkness into the
   light.

194 Ascribed to St Thomas Aquinas (1227-1274), trans. Gerard Manley Hopkins (1844-1889), alt.

1. Godhead here in hiding,
   whom I do adore,
   masked by these bare shadows,
   shape and nothing more,
   see, Lord, at thy service
   low lies here a heart
   lost, all lost in wonder
   at the God thou art.

2. Seeing, touching, tasting
   are in thee deceived;
   how, says trusty hearing,
   that shall be believed?
   What God's Son hath told me,
   take for truth I do;
   truth himself speaks truly,
   or there's nothing true.

3. On the cross thy Godhead
   made no sign to men;
   here thy very manhood
   steals from human ken;
   both are my confession,
   both are my belief;
   and I pray the prayer
   of the dying thief.

4. I am not like Thomas,
   wounds I cannot see,
   but can plainly call thee
   Lord and God as he;
   this faith each day deeper
   be my holding of,
   daily make me harder
   hope and dearer love.

5. O thou our reminder
   of Christ crucified,
   living Bread, the life of
   us for whom he died,
   lend this life to me then,
   feed and feast my mind,
   there be thou the sweetness
   man was meant to find.

6. Jesu, whom I look at
   shrouded here below,
   I beseech thee send me
   what I long for so,
   some day to gaze on thee
   face to face in light
   and be blest for ever
   with thy glory's sight.

195

Hubert J. Richards (b. 1921)
© 1982 Kevin Mayhew Ltd.

1. God's Spirit is in my heart.
   He has called me and set me apart.
   This is what I have to do,
   what I have to do.

   *He sent me to give the Good News to
      the poor,*
   *tell pris'ners that they are pris'ners no
      more,*
   tell blind people that they can see,
   and set the downtrodden free,
   and go tell ev'ryone the news
   that the kingdom of God has come,
   *and go tell ev'ryone the news that God's
      kingdom has come.*

2. Just as the Father sent me,
   so I'm sending you out to be
   my witnesses throughout the world,
   the whole of the world.

3. Don't carry a load in your pack,
   you don't need two shirts on your back.
   A workman can earn his own keep,
   can earn his own keep.

4. Don't worry what you have to say,
   don't worry because on that day
   God's Spirit will speak in your heart,
   will speak in your heart.

196

Michael Forster (b. 1946). Alternative words
overleaf by William Arms Fisher
© 1999 Kevin Mayhew Ltd

1. Going home, moving on,
   through God's open door;
   hush, my soul, have no fear,
   Christ has gone before.
   Parting hurts, love protests,
   pain is not denied;
   yet, in Christ, life and hope
   span the great divide.
   Going home, moving on,
   through God's open door;
   hush, my soul, have no fear,
   Christ has gone before,
   Christ has gone before.

2. No more guilt, no more fear,
   all the past is healed:
   broken dreams now restored,
   perfect grace revealed.
   Christ has died, Christ is ris'n,
   Christ will come again:
   death destroyed, life restored,
   love alone shall reign.
   Going home, moving on,
   through God's open door;
   hush, my soul, have no fear,
   Christ has gone before,
   Christ has gone before.

An alternative text will be found overleaf

Alternative text:

1. Going home, going home,
   I'm a-going home.
   Quiet like, some still day,
   I'm just going home.
   It's not far, just close by,
   through an open door.
   Work all done, care laid by,
   going to fear no more.
   Mother's there expecting me,
   father's waiting too.
   Lots of folk gathered there,
   all the friends I knew,
   all the friends I knew.

2. Morning star lights the way,
   restless dreams all done.
   Shadows gone, break of day,
   real life just begun.
   There's no break, there's no end,
   just a-living on,
   wide awake, with a smile,
   going on and on.
   Going home, going home,
   I'm just going home.
   It's not far, just close by,
   through an open door.
   I'm just going home.

197 John Mason Neale (1818-1866) alt.

1. Good Christians all, rejoice
   with heart and soul and voice!
   Give ye heed to what we say:
   News! News! Jesus Christ is born today;
   ox and ass before him bow,
   and he is in the manger now:
   Christ is born today,
   Christ is born today!

2. Good Christians all, rejoice
   with heart and soul and voice!
   Now ye hear of endless bliss:
   Joy! Joy! Jesus Christ was born for this.
   He hath opened heaven's door,
   and we are blest for evermore:
   Christ was born for this,
   Christ was born for this.

3. Good Christians all, rejoice
   with heart and soul and voice!
   Now ye need not fear the grave:
   Peace! Peace! Jesus Christ was born to
      save;
   calls you one, and calls you all,
   to gain his everlasting hall:
   Christ was born to save,
   Christ was born to save.

198 John Mason Neale (1818-1866) alt.

1. Good King Wenceslas looked out
   on the feast of Stephen,
   when the snow lay round about,
   deep, and crisp, and even;
   brightly shone the moon that night,
   though the frost was cruel,
   when a poor man came in sight,
   gath'ring winter fuel.

2. 'Hither, page, and stand by me,
   if thou know'st it, telling,
   yonder peasant, who is he,
   where and what his dwelling?'
   'Sire, he lives a good league hence,
   underneath the mountain,
   right against the forest fence,
   by Saint Agnes' fountain.'

3. 'Bring me flesh, and bring me wine,
   bring me pine logs hither:
   thou and I will see him dine,
   when we bring him thither.'
   Page and monarch, forth they went,
   forth they went together;
   through the rude wind's wild lament,
   and the bitter weather.

4. 'Sire, the night is darker now,
   and the wind blows stronger;
   fails my heart, I know not how;
   I can go no longer.'
   'Mark my footsteps good, my page;
   tread thou in them boldly:
   thou shalt find the winter's rage
   freeze thy blood less coldly.'

5. In his master's steps he trod,
   where the snow lay dinted;
   heat was in the very sod
   which the Saint had printed.
   Therefore, Christians all, be sure,
   wealth or rank possessing,
   ye who now will bless the poor,
   shall yourselves find blessing.

199 Lucien Deiss (b. 1921), adapted from
Ezekiel 36:26 and Jeremiah 31:31-34
© 1965, 1973, 1996 World Library Publications Inc.

Grant to us, O Lord, a heart renewed;
recreate in us your own Spirit, Lord!

1. Behold, the days are coming, says the
   Lord our God,
   when I will make a new covenant
   with the house of Israel.

2. Deep within their being I will
   implant my law;
   I will write it in their hearts.

3. I will be their God,
   and they shall be my people.

4. And for all their faults I will grant
   forgiveness;
   never more will I remember their sins.

200 Jean Holloway (b. 1939)
© 1998 Kevin Mayhew Ltd

1. Grant us the courage, gracious God,
   to change the things we can,
   pursuing justice, spreading hope
   that Jesus Christ began.

2. Give us serenity to bear
   the things we cannot change;
   acceptance of the things we find
   mysterious or strange.

3. We ask for wisdom to discern
   the changes we can make;
   and pray for your sustaining love
   through risks we choose to take.

4. Encourage all who love your church
   to try the bold and new;
   foresaking safe, familiar ways
   for greater trust in you.

5. Your Holy Spirit leads the way
   to change we dream not of –
   through fear of the unknown, and on
   to costly deeds of love.

201 William Williams (1717-1791)
trans. Peter Williams (1727-1796) and others

1. Guide me, O thou great Redeemer,
   pilgrim through this barren land;
   I am weak, but thou art mighty,
   hold me with thy pow'rful hand:
   Bread of Heaven, Bread of Heaven,
   feed me till I want no more,
   feed me till I want no more.

Continued overleaf

2. Open now the crystal fountain,
   whence the healing stream doth flow;
   let the fire and cloudy pillar
   lead me all my journey through;
   strong deliv'rer, strong deliv'rer,
   be thou still my strength and shield,
   be thou still my strength and shield.

3. When I tread the verge of Jordan,
   bid my anxious fears subside;
   death of death, and hell's destruction,
   land me safe on Canaan's side;
   songs of praises, songs of praises,
   I will ever give to thee,
   I will ever give to thee.

202 Sister Agnes

1. Hail, glorious Saint Patrick,
   dear saint of our isle,
   on us thy poor children
   bestow a sweet smile;
   and now thou art high
   in thy mansions above,
   on Erin's green valleys
   look down in thy love.

   On Erin's green valleys (x3)
   look down in thy love.

2. Hail, glorious Saint Patrick,
   thy words were once strong,
   against Satan's wiles and
   an infidel throng;
   not less is thy might
   where in heaven thou art;
   O, come to our aid,
   in our battle take part.

3. In the war against sin,
   in the fight for the faith,
   dear saint, may thy children
   resist unto death;
   may their strength be in meekness,
   in penance, in prayer,
   their banner the Cross
   which they glory to bear.

4. Thy people, now exiles
   on many a shore,
   shall love and revere thee
   till time be no more;
   and the fire thou has kindled
   shall ever burn bright,
   its warmth undiminished,
   undying its light.

5. Ever bless and defend
   the sweet land of our birth,
   where the shamrock still blooms
   as when thou wert on earth,
   and our hearts shall yet burn,
   wheresoever we roam,
   for God and Saint Patrick,
   and our native home.

203

Carey Landry (b. 1944), based on Luke 1:28-30
© *1975 Carey Landry and North American Liturgy Resources*

Hail, Mary, full of grace,
the Lord is with you.
Blessèd are you among women,
and blest is the fruit of your womb,
   Jesus.
Holy Mary, Mother of God,
pray for us sinners, now
and at the hour of death. Amen.

Gentle woman, quiet light,
morning star, so strong and bright,
gentle mother, peaceful dove,
teach us wisdom; teach us love.

1. You were chosen by the Father;
   you were chosen for the Son.
   You were chosen from all women
   and for woman, shining one.

2. Blessèd are you among women;
   blest, in turn, all women, too.
   Blessèd they with peaceful spirits;
   blessèd they with gentle hearts.

204 John Lingard (1771-1851)

1. Hail, Queen of heav'n, the ocean star,
   guide of the wand'rer here below;
   thrown on life's surge, we claim thy
       care;
   save us from peril and from woe.
   Mother of Christ, star of the sea,
   pray for the wand'rer, pray for me.

2. O gentle, chaste and spotless maid,
   we sinners make our prayers through
       thee;
   remind us all that we are saved
   in spite of our iniquity.
   Virgin most pure, star of the sea,
   pray for the sinner, pray for me.

3. Sojourners in this vale of tears,
   to thee, blest advocate, we cry;
   pity our sorrows, calm our fears,
   and soothe with hope our misery.
   Refuge in grief, star of the sea,
   pray for the mourner, pray for me.

4. And while to him who reigns above,
   in Godhead One, in persons Three,
   the source of life, of grace, of love,
   homage we pay on bended knee,
   do thou, bright Queen, star of the sea,
   pray for thy children, pray for me.

205 Patrick Brennan (1877-1952)
© Burns & Oates Ltd./Continuum Int.

1. Hail, Redeemer, King divine!
   Priest and Lamb, the throne is thine,
   King, whose reign shall never cease,
   Prince of everlasting peace.

   Angels, saints and nations sing:
   'Praised be Jesus Christ, our King,
   Lord of life, earth, sky and sea,
   King of love on Calvary.'

2. King whose name creation thrills,
   rule our minds, our hearts, our wills,
   till in peace each nation rings
   with thy praises, King of kings.

3. King most holy, King of truth,
   guide the lowly, guide the youth;
   Christ thou King of glory bright,
   be to us eternal light.

4. Shepherd-King, o'er mountains steep,
   homeward bring the wand'ring sheep,
   shelter in one royal fold
   states and kingdoms, new and old.

206 Charles Wesley (1707-1788)
Thomas Cotterill (1779-1823) and others, alt.

1. Hail the day that sees him rise,
       alleluia!
   to his throne above the skies;
       alleluia!
   Christ the Lamb, for sinners giv'n,
       alleluia!
   enters now the highest heav'n!
       alleluia!

2. There for him high triumph waits;
   lift your heads, eternal gates!
   He hath conquered death and sin;
   take the King of Glory in!

Continued overleaf

*3. Circled round with angel-pow'rs,
their triumphant Lord and ours;
wide unfold the radiant scene,
take the King of Glory in!

*4. Lo, the heav'n its Lord receives,
yet he loves the earth he leaves;
though returning to his throne,
calls the human race his own.

*5. See, he lifts his hands above;
see, he shows the prints of love;
hark, his gracious lips bestow
blessings on his Church below.

*6. Still for us he intercedes,
his prevailing death he pleads;
near himself prepares our place,
he the first-fruits of our race.

7. Lord, though parted from our sight,
far above the starry height,
grant our hearts may thither rise,
seeking thee above the skies.

8. Ever upward let us move,
wafted on the wings of love;
looking when our Lord shall come,
longing, sighing after home.

*2. He who was nailed to the cross
is Lord and the ruler of all things;
all things created on earth
sing to the glory of God:

*3. Daily the loveliness grows,
adorned with the glory of blossom;
heaven her gates unbars,
flinging her increase of light:

4. Rise from the grave now, O Lord,
who art author of life and creation.
Treading the pathway of death,
life thou bestowest on all:

*5. God the All-Father, the Lord,
who rulest the earth and the heavens,
guard us from harm without,
cleanse us from evil within:

*6. Jesus the health of the world,
enlighten our minds, thou Redeemer,
Son of the Father supreme,
only begotten of God:

7. Spirit of life and of pow'r,
now flow in us, fount of our being,
light that dost lighten all,
life that in all dost abide:

8. Praise to the Giver of good!
Thou Love who art author of concord,
pour out thy balm on our souls,
order our ways in thy peace.

207 The editors of *The English Hymnal* based on the Latin of Venantius Fortunatus (530-609) © *Hymns Ancient & Modern*

Hail thee, festival day!
Blest day that art hallowed for ever;
day whereon Christ arose,
breaking the kingdom of death.

1. Lo, the fair beauty of earth
from the death of the winter arising!
Ev'ry good gift of the year,
now with its Master returns.

208 *Ave, maris stella,* 9th century, trans. Edward Caswall (1814-1878)

1. Hail, thou star of ocean, portal of the sky,
ever virgin mother of the Lord most high.
O, by Gabriel's 'Ave', uttered long ago,
Eva's name reversing, 'stablish peace below.

2. Break the captive's fetters, light on
      blindness pour,
   all our ills expelling, ev'ry bliss implore.
   Show thyself a mother; offer him our
      sighs,
   who for us incarnate did not thee
      despise.

3. Virgin of all virgins, to thy shelter
      take us;
   gentlest of the gentle, chaste and
      gentle make us.
   Still, as on we journey, help our weak
      endeavour;
   till with thee and Jesus we rejoice for
      ever.

4. Through the highest heaven, to
      th'almighty Three,
   Father, Son and Spirit, One same
      glory be.

209 Paraphrase of Psalm 72 by James Montgomery (1771-1854)

1. Hail to the Lord's anointed,
   great David's greater son!
   Hail, in the time appointed,
   his reign on earth begun!
   He comes to break oppression,
   to set the captive free;
   to take away transgression,
   and rule in equity.

2. He comes with succour speedy
   to those who suffer wrong;
   to help the poor and needy,
   and bid the weak be strong;
   to give them songs for sighing,
   their darkness turn to light,
   whose souls, condemned and dying,
   were precious in his sight.

3. He shall come down like showers
   upon the fruitful earth,
   and love, joy, hope, like flowers,
   spring in his path to birth:
   before him on the mountains
   shall peace the herald go;
   and righteousness in fountains
   from hill to valley flow.

4. Kings shall fall down before him,
   and gold and incense bring;
   all nations shall adore him,
   his praise all people sing;
   to him shall prayer unceasing
   and daily vows ascend;
   his kingdom still increasing,
   a kingdom without end.

5. O'er ev'ry foe victorious,
   he on his throne shall rest,
   from age to age more glorious,
   all-blessing and all-blest;
   the tide of time shall never
   his covenant remove;
   his name shall stand for ever;
   that name to us is love.

210 Unknown

Hallelu, hallelu, hallelu, hallelujah;
we'll praise the Lord! *(Repeat)*
We'll praise the Lord, hallelujah! *(x3)*
We'll praise the Lord!

211 *Vox clara ecce intonat*, 6th century, trans. Edward Caswall (1814-1878)

1. Hark! a herald voice is calling:
   'Christ is nigh!' it seems to say;
   'Cast away the dreams of darkness,
   O ye children of the day!'

Continued overleaf

2. Startled at the solemn warning,
let the earth-bound soul arise;
Christ, her sun, all sloth dispelling,
shines upon the morning skies.

3. Lo, the Lamb, so long expected,
comes with pardon down from heav'n;
let us haste, with tears of sorrow,
one and all to be forgiv'n.

4. So when next he comes with glory,
wrapping all the earth in fear,
may he then, as our defender,
on the clouds of heav'n appear.

5. Honour, glory, virtue, merit,
to the Father and the Son,
with the co-eternal Spirit,
while unending ages run.

212 Charles Wesley (1707-1788),
George Whitefield (1714-1770),
Martin Madan (1726-1790) and others, alt.

1. Hark, the herald-angels sing
glory to the new-born King;
peace on earth and mercy mild,
God and sinners reconciled:
joyful, all ye nations rise,
join the triumph of the skies,
with th'angelic host proclaim,
'Christ is born in Bethlehem.'

Hark, the herald-angels sing
glory to the new-born King.

2. Christ, by highest heav'n adored,
Christ, the everlasting Lord,
late in time behold him come,
offspring of a virgin's womb!
Veiled in flesh the Godhead see,
hail, th'incarnate Deity!
Pleased as man with us to dwell,
Jesus, our Emmanuel.

3. Hail, the heav'n-born Prince of Peace!
Hail, the Sun of Righteousness!
Light and life to all he brings,
ris'n with healing in his wings;
mild he lays his glory by,
born that we no more may die,
born to raise us from the earth,
born to give us second birth.

213 Christian Strover (b. 1932)
© *Christian Strover/Jubilate Hymns*
Used by permission.

1. Have you heard the raindrops
drumming on the rooftops?
Have you heard the raindrops
dripping on the ground?
Have you heard the raindrops
splashing in the streams
and running to the rivers all around?

There's water, water of life,
Jesus gives us the water of life;
there's water, water of life,
Jesus gives us the water of life.

2. There's a busy worker
digging in the desert,
digging with a spade that
flashes in the sun;
soon there will be water
rising in the well-shaft,
spilling from the bucket as it comes.

3. Nobody can live
who hasn't any water,
when the land is dry,
then nothing much grows;
Jesus gives us life if we drink
the living water,
sing it so that ev'rybody knows.

214 Traditional

1. He brings us in to his banqueting table,
his banner over me is love;
he brings us in to his banqueting table,
his banner over me is love;
he brings us in to his banqueting table,
his banner over me is love;
his banner over me is love.

2. The one way to peace is the pow'r of
the cross,
his banner over me is love . . .

3. He builds his Church on a firm
foundation,
his banner over me is love . . .

4. In him we find a new creation,
his banner over me is love . . .

5. He lifts us up to heavenly places,
his banner over me is love . . .

215 Unknown

1. He is Lord, he is Lord.
He is risen from the dead and he is
Lord.
Ev'ry knee shall bow, ev'ry tongue
confess
that Jesus Christ is Lord.

2. He is King, he is King.
He is risen from the dead and he is
King.
Ev'ry knee shall bow, ev'ry tongue
confess
that Jesus Christ is King.

3. He is love, he is love.
He is risen from the dead and he is love.
Ev'ry knee shall bow, ev'ry tongue
confess
that Jesus Christ is love.

216 Willard F. Jabusch (b. 1930)
© 1998 Willard F. Jabusch

1. He is risen, tell the story
to the nations of the night;
from their sin and from their blindness,
let them walk in Easter light.
Now begins a new creation,
now has come our true salvation,
Jesus Christ, the Son of God.

2. Mary goes to tell the others
of the wonders she has seen;
John and Peter come a-running –
what can all this truly mean?
O Rabboni, Master holy,
to appear to one so lowly!
Jesus Christ, the Son of God!

3. He has cut down death and evil,
he has conquered all despair;
he has lifted from our shoulders
all the weight of anxious care.
Risen Brother, now before you,
we will worship and adore you,
Jesus Christ, the Son of God!

4. Now get busy, bring the message,
so that all may come to know
there is hope for saint and sinner,
for our God has loved us so.
Ev'ry church bell is a-ringing,
ev'ry Christian now is singing,
Jesus Christ, the Son of God!

217 Francesca Leftley (b. 1955)
© 1999 Kevin Mayhew Ltd

1. Healer of the sick,
Lord Jesus, Son of God;
Lord, how we long for you:
walk here among us.

Continued overleaf

Bind up our broken lives,
comfort our broken hearts,
banish our hidden fears.
Lord, come with pow'r,
bring new light to the blind,
bring peace to troubled minds,
hold us now in your arms, set us free now.

2. Bearer of our pain,
   Lord Jesus, Lamb of God;
   Lord, how we cry to you:
   walk here among us.

3. Calmer of our fears,
   Lord Jesus, Prince of Peace;
   Lord, how we yearn for you:
   walk here among us.

4. Saviour of the world,
   Lord Jesus, mighty God;
   Lord, how we sing to you:
   walk here among us.

218 Anthony D'Souza (b. 1950), based on Psalm 60
© 1984 Kevin Mayhew Ltd

Hear my cry, O Lord, my God,
listen to my prayer;
from earth's end I call to you
when my heart is faint.

1. Set me high on a rock;
   you are my refuge, O Lord.

2. Let me stay in your tent;
   safe in the shade of your wings.

3. I will echo your praise;
   pay my vows day after day.

219 Ralph Wright OSB (b. 1938)
© 1989 GIA Publications Inc.

1. Hear our prayer, O gentle mother,
   help us worship as we gather
   that with you we may give praise
   to the Father all our days.

2. Mirror of a true believer,
   putting on the mind of Jesus
   in the word of your own Son
   you could see the Kingdom come.

3. Hear our prayer, most loving Father,
   through the virgin-born, our brother;
   in the Spirit may we bring
   this our homage as we sing.

Verse 2 may be replaced with an
appropriate stanza from the following:

1st January
Mary, Mother of God
Woman, raised above all nations,
chosen out of all creation,
Mary, you have brought to birth
Jesus, Lord of all the earth.

25th March
Annunciation
Humbly you received the greeting
brought by Gabriel to your dwelling.
Though in darkness you believed,
through the Spirit you conceived.

31st May
Visitation
As your cousin comes to meet you,
'Blest of women,' so she greets you.
John who leaps within her womb
knows the Bridegroom will come
   soon.

15th August
Assumption

8th December
Immaculate Conception
Mary, virgin, sinless mother,
humble, pow'rful, full of wonder,
help us have the calm to see
what your Son calls us to be.

15th September

Our Lady of Sorrows

Mary, standing still and grieving
as your Son in pain hung bleeding,
you have known within your heart
all the torment of the dark.

220 Marty Haugen (b. 1950)
© 1982 GIA Publications Inc.

1. Here in this place new light is
     streaming,
   now is the darkness vanished away,
   see in this space our fears and our
     dreamings,
   brought here to you in the light of
     this day.
   Gather us in – the lost and forsaken,
   gather us in – the blind and the lame;
   call to us now, and we shall awaken,
   we shall arise at the sound of our name.

2. We are the young – our lives are a
     myst'ry,
   we are the old – who yearn for your
     face,
   we have been sung throughout all of
     hist'ry,
   called to be light to the whole human
     race.
   Gather us in – the rich and the
     haughty,
   gather us in – the proud and the strong;
   give us a heart so meek and so lowly,
   give us the courage to enter the song.

3. Here we will take the wine and the
     water,
   here we will take the bread of new birth,
   here you shall call your sons and your
     daughters,
   call us anew to be salt for the earth.
   Give us to drink the wine of
     compassion,
   give us to eat the bread that is you;
   nourish us well, and teach us to fashion
   lives that are holy and hearts that are
     true.

4. Not in the dark of buildings confining,
   not in some heaven, light-years away.
   But here in this place the new light is
     shining,
   now is the Kingdom, and now is the
     day.
   Gather us in and hold us for ever,
   gather us in and make us your own;
   gather us in – all peoples together,
   fire of love in our flesh and our bone.

221 Traditional

1. He's got the whole world in his hand.
   (x4)

2. He's got you and me, brother . . .

3. He's got you and me, sister . . .

4. He's got the little tiny baby . . .

5. He's got ev'rybody here . . .

222 Charles Edward Oakley (1832-1865), adapted

1. Hills of the north, rejoice,
   echoing songs arise,
   hail with united voice
   him who made earth and skies:
   he comes in righteousness and love,
   he brings salvation from above.

Continued overleaf

2. Isles of the southern seas
   sing to the list'ning earth,
   carry on ev'ry breeze
   hope of a world's new birth:
   in Christ shall all be made anew,
   his word is sure, his promise true.

3. Lands of the east, arise,
   he is your brightest morn,
   greet him with joyous eyes,
   praise shall his path adorn:
   the God whom you have longed to
      know
   in Christ draws near, and calls you
      now.

4. Shores of the utmost west,
   lands of the setting sun,
   welcome the heav'nly guest
   in whom the dawn has come:
   he brings a never-ending light
   who triumphed o'er our darkest
      night.

5. Shout, as you journey on,
   songs be in ev'ry mouth,
   lo, from the north they come,
   from east and west and south:
   in Jesus all shall find their rest,
   in him the longing earth be blest.

223 Adaptation of a hymn by Ambrose (d. 397)
Ascribed to Ignaz Franz (1719-1790),
trans. Clarence Walworth (1820-1900)

1. Holy God, we praise thy name;
   Lord of all, we bow before thee.
   All on earth thy sceptre own,
   all in heav'n above adore thee.
   Infinite thy vast domain,
   everlasting is thy reign.

2. Hark, the loud celestial hymn,
   angel choirs above are raising;
   cherubim and seraphim,
   in unceasing chorus praising,
   fill the heav'ns with sweet accord,
   holy, holy, holy Lord.

3. Holy Father, Holy Son,
   Holy Spirit, three we name thee,
   while in essence only one
   undivided God we claim thee;
   and adoring bend the knee,
   while we own the mystery.

4. Spare thy people, Lord, we pray,
   by a thousand snares surrounded;
   keep us without sin today;
   never let us be confounded.
   Lo, I put my trust in thee,
   never, Lord, abandon me.

224 Jimmy Owens (b. 1930)
© 1972 Bud John Songs/EMI Christian Music
Publishing. Administered by Kevin Mayhew Ltd

1. Holy, holy, holy, holy.
   Holy, holy, holy Lord God almighty;
   and we lift our hearts before you
   as a token of our love,
   holy, holy, holy, holy.

2. Gracious Father, gracious Father,
   we are glad to be your children,
      gracious Father;
   and we lift our heads before you
   as a token of our love,
   gracious Father, gracious Father.

3. Risen Jesus, risen Jesus,
   we are glad you have redeemed us,
      risen Jesus;
   and we lift our hands before you
   as a token of our love,
   risen Jesus, risen Jesus.

4. Holy Spirit, Holy Spirit,
   come and fill our hearts anew,
      Holy Spirit;
   and we lift our voice before you
   as a token of our love,
   Holy Spirit, Holy Spirit.

5. Hallelujah, hallelujah,
   hallelujah, hallelujah, hallelujah;
   and we lift our hearts before you
   as a token of our love,
   hallelujah, hallelujah.

225 Unknown

1. Holy, holy, holy is the Lord,
   holy is the Lord God almighty.
   Holy, holy, holy is the Lord,
   holy is the Lord God almighty:
   who was, and is, and is to come;
   holy, holy, holy is the Lord.

2. Jesus, Jesus, Jesus is the Lord,
   Jesus is the Lord God almighty:
      (Repeat)
   who was, and is, and is to come;
   Jesus, Jesus, Jesus is the Lord.

3. Worthy, worthy, worthy is the Lord,
   worthy is the Lord God almighty:
      (Repeat)
   who was, and is and is to come;
   worthy, worth, worthy is the Lord.

4. Glory, glory, glory to the Lord,
   glory to the Lord God almighty:
      (Repeat)
   who was, and is, and is to come;
   glory, glory, glory to the Lord.

226 Reginald Heber (1783-1826)

1. Holy, holy, holy!
   Lord God almighty!
   Early in the morning
   our song shall rise to thee;
   holy, holy, holy!
   Merciful and mighty!
   God in three persons,
   blessèd Trinity!

2. Holy, holy, holy!
   All the saints adore thee,
   casting down their golden crowns
   around the glassy sea;
   cherubim and seraphim
   falling down before thee,
   which wert, and art,
   and evermore shall be.

3. Holy, holy, holy!
   Though the darkness hide thee,
   though the sinful mortal eye
   thy glory may not see,
   only thou art holy,
   there is none beside thee,
   perfect in pow'r,
   in love, and purity.

4. Holy, holy, holy!
   Lord God almighty!
   All thy works shall praise thy name,
   in earth and sky and sea;
   holy, holy, holy!
   Merciful and mighty!
   God in three persons,
   blessèd Trinity!

227 Damian Lundy (1944-1977)
© 1987, 1999 Kevin Mayhew Ltd

1. Holy Mary, you were chosen
   by the Father, the God of life,
   joyfully responding, you became a
      mother.
   Pray now for us, and show a mother's
      love.

Continued overleaf

2. Holy Mary, you were chosen,
   called to carry the Son of God.
   Gratefully responding,
   you became his mother.
   Pray now for us, and show a mother's
     love.

3. Holy Mary, you were chosen,
   so the Spirit could work in you.
   Faithfully responding,
   you became God's mother.
   Pray now for us, and show a mother's
     love.

4. Holy Mary, you were chosen,
   all God's children are blessed in you.
   Joyfully responding,
   you became our mother.
   Pray now for us, and show a mother's
     love.

228

Brian Foley (1919-2000)
© 1971 Faber Music Ltd

1. Holy Spirit, come, confirm us
   in the truth that Christ makes known;
   we have faith and understanding
   through your promised light alone.

2. Holy Spirit, come, console us,
   come as Advocate to plead;
   loving Spirit from the Father,
   grant in Christ the help we need.

3. Holy Spirit, come, renew us,
   come yourself to make us live;
   holy through your loving presence,
   holy through the gifts you give.

4. Holy Spirit, come, possess us,
   you the love of Three in One,
   Holy Spirit of the Father,
   Holy Spirit of the Son.

229

Ascribed to Stephen Langton (d. 1228)
trans. Edward Caswall (1814-1878) alt.

1. Holy Spirit, Lord of light,
   from the clear celestial height,
   thy pure beaming radiance give;
   come, thou Father of the poor,
   come with treasures which endure;
   come, thou light of all that live!

2. Thou, of all consolers best,
   thou, the soul's delightsome guest,
   dost refreshing peace bestow:
   thou in toil art comfort sweet;
   pleasant coolness in the heat;
   solace in the midst of woe.

3. Light immortal, light divine,
   visit thou these hearts of thine,
   and our inmost being fill:
   if thou take thy grace away,
   nothing pure in us will stay;
   all his good is turned to ill.

4. Heal our wounds, our strength renew;
   on our dryness pour thy dew;
   wash the stains of guilt away;
   bend the stubborn heart and will;
   melt the frozen, warm the chill;
   guide the steps that go astray.

5. Thou, on those who evermore
   thee confess and thee adore,
   in thy sev'nfold gifts descend:
   give them comfort when they die;
   give them life with thee on high;
   give them joys that never end.

230

John Glynn (b. 1948)
© 1976 Kevin Mayhew Ltd

1. Holy Spirit of fire,
   flame everlasting, so bright and clear,
   speak this day in our hearts.
   Lighten our darkness and purge us of
     fear,
   Holy Spirit of fire.

The wind can blow or be still,
or water be parched by the sun.
A fire can die into dust:
but here the eternal Spirit of God
tells us a new world's begun.

2. Holy Spirit of love,
strong are the faithful who trust your
pow'r.
Love who conquers our will,
teach us the words of the gospel of
peace,
Holy Spirit of love.

3. Holy Spirit of God,
flame everlasting, so bright and clear,
speak this day in our hearts.
Lighten our darkness and purge us of
fear,
Holy Spirit of God.

231 Jean-Paul Lécot (b. 1947), trans. W. R. Lawrence (1925-1997), alt. © 1988 Kevin Mayhew Ltd

1. Holy virgin, by God's decree,
you were called eternally;
that he could give his Son to our race.
Mary, we praise you, hail, full of grace.

Ave, ave, ave, Maria.

2. By your faith and loving accord,
as the handmaid of the Lord,
you undertook God's plan to embrace.
Mary, we thank you, hail, full of grace.

3. Joy to God you gave and expressed,
of all women none more blessed,
when in our flesh your Son took his
place.
Mary, we love you, hail, full of grace.

4. Refuge for your children so weak,
sure protection all can seek.
Problems of life you help us to face.
Mary, we trust you, hail, full of grace.

5. To our needy world of today
love and beauty you portray,
showing the path to Christ we must
trace.
Mary, our mother, hail, full of grace.

232 Carl Tuttle (b. 1953). © 1985 Firmpaths Music. Administered by CopyCare

1. Hosanna, hosanna,
hosanna in the highest! *(Repeat)*

Lord, we lift up your name,
with hearts full of praise;
be exalted, O Lord, my God!
Hosanna in the highest!

2. Glory, glory, glory
to the King of kings! *(Repeat)*

233 Martin E. Leckebusch (b. 1962) © 2000 Kevin Mayhew Ltd.

1. How good it is to trust in you,
the mighty King of kings;
how sheltered is the hiding place
we find beneath your wings.

2. No better refuge could we reach –
protection here is sure!
However fierce the storms of life,
with you we are secure.

3. Your presence stills our troubled hearts;
our doubts and fears decrease –
in Christ you give us lasting joy
and all-pervading peace.

4. You see our needs before we ask;
you hear our ev'ry cry;
and on your utter faithfulness
we know we can rely.

5. Within the haven of your love
our strength is forged anew,
enabling us to rise and soar
on eagles' wings with you!

234 Unknown

How great is our God,
how great is his name!
How great is our God,
for ever the same!

1. He rolled back the waters
   of the mighty Red Sea,
   and he said: 'I'll never leave you.
   Put your trust in me.'

2. He sent his Son, Jesus,
   to set us all free,
   and he said: 'I'll never leave you.
   Put your trust in me.'

3. He gave us his Spirit,
   and now we can see.
   And he said: 'I'll never leave you.
   Put your trust in me.'

235 v. 1 Leonard E. Smith Jnr (b. 1942), based on Isaiah 52:7-10, vs. 2-4 unknown. © 1974 Thankyou Music. Administered by worshiptogether.com songs

1. How lovely on the mountains
   are the feet of him
   who brings good news, good news,
   announcing peace,
   proclaiming news of happiness:
   our God reigns, our God reigns.

   Our God reigns. (x4)

2. You watchmen, lift your voices
   joyfully as one,
   shout for your King, your King!
   See eye to eye,
   the Lord restoring Zion:
   our God reigns, our God reigns.

3. Wasteplaces of Jerusalem,
   break forth with joy!
   We are redeemed, redeemed.
   The Lord has saved
   and comforted his people:
   our God reigns, our God reigns.

4. Ends of the earth, see
   the salvation of our God!
   Jesus is Lord, is Lord!
   Before the nations,
   he has bared his holy arm:
   our God reigns, our God reigns!

236 Martin E. Leckebusch (b. 1962) © 2000 Kevin Mayhew Ltd

1. How privileged we are,
   that we are called to bring
   our offerings and gifts to you,
   our Sov'reign Lord and King!

2. It humbles us to see
   the riches you provide:
   to ev'ryone who seeks your help
   your hand is open wide.

3. What joys you pour on those
   who give with pure delight –
   for all who share with cheerful hearts
   are precious in your sight.

4. Lord, as we bring our gifts
   this longing we express:
   that we may serve you faithfully
   with all that we possess.

5. Within this broken world
   so many needs arise;
   Lord, may our use of wealth become
   creative, bold and wise.

6. So, may we worship you
   with ev'rything we own,
   for all we have and give and are
   belong to you alone.

237 Suzanne Toolan (b. 1927)
© 1966, 1970, 1986, 1993 GIA Publications Inc.

1. I am the bread of life.
   You who come to me shall not hunger;
   and who believe in me shall not thirst.
   No one can come to me
   unless the Father beckons.

   And I will raise you up,
   and I will raise you up,
   and I will raise you up on the last day.

2. The bread that I will give
   is my flesh for the life of the world,
   and if you eat of this bread,
   you shall live for ever,
   you shall live for ever.

3. Unless you eat
   of the flesh of the Son of Man,
   and drink of his blood,
   and drink of his blood,
   you shall not have life within you.

4. I am the resurrection,
   I am the life.
   If you believe in me,
   even though you die,
   you shall live for ever.

5. Yes, Lord, I believe
   that you are the Christ,
   the Son of God,
   who has come
   into the world.

238 Attributed to St Patrick (372-466),
trans. Cecil Frances Alexander (1818-1895) alt.

1. I bind unto myself today
   the strong name of the Trinity,
   by invocation of the same,
   the Three in One, and One in Three.

2. I bind unto myself today
   the virtues of the starlit heav'n,
   the glorious sun's life-giving ray
   the whiteness of the moon at even,
   the flashing of the lightning free,
   the whirling wind's tempestuous
      shocks,
   the stable earth, the deep salt sea
   around the old eternal rocks.

3. I bind unto myself today
   the pow'r of God to hold and lead,
   his eye to watch, his might to stay,
   his ear to hearken to my need;
   the wisdom of my God to teach,
   his hand to guide, his shield to ward,
   the word of God to give me speech,
   his heav'nly host to be my guard.

PART TWO

4. Christ be with me, Christ within me,
   Christ behind me, Christ before me,
   Christ beside me, Christ to win me,
   Christ to comfort and restore me;
   Christ beneath me, Christ above me,
   Christ in quiet, Christ in danger,
   Christ in hearts of all that love me,
   Christ in mouth of friend and
      stranger.

DOXOLOGY

5. I bind unto myself the name,
   the strong name of the Trinity,
   by invocation of the same,
   the Three in One, and One in Three,
   of whom all nature hath creation,
   eternal Father, Spirit, Word.
   Praise to the Lord of my salvation:
   salvation is of Christ the Lord.
   Amen.

239 William Young Fullerton (1857-1932) alt.

1. I cannot tell
   how he whom angels worship
   should stoop to love
   the peoples of the earth,
   or why as shepherd
   he should seek the wand'rer
   with his mysterious promise
   of new birth.
   But this I know,
   that he was born of Mary,
   when Bethl'em's manger
   was his only home,
   and that he lived at
   Nazareth and laboured,
   and so the Saviour,
   Saviour of the world, is come.

*2. I cannot tell
   how silently he suffered,
   as with his peace
   he graced this place of tears,
   or how his heart
   upon the cross was broken,
   the crown of pain
   to three and thirty years.
   But this I know,
   he heals the broken-hearted,
   and stays our sin,
   and calms our lurking fear,
   and lifts the burden
   from the heavy laden,
   for yet the Saviour,
   Saviour of the world, is here.

*3. I cannot tell
   how he will win the nations,
   how he will claim
   his earthly heritage,
   how satisfy
   the needs and aspirations
   of east and west,

of sinner and of sage.
But this I know,
all flesh shall see his glory,
and he shall reap
the harvest he has sown,
and some glad day
his sun shall shine in splendour
when he the Saviour,
Saviour of the world, is known.

4. I cannot tell
   how all the lands shall worship,
   when, at his bidding,
   ev'ry storm is stilled,
   or who can say
   how great the jubilation
   when ev'ry heart
   with perfect love is filled.
   But this I know,
   the skies will thrill with rapture,
   and myriad, myriad
   human voices sing,
   and earth to heav'n,
   and heav'n to earth, will answer:
   'At last the Saviour,
   Saviour of the world, is King!'

240 Sydney Carter (1915-2004)
© 1963 Stainer & Bell Ltd

1. I danced in the morning
   when the world was begun,
   and I danced in the moon
   and the stars and the sun,
   and I came down from heaven
   and I danced on the earth,
   at Bethlehem I had my birth.

   Dance then, wherever you may be,
   I am the Lord of the Dance, said he,
   and I'll lead you all, wherever you may
     be,
   and I'll lead you all in the dance, said he.

2. I danced for the scribe
   and the Pharisee,
   but they would not dance
   and they wouldn't follow me.
   I danced for the fishermen,
   for James and John –
   they came with me
   and the dance went on.

3. I danced on the Sabbath
   and I cured the lame;
   the holy people
   said it was a shame.
   They whipped and they stripped
   and they hung me on high,
   and they left me there
   on a cross to die.

4. I danced on a Friday
   when the sky turned black –
   it's hard to dance
   with the devil on your back.
   They buried my body,
   and they thought I'd gone,
   but I am the dance,
   and I still go on.

5. They cut me down
   and I leapt up high;
   I am the life
   that'll never, never die;
   I'll live in you
   if you'll live in me –
   I am the Lord
   of the Dance, said he.

241 *Estelle White (b. 1925)*
© 1978 Kevin Mayhew Ltd

1. I give my hands to do your work
   and, Jesus Lord, I give them willingly.
   I give my feet to go your way
   and ev'ry step I shall take cheerfully.

O, the joy of the Lord is my strength,
my strength!
O, the joy of the Lord is my help, my help!
For the pow'r of his Spirit is in my soul
and the joy of the Lord is my strength.

2. I give my eyes to see the world
   and ev'ryone, in just the way you do.
   I give my tongue to speak your words,
   to spread your name and freedom-
   giving truth.

3. I give my mind in ev'ry way
   so that each thought I have will come
   from you.
   I give my spirit to you, Lord,
   and ev'ry day my prayer will spring
   anew.

4. I give my heart that you may love
   in me your Father and the human race.
   I give myself that you may grow
   in me and make my life a song of
   praise.

242 *Michael Forster (b. 1946)*
based on the Good Friday Reproaches.
© 1996 Kevin Mayhew Ltd

1. I give you love, and how do you repay?
   When you were slaves I strove to set
   you free;
   I led you out from under Pharaoh's
   yoke,
   but you led out your Christ to Calvary.

My people, tell me, what is my offence?
What have I done to harm you?
Answer me!

2. For forty years I was your constant
   guide,
   I fed you with my manna from on
   high.
   I led you out to live in hope and peace,
   but you led out my only Son to die.

Continued overleaf

3. With cloud and fire I marked the
     desert way,
   I heard your cries of rage and calmed
     your fear.
   I opened up the sea and led you
     through,
   but you have opened Christ with nail
     and spear.

   My people, tell me, what is my offence?
   What have I done to harm you?
   Answer me!

4. When in distress you cried to me for
     food,
   I sent you quails in answer to your call,
   and saving water from the desert rock,
   but to my Son you offered bitter gall.

5. I gave you joy when you were in despair,
   with songs of hope, I set your hearts
     on fire;
   crowned you with grace, the people
     of my choice,
   but you have crowned my Christ
     with thorny briar.

6. When you were weak, exploited and
     oppressed,
   I heard your cry and listened to your
     plea.
   I raised you up to honour and renown,
   but you have raised me on a shameful
     tree.

243 Horatius Bonar (1808-1889)

1. I heard the voice of Jesus say,
   'Come unto me and rest;
   lay down, thou weary one, lay down
   thy head upon my breast.'
   I came to Jesus as I was,
   so weary, worn and sad;
   I found in him a resting-place,
   and he has made me glad.

2. I heard the voice of Jesus say,
   'Behold, I freely give
   the living water, thirsty one;
   stoop down and drink and live.'
   I came to Jesus, and I drank
   of that life-giving stream;
   my thirst was quenched, my soul
     revived,
   and now I live in him.

3. I heard the voice of Jesus say,
   'I am this dark world's light;
   look unto me, thy morn shall rise,
   and all thy day be bright.'
   I looked to Jesus, and I found
   in him my star, my sun;
   and in that light of life I'll walk
   till trav'lling days are done.

244 Unknown

1. I know that my Redeemer lives,
   and on that final day of days
   his voice shall bid me rise again;
   unending joy, unceasing praise.

2. This hope I cherish in my heart:
   to stand on earth, my flesh restored,
   and, not a stranger but a friend,
   behold my Saviour and my Lord.

245 From the Gospel of John

I received the living God,
and my heart is full of joy.
I received the living God,
and my heart is full of joy.

1. Jesus said: 'I am the Bread,
   kneaded long to give you life;
   you who will partake of me
   need not ever fear to die.'

2. Jesus said: 'I am the Way,
   and my Father longs for you;
   so I come to bring you home
   to be one with him anew.'

3. Jesus said: 'I am the Truth;
   if you follow close to me,
   you will know me in your heart,
   and my word shall make you free.'

4. Jesus said: 'I am the Life,
   far from whom no thing can grow,
   but receive this living bread,
   and my Spirit you shall know.'

246 Richard Beaumont
© 1974 Shalom Community

I sing a song to you, Lord,
a song of love and praise.
All glory be to you, Lord,
through everlasting days.

1. Holy holy, holy, mighty Lord and God.
   He who was and is now, and who is
      to come.

2. Worthy is the slain Lamb,
   honour him and praise.
   We rejoice with gladness,
   sing our love today.

3. He has used his power,
   has begun his reign.
   So rejoice, you heavens,
   and proclaim his name.

4. Shine your light on us, Lord,
   let us know your way.
   Be our guide for ever,
   make us yours today.

247 Daniel L. Schutte (b. 1947), based on Isaiah 6
© 1981 Daniel L. Schutte and New Dawn Music

1. I, the Lord of sea and sky,
   I have heard my people cry.
   All who dwell in dark and sin
   my hand will save.
   I who made the stars of night,
   I will make their darkness bright.
   Who will bear my light to them?
   Whom shall I send?

Here I am, Lord. Is it I, Lord?
I have heard you calling in the night.
I will go, Lord, if you lead me.
I will hold your people in my heart.

2. I, the Lord of snow and rain,
   I have borne my people's pain.
   I have wept for love of them.
   They turn away.
   I will break their hearts of stone,
   give them hearts for love alone.
   I will speak my word to them.
   Whom shall I send?

3. I, the Lord of wind and flame,
   I will tend the poor and lame.
   I will set a feast for them.
   My hand will save.
   Finest bread I will provide
   till their hearts be satisfied.
   I will give my life to them.
   Whom shall I send?

248 John Glynn (b. 1948)
© 1976 Kevin Mayhew Ltd.

1. I watch the sunrise lighting the sky,
   casting its shadows near.
   And on this morning, bright though
      it be,
   I feel those shadows near me.

Continued overleaf

But you are always close to me,
following all my ways.
May I be always close to you,
following all your ways, Lord.

2. I watch the sunlight shine through
   the clouds,
   warming the earth below.
   And at the mid-day, life seems to say:
   'I feel your brightness near me.'
   For you are always . . .

3. I watch the sunset fading away,
   lighting the clouds with sleep.
   And as the evening closes its eyes,
   I feel your presence near me.
   For you are always . . .

4. I watch the moonlight guarding the
   night,
   waiting till morning comes.
   The air is silent, earth is at rest –
   only your peace is near me.
   Yes, you are always . . .

249 Gerard Markland (b. 1953)
© 1978 Kevin Mayhew Ltd

I will be with you wherever you go.
Go now throughout the world!
I will be with you in all that you say.
Go now and spread my word!

1. Come, walk with me on stormy
   waters.
   Why fear? Reach out, and I'll be there.

2. And you, my friend, will you now
   leave me,
   or do you know me as your Lord?

3. Your life will be transformed with
   power
   by living truly in my name.

4. And if you say: 'Yes, Lord, I love you,'
   then feed my lambs and feed my sheep.

250 Carey Landry (b. 1944) based on Isaiah 49:15-16
© 1983 Carey Landry and
North American Liturgy Resources

1. I will never forget you, my people;
   I have carved you on the palm of my
   hand.
   I will never forget you;
   I will not leave you orphaned.
   I will never forget my own.

2. Does a mother forget her baby?
   Or a woman the child within her
   womb?
   Yet even if these forget, yes,
   even if these forget,
   I will never forget my own.

251 Max Dyer (b. 1951)
© 1974 Celebration/kingswaysongs.com

1. I will sing, I will sing a song unto the
   Lord.
   I will sing, I will sing a song unto the
   Lord.
   I will sing I will sing a song unto the
   Lord.
   Alleluia, glory to the Lord.

   Alleluia, alleluia, glory to the Lord.
   Alleluia, alleluia, glory to the Lord.
   Alleluia, alleluia, glory to the Lord
   Alleluia, alleluia, glory to the Lord.

2. We will come, we will come as one
   before the Lord. *(x3)*
   Alleluia, glory to the Lord.

3. If the Son, if the Son shall make you
   free, *(x3)*
   you shall be free indeed.

4. They that sow in tears shall reap in
   joy. *(x3)*
   Alleluia, glory to the Lord.

5. Ev'ry knee shall bow and ev'ry tongue
   confess *(x3)*
   that Jesus Christ is Lord.

6. In his name, in his name we have the
victory. *(x3)*
Alleluia, glory to the Lord.

252 Francis Harold Rowley (1854-1952). © *Harper CollinsReligious. Administered by CopyCare*

1. I will sing the wondrous story
of the Christ who died for me,
how he left the realms of glory
for the cross on Calvary.
Yes, I'll sing the wondrous story
of the Christ who died for me –
sing it with his saints in glory,
gathered by the crystal sea.

2. I was lost but Jesus found me,
found the sheep that went astray,
raised me up and gently led me
back into the narrow way.
Days of darkness still may meet me,
sorrow's path I oft may tread;
but his presence still is with me,
by his guiding hand I'm led.

3. He will keep me till the river
rolls its waters at my feet:
then he'll bear me safely over,
made by grace for glory meet.
Yes, I'll sing the wondrous story
of the Christ who died for me –
sing it with his saints in glory,
gathered by the crystal sea.

253 John B. Foley (b. 1939), based on Romans 8:31-39 © *1975 John B. Foley, SJ and New Dawn Music*

If God is for us, who can be against,
if the Spirit of God has set us free?
(Repeat)

1. I know that nothing in this world
can ever take us from his love.

2. Nothing can take us from his love,
poured out in Jesus, the Lord.

3. And nothing present or to come
can ever take us from his love.

4. I know that neither death nor life
can ever take us from his love.

254 Brian Howard (b. 1930). © *1975 Mission Hills Music. Administered by CopyCare*

1. If I were a butterfly,
I'd thank you, Lord, for giving me
wings,
and if I were a robin in a tree,
I'd thank you, Lord, that I could sing,
and if I were a fish in the sea,
I'd wiggle my tail and I'd giggle with
glee,
but I just thank you, Father,
for making me 'me'.

For you gave me a heart,
and you gave me a smile,
you gave me Jesus
and you made me your child,
and I just thank you, Father,
for making me 'me'.

2. If I were an elephant,
I'd thank you, Lord, by raising my
trunk,
and if I were a kangaroo,
you know I'd hop right up to you,
and if I were an octopus,
I'd thank you, Lord, for my fine
looks,
but I just thank you, Father,
for making me 'me'.

Continued overleaf

3. If I were a wiggly worm,
   I'd thank you, Lord, that I could
      squirm,
   and if I were a billy goat,
   I'd thank you, Lord, for my strong
      throat,
   and if I were a fuzzy wuzzy bear,
   I'd thank you, Lord, for my fuzzy
      wuzzy hair,
   but I just thank you, Father,
   for making me 'me'.

   For you gave me a heart,
   and you gave me a smile,
   you gave me Jesus
   and you made me your child,
   and I just thank you, Father,
   for making me 'me'.

255 John Wyse (1825-1898), alt.

1. I'll sing a hymn to Mary,
   the mother of my God,
   the virgin of all virgins,
   of David's royal blood.
   O teach me, holy Mary,
   a loving song to frame,
   when wicked ones blaspheme thee,
   to love and bless thy name.

2. O noble Tower of David,
   of gold and ivory,
   the Ark of God's own promise,
   the gate of heav'n to me,
   to live and not to love thee,
   would fill my soul with shame;
   when wicked ones blaspheme thee,
   I'll love and bless thy name.

3. The saints are high in glory,
   with golden crowns so bright;
   but brighter far is Mary,
   upon her throne of light.

O that which God did give thee,
let mortals ne'er disclaim;
when wicked ones blaspheme thee,
I'll love and bless thy name.

4. But in the crown of Mary,
   there lies a wondrous gem,
   as queen of all the angels,
   which Mary shares with them:
   no sin hath e'er defiled thee,
   so doth our faith proclaim;
   when wicked ones blaspheme thee,
   I'll love and bless thy name.

256 Unknown

1. Immaculate Mary!
   Our hearts are on fire;
   that title so wondrous
   fills all our desire.

   Ave, ave, ave Maria!
   Ave, ave, ave Maria!

2. We pray for God's glory,
   may his kingdom come!
   We pray for his vicar,
   our father, and Rome.

3. We pray for our mother
   the Church upon earth,
   and bless, sweetest lady,
   the land of our birth.

4. For poor, sick, afflicted
   thy mercy we crave;
   and comfort the dying,
   thou light of the grave.

5. In grief and temptation,
   in joy or in pain,
   we'll ask thee, our mother,
   nor seek thee in vain.

6. In death's solemn moment,
   our mother, be nigh;
   as children of Mary,
   O teach us to die.

7. And crown thy sweet mercy
   with this special grace,
   and worship in heaven
   God's ravishing face.

8. To God be all glory
   and worship for aye;
   to God's virgin mother
   an endless Ave.

257
Walter Chalmers Smith (1824-1908)
based on 1 Timothy 1:17

1. Immortal, invisible,
   God only wise,
   in light inaccessible hid
   from our eyes,
   most blessèd, most glorious,
   the Ancient of Days,
   almighty, victorious,
   thy great name we praise.

2. Unresting, unhasting,
   and silent as light,
   nor wanting, nor wasting,
   thou rulest in might;
   thy justice like mountains
   high soaring above
   thy clouds which are fountains
   of goodness and love.

3. To all life thou givest,
   to both great and small;
   in all life thou livest,
   the true life of all;
   we blossom and flourish
   as leaves on the tree,
   and wither and perish;
   but naught changeth thee.

4. Great Father of glory,
   pure Father of light,
   thine angels adore thee,
   all veiling their sight;
   all laud we would render,
   O help us to see
   'tis only the splendour
   of light hideth thee.

258
Kevin Nichols (1929 – 2006)
© 1976 Kevin Mayhew Ltd

1. In bread we bring you, Lord,
   our bodies' labour.
   In wine we offer you our spirits' grief.
   We do not ask you, Lord,
   who is my neighbour,
   but stand united now, one in belief.
   O we have gladly heard
   your Word, your holy Word,
   and now in answer, Lord,
   our gifts we bring.
   Our selfish hearts make true,
   our failing faith renew,
   our lives belong to you, our Lord and
      King.

2. The bread we offer you
   is blessed and broken,
   and it becomes for us our spirits' food.
   Over the cup we bring
   your Word is spoken;
   make it your gift to us,
   your healing blood.
   Take all that daily toil
   plants in our hearts' poor soil,
   take all we start and spoil,
   each hopeful dream,
   the chances we have missed,
   the graces we resist,
   Lord, in thy Eucharist, take and
      redeem.

259 Stuart Townend (b. 1963) and Keith Getty
© 2001 Kingsway's Thankyou Music.
Administered by worshiptogether.com songs

1. In Christ alone my hope is found,
   he is my light, my strength, my song;
   this cornerstone, this solid ground,
   firm through the fiercest drought and
      storm.
   What heights of love, what depths of
      peace,
   when fears are stilled, when strivings
      cease!
   My comforter, my all in all,
   here in the love of Christ I stand.

2. In Christ alone! – who took on flesh,
   fullness of God in helpless babe!
   This gift of love and righteousness,
   scorned by the ones he came to save:
   till on that cross as Jesus died,
   the wrath of God was satisfied –
   for ev'ry sin on him was laid;
   here in the death of Christ I live.

3. There in the ground his body lay,
   light of the world by darkness slain:
   then bursting forth in glorious day
   up from the grave he rose again!
   And as he stands in victory
   sin's curse has lost its grip on me,
   for I am his and he is mine –
   bought with the precious blood of
      Christ.

4. No guilt in life, no fear in death,
   this is the pow'r of Christ in me;
   from life's first cry to final breath,
   Jesus commands my destiny.
   No pow'r of hell, no scheme of man,
   can ever pluck me from his hand;
   till he returns or calls me home,
   here in the pow'r of Christ I'll stand!

260 John Oxenham (1852-1941) alt.
© Desmond Dunkerley

1. In Christ there is no east or west,
   in him no south or north,
   but one great fellowship of love
   throughout the whole wide earth.

2. In him shall true hearts ev'rywhere
   their high communion find;
   his service is the golden cord,
   close binding humankind.

3. Join hands, united in the faith,
   whate'er your race may be;
   who serve my Father as their own
   are surely kin to me.

4. In Christ now meet both east and west,
   in him meet south and north;
   all Christlike souls are one in him,
   throughout the whole wide earth.

261 vs. 1-3, Henry J. Pye (1825-1903)
v. 4, William Cooke (1821-1894)

1. In his temple now behold him,
   see the long-expected Lord;
   ancient prophets had foretold him,
   God has now fulfilled his word,
   now to praise him, his redeemèd
   shall break forth with one accord.

2. In the arms of her who bore him,
   Virgin pure, behold him lie,
   while his aged saints adore him
   ere in faith and hope they die.
   Alleluia! Alleluia!
   See th'incarnate God most high.

3. Jesus, by your presentation,
   when they blessed you, weak and poor,
   make us see our great salvation,
   seal us with your promise sure,
   and present us in your glory
   to your Father, cleansed and pure.

4. Prince and author of salvation,
   be your boundless love our theme!
   Jesus, praise to you be given,
   by the world you did redeem,
   with the Father and the Spirit,
   Lord of majesty supreme.

5. What can I give him,
   poor as I am?
   If I were a shepherd
   I would bring a lamb;
   if I were a wise man
   I would do my part,
   yet what I can I give him:
   give my heart.

262 Christina Georgina Rossetti (1830-1894)

1. In the bleak mid-winter
   frosty wind made moan,
   earth stood hard as iron,
   water like a stone;
   snow had fallen, snow on snow,
   snow on snow,
   in the bleak mid-winter, long ago.

2. Our God, heav'n cannot hold him
   nor earth sustain;
   heav'n and earth shall flee away
   when he comes to reign.
   In the bleak mid-winter
   a stable-place sufficed
   the Lord God almighty, Jesus Christ.

3. Enough for him, whom cherubim
   worship night and day,
   a breastful of milk,
   and a mangerful of hay:
   enough for him, whom angels
   fall down before,
   the ox and ass and camel which adore.

4. Angels and archangels
   may have gathered there,
   cherubim and seraphim
   thronged the air;
   but only his mother
   in her maiden bliss
   worshipped the belovèd with a kiss.

263 Christopher Walker (b. 1947)
© 1997 Christopher Walker OCP Publications

Laudate, laudate Dominum,
omnes gentes, laudate Dominum.
Exsultate, jubilate
per annos Domini, omnes gentes.
Laudate, laudate Dominum,
omnes gentes, laudate Dominum.
Exsultate, jubilate
per annos Domini, omnes gentes.

or

We praise you, we praise your holy name,
God of justice, eternally the same.
May our living be thanksgiving,
rejoicing in your name now and always.
We praise you, we praise your holy name,
God of justice, eternally the same.
May our living be thanksgiving,
rejoicing in your name now and always.

1. In the faith of Christ we walk hand
      in hand,
   light before our path as the Lord has
      planned;
   shining the torch of faith in our land:
   in the name of Christ Jesus.

Continued overleaf

2. In the name of Christ we will spread
the seed;
share the Word of God with all those
in need,
faithful in thought and word and deed:
in the name of Christ Jesus.

Laudate, laudate Dominum,
omnes gentes, laudate Dominum.
Exsultate, jubilate
per annos Domini, omnes gentes.
Laudate, laudate Dominum,
omnes gentes, laudate Dominum.
Exsultate, jubilate
per annos Domini, omnes gentes.

or

We praise you, we praise your holy name,
God of justice, eternally the same.
May our living be thanksgiving,
rejoicing in your name now and always.
We praise you, we praise your holy name,
God of justice, eternally the same.
May our living be thanksgiving,
rejoicing in your name now and always.

3. In the pow'r of Christ we proclaim
one Lord.
All who put on Christ are by faith
restored;
sharing new life, salvation's reward:
in the name of Christ Jesus.

4. In the life of Christ, through the
blood he shed,
we are justified, and by him are fed,
nourished by word and living bread:
in the name of Christ Jesus.

5. In the Church of God we are unified,
by the Spirit's pow'r we are sanctified,
temples of grace, where God may
abide:
by the pow'r of the Spirit.

6. Praise to God the Father while ages
run,
praise to Christ the Saviour, God's
only Son,
praise to the Holy Spirit be sung:
omnes gentes, laudate.

264 Martin E. Leckebusch (b. 1962)
© 2000 Kevin Mayhew Ltd

1. In the garden Mary lingers,
broken and forlorn,
then an unexpected greeting
names her in the dawn:
so she meets her risen Saviour
on the resurrection morn.

2. Evening journey: two disciples,
grieving for the dead,
find a stranger walks beside them,
cheers their hearts instead –
finally they recognise him
as he breaks and shares the bread.

3. Ten distraught, confused apostles
hide away in fear;
rumours that the grave is empty
they are shocked to hear –
yet when Jesus stands among them
dread and sorrow disappear.

4. Fishermen who toiled for nothing
on the lake all night
hear the sound of Jesus' welcome
in the morning light:
in the friendship shared at breakfast
old mistakes are lost to sight.

5. Ev'ry day a fresh beginning –
newness, come what may!
In the most unlikely places
Jesus reigns today;
from the past to new horizons
Christ our Saviour leads the way.

265 Taizé Community
© Ateliers et Presses de Taizé

In the Lord I'll be ever thankful,
in the Lord I will rejoice!
Look to God, do not be afraid;
lift up your voices:
the Lord is near,
lift up your voices:
the Lord is near.

266 Margaret Rizza (b. 1929)
© 1998 Kevin Mayhew Ltd

In the Lord is my joy and salvation,
he gives light to all his creation.
In the Lord is my joy and salvation,
he gives peace and true consolation.
In the Lord is my salvation.
In the Lord is my salvation.

267 Francesca Leftley (b. 1955)
© 1978 Kevin Mayhew Ltd

1. In you, my God,
   may my soul find its peace;
   you are my refuge,
   my rock and my strength,
   calming my fears
   with the touch of your love.
   Here in your presence
   my troubles will cease.

2. In you, my God,
   may my soul find its joy;
   you are the radiance,
   the song of my heart,
   drying my tears
   with the warmth of your love.
   Here in your presence
   my troubles will cease.

3. In you, my God,
   may my soul find its rest;
   you are the meaning,
   the purpose of life,
   drawing me near
   to the fire of your love,
   safe in your presence
   my yearning will cease.

268 Traditional Polish, trans. Edith Margaret
Gellibrand Reed (1885-1933)

1. Infant holy, infant lowly,
   for his bed a cattle stall;
   oxen lowing, little knowing
   Christ the babe is Lord of all.
   Swift are winging angels singing,
   nowells ringing, tidings bringing,
   Christ the babe is Lord of all,
   Christ the babe is Lord of all.

2. Flocks were sleeping, shepherds
      keeping
   vigil till the morning new;
   saw the glory, heard the story,
   tidings of a gospel true.
   Thus rejoicing, free from sorrow,
   praises voicing, greet the morrow,
   Christ the babe was born for you,
   Christ the babe was born for you.

269 John L. Bell (b. 1949) and
Graham Maule (b. 1958).
© 1987, 1997 WGRG, Iona Community

1. Inspired by love and anger,
   disturbed by endless pain,
   aware of God's own bias,
   we ask him once again:
   'How long must some folk suffer?
   How long can few folk mind?
   How long dare vain self-int'rest
   turn prayer and pity blind?'

Continued overleaf

2. From those for ever victims
   of heartless human greed,
   their cruel plight composes
   a litany of need:
   'Where are the fruits of justice?
   Where are the signs of peace?
   When is the day when pris'ners
   and dreams find their release?'

3. From those for ever shackled
   to what their wealth can buy,
   the fear of lost advantage
   provokes the bitter cry:
   'Don't query our position!
   Don't criticise our wealth!
   Don't mention those exploited
   by politics and stealth!'

4. To God, who through the prophets
   proclaimed a diff'rent age,
   we offer earth's indiff'rence,
   its agony and rage:
   'When will the wronged be righted?
   When will the kingdom come?
   When will the world be gen'rous
   to all instead of some?'

5. God asks: 'Who will go for me?
   Who will extend my reach?
   And who, when few will listen,
   will prophesy and preach?
   And who, when few bid welcome,
   will offer all they know?
   And who, when few dare follow,
   will walk the road I show?'

6. Amused in someone's kitchen,
   asleep in someone's boat,
   attuned to what the ancients
   exposed, proclaimed and wrote,
   a Saviour without safety,
   a tradesman without tools
   has come to tip the balance
   with fishermen and fools.

270 Michael Cockett (b. 1938), adapted from *Ubi Caritas*. © McCrimmon Publishing Co. Ltd

1. Into one we all are gathered
   through the love of Christ.
   Let us then rejoice with gladness.
   In him we find love.
   Let us fear and love the living God,
   and love and cherish humankind.

   Where charity and love are, there is God.

2. Therefore, when we are together
   in the love of Christ,
   let our minds know no division,
   strife or bitterness;
   may the Christ our God be in our
       midst.
   Through Christ our Lord all love is
       found.

3. May we see your face in glory,
   Christ our loving God.
   With the blessèd saints of heaven
   give us lasting joy.
   We will then possess true happiness,
   and love for all eternity.

271 Edmund Hamilton Sears (1810-1876) alt.

1. It came upon the midnight clear,
   that glorious song of old,
   from angels bending near the earth
   to touch their harps of gold:
   'Peace on the earth, goodwill to all,
   from heav'n's all-gracious King!'
   The world in solemn stillness lay
   to hear the angels sing.

2. Still through the cloven skies they
       come,
   with peaceful wings unfurled;
   and still their heav'nly music floats
   o'er all the weary world:

above its sad and lowly plains
they bend on hov'ring wing;
and ever o'er its Babel-sounds
the blessèd angels sing.

*3. Yet with the woes of sin and strife
the world has suffered long;
beneath the angel-strain have rolled
two thousand years of wrong;
and warring humankind hears not
the love-song which they bring;
O hush the noise of mortal strife,
and hear the angels sing!

*4. And ye, beneath life's crushing load,
whose forms are bending low,
who toil along the climbing way
with painful steps and slow:
look now! for glad and golden hours
come swiftly on the wing;
O rest beside the weary road,
and hear the angels sing.

5. For lo, the days are hast'ning on,
by prophets seen of old,
when with the ever-circling years
comes round the age of gold;
when peace shall over all the earth
its ancient splendours fling,
and all the world give back the song
which now the angels sing.

272 Spiritual

It's me, it's me, it's me, O Lord,
standing in the need of prayer. (Repeat)

1. Not my brother or my sister,
but it's me, O Lord,
standing in the need of prayer.
(Repeat)

2. Not my mother or my father . . .

3. Not the stranger or my neighbour . . .

273 Michael Forster (b. 1946)
© 2005 Kevin Mayhew Ltd

1. Jerusalem, the kingdom
God's faithful long to see,
where peace and wholeness prosper
and ev'ry heart is free;
where justice flows like fountains
and praises never cease,
come make your home among us,
and give this world your peace.

2. Among us and around us,
yet veiled from mortal sight,
the vision of the prophets
and God's proclaimed delight;
where tears find consolation,
and open wounds are healed,
where eyes and ears are opened,
the kingdom is revealed.

3. O call us to your table,
invite us to the feast,
where Christ will bring together
the greatest and the least;
where grace will flow among us
like rich, abundant wine,
and those the world rejected
will feast on love divine.

4. By grace alone united,
we join the heav'nly throng;
with countless saints and martyrs,
we sing the kingdom's song.
'O holy, holy, holy!'
the universe resounds
with praise and adoration
and endless grace abounds.

274

Tom S. Colvin (b. 1925) based on a song from North Ghana. © 1969 Hope Publishing. Administered by CopyCare

Jesu, Jesu, fill us with your love,
show us how to serve
the neighbours we have from you.

1. Kneels at the feet of his friends,
   silently washes their feet,
   Master who acts as a slave to them.

2. Neighbours are wealthy and poor,
   varied in colour and race,
   neighbours are near us and far away.

3. These are the ones we should serve,
   these are the ones we should love,
   all these are neighbours to us and you.

4. Loving puts us on our knees,
   silently washing their feet,
   this is the way we should live with you.

275 Charles Wesley (1707-1788) alt.

1. Jesu, lover of my soul,
   let me to thy bosom fly,
   while the gath'ring waters roll,
   while the tempest still is high:
   hide me, O my Saviour, hide,
   till the storm of life is past;
   safe into the haven guide,
   O receive my soul at last.

2. Other refuge have I none,
   hangs my helpless soul on thee;
   leave, ah, leave me not alone,
   still support and comfort me.
   All my trust on thee is stayed,
   all my help from thee I bring;
   cover my defenceless head
   with the shadow of thy wing.

3. Plenteous grace with thee is found,
   grace to cleanse from ev'ry sin;
   let the healing streams abound,
   make and keep me pure within.

Thou of life the fountain art,
freely let me take of thee,
spring thou up within my heart,
rise to all eternity.

276 Patrick Matsikenyiri
© Copyright Control

Jesu, tawa pano;
Jesu, tawa pano;
Jesu, tawa pano;
tawa pano, mu zita renyu.

English version

Jesus, we are here,
Jesus, we are here,
Jesus, we are here,
Jesus, we are here for you.

277 St Bernard of Clairvaux (1091-1153)
trans. Edward Caswall (1814-1878) alt.

1. Jesu, the very thought of thee
   with sweetness fills the breast;
   but sweeter far thy face to see,
   and in thy presence rest.

2. No voice can sing, no heart can frame,
   nor can the mem'ry find,
   a sweeter sound than Jesu's name,
   the Saviour of mankind.

3. O hope of ev'ry contrite heart,
   O joy of all the meek,
   to those who ask how kind thou art,
   how good to those who seek!

4. But what to those who find? Ah, this
   nor tongue nor pen can show;
   the love of Jesus, what it is
   his true disciples know.

5. Jesu, our only joy be thou,
   as thou our prize wilt be;
   in thee be all our glory now,
   and through eternity.

278

Matt Redman
© 1995 Thankyou Music.
Administered by worshiptogether.com songs

1. Jesus Christ, I think upon your
     sacrifice;
   you became nothing, poured out to
     death.
   Many times I've wondered at your
     gift of life,
   and I'm in that place once again,
   I'm in that place once again.

   And once again I look upon
   the cross where you died,
   I'm humbled by your mercy
   and I'm broken inside.
   Once again I thank you,
   once again I pour out my life.

2. Now you are exalted to the highest
     place,
   King of the heavens, where one day
     I'll bow.
   But for now I marvel at this saving
     grace,
   and I'm full of praise once again,
   I'm full of praise once again.

   Thank you for the cross, thank you
     for the cross,
   thank you for the cross, my friend.
   Thank you for the cross, thank you
     for the cross,
   thank you for the cross, my friend.

279

v. 1: *Surrexit hodie* (14th century) trans. anon.
as in *Lyra Davidica* (1708), vs. 2-3 from
J. Arnold's *Compleat Psalmodist* (1749)

1. Jesus Christ is ris'n today, alleluia!
   our triumphant holy day, alleluia!
   who did once, upon the cross,
     alleluia!
   suffer to redeem our loss, alleluia!

2. Hymns of praise then let us sing,
     alleluia!
   unto Christ, our heav'nly King,
     alleluia!
   who endured the cross and grave,
     alleluia!
   sinners to redeem and save, alleluia!

3. But the pains that he endured, alleluia!
   our salvation have procured; alleluia!
   now above the sky he's King, alleluia!
   where the angels ever sing, alleluia!

280

John L. Bell (b. 1949) and Graham Maule
(b. 1958). © WGRG, Iona Community.
Used by permission from 'Enemy of Apathy'
(Wild Goose Publications, 1988)

1. Jesus Christ is waiting,
   waiting in the streets:
   no one is his neighbour,
   all alone he eats.
   Listen, Lord Jesus,
   I am lonely too;
   make me, friend or stranger,
   fit to wait on you.

2. Jesus Christ is raging,
   raging in the streets,
   where injustice spirals
   and real hope retreats.
   Listen, Lord Jesus,
   I am angry too;
   in the Kingdom's causes
   let me rage with you.

3. Jesus Christ is healing,
   healing in the streets
   curing those who suffer,
   touching those he greets.
   Listen, Lord Jesus,
   I have pity too;
   let my care be active,
   healing, just like you.

Continued overleaf

4. Jesus Christ is dancing,
   dancing in the streets,
   where each sign of hatred
   he, with love, defeats.
   Listen, Lord Jesus,
   I should triumph too;
   where good conquers evil,
   let me dance with you.

5. Jesus Christ is calling,
   calling in the streets,
   'Who will join my journey?
   I will guide their feet.'
   Listen, Lord Jesus,
   let my fears be few;
   walk one step before me,
   I will follow you.

281

David J. Mansell (b. 1936)
© 1982 Authentic Publishing
Administered by CopyCare

1. Jesus is Lord!
   Creation's voice proclaims it,
   for by his pow'r each tree and flow'r
   was planned and made.
   Jesus is Lord!
   The universe declares it;
   sun, moon and stars in heaven cry:
   Jesus is Lord!

   Jesus is Lord! Jesus is Lord!
   Praise him with alleluias,
   for Jesus is Lord!

2. Jesus is Lord!
   Yet from his throne eternal
   in flesh he came to die in pain
   on Calv'ry's tree.
   Jesus is Lord!
   From him all life proceeding,
   yet gave his life as ransom
   thus setting us free.

3. Jesus is Lord!
   O'er sin the mighty conqu'ror,
   from death he rose and all his foes
   shall own his name.
   Jesus is Lord!
   God sends his Holy Spirit
   to show by works of power
   that Jesus is Lord.

282

Adoro te devote ascribed to St Thomas Aquinas
(1227-1274), trans. James Quinn (b. 1919)
© *Geoffrey Chapman, an imprint of Continuum*

1. Jesus, Lord of glory,
   clothed in heaven's light,
   here I bow before you,
   hidden from my sight.
   Lord, to whom my body,
   mind and heart belong,
   mind and heart here falter,
   Love so deep, so strong.

*2. Here distrust, my spirit,
   eye and tongue and hand,
   trust faith's ear and listen,
   hear and understand.
   Hear the voice of Wisdom,
   speaking now to you;
   when God's Word has spoken,
   what can be more true?

3. Once you hid your glory,
   Jesus crucified,
   now you hide your body,
   Jesus glorified.
   When you come in judgement,
   plain for all to see,
   God and man in splendour,
   Lord, remember me.

4. Once you showed to Thomas
wounded hands and side.
Here I kneel adoring,
faith alone my guide.
Help me grow in faith, Lord,
grow in hope and love,
living by your Spirit,
gift of God above.

*5. Here I see your dying,
Jesus, victim-priest,
here I know your rising,
host and guest and feast.
Let me taste your goodness,
manna from the skies,
feed me, heal me, save me,
food of Paradise.

*6. Heart of Jesus, broken,
pierced and open wide,
wash me in the water
flowing from your side.
Jesus' blood so precious
that one drop could free
all the world from evil,
come and ransom me.

7. How I long to see you,
Jesus, face to face,
how the heart is thirsting,
living spring of grace.
Show me soon your glory,
be my great reward,
be my joy for ever,
Jesus, gracious Lord.

283 Frederick William Faber (1814-1863)

1. Jesus, my Lord, my God, my all,
how can I love thee as I ought?
And how revere this wondrous gift
so far surpassing hope or thought?

Sweet Sacrament, we thee adore;
O make us love thee more and more.

2. Had I but Mary's sinless heart
to love thee with, my dearest King,
O, with what bursts of fervent praise
thy goodness, Jesus, would I sing!

3. Ah, see, within a creature's hand
the vast Creator deigns to be,
reposing, infant-like, as though
on Joseph's arm, or Mary's knee.

4. Thy body, soul and Godhead, all;
O mystery of love divine!
I cannot compass all I have,
for all thou hast and art are mine.

5. Sound, sound, his praises higher still,
and come, ye angels, to our aid;
'tis God, 'tis God, the very God
whose pow'r both us and angels made.

284 Naida Hearn (b. 1944)
© 1974 Scripture in Song/ Marantha! Music.
Administered by CopyCare

Jesus, Name above all names,
beautiful Saviour, glorious Lord,
Emmanuel, God is with us,
blessed Redeemer, living Word.

285 Taizé Community, based on Scripture
© Ateliers et Presses de Taizé

Jesus, remember me
when you come into your kingdom.

286 Damian Lundy (1944-1997)
© 1988, 2005 Kevin Mayhew Ltd

1. Jesus rose on Easter Day,
alleluia, now we pray.
Resurrexit, let us say,
for he is Lord and mighty God for ever.

Continued overleaf

2. He has conquered death and sin.
   All God's people now begin
   singing praises unto him,
   for he is Lord and mighty God for ever.

3. 'Alleluia' is our cry,
   for he lives, no more to die.
   Glory be to God on high,
   for he is Lord and mighty God for ever.

4. Alleluia! May we know
   all the joy which long ago
   set the Easter sky aglow,
   for he is Lord and mighty God for ever.

5. Alleluia! Let us be
   filled with love, our hearts set free
   as we praise his victory,
   for he is Lord and mighty God for ever.

287 Graham Kendrick (b. 1950)
© 1977 Thankyou Music.
Administered by worshiptogether.com songs

1. Jesus, stand among us
   at the meeting of our lives,
   be our sweet agreement
   at the meeting of our eyes.
   O Jesus, we love you,
   so we gather here,
   join our hearts in unity
   and take away our fear.

2. So to you we're gath'ring
   out of each and ev'ry land,
   Christ the love between us
   at the joining of our hands.
   O Jesus, we love you,
   so we gather here,
   join our hearts in unity
   and take away our fear.

3. Jesus stand among us
   at the breaking of the bread;
   join us as one body
   as we worship you, our Head.

O Jesus, we love you,
so we gather here,
join our hearts in unity
and take away our fear.

288 Unknown. Trans. Dermott Monahan
(1906-1957). © *The Trustees for Methodist Church Purposes*

1. Jesus the Lord said: 'I am the Bread,
   the Bread of Life for mankind am I.
   The Bread of Life for mankind am I,
   the Bread of Life for mankind am I.'
   Jesus the Lord said: 'I am the Bread,
   the Bread of Life for mankind am I.'

2. Jesus the Lord said: 'I am the Door,
   the Way and the Door for the poor
      am I.
   The Way and the Door for the poor
      am I,
   the Way and the Door for the poor
      am I.'
   Jesus the Lord said: 'I am the Door,
   the Way and the Door for the poor
      am I.'

3. Jesus the Lord said: 'I am the Light,
   the one true Light of the world am I.
   The one true Light of the world am I,
   the one true Light of the world am I.'
   Jesus the Lord said: 'I am the Light,
   the one true Light of the world am I.'

4. Jesus the Lord said: 'I am the Shepherd,
   the one good Shepherd of the sheep
      am I.
   The one good Shepherd of the sheep
      am I,
   the one good Shepherd of the sheep
      am I.'
   Jesus the Lord said: 'I am the Shepherd,
   the one good Shepherd of the sheep
      am I.'

5. Jesus the Lord said: 'I am the Life,
   the Resurrection and the Life am I.
   The Resurrection and the Life am I,
   the Resurrection and the Life am I.'
   Jesus the Lord said: 'I am the Life,
   the Resurrection and the Life am I'.

289 Michael Forster (b. 1946)
    © 1997 Kevin Mayhew Ltd

A hymn for the Stations of the Cross

1. Jesus, who condemns you?
   Who cries 'crucify'?
   Priest or politician?
   Jesus, is it I?

2. Heavy, oh too heavy,
   weighs a world of hate;
   Christ, be our Redeemer,
   Jesus, bear the weight.

3. Perfect in obedience
   to your Father's call,
   Christ, creation's glory,
   shares creation's fall.

4. Where the humble suffer,
   and the proud deride,
   Mary, blessèd Mother,
   calls us to your side.

5. Christ, our only Saviour,
   you must bear the loss;
   yet give us compassion,
   let us bear the cross.

6. Christ, where now you suffer,
   in each painful place,
   let each act of kindness
   still reveal your face.

7. Mortal flesh exhausted,
   tortured sinews fail,
   yet the spirit triumphs,
   and the will prevails.

8. Still the faithful women
   stand beside the way,
   weeping for the victims
   of the present day.

9. Bowed beneath the burden
   of creation's pain,
   Saviour, be beside us
   when we fall again.

10. Church of God, resplendent
    in the robes of pow'r,
    be the Saviour's body,
    share his triumph hour!

11. All the pow'rs of evil
    join to strike the nail;
    patience and compassion
    silently prevail.

12. Lonely and forsaken,
    in this dying breath,
    love alone can bear him
    through the veil of death.

13. Arms that cradled Jesus,
    both at death and birth,
    cradle all who suffer
    in the pains of earth.

14. Christ, who came with nothing
    from your Mother's womb,
    rest in destitution,
    in a borrowed tomb.

15. Broken but triumphant,
    birthing gain from loss,
    let us share your glory,
    let us share your cross.

290 Mary Barrett, based on John 14:6
© 1978 Kevin Mayhew Ltd

Jesus, you are Lord.
You are risen from the dead and you
are Lord.
Ev'ry knee shall bow,
and ev'ry tongue confess that Jesus, you
are Lord.
You are the Way.

1. I am the Way.
   No one knows the Father but it be
      through me.
   I am in my Father,
   and my Father is in me, and we come
      in love
   to live within your heart.

2. I am the Truth.
   And I set my Spirit deep within your
      hearts,
   and you will know me, and love me,
   and the truth I give to you will set
      you free.

3. I am the Life.
   The living waters I pour out for you.
   Anyone who drinks of the waters that
      I give
   will have eternal life.

4. I am the Word,
   the true light that shines brightly in
      the dark,
   a light that darkness could not overpow'r,
   the Word made flesh, risen among you.

291 Daniel L. Schutte (b. 1947)
© 1991 Daniel L. Schutte/OCP Publications

Join in the dance of the earth's jubilation!
This is the feast of the love of God.
Shout from the heights to the ends of
creation:
Jesus the Saviour is risen from the grave!

1. Wake, O people; sleep no longer;
   greet the breaking day!
   Christ, Redeemer, Lamb and Lion,
   turns the night away!

2. All creation, like a mother,
   labours to give birth.
   Soon the pain will be forgotten,
   joy for all the earth!

3. Now our shame becomes our glory
   on this holy tree.
   Now the reign of death is ended;
   now we are set free!

4. None on earth, no prince or power,
   neither death nor life,
   nothing now can ever part us
   from the love of Christ!

5. Love's triumphant day of vict'ry
   heaven opens wide.
   On the tree of hope and glory
   death itself has died!

6. Christ for ever, Lord of ages,
   Love beyond our dreams:
   Christ, our hope of heaven's glory
   all that yet will be!

292 Isaac Watts (1674-1748),
based on Psalm 98, alt.

1. Joy to the world! The Lord is come;
   let earth receive her King;
   let ev'ry heart prepare him room,
   and heav'n and nature sing,
   and heav'n and nature sing,
   and heav'n and heav'n and nature sing.

2. Joy to the earth! The Saviour reigns;
   let us our songs employ;
   while fields and floods, rocks,
      hills and plains
   repeat the sounding joy,
   repeat the sounding joy,
   repeat, repeat the sounding joy.

3. He rules the world with truth and grace,
and makes the nations prove
the glories of his righteousness,
and wonders of his love,
and wonders of his love,
and wonders, and wonders of his love.

294 From Psalm 32

Jubilate Deo,
jubilate Deo, alleluia.

Translation: Rejoice in God.

293 Jean-Paul Lécot (b. 1947) based on Psalm 32
Trans. W. R. Lawrence alt.
© 1988 Kevin Mayhew Ltd

Jubilate Deo, cantate Domino!
Jubilate Deo, cantate Domino!

1. All of you who accept to be servants of God,
by your songs of joy praise him now and evermore.

2. To the Lord offer thanks and give praise to his name;
sing aloud new songs to proclaim his mighty power.

3. For the Word of the Lord is both faithful and sure;
all the things he does show his justice, truth and love.

4. All creation is filled with the love of the Lord;
everything that is was created through the Word.

5. May the People of God in all ages be bless'd;
day by day his grace is outpoured upon us all.

6. May our hearts never waver, but trust in the Lord;
he, the living God, is both merciful and good.

295 Traditional
© Ateliers et Presses de Taizé

Jubilate Deo omnis terra.
Servite Domino in laetitia.
Alleluia, alleluia, in laetitia.

Translation: Rejoice in God, all the
earth. Serve the Lord
with gladness.

296 Fred Dunn (1907-1979). © 1977 Thankyou
Music. Administered by worshiptogether.com songs

Jubilate, ev'rybody,
serve the Lord in all your ways and
come before his presence singing;
enter now his courts with praise.
For the Lord our God is gracious,
and his mercy everlasting.
Jubilate, jubilate, jubilate Deo!

297 Lucien Deiss (b. 1921), based on 2 Timothy
2:8-11. © 1965 World Library Publications

Keep in mind that Jesus Christ has died
for us
and is risen from the dead.
He is our saving Lord,
he is joy for all ages

1. If we die with the Lord,
we shall live with the Lord.

Continued overleaf

2. If we endure with the Lord,
we shall reign with the Lord.

Keep in mind that Jesus Christ has died
for us
and is risen from the dead.
He is our saving Lord,
he is joy for all ages

3. In him hope of glory,
in him all our love.

4. In him our redemption,
in him all our grace

5. In him our salvation,
in him all our peace.

298 Refrain: Paul Inwood (b. 1947). Verses: *The Grail.* Refrain: © *1985 Paul Inwood.* Verses: © *1963 The Grail/Harper Collins Religious*

O Lord, you are the centre of my life:
I will always praise you,
I will always serve you,
I will always keep you in my sight.

1. Keep me safe, O God,
I take refuge in you.
I say to the Lord,
'You are my God.
My happiness lies in you alone;
my happiness lies in you alone.'

2. I will bless the Lord
who gives me counsel,
who even at night directs my heart.
I keep the Lord ever in my sight:
since he is at my right hand,
I shall stand firm.

3. And so my heart rejoices,
my soul is glad;
even in safety shall my body rest.
For you will not leave
my soul among the dead,
nor let your belovèd know decay.

299 John L. Bell (b. 1949) and Graham Maule (b. 1958). © *1989, 1996 WRGR, Iona Community*

Kindle a flame to lighten the dark
and take all fear away.

300 George Herbert (1593-1633)

1. King of glory, King of peace,
I will love thee;
and, that love may never cease,
I will move thee.
Thou hast granted my appeal,
thou hast heard me;
thou didst note my ardent zeal,
thou hast spared me.

2. Wherefore with my utmost art,
I will sing thee,
and the cream of all my heart
I will bring thee.
Though my sins against me cried,
thou didst clear me,
and alone, when they replied,
thou didst hear me.

3. Sev'n whole days, not one in sev'n,
I will praise thee;
in my heart, though not in heav'n,
I can raise thee.
Small it is, in this poor sort
to enrol thee:
e'en eternity's too short
to extol thee.

301 Naomi Batya and Sophie Conty © *1980 Maranatha! Music. Administered by CopyCare*

King of kings and Lord of lords,
glory, hallelujah.
King of kings and Lord of lords,
glory, hallelujah.
Jesus, Prince of Peace,
glory, hallelujah.
Jesus, Prince of Peace,
glory, hallelujah.

302 Spiritual

1. Kum ba yah, my Lord, kum ba yah,
   (x3)
   O Lord, kum ba yah.

2. Someone's crying, Lord, kum ba yah,
   (x3)
   O Lord, kum ba yah.

3. Someone's singing, Lord, kum ba yah,
   (x3)
   O Lord, kum ba yah.

4. Someone's praying, Lord, kum ba yah,
   (x3)
   O Lord, kum ba yah.

303 Chris Bowater (b. 1947) © 1988 Sovereign Music UK

Lamb of God, Holy One,
Jesus Christ, Son of God,
lifted up willingly to die;
that I the guilty one may know
the blood once shed
still freely flowing,
still cleansing, still healing.
I exalt you, Jesus, my sacrifice,
I exalt you, my Redeemer and my Lord.
I exalt you, worthy Lamb of God,
and in honour I bow down before
   your throne.

304 Psalm 147

Lauda Jerusalem, Dominum.
Lauda Deum tuum Zion.
Hosanna! Hosanna!
Hosanna filio David!

*Translation: Jerusalem, praise the Lord,
   Zion, praise God.
   Hosanna to the Son of
   David.*

305 Taizé Community, based on Scripture © Ateliers et Presses de Taizé

*Laudate Dominum,
laudate Dominum,
omnes gentes, alleluia.* (Repeat)

or

*Sing praise and bless the Lord,
sing praise and bless the Lord,
peoples, nations, alleluia.* (Repeat)

*The following verses may be sung by a
Cantor:*

1. Praise the Lord, all you nations,
   praise God, all you peoples.
   Alleluia.
   Strong is God's love and mercy,
   always faithful for ever.
   Alleluia.

2. Alleluia, alleluia.
   Let ev'rything living give praise to
      the Lord.
   Alleluia, alleluia.
   Let ev'rything living give praise to
      the Lord.

306 From Psalm 116 © Ateliers et Presses de Taizé

Laudate omnes gentes,
laudate Dominum.

*Translation: All peoples, praise the
Lord.*

Continued overleaf

307

Carey Landry (b. 1944)
© 1977 Carey Landry and North American
Liturgy Resources

Lay your hands gently upon us,
let their touch render your peace,
let them bring your forgiveness and
*   healing,*
lay your hands, gently lay your hands.

1. You were sent to free the broken-
      hearted.
   You were sent to give sight to the
      blind.
   You desire to heal all our illness.
   Lay your hands, gently lay your hands.

2. Lord, we come to you through one
      another,
   Lord, we come to you in all our need.
   Lord, we come to you seeking
      wholeness.
   Lay your hands, gently lay your hands.

308

John Henry Newman (1801-1890)

1. Lead, kindly light,
   amid th'encircling gloom,
   lead thou me on;
   the night is dark,
   and I am far from home;
   lead thou me on.
   Keep thou my feet;
   I do not ask to see
   the distant scene;
   one step enough for me.

2. I was not ever thus,
   nor prayed that thou
   shouldst lead me on;
   I loved to choose
   and see my path; but now
   lead thou me on.

I loved the garish day,
and, spite of fears,
pride ruled my will:
remember not past years.

3. So long thy pow'r
   hath blest me, sure it still
   will lead me on,
   o'er moor and fen,
   o'er crag and torrent, till
   the night is gone;
   and with the morn
   those angel faces smile,
   which I have loved long since,
   and lost awhile.

309

James Edmeston (1791-1867)

1. Lead us, heav'nly Father, lead us
   o'er the world's tempestuous sea;
   guard us, guide us, keep us, feed us,
   for we have no help but thee;
   yet possessing ev'ry blessing
   if our God our Father be.

2. Saviour, breathe forgiveness o'er us,
   all our weakness thou dost know,
   thou didst tread this earth before us,
   thou didst feel its keenest woe;
   lone and dreary, faint and weary,
   through the desert thou didst go.

3. Spirit of our God, descending,
   fill our hearts with heav'nly joy,
   love with ev'ry passion blending,
   pleasure that can never cloy;
   thus provided, pardoned, guided,
   nothing can our peace destroy.

310

Joseph W. Reeks (1849-1900)
Alternative text Michael Forster (b. 1946)
© Alternative text 2005 Kevin Mayhew Ltd

1. Leader, now on earth no longer,
   soldier of th'eternal King,
   victor in the fight for heaven,
   we thy loving praises sing.

Great Saint George, our patron,
help us, in the conflict be thou nigh;
help us in that daily battle,
where each one must win or die.

2. Praise him who in deadly battle
   never shrank from foeman's sword,
   proof against all earthly weapon,
   gave his life for Christ the Lord.

3. Who, when earthly war was over,
   fought, but not for earth's renown;
   fought, and won a nobler glory,
   won the martyr's purple crown.

4. Help us when temptation presses,
   we have still our crown to win;
   help us when our soul is weary
   fighting with the pow'rs of sin.

5. Clothe us in thy shining armour,
   place thy good sword in our hand;
   teach us how to wield it, fighting
   onward t'wards the heav'nly land.

6. Onward till, our striving over,
   on life's battlefield we fall,
   resting then, but ever ready,
   waiting for the angel's call.

Alternative text to the same tune:

1. God of hope and God of courage,
   strength in weakness, hope in fear,
   give us holy inspiration
   through Saint George we honour here.
   By the promise of salvation,
   and assurance of your grace,
   fit us for the confrontation
   with the selves we fear to face.

2. Help us face the fears we harbour,
   slay the 'dragons' deep inside:
   prejudices unacknowledged,
   hurt and anger long-denied.

Then, in joyful recognition
of the beauty they concealed,
let us celebrate the glory
of humanity revealed.

3. Give us grace to see your image
   in our own humanity,
   trust the process of becoming,
   and become what we might be.
   Then, with boldness unabated,
   may we rise where eagles soar,
   where the human soul rejoices
   and the 'dragons' are no more.

4. God of hope and God of courage,
   kindle ev'ry human soul,
   with the great prophetic vision
   of creation truly whole.
   No more talk of mortal conflict!
   Let your majesty be shown,
   in humanity made perfect,
   fully knowing, fully known.

311 Michael Forster (b.1946)
© 2008 Kevin Mayhew Ltd

1. Lest we forget, O God of love,
      remind us
   how you detest the spectacle of war;
   let us recall the errors now behind us,
   firmly resolved to tread that path no
      more.
   When passions rage, when fear and
      hatred blind us,
   lest we forget, O God, let us recall.

2. Lest we forget the agony and slaughter
   that lie behind the victor's public face,
   let us recall the tears of wives and
      daughters,
   the broken dreams fine words cannot
      replace.
   Let not our hopes dissolve in fire and
      water;
   lest we forget, O God, let us recall.

Continued overleaf

3. Lest we forget the rapid escalation,
   beyond our pow'r to forecast or control,
   let us recall how nuclear conflagration
   scarred for all time creation's very soul.
   Then fire with hope the hearts of
       ev'ry nation;
   lest we forget, O God, let us recall.

4. Lest we forget the power and the glory
   that brought us through the desert
       and the grave,
   let us recall your people's ancient story:
   the pow'r of love to reconcile and save.
   Love has redeemed the world from
       pain and fury;
   lest we forget, O God, let us recall.

312 Liturgy of St James, trans. G. Moultrie (1829-1885)

1. Let all mortal flesh keep silence
   and with fear and trembling stand;
   ponder nothing earthly-minded,
   for with blessing in his hand
   Christ our God on earth descendeth,
   our full homage to demand.

2. King of kings, yet born of Mary,
   as of old on earth he stood,
   Lord of lords, in human vesture,
   in the body and the blood.
   He will give to all the faithful
   his own self for heav'nly food.

3. Rank on rank the host of heaven
   spreads its vanguard on the way,
   as the Light of light descendeth
   from the realms of endless day,
   that the pow'rs of hell may vanish
   as the darkness clears away.

4. At his feet the six-winged seraph;
   cherubim, with sleepless eye,
   veil their faces to the Presence,
   as with ceaseless voice they cry,
   alleluia, alleluia,
   alleluia, Lord most high.

313 Unknown

1. Let all that is within me cry: holy.
   Let all that is within me cry: holy.
   Holy, holy,
   holy is the Lamb that was slain.

2. Let all that is within me cry: mighty.
      (x2)
   Mighty, mighty,
   mighty is the Lamb that was slain.

3. Let all that is within me cry: worthy.
      (x2)
   Worthy, worthy,
   worthy is the Lamb that was slain.

4. Let all that is within me cry: blessèd.
      (x2)
   Blessèd, blessèd,
   blessèd is the Lamb that was slain.

5. Let all that is within me cry: Jesus.
      (x2)
   Jesus, Jesus,
   Jesus is the Lamb that was slain.

314 George Herbert (1593-1633)

1. Let all the world in ev'ry corner sing,
      my God and King!
   The heav'ns are not too high,
   his praise may thither fly;
   the earth is not too low,
   his praises there may grow.
   Let all the world in ev'ry corner sing,
      my God and King!

2. Let all the world in ev'ry corner sing,
   my God and King!
   The Church with psalms must shout,
   no door can keep them out;
   but, above all, the heart
   must bear the longest part.
   Let all the world in ev'ry corner sing,
   my God and King!

5. So on this day, O Christ, our mighty
   King,
   let all the faithful, praise and honour
   bring,
   our voices blend with heaven's choirs
   to sing:
   Alleluia! Alleluia!

315 Peter Simpson and Michael Saward (b. 1932)
© Michael Saward/Jubilate Hymns

1. Let earth rejoice! Let all creation sing!
   Heav'n adds its praises to the Saviour
   King.
   Around the throne the shouts of
   triumph ring.
   Alleluia! Alleluia!

2. To earth he came, a child so long ago,
   light in our darkness, grace and truth
   to show.
   The Word of life, whose gospel now
   we know.
   Alleluia! Alleluia!

3. Despised, rejected, he was crucified;
   Suffering Servant, on the cross he died;
   true Lamb of God, salvation to
   provide.
   Alleluia! Alleluia!

4. He rose again, and bursting from the
   grave
   reigns high in glory, who our sins
   forgave,
   now we rejoice, as those he came to
   save.
   Alleluia! Alleluia!

316 Mike Anderson (b. 1956)
© 2004 Kevin Mayhew Ltd

Let me wash your feet,
although I am the Master.
Let me wash your feet,
now go and do the same.

1. If there is love among you,
   all will know you follow me.
   I give a new commandment,
   that you love as I love you!

2. Let faith and hope and love live,
   with the greatest being love.
   So take my new commandment,
   go and love as I love you!

317 Dave Bilbrough
© 1979 Thankyou Music.
Administered by worshiptogether.com songs

Let there be love shared among us,
let there be love in our eyes.
May now your love sweep this nation;
cause us, O Lord, to arise.
Give us a fresh understanding
of brotherly (sisterly) love that is real.
Let there be love shared among us,
let there be love.

318 Unknown

1. Let us break bread together
on our knees.
Let us break bread together
on our knees.
When I fall on my knees
with my face to the rising sun,
O Lord, have mercy on me.

2. Let us drink wine together . . .

3. Let us praise God together . . .

319 Marty Haugen (b. 1952)
© 1994 GIA Publications Inc.

1. Let us build a house where love can
dwell
and all can safely live,
a place where saints and children tell
how hearts learn to forgive.
Built of hopes and dreams and visions,
rock of faith and vault of grace;
here the love of Christ shall end
divisions:

all are welcome, all are welcome,
all are welcome in this place.

2. Let us build a house where prophets
speak,
and words are strong and true,
where all God's children dare to seek
to dream God's reign anew.
Here the cross shall stand as witness
and symbol of God's grace;
here as one we claim the faith of Jesus:

3. Let us build a house where love is
found
in water, wine and wheat:
a banquet hall on holy ground,
where peace and justice meet.
Here the love of God, through Jesus,
is revealed in time and space;
as we share in Christ the feast that
frees us:

4. Let us build a house where hands will
reach
beyond the wood and stone
to heal and strengthen, serve and
teach,
and live the Word they've known.
Here the outcast and the stranger
bear the image of God's face;
let us bring an end to fear and danger:

5. Let us build a house where all are
named,
their songs and visions heard
and loved and treasured, taught and
claimed
as words within the Word.
Built of tears and cries and laughter,
pray'rs of faith and songs of grace,
let this house proclaim from floor to
rafter:

320 John Milton (1608-1674),
based on Psalm 136

1. Let us, with a gladsome mind,
praise the Lord, for he is kind;

for his mercies ay endure,
ever faithful, ever sure.

2. Let us blaze his name abroad,
for of gods he is the God;

3. He, with all-commanding might,
filled the new-made world with light;

4. He the golden-tressèd sun
   caused all day his course to run;

5. And the moon to shine at night,
   'mid her starry sisters bright;

6. All things living he doth feed,
   his full hand supplies their need;

7. Let us, with a gladsome mind,
   praise the Lord, for he is kind;

321 George William Kitchin (1827-1912) and
Michael Robert Newbolt (1874-1956) alt.
© Hymns Ancient & Modern Ltd

*Lift high the Cross,
the love of Christ proclaim
till all the world adore his sacred name!*

1. Come, Christians,
   follow where our Saviour trod,
   o'er death victorious,
   Christ the Son of God.

2. Led on their way by this
   triumphant sign,
   the hosts of God in joyful
   praise combine:

*3. Each new disciple
   of the Crucified
   is called to bear the seal
   of him who died:

*4. Saved by the Cross
   whereon their Lord was slain,
   now Adam's children
   their lost home regain:

5. From north and south,
   from east and west they raise
   in growing harmony
   their song of praise:

*6. O Lord, once lifted
   on the glorious tree,
   as thou hast promised,
   draw us unto thee:

7. Let ev'ry race
   and ev'ry language tell
   of him who saves
   from fear of death and hell:

*8. From farthest regions,
   let them homage bring,
   and on his Cross
   adore their Saviour King:

*9. Set up thy throne,
   that earth's despair may cease
   beneath the shadow
   of its healing peace:

322 Nick Fawcett (b. 1957)
© 2004 Kevin Mayhew Ltd

1. Lift up your voice, give thanks with
      songs of praise,
   sing to our God, your hymns of
      worship raise;
   tell of his grace, so wonderful and free,
   his mercy reaching out to you and me.

2. Lift up your voice, give thanks with
      songs of love,
   sing of the Saviour sent from God
      above;
   tell of the one who, at the Father's call,
   through gracious service showed his
      care for all.

3. Lift up your voice, give thanks with
      songs of joy,
   sing of a love that nothing can destroy;
   tell of the friend, who died that we
      might live,
   who offers hope that no one else can
      give.

Continued overleaf

4. Lift up your voice, give thanks with
    songs of trust,
  sing of the God who lifts hope from
    the dust;
  tell of the Christ, who, just as he had
    said,
  defeated evil, rising from the dead.

5. Lift up your voice, give thanks with
    songs of awe,
  sing to the Lord who lives for evermore;
  tell of the king whose glory fills the sky,
  the Lord of lords who reigns
    enthroned on high.

323 Estelle White (b. 1925)
    © 1976 Kevin Mayhew Ltd

1. Like a sea without a shore,
  love divine is boundless.
  Time is now and evermore,
  and his love surrounds us.

  Maranatha! Maranatha!
  Maranatha! Come, Lord Jesus, come!

2. So that we could all be free,
  he appeared among us.
  Blest are those who have not seen,
  yet believe his promise.

3. All our visions, all our dreams,
  are but ghostly shadows
  of the radiant clarity
  waiting at life's close.

4. Death, where is your victory?
  Death, where is your sting?
  Closer than the air we breathe
  is our risen King.

  'Maranatha' is an Aramaic expression
  meaning 'Lord, come!'
  (See 1 Corinthians 16:22)

324 Verses: Psalm 41, Grail translation
    Refrain: Charles Watson
    Verses text: © 1963, 1986, 1993 The Grail,
    England/HarperCollins Religious
    Refrain text: © Charles Watson

Like as the deer that yearns for flowing
    waters,
so longs my soul for God, the living God.

1. My soul is thirsting for God, the God
    of my life;
  when can I enter and see the face of
    God?

2. These things will I remember as
    I pour out my soul:
  how I would lead the rejoicing crowd
    into the house of God.

3. Send forth your light and your truth,
    let these be my guide;
  let them bring me to your holy
    mountain, to the place where you
    dwell.

4. And I will come to the altar of God,
    the God of my joy!
  My Redeemer, I will thank you on
    the harp, O God, my God!

325 Aniceto Nazareth
    © 1984 Kevin Mayhew Ltd

Listen, let your heart keep seeking;
listen to his constant speaking;
listen to the Spirit calling you.
Listen to his inspiration;
listen to his invitation;
listen to the Spirit calling you.

1. He's in the sound of the thunder,
  in the whisper of the breeze.
  He's in the might of the whirlwind,
  in the roaring of the seas.

2. He's in the laughter of children,
   in the patter of the rain.
   Hear him in cries of the suff'ring,
   in their moaning and their pain.

3. He's in the noise of the city,
   in the singing of the birds.
   And in the night-time the stillness
   helps you listen to his word.

326 Eric Boswell (b. 1959)
© 1959 Warner/Chappell Music Ltd.

1. Little donkey, little donkey,
   on the dusty road,
   got to keep on plodding onwards
   with your precious load.
   Been a long time, little donkey,
   through the winter's night;
   don't give up now, little donkey,
   Bethlehem's in sight.

   Ring out those bells tonight,
   Bethlehem, Bethlehem,
   follow that star tonight,
   Bethlehem, Bethlehem.
   Little donkey, little donkey,
   had a heavy day,
   little donkey, carry Mary
   safely on her way.

2. Little donkey, little donkey,
   journey's end is near.
   There are wise men, waiting for a
   sign to bring them here.
   Do not falter, little donkey,
   there's a star ahead;
   it will guide you, little donkey,
   to a cattle shed.

327 Traditional Czech carol
trans. Percy Dearmer (1867-1936)
Alternative words: Christopher Massey (b. 1956)
© 1999 Kevin Mayhew Ltd

1. Little Jesus, sweetly sleep, do not stir;
   we will lend a coat of fur;
   we will rock you, rock you, rock you,
   we will rock you, rock you, rock you;
   see the fur to keep you warm,
   snugly round your tiny form.

2. Mary's little baby sleep, sweetly sleep,
   sleep in comfort, slumber deep;
   we will rock you, rock you, rock you,
   we will rock you, rock you, rock you;
   we will serve you all we can,
   darling, darling little man.

Alternative words:

1. Little Jesus, sleep away, in the hay,
   while we worship, watch and pray.
   We will gather at the manger,
   worship this amazing stranger:
   little Jesus born on earth,
   sign of grace and human worth.

2. Little Jesus, sleep away, while you may;
   pain is for another day.
   While you sleep, we will not wake you,
   when you cry we'll not forsake you.
   Little Jesus, sleep away,
   we will worship you today.

328 Charles Wesley (1707-1788), John Cennick
(1718-1755) and Martin Madan (1728-1790) alt.

1. Lo, he comes with clouds descending,
   once for mortal sinners slain;
   thousand thousand saints attending
   swell the triumph of his train.
   Alleluia! Alleluia! Alleluia!
   Christ appears on earth to reign.

Continued overleaf

2. Ev'ry eye shall now behold him
   robed in dreadful majesty;
   we who set at naught and sold him,
   pierced and nailed him to the tree,
   deeply grieving, deeply grieving,
      deeply grieving,
   shall the true Messiah see.

3. Those dear tokens of his passion
   still his dazzling body bears,
   cause of endless exultation
   to his ransomed worshippers:
   with what rapture, with what rapture,
      with what rapture
   gaze we on those glorious scars!

4. Yea, amen, let all adore thee,
   high on thine eternal throne;
   Saviour, take the pow'r and glory,
   claim the kingdom for thine own.
   Alleluia! Alleluia! Alleluia!
   Thou shalt reign, and thou alone.

329 Bernadette Farrell (b. 1957)
© 1993 Bernadette Farrell/ OCP Publications

1. Longing for light, we wait in darkness.
   Longing for truth, we turn to you.
   Make us your own, your holy people,
   light for the world to see.

   Christ, be our light!
   Shine in our hearts,
   shine through the darkness.
   Christ, be our light!
   Shine in your Church
   gathered today.

2. Longing for peace, our world is
      troubled.
   Longing for hope, many despair.
   Your word alone has power to save us.
   Make us your living voice.

3. Longing for food, many are hungry.
   Longing for water, many still thirst.
   Make us your bread, broken for others,
   shared until all are fed.

4. Longing for shelter, many are homeless.
   Longing for warmth, many are cold.
   Make us your building, sheltering
      others,
   walls made of living stone.

5. Many the gifts, many the people,
   many the hearts that yearn to belong.
   Let us be servants to one another,
   making your kingdom come.

330 Jodi Page Clark (b. 1941)
© 1976 Celebration.
Administered by kingswaysongs.com

1. Look around you, can you see?
   Times are troubled, people grieve.
   See the violence, feel the hardness;
   all my people, weep with me.

   Kyrie, eleison. Christe, eleison.
   Kyrie eleison.

2. Walk among them, I'll go with you.
   Reach out to them with my hands.
   Suffer with me, and together
   we will serve them, help them stand.

3. Forgive us, Father; hear our prayer.
   We'll walk with you anywhere,
   through your suff'ring, with forgiveness,
   take your life into the world.

331 Dal tuo celeste by St Alphonsus (1696-1787),
trans. Edmund Vaughan (1827-1908)

1. Look down, O mother Mary,
   from thy bright throne above;
   cast down upon thy children
   one only glance of love;
   and if a heart so tender
   with pity flows not o'er,
   then turn away, O mother,
   and look on us no more.

Look down, O mother Mary,
from thy bright throne above,
cast down upon thy children
one only glance of love.

2. See how, ungrateful sinners,
   we stand before thy Son;
   his loving heart upbraids us
   the evil we have done,
   but if thou wilt appease him,
   speak for us but one word;
   for thus thou canst obtain us,
   the pardon of our Lord.

3. O Mary, dearest mother,
   if thou wouldst have us live,
   say that we are thy children,
   and Jesus will forgive.
   Our sins make us unworthy
   that title still to bear,
   but thou art still our mother;
   then show a mother's care.

4. Unfold to us thy mantle,
   there stay we without fear;
   what evil can befall us
   if, mother, thou art near?
   O kindest, dearest mother,
   thy sinful children save;
   look down on us with pity,
   who thy protection crave.

332 Sister M. Teresine (1897-1988)
© The successor to Sister M. Teresine, OSF

1. Lord, accept the gifts we offer
   at this Eucharistic feast,
   bread and wine to be transformed now
   through the action of thy priest.
   Take us too, Lord, and transform us,
   be thy grace in us increased.

2. May our souls be pure and spotless
   as the host of wheat so fine;
   may all stain of sin be crushed out,
   like the grape that forms the wine,
   as we, too, become partakers,
   in the sacrifice divine.

3. Take our gifts, almighty Father,
   living God, eternal, true,
   which we give through Christ our
      Saviour,
   pleading here for us anew.
   Grant salvation to all present,
   and our faith and love renew.

333 George Hugh Bourne (1840-1925)

1. Lord, enthroned in heav'nly splendour,
   first begotten from the dead,
   thou alone, our strong defender,
   liftest up thy people's head.
   Alleluia, alleluia,
   Jesu, true and living bread.

2. Here our humblest homage pay we,
   here in loving rev'rence bow;
   here for faith's discernment pray we,
   lest we fail to know thee now.
   Alleluia, alleluia,
   thou art here, we ask not how.

3. Though the lowliest form doth veil thee
   as of old in Bethlehem,
   here as there thine angels hail thee,
   Branch and Flow'r of Jesse's Stem.
   Alleluia, alleluia,
   we in worship join with them.

4. Paschal Lamb, thine off'ring, finished
   once for all when thou wast slain,
   in its fullness undiminished
   shall for evermore remain.
   Alleluia, alleluia,
   cleansing souls from ev'ry stain.

Continued overleaf

5. Life-imparting heav'nly manna,
   stricken rock with streaming side,
   heav'n and earth with loud hosanna
   worship thee, the Lamb who died.
   Alleluia, alleluia,
   ris'n, ascended, glorified!

334 Timothy Dudley-Smith (b. 1926)
© *Timothy Dudley-Smith*

1. Lord, for the years
   your love has kept and guided,
   urged and inspired us,
   cheered us on our way,
   sought us and saved us,
   pardoned and provided,
   Lord of the years,
   we bring our thanks today.

2. Lord, for that word,
   the word of life which fires us,
   speaks to our hearts
   and sets our souls ablaze,
   teaches and trains,
   rebukes us and inspires us,
   Lord of the word,
   receive your people's praise.

3. Lord, for our land,
   in this our generation,
   spirits oppressed by pleasure,
   wealth and care;
   for young and old,
   for commonwealth and nation,
   Lord of our land,
   be pleased to hear our prayer.

4. Lord, for our world;
   when we disown and doubt him,
   loveless in strength,
   and comfortless in pain;
   hungry and helpless,
   lost indeed without him:
   Lord of the world,
   we pray that Christ may reign.

5. Lord, for ourselves;
   in living pow'r remake us,
   self on the cross
   and Christ upon the throne;
   past put behind us,
   for the future take us,
   Lord of our lives,
   to live for Christ alone.

335 Sister M. Xavier (1856-1917)

1. Lord, for tomorrow and its needs
   I do not pray;
   keep me, my God, from stain of sin,
   just for today.

2. Let me both diligently work
   and duly pray;
   let me be kind in word and deed,
   just for today.

3. Let me no wrong or idle word
   unthinking say;
   set thou a seal upon my lips,
   just for today.

4. And if today my tide of life
   should ebb away,
   give me thy sacraments divine,
   sweet Lord, today.

5. So, for tomorrow and its needs
   I do not pray;
   but keep me, guide me, love me, Lord,
   just for today.

336 Gerard Markland (b. 1953), based on Ezekiel
© *1978 Kevin Mayhew Ltd*

Lord, have mercy. Lord, have mercy.
Lord, have mercy on your people.
   (Repeat)

1. Give me the heart of stone within you,
   and I'll give you a heart of flesh.
   Clean water I will use to cleanse all
      your wounds.
   My Spirit I give to you.

2. You'll find me near the broken-hearted:
   those crushed in spirit I will save.
   So turn to me, for my pardon is great;
   my word will heal all your wounds.

4. Reach out and touch with healing
      pow'r
   the wounds we have received,
   that in forgiveness we may love
   and may no longer grieve.

5. Then stay with us when evening comes
   and darkness makes us blind,
   O stay until the light of dawn
   may fill both heart and mind.

337 Nick Fawcett (b. 1957)
© 2004 Kevin Mayhew Ltd

1. Lord, I lift
   my hands to you in prayer,
   my mind in turmoil,
   heart overwhelmed by care.

2. Come to me;
   and let me still your soul.
   No need to fret now;
   love waits to make you whole.

3. Lord, I come;
   your word has been fulfilled.
   Your peace flows freely;
   storms deep within are stilled.

338 Ralph Wright
© 1980 ICEL, Inc.

1. Lord Jesus, as we turn from sin
   with strength and hope restored,
   receive the homage that we bring
   to you, our risen Lord.

2. We call on you whose living word
   has made the Father known,
   O Shepherd, we have wandered far,
   find us and lead us home.

3. Your glance at Peter helped him know
   the love he had denied,
   now gaze on us and heal us, Lord,
   of selfishness and pride.

339 Patrick Appleford (b. 1925)
© 1960 Josef Weinberger Ltd

1. Lord Jesus Christ, you have come to us,
   you are one with us, Mary's Son.
   Cleansing our souls from all their sin,
   pouring your love and goodness in,
   Jesus, our love for you we sing,
   living Lord.

2. Lord Jesus Christ, now and ev'ry day
   teach us how to pray, Son of God.
   You have commanded us to do
   this in remembrance, Lord, of you.
   Into our lives your pow'r breaks
      through,
   living Lord.

3. Lord Jesus Christ, you have come to us,
   born as one of us, Mary's Son.
   Led out to die on Calvary,
   risen from death to set us free,
   living Lord Jesus, help us see
   you are Lord.

4. Lord Jesus Christ, I would come to
      you,
   live my life for you, Son of God.
   All your commands I know are true,
   your many gifts will make me new,
   into my life your pow'r breaks through,
   living Lord.

340

Mnōeo Christe by Bishop Synesius (375-430)
trans. Allen William Chatfield (1808-1896)

1. Lord Jesus, think on me,
   and purge away my sin;
   from earth-born passions set me free,
   and make me pure within.

2. Lord Jesus, think on me,
   with care and woe opprest;
   let me thy loving servant be
   and taste thy promised rest.

3. Lord Jesus, think on me
   amid the battle's strife;
   in all my pain and misery
   be thou my health and life.

4. Lord Jesus, think on me,
   nor let me go astray;
   through darkness and perplexity
   point thou the heav'nly way.

5. Lord Jesus, think on me,
   when flows the tempest high:
   when on doth rush the enemy,
   O Saviour, be thou nigh.

6. Lord Jesus, think on me,
   that, when the flood is past,
   I may th'eternal brightness see,
   and share thy joy at last.

341

John B. Foley (b. 1939),
based on the Prayer of St Francis
© 1976 John B. Foley, SJ/New Dawn Music

1. Lord, make me a means of your peace.
   Where there's hatred grown,
   let me sow your love.
   Where there's inj'ry, Lord,
   let forgiveness be my sword.
   Lord, make me a means of your peace.

2. Lord, make me a means of your peace.
   Where there's doubt and fear,
   let me sow your faith.
   In this world's despair,
   give me hope in you to share.
   Lord, make me a means of your peace.

3. Lord, make me a means of your peace.
   When there's sadness here,
   let me sow your joy.
   When the darkness nears,
   may your light dispel our fears.
   Lord, make me a means of your peace.

4. Lord, grant me to seek and to share:
   less to be consoled
   than to help console,
   less to be understood
   than to understand your good.
   Lord, make me a means of your peace.

5. Lord, grant me to seek and to share:
   to receive love less
   than to give love free,
   just to give in thee,
   just receiving from your tree.
   Lord, make me a means of your peace.

6. Lord, grant me to seek and to share:
   to forgive in thee,
   you've forgiven me;
   for to die in thee
   is eternal life to me.
   Lord, make me a means of your peace.

342

Jan Struther (1901-1953)
© Oxford University Press

1. Lord of all hopefulness,
   Lord of all joy,
   whose trust, ever childlike,
   no cares could destroy,
   be there at our waking,
   and give us, we pray,
   your bliss in our hearts, Lord,
   at the break of the day.

2. Lord of all eagerness,
   Lord of all faith,
   whose strong hands were skilled
   at the plane and the lathe,
   be there at our labours,
   and give us, we pray,
   your strength in our hearts, Lord,
   at the noon of the day.

3. Lord of all kindliness,
   Lord of all grace,
   your hands swift to welcome,
   your arms to embrace,
   be there at our homing,
   and give us, we pray,
   your love in our hearts, Lord,
   at the eve of the day.

4. Lord of all gentleness,
   Lord of all calm,
   whose voice is contentment,
   whose presence is balm,
   be there at our sleeping,
   and give us, we pray,
   your peace in our hearts, Lord,
   at the end of the day.

343 Catherine Walker (b. 1958)
© *Catherine Walker/St Mungo Music*

Lord of life, I come to you;
Lord of all, my Saviour be;
Lord of love, come bless us
with the light of your love.

344 Graham Kendrick (b. 1950)
© *1987 Make Way Music*

1. Lord, the light of your love is shining,
   in the midst of the darkness, shining;
   Jesus, Light of the World, shine upon
   us,
   set us free by the truth you now bring
   us.
   Shine on me, shine on me.

Shine, Jesus, shine,
fill this land with the Father's glory;
blaze, Spirit, blaze,
set our hearts on fire.
Flow, river, flow,
flood the nations with grace and mercy;
send forth your word, Lord,
and let there be light.

2. Lord, I come to your awesome
      presence,
   from the shadows into your radiance;
   by the blood I may enter your
      brightness,
   search me, try me, consume all
      my darkness.
   Shine on me, shine on me.

3. As we gaze on your kingly brightness,
   so our faces display your likeness,
   ever changing from glory to glory;
   mirrored here may our lives tell your
      story.
   Shine on me, shine on me.

345 Henry Williams Baker (1821-1877)

1. Lord, thy word abideth,
   and our footsteps guideth;
   who its truth believeth
   light and joy receiveth.

2. When our foes are near us,
   then thy word doth cheer us,
   word of consolation,
   message of salvation.

3. When the storms are o'er us,
   and dark clouds before us,
   then its light directeth,
   and our way protecteth.

Continued overleaf

4. Who can tell the pleasure,
   who recount the treasure,
   by thy word imparted
   to the simple-hearted?

5. Word of mercy, giving
   succour to the living;
   word of life, supplying
   comfort to the dying.

6. O that we, discerning
   its most holy learning,
   Lord, may love and fear thee,
   evermore be near thee.

346 Nick Fawcett (b. 1957)
© 2004 Kevin Mayhew Ltd

1. Lord, today your voice is calling,
   lifting thoughts to things above;
   life is wonderful, enthralling,
   touched by your unfailing love.
   Suddenly I see the beauty
   often hidden from my gaze,
   so I come, not out of duty,
   but with glad and grateful praise.

2. Lord, I sometimes fail to value
   all your blessings as I should.
   Slow to make the time to thank you,
   blind to so much that is good.
   Days are lived in such a hurry
   there's no time to stop and stare,
   joy is crushed by weight of worry,
   happiness obscured by care.

3. Lord, today I come rejoicing,
   vowed to waste your gifts no more;
   bringing praise and gladly voicing
   what I should have voiced before.
   Pouring out my adoration,
   scarcely knowing where to start,
   with a song of exultation,
   Lord, I thank you from the heart.

347 Jean Holloway (b. 1939)
© 1995 Kevin Mayhew Ltd

1. Lord, we come to ask your healing,
   teach us of love;
   all unspoken shame revealing,
   teach us of love.
   Take our selfish thoughts and actions,
   petty feuds, divisive factions,
   hear us now to you appealing,
   teach us of love.

2. Soothe away our pain and sorrow,
   hold us in love;
   grace we cannot buy or borrow,
   hold us in love.
   Though we see but dark and danger,
   though we spurn both friend and
       stranger,
   though we often dread tomorrow,
   hold us in love.

3. When the bread is raised and broken,
   fill us with love;
   words of consecration spoken,
   fill us with love.
   As our grateful prayers continue,
   make the faith that we have in you
   more than just an empty token,
   fill us with love.

4. Help us live for one another,
   bind us in love;
   stranger, neighbour, father, mother –
   bind us in love.
   All are equal at your table,
   through your Spirit make us able
   to embrace as sister, brother,
   bind us in love.

348 Claudia Frances Hernaman (1838-1898)

1. Lord, who throughout these forty days
   for us didst fast and pray,
   teach us with thee to mourn our sins,
   and at thy side to stay.

2. As thou with Satan didst contend
   and didst the vict'ry win,
   O give us strength in thee to fight,
   in thee to conquer sin.

3. As thirst and hunger thou didst bear,
   so teach us, gracious Lord,
   to die to self, and daily live
   by thy most holy word.

4. And through these days of penitence,
   and through thy Passiontide,
   yea, evermore, in life and death,
   Lord Christ, with us abide.

349
Nick Fawcett (b. 1957)
© 2004 Kevin Mayhew Ltd

1. Lord, you created a world rich in
   splendour,
   touched with a beauty no words can
   express.
   Able to move us to outbursts of
   wonder,
   so much to thrill us and so much to
   bless.

2. Mountains and moorlands rise up to
   the heavens,
   rivers and streams tumble down to
   the sea,
   gifts that amaze in profusion
   surround us,
   each a reflection of your majesty.

3. Promise of springtime and harvest of
   autumn,
   cold winter mornings and warm
   summer days,
   season by season brings new joys to
   greet us,
   reason to thank you and reason to
   praise.

4. Deep in the forest, remote in the
   desert,
   down in the ocean or high in the air;
   life in abundance is ev'rywhere round
   us,
   proof of your power and sign of your
   care.

5. Lord, you have given a world rich in
   splendour,
   touched with a beauty that fills us
   with awe;
   hear now our praises, we bring you
   our worship,
   with all creation we kneel and adore.

350
Jeffrey Rowthorn (b. 1934)
*© 1978 Hope Publishing.
Administered by CopyCare*

1. Lord, you give the great commission:
   'Heal the sick and preach the word.'
   Lest the Church neglect its mission,
   and the Gospel go unheard,
   help us witness to your purpose
   with renewed integrity;
   with the Spirit's gifts empow'r us
   for the work of ministry.

2. Lord, you call us to your service:
   'In my name baptise and teach,'
   that the world may trust your promise,
   life abundant meant for each,
   give us all new fervour, draw us
   closer in community;
   with the Spirit's gifts empow'r us
   for the work of ministry.

3. Lord, you make the common holy:
   'This my body, this my blood.'
   Let us all, for earth's true glory,
   daily lift life heavenward,
   asking that the world around us
   share your children's liberty;
   with the Spirit's gifts empow'r us
   for the work of ministry.

Continued overleaf

4. Lord, you show us love's true measure;
   'Father what they do, forgive.'
   Yet we hoard as private treasure
   all that you so freely give.
   May your care and mercy lead us
   to a just society;
   with the Spirit's gifts empow'r us
   for the work of ministry.

5. Lord, you bless with words assuring:
   'I am with you to the end.'
   Faith and hope and love restoring,
   may we serve as you intend,
   and, amid the cares that claim us,
   hold in mind eternity;
   with the Spirit's gifts empow'r us
   for the work of ministry.

351 Christina Georgina Rossetti (1830-1894)

1. Love came down at Christmas,
   Love all lovely, Love divine;
   Love was born at Christmas,
   star and angels gave the sign.

2. Worship we the Godhead,
   Love incarnate, Love divine;
   worship we our Jesus:
   but wherewith for sacred sign?

3. Love shall be our token,
   love be yours and love be mine,
   love to God and all men,
   love for plea and gift and sign.

352 Charles Wesley (1707-1788) alt.

1. Love divine, all loves excelling,
   joy of heav'n, to earth come down,
   fix in us thy humble dwelling,
   all thy faithful mercies crown.

2. Jesu, thou art all compassion,
   pure unbounded love thou art;
   visit us with thy salvation,
   enter ev'ry trembling heart.

3. Breathe, O breathe thy loving Spirit
   into ev'ry troubled breast;
   let us all in thee inherit,
   let us find thy promised rest.

*4. Take away the love of sinning,
   Alpha and Omega be;
   end of faith, as its beginning,
   set our hearts at liberty.

5. Come, almighty to deliver,
   let us all thy grace receive;
   suddenly return, and never,
   never more thy temples leave.

*6. Thee we would be always blessing,
   serve thee as thy hosts above;
   pray, and praise thee without ceasing,
   glory in thy perfect love.

*7. Finish then thy new creation,
   pure and spotless let us be;
   let us see thy great salvation
   perfectly restored in thee.

8. Changed from glory into glory,
   till in heav'n we take our place,
   till we cast our crowns before thee,
   lost in wonder, love, and praise.

353 Luke Connaughton (1917-1979) alt.
© McCrimmon Publishing Co. Ltd

1. Love is his word, love is his way,
   feasting with all, fasting alone,
   living and dying, rising again,
   love, only love, is his way.

   Richer than gold is the love of my Lord:
   better than splendour and wealth.

2. Love is his way, love is his mark,
   sharing his last Passover feast,
   Christ at the table, host to the twelve,
   love, only love, is his mark.

3. Love is his mark, love is his sign,
   bread for our strength, wine for our joy,
   'This is my body, this is my blood.'
   Love, only love, is his sign.

4. Love is his sign, love is his news,
   'Do this,' he said, 'lest you forget
   all my deep sorrow, all my dear blood.'
   Love, only love, is his news.

5. Love is his news, love is his name,
   we are his own, chosen and called,
   family, brethren, cousins and kin.
   Love, only love, is his name.

6. Love is his name, love is his law,
   hear his command, all who are his,
   'Love one another, I have loved you.'
   Love, only love, is his law.

7. Love is his law, love is his word:
   love of the Lord, Father and Word,
   love of the Spirit, God ever one,
   love, only love, is his word.

354 Pamela Hayes
© 1998 Kevin Mayhew Ltd

1. Lovely in your littleness,
   longing for our lowliness,
   longing for our lowliness,
   searching for our meekness:
   Jesus is our joy, Jesus is our joy.

2. Peace within our pow'rlessness,
   hope within our helplessness,
   hope within our helplessness,
   love within our loneliness:
   Jesus is our joy, Jesus is our joy.

3. Held in Mary's tenderness,
   tiny hands are raised to bless,
   tiny hands are raised to bless,
   touching us with God's caress:
   Jesus is our joy, Jesus is our joy.

4. Joy, then, in God's graciousness,
   peace comes with gentleness,
   peace comes with gentleness,
   filling hearts with gladness:
   Jesus is our joy, Jesus is our joy.

355 Jane Elizabeth Leeson (1809-1881)

1. Loving Shepherd of thy sheep,
   keep me, Lord, in safety keep;
   nothing can thy pow'r withstand,
   none can pluck me from thy hand.

2. Loving Shepherd, thou didst give
   thine own life that I might live;
   may I love thee day by day,
   gladly thy sweet will obey.

3. Loving Shepherd, ever near,
   teach me still thy voice to hear;
   suffer not my steps to stray
   from the straight and narrow way.

4. Where thou leadest may I go,
   walking in thy steps below;
   then, before thy Father's throne,
   Jesu, claim me for thine own.

356 Ray Simpson (b. 1940)
© 2000 Ray Simpson

Magnificat, magnificat,
praise God my soul, praise God.
The proud are downed,
the poor raised up,
magnificat, my soul.

357 Luke 1:46

Magnificat, magnificat,
anima mea Dominum.

Translation: My soul praises and
magnifies the Lord.

358 Jack W. Hayford (b. 1934)
© 1976 Rocksmith Music Inc.
Administered by Kevin Mayhew Ltd

Majesty, worship his majesty;
unto Jesus be glory, honour and praise.
Majesty, kingdom, authority
flow from his throne unto his own:
his anthem raise.
So exalt, lift up on high the name of
Jesus;
magnify, come glorify
Christ Jesus the King.
Majesty, worship his majesty,
Jesus who died, now glorified,
King of all kings.

359 Sebastian Temple (1928-1997)
based on the Prayer of St Francis
© 1967 Sebastian Temple/OCP Publications

1. Make me a channel of your peace.
   Where there is hatred, let me bring
      your love.
   Where there is injury, your pardon,
      Lord;
   and where there's doubt, true faith in
      you.

   O, Master, grant that I may never seek
   so much to be consoled as to console,
   to be understood as to understand,
   to be loved as to love with all my soul.

2. Make me a channel of your peace.
   Where there's despair in life, let me
      bring hope.
   Where there is darkness, only light,
   and where there's sadness, ever joy.

3. Make me a channel of your peace.
   It is in pardoning that we are pardoned,
   in giving of ourselves that we receive,
   and in dying that we're born to
      eternal life.

360 Graham Kendrick (b. 1950)
© 1986 Thankyou Music.
Administered by worshiptogether.com songs

1. Make way, make way, for Christ the
      King
   in splendour arrives;
   fling wide the gates and welcome him
   into your lives.

   Make way (make way),
   make way (make way),
   for the King of kings
   (for the King of kings);
   make way (make way),
   make way (make way),
   and let his kingdom in!

2. He comes the broken hearts to heal,
   the pris'ners to free;
   the deaf shall hear, the lame shall dance,
   the blind shall see.

3. And those who mourn with heavy
      hearts,
   who weep and sigh,
   with laughter, joy and royal crown
   he'll beautify.

4. We call you now to worship him
   as Lord of all,
   to have no gods before him,
   their thrones must fall.

361 West Indian Spiritual, alt.
© 1999, 2004 Kevin Mayhew Ltd

1. Mary had a baby, yes, Lord,
   Mary had a baby, yes, my Lord,
   Mary had a baby, yes, Lord,
   the people came to Bethlehem
   to see her son.

2. What did she name him, yes, Lord?
   (x3)

3. Mary named him Jesus, yes, Lord, *(x3)*

4. Where was he born, yes, Lord? *(x3)*

5. Born in a stable, yes, Lord, *(x3)*

6. Where did she lay him, yes, Lord? *(x3)*

7. Laid him in a manger, yes, Lord, *(x3)*

362 Brian Foley (1919-2000)
© 1971 Faber Music Ltd

1. Mary, how lovely the light of your
   glory!
   From David's house, royal daughter,
   you come,
   holier, higher than angels in heaven,
   holiest, highest through all God has
   done.

2. Blest of all women, both virgin and
   mother,
   favoured in grace for the Son whom
   you bore;
   Christ is your Son whom all peoples
   must worship,
   Christ is your Son whom all angels
   adore.

3. Pray for us, plead for us, exiles in
   darkness,
   pray with us, praying to Christ in
   our needs;
   all pow'r is given him here and in
   heaven,
   Christ ever lives for us and intercedes.

4. Father, the prayer of your Son
   interceding
   wins for us life and light for all our
   days;
   praise to you, Father, to Christ and
   your Spirit,
   glory, eternal God, glory and praise!

363 F. W. Weatherell

1. Mary immaculate,
   star of the morning,
   chosen before
   the creation began,
   chosen to bring,
   for thy bridal adorning,
   woe to the serpent
   and rescue to man.

2. Here, in an orbit
   of shadow and sadness
   veiling thy splendour,
   thy course thou hast run;
   now thou art throned
   in all glory and gladness,
   crowned by the hand
   of thy Saviour and Son.

3. Sinners, we worship
   thy sinless perfection,
   fallen and weak,
   for thy pity we plead;
   grant us the shield
   of thy sov'reign protection,
   measure thine aid
   by the depth of our need.

4. Frail is our nature
   and strict our probation,
   watchful the foe
   that would lure us to wrong,
   succour our souls
   in the hour of temptation,
   Mary immaculate,
   tender and strong.

5. See how the wiles
   of the serpent assail us,
   see how we waver
   and flinch in the fight;
   let thine immaculate
   merit avail us,
   make of our weakness
   a proof of thy might.

Continued overleaf

6. Bend from thy throne
   at the voice of our crying;
   bend to this earth
   which thy footsteps have trod;
   stretch out thine arms
   to us living and dying,
   Mary immaculate,
   mother of God.

364
Sister Colm Keane
© 2003 Kevin Mayhew Ltd

1. Mary most holy, from your hands
   falling
   are heaven's blessings. Hear us,
   now calling.
   Teach us to pray, and work for God's
   glory.
   Ave Maria, ave.

2. Help us to witness Christ is still
   living,
   service to others cheerfully giving.
   Teach us to pray, and work for God's
   glory.
   Ave Maria, ave.

3. Through joy and sorrow, each day's
   condition,
   ever, dear Mother, hear our petition.
   Teach us to pray, and work for God's
   glory.
   Ave Maria, ave.

365
Ernest Sands
© 1990 Ernest Sands/ OCP Publications

May the choirs of angels come to greet
you.
May they speed you to paradise.
May the Lord enfold you in his mercy.
May you find eternal life.

1. The Lord is my light and my help;
   it is he who protects me from harm.
   The Lord is the strength of my days;
   before whom should I tremble with
   fear?

2. There is one thing I ask of the Lord;
   that he grant me my heart-felt desire.
   To dwell in the courts of our God
   ev'ry day of my life in his presence.

3. O Lord, hear my voice when I cry;
   have mercy on me and give answer.
   Do not cast me away in your anger,
   for you are the God of my help.

4. I am sure I shall see the Lord's
   goodness;
   I shall dwell in the land of the living.
   Hope in God, stand firm and take
   heart,
   place all your trust in the Lord.

366
Gaelic blessing adpt. by Margaret Rizza (b.1929)
© 1998 Kevin Mayhew Ltd

May the Lord bless you,
may the Lord protect you and guide
you,
may his strength uphold you,
his light shine upon you,
his peace surround you,
his love enfold you.

367
Graham Kendrick (b. 1950)
© 1986 Thankyou Music.
Administered by worshiptogether.com songs

1. Meekness and majesty,
   manhood and deity,
   in perfect harmony,
   the Man who is God.
   Lord of eternity
   dwells in humanity,
   kneels in humility
   and washes our feet.

O what a mystery,
meekness and majesty.
Bow down and worship
for this is your God,
this is your God.

2. Father's pure radiance,
   perfect in innocence,
   yet learns obedience
   to death on a cross.
   Suff'ring to give us life,
   conqu'ring through sacrifice,
   and as they crucify
   prays: 'Father forgive.'

3. Wisdom unsearchable,
   God the invisible,
   love indestructible
   in frailty appears.
   Lord of infinity,
   stooping so tenderly,
   lifts our humanity
   to the heights of his throne.

368 Eleanor Farjeon (1881-1965)
© *David Higham Associates. Used by permission*
from 'The Children's Bells', Oxford University Press

1. Morning has broken like the first
   morning,
   blackbird has spoken like the first bird.
   Praise for the singing! Praise for the
   morning!
   Praise for them, springing fresh from
   the Word!

2. Sweet the rain's new fall, sunlit from
   heaven,
   like the first dew-fall on the first grass.
   Praise for the sweetness of the wet
   garden,
   sprung in completeness where his feet
   pass.

3. Mine is the sunlight! Mine is the
   morning
   born of the one light Eden saw play!
   Praise with elation, praise ev'ry morning,
   God's re-creation of the new day!

369 Estelle White (b. 1925)
© *McCrimmon Publishing Co. Ltd*

1. 'Moses, I know you're the man,'
   the Lord said.
   'You're going to work out my plan,'
   the Lord said.
   'Lead all the Israelites out of slavery,
   and I shall make them a wandering
   race
   called the people of God.'

So ev'ry day we're on our way,
for we're a travelling, wandering race
called the people of God.

2. 'Don't get too set in your ways,'
   the Lord said.
   'Each step is only a phase,'
   the Lord said.
   'I'll go before you and I shall be a sign
   to guide my travelling, wandering
   race.
   You're the people of God.'

*3. 'No matter what you may do,'
   the Lord said,
   'I shall be faithful and true,'
   the Lord said.
   'My love will strengthen you as you
   go along,
   for you're my travelling, wandering
   race.
   You're the people of God.'

Continued overleaf

4. 'Look at the birds in the air,'
   the Lord said.
   'They fly unhampered by care,'
   the Lord said.
   'You will move easier if you're
   trav'lling light,
   for you're a wandering, vagabond
   race.
   You're the people of God.'

   So ev'ry day we're on our way,
   for we're a travelling, wandering race
   called the people of God.

5. 'Foxes have places to go,'
   the Lord said,
   'but I've no home here below,'
   the Lord said.
   'So if you want to be with me all
   your days,
   keep up the moving and travelling on.
   You're the people of God.'

370 Nick Fawcett (b. 1957)
    © 2005 Kevin Mayhew Ltd

1. Mother of Christ, called from above,
   chosen to serve, chosen to love,
   freely you offered your body, your all,
   no price too costly to answer God's call.

2. Mother of Christ, called from on high,
   wondering how, wondering why;
   yet you were willing to bow to God's
   will,
   ready to serve him in good times or ill.

3. Mother of Christ, called from the
   crowd,
   handmaid of God, singing aloud,
   gladly rejoicing, you poured out your
   praise,
   heart overflowing and spirit ablaze.

4. Mother of Christ, called to respond,
   bearing a child, gift from beyond.
   Angels in splendour have gathered to
   sing.
   Shepherds and magi revere him as king.

5. Mother of Christ, called here today,
   we too would serve; guide us, we pray.
   Speak to us, teach us – from you we
   would learn;
   help us to honour the Saviour in turn.

371 Damian Lundy (1944-1997)
    © 1978 Kevin Mayhew Ltd

1. Mother of God's living Word,
   glorifying Christ your Lord;
   full of joy, God's people sing,
   grateful for your mothering.

2. Virgin soil, untouched by sin,
   for God's seed to flourish in;
   watered by the Spirit's dew,
   in your womb the Saviour grew.

3. Sharing his humility,
   Bethlehem and Calvary,
   with him in his bitter pain,
   now as queen with him you reign.

4. We are God's new chosen race,
   new-born children of his grace,
   citizens of heaven who
   imitate and honour you.

5. We, God's people on our way,
   travelling by night and day,
   moving to our promised land,
   walk beside you hand in hand.

6. Christ, your Son, is always near,
   so we journey without fear,
   singing as we walk along:
   Christ our joy, and Christ our song!

7. Sing aloud to Christ with joy,
who was once a little boy.
Sing aloud to Mary, sing,
grateful for her mothering.

372 Matthew Bridges (1800-1894)

1. My God, accept my heart this day,
and make it wholly thine,
that I from thee no more may stray,
no more from thee decline.

2. Before the cross of him who died,
behold, I prostrate fall;
let ev'ry sin be crucified,
and Christ be all in all.

3. Anoint me with thy heav'nly grace,
and seal me for thine own,
that I may see thy glorious face,
and worship at thy throne.

4. Let ev'ry thought and work and word
to thee be ever giv'n;
then life shall be thy service, Lord,
and death the gate of heav'n.

5. All glory to the Father be,
all glory to the Son,
all glory, Holy Ghost, to thee,
while endless ages run.

373
Philip Doddridge (1702-1751), alt.
v. 3 Michael Forster (b. 1946)
© This version 1996 Kevin Mayhew Ltd

1. My God, and is thy table spread,
and does thy cup with love o'erflow?
Thither be all thy children led,
and let them all thy sweetness know.

2. Hail, sacred feast, which Jesus makes!
Rich banquet of his flesh and blood!
Thrice happy all, who here partake
that sacred stream, that heav'nly food.

3. What wondrous love! What perfect
grace,
for Jesus, our exalted host,
invites us to this special place
who offer least and need the most.

4. O let thy table honoured be,
and furnished well with joyful guests;
and may each soul salvation see,
that here its sacred pledges tastes.

374
Frederick William Faber (1814-1863) alt.
© Jubilate Hymns. Used by permission

1. My God, how wonderful you are,
your majesty how bright;
how beautiful your mercy-seat,
in depths of burning light!

2. Creator from eternal years
and everlasting Lord,
by holy angels day and night
unceasingly adored!

3. How wonderful, how beautiful
the sight of you must be –
your endless wisdom, boundless pow'r,
and awesome purity!

4. O how I fear you, living God,
with deepest, tend'rest fears,
and worship you with trembling hope
and penitential tears!

5. But I may love you too, O Lord,
though you are all-divine,
for you have stooped to ask of me
this feeble love of mine.

6. Father of Jesus, love's reward,
great King upon your throne,
what joy to see you as you are
and know as I am known!

375

17th century Latin
trans. Edward Caswall (1814-1878)

1. My God, I love thee; not because
I hope for heav'n thereby,
nor yet because who love thee not
are lost eternally.
Thou, O my Jesus, thou didst me
upon the cross embrace;
for me didst bear the nails and spear,
and manifold disgrace.

2. And griefs and torments numberless,
and sweat of agony;
yea, death itself – and all for me
who was thine enemy.
Then why, O blessèd Jesu Christ,
should I not love thee well?
Not for the sake of winning heav'n,
nor of escaping hell.

3. Not from the hope of gaining aught,
not seeking a reward;
but as thyself hast lovèd me,
O ever-loving Lord.
So would I love thee, dearest Lord,
and in thy praise will sing;
solely because thou art my God,
and my most loving King.

376

Robin Mark (b. 1955)
© Daybreak Music Ltd

1. My heart will sing to you
because of your great love,
a love so rich, so pure,
a love beyond compare;
the wilderness, the barren place,
become a blessing
in the warmth of your embrace.

May my heart sing your praise for ever,
may my voice lift your name, my God;
may my soul know no other treasure
than your love, than your love.

2. When earthly wisdom dims
the light of knowing you,
or if my search for understanding
clouds your way,
to you I fly, my hiding-place,
where revelation
is beholding face to face.

377

Darlene Zschech (b. 1965)
© 1993 Darlene Zschech/Hillsong Publishing/
kingswaysongs.com

1. My Jesus, my Saviour,
Lord, there is none like you.
All of my days I want to praise
the wonders of your mighty love.

2. My comfort, my shelter,
tower of refuge and strength,
let ev'ry breath, all that I am,
never cease to worship you.

Shout to the Lord,
all the earth, let us sing
power and majesty,
praise to the King.
Mountains bow down
and the seas will roar
at the sound of your name.
I sing for joy
at the work of your hands.
For ever I'll love you,
for ever I'll stand.
Nothing compares to the promise
I have in you.

378

Psalm 22, Grail translation
© 1963, 1986, 1993 The Grail/Harper Collins
Religious

Response 1:
My shepherd is the Lord,
nothing indeed shall I want.

Response 2:
His goodness shall follow me always
to the end of my days.

The following verses may be sung by a Cantor:

1. The <u>Lord</u> is my <u>shep</u>herd;
there is <u>noth</u>ing I shall <u>want</u>.
<u>Fresh</u> and <u>green</u> are the <u>pas</u>tures
where he <u>gives</u> me re<u>pose</u>.
Near <u>rest</u>ful <u>wat</u>ers he <u>leads</u> me,
to re<u>vive</u> my drooping <u>spir</u>it.

2. He <u>guides</u> me a<u>long</u> the right <u>path</u>;
he is <u>true</u> to his <u>name</u>.
If I should <u>walk</u> in the <u>val</u>ley of
<u>dark</u>ness
no <u>evil</u> would I <u>fear</u>.
You are <u>there</u> with your <u>crook</u> and
your <u>staff</u>;
with <u>these</u> you give me <u>comfort</u>.

3. You have pre<u>pared</u> a <u>banquet</u> for <u>me</u>
in the <u>sight</u> of my <u>foes</u>.
My <u>head</u> you have a<u>noint</u>ed with <u>oil</u>;
my <u>cup</u> is over<u>flow</u>ing.

4. Surely <u>good</u>ness and <u>kind</u>ness shall
<u>fol</u>low me
all the <u>days</u> of my <u>life</u>.
In the <u>Lord's</u> own <u>house</u> shall I <u>dwell</u>
for <u>ever</u> and <u>ever</u>.

5. To the <u>Fa</u>ther and <u>Son</u> give glory,
give <u>glo</u>ry to the Spirit.
To God who <u>is</u>, who <u>was</u>, and who
<u>will</u> be
for <u>ever</u> and <u>ever</u>.

379 Samuel Crossman (c. 1624-1684) alt.

1. My song is love unknown,
my Saviour's love to me,
love to the loveless shown,
that they might lovely be.
O who am I, that for my sake,
my Lord should take frail flesh and
die?

2. He came from his blest throne,
salvation to bestow;
but men refused, and none
the longed-for Christ would know.
But O, my friend, my friend indeed,
who at my need his life did spend!

3. Sometimes they strew his way,
and his sweet praises sing:
resounding all the day
hosannas to their King:
then 'Crucify!' is all their breath,
and for his death they thirst and cry.

*4. Why, what hath my Lord done?
What makes this rage and spite?
He made the lame to run,
he gave the blind their sight.
Sweet injuries! Yet they at these
themselves displease,
and 'gainst him rise.

*5. They rise, and needs will have
my dear Lord made away;
a murderer they save,
the Prince of Life they slay.
Yet cheerful he to suff'ring goes,
that he his foes from thence might
free.

6. Here might I stay and sing,
no story so divine;
never was love, dear King,
never was grief like thine.
This is my friend in whose sweet
praise
I all my days could gladly spend.

380 Unknown, based on Luke 1:46-55

1. My soul is filled with joy
as I sing to God my Saviour:
he has looked upon his servant,
he has visited his people.

Continued overleaf

And holy is his name
through all generations!
Everlasting is his mercy
to the people he has chosen,
and holy is his name!

2. I am lowly as a child,
   but I know from this day forward
   that my name will be remembered
   and the world will call me blessèd.

3. I proclaim the pow'r of God!
   He does marvels for his servants;
   though he scatters the proud-hearted
   and destroys the might of princes.

4. To the hungry he gives food,
   sends the rich away empty.
   In his mercy he is mindful
   of the people he has chosen.

5. In his love he now fulfils
   what he promised to our fathers.
   I will praise the Lord, my Saviour.
   Everlasting is his mercy.

381
Lucien Deiss (b. 1921), based on Psalm 130
© 1965 World Library Publications

My soul is longing for your peace,
near to you my God.

1. Lord, you know that my heart is not
   proud
   and my eyes are not lifted from the
   earth.

2. Lofty thoughts have never filled my
   mind,
   far beyond my sight all ambitious
   deeds.

3. In your peace I have maintained my
   soul,
   I have kept my heart in your quiet
   peace.

4. As a child rests on a mother's knee,
   so I place my soul in your loving care.

5. Israel, put all your hope in God,
   place your trust in him, now and
   evermore.

382
Francesca Leftley (b. 1955)
© 1978 Kevin Mayhew Ltd

1. My soul is sad, my heart is breaking
   tonight.
   Could you not watch and comfort
   me until light?
   Am I alone, surrounded only by night?
   Could you not watch one hour with
   me?

2. Could you not keep awake for one
   hour with me?
   Is it so hard that you should do this
   for me?
   I die for you that you might always
   be free.
   Could you not watch one hour with
   me?

3. And so I weep, and there is no one to
   hear.
   I am in pain; will no one witness my
   tears?
   I am your God, and as my Passion
   draws near,
   could you not watch one hour with me?

383
Owen Alstott, based on Luke 1:46-55
© 1993 Owen Alstott/OCP Publications

1. My soul proclaims the greatness of
   the Lord,
   my spirit sings to God, my saving God,
   who on this day above all others
   favoured me
   and raised me up, a light for all to see.

2. Through me great deeds will God
   make manifest,
   and all the earth will come to call me
   blest.
   Unbounded love and mercy sure will
   I proclaim
   for all who know and praise God's
   holy name.

3. God's mighty arm, protector of the
   just,
   will guard the weak and raise them
   from the dust.
   But mighty kings will swiftly fall
   from thrones corrupt,
   the strong brought low, the lowly
   lifted up.

4. Soon will the poor and hungry of the
   earth
   be richly blest, be given greater worth:
   and Israel, as once foretold to Abraham,
   will live in peace throughout the
   promised land.

5. All glory be to God, Creator blest,
   to Jesus Christ, God's love made
   manifest,
   and to the Holy Spirit, gentle
   Comforter,
   all glory be, both now and evermore.

384 Anne Carter (1944-1993), based on Luke 1:46-55
© 1988 Society of the Sacred Heart

1. My soul proclaims you, mighty God.
   My spirit sings your praise.
   You look on me, you lift me up,
   and gladness fills my days.

2. All nations now will share my joy;
   your gifts you have outpoured.
   Your little one you have made great;
   I magnify my God.

3. For those who love your holy name,
   your mercy will not die.
   Your strong right arm puts down the
   proud
   and lifts the lowly high.

4. You fill the hungry with good things,
   the rich you send away.
   The promise made to Abraham
   is filled to endless day.

5. Magnificat, magnificat,
   magnificat, praise God!
   Praise God, praise God, praise God,
   praise God,
   magnificat, praise God!

385 St Teresa of Avila (1545-1582)
© Ateliers et Presses de Taizé

Nada te turbe, nada te espante.
Quien a Dios tiene nada le falta.
Nada te turbe, nada te espante.
Solo Dios basta.

or

Nothing can trouble, nothing can
   frighten.
Those who seek God shall never go
   wanting.
Nothing can trouble, nothing can
   frighten.
God alone fills us.

386 *Hymnum canamus gloria* by the Venerable Bede
(673-735), trans. Ronald Arbuthnott Knox
(1888-1957). © Burns & Oates Ltd/
Continuum Int. Publishing group

1. New praises be given
   to Christ newly crowned,
   who back to his heaven
   a new way hath found;
   God's blessedness sharing
   before us he goes,
   what mansions preparing,
   what endless repose!

Continued overleaf

2. His glory still praising
on thrice holy ground,
th'apostles stood gazing,
his mother around;
with hearts that beat faster,
with eyes full of love,
they watched while their
master ascended above.

3. 'No star can disclose him,'
the bright angels said;
'eternity knows him,
your conquering head;
those high habitations,
he leaves not again,
till, judging all nations,
on earth he shall reign.'

4. Thus spoke they and straightway,
where legions defend
heav'n's glittering gateway,
their Lord they attend,
and cry, looking thither,
'Your portals let down
for him who rides hither
in peace and renown.'

5. They asked, who keep sentry
in that blessèd town,
'Who thus claimeth entry,
a king of renown?'
'The Lord of all valiance,'
that herald replied,
'who Satan's battalions
laid low in their pride.'

6. Grant, Lord, that our longing
may follow thee there,
on earth who are thronging
thy temples with prayer;
and unto thee gather,
Redeemer, thine own,
where thou with thy Father
dost sit on the throne.

387 Michael Forster (b. 1946),
based on *Te lucis ante terminum*
© 1999 Kevin Mayhew Ltd

1. Now as the evening shadows fall,
God our Creator, hear our call:
help us to trust your constant grace,
though darkness seems to hide your
face.

2. Help us to find, in sleep's release,
bodily rest and inner peace;
so may the darkness of the night
refresh our eyes for morning light.

3. Father almighty, holy Son,
Spirit eternal, three in One,
grant us the faith that sets us free
to praise you for eternity.

388 *Nun danket alle Gott* by Martin Rinkart (1586-
1649), trans. Catherine Winkworth (1827-1878)

1. Now thank we all our God,
with hearts and hands and voices,
who wondrous things hath done,
in whom his world rejoices;
who from our mother's arms
hath blessed us on our way
with countless gifts of love,
and still is ours today.

2. O may this bounteous God
through all our life be near us,
with ever joyful hearts
and blessèd peace to cheer us;
and keep us in his grace,
and guide us when perplexed,
and free us from all ills
in this world and the next.

3. All praise and thanks to God
   the Father now be given,
   the Son and him who reigns
   with them in highest heaven,
   the one eternal God,
   whom earth and heav'n adore;
   for thus it was, is now,
   and shall be evermore.

389 John Macleod Campbell Crum (1872-1958) alt.
© Oxford University Press

1. Now the green blade riseth
   from the buried grain,
   wheat that in the dark earth
   many days has lain;
   Love lives again,
   that with the dead has been:
   Love is come again,
   like wheat that springeth green.

2. In the grave they laid him,
   Love by hatred slain,
   thinking that never
   he would wake again,
   laid in the earth
   like grain that sleeps unseen:
   Love is come again,
   like wheat that springeth green.

3. Forth he came at Easter,
   like the risen grain,
   he that for three days
   in the grave had lain;
   quick from the dead,
   my risen Lord is seen:
   Love is come again,
   like wheat that springeth green.

4. When our hearts are wintry,
   grieving or in pain,
   thy touch can call us
   back to life again;

fields of our hearts,
that dead and bare have been:
Love is come again,
like wheat that springeth green.

390 Willard F. Jabusch (b. 1930)
© Willard F. Jabusch

1. Now watch for God's coming, be
   patient till then;
   like sunshine he'll brighten all
   women and men;
   who hope in the Lord will possess
   fertile land;
   the poor he will welcome and grasp
   by the hand.

2. Our steps are directed, God watches
   our path;
   he guides us and holds us and saves
   us from wrath,
   and though we may fall we will not
   go headlong,
   for God gives sound footing and
   keeps us from wrong.

3. So wait for his coming, be patient till
   then;
   the wicked are armed and would kill
   honest men.
   Their arms shall be broken, no refuge
   they'll see,
   but saved are the needy by God's own
   decree.

4. Now those who do evil will wither
   like grass,
   like green of the springtime they fade
   and they pass,
   so trust in the Lord and to him give
   your life,
   he'll bring heart's desires and peace in
   our strife.

391

Te lucis ante terminum
trans. Edward Caswall (1814-1878)

1. Now with the fast-departing light,
   maker of all, we ask of thee,
   of thy great mercy, through the night
   our guardian and defence to be.

2. Far off let idle visions fly,
   no phantom of the night molest;
   curb thou our raging enemy,
   that we in chaste repose may rest.

3. Father of mercies, hear our cry,
   hear us, O sole-begotten Son
   who, with the Holy Ghost most high,
   reignest while endless ages run.

392

St Alphonus (1696-1787),
trans. Edmund Vaughan (1827-1908)

1. O bread of heaven beneath this veil
   thou dost my very God conceal;
   my Jesus, dearest treasure, hail;
   I love thee and adoring kneel;
   each loving soul by thee is fed
   with thine own self in form of bread.

2. O food of life, thou who dost give
   the pledge of immortality;
   I live; no, 'tis not I that live;
   God gives me life, God lives in me;
   he feeds my soul, he guides my ways,
   and ev'ry grief with joy repays.

3. O bond of love, that dost unite
   the servant to his living Lord;
   could I dare live, and not requite
   such love – then death were meet
     reward:
   I cannot live unless to prove
   some love for such unmeasured love.

4. Belovèd Lord in heav'n above,
   there, Jesus, thou awaitest me;
   to gaze on thee with changeless love,
   yes, thus I hope, thus shall it be:
   for how can he deny me heav'n
   who here on earth himself hath giv'n?

393

Psalm 22
© 1963, 1986, 1993 The Grail/Harper Collins
Religious

O Christe, Domine Jesu,
O Christe, Domine Jesu!

Translation: O Christ, Lord Jesus.

The following verses may be sung by a
Cantor:

1. The Lord is my shepherd;
   there is nothing I shall want.
   Fresh and green are the pastures
   where he gives me repose.
   Near restful waters he leads me,
   to revive my drooping spirit.
   He guides me along the right path;
   he is true to his name.
   If I should walk in the valley of
     darkness
   no evil would I fear.

2. You are there with your rod and staff;
   with these you give me comfort.
   You have prepared a banquet for me
   in the sight of my foes.
   My head you have anointed with oil;
   my cup is overflowing.
   Surely goodness and kindness shall
     follow me
   all the days of my life.
   In the Lord's house shall I dwell for
     ever and ever.

394

Attributed to John Francis Wade (1711-1786)
trans. Frederick Oakeley (1802-1880)

1. O come, all ye faithful,
   joyful and triumphant,
   O come ye, O come ye to Bethlehem;
   come and behold him,
   born the king of angels:

   O come, let us adore him,
   O come, let us adore him,
   O come, let us adore him,
   Christ the Lord.

2. God of God,
   Light of Light,
   lo, he abhors not the Virgin's womb;
   very God, begotten not created:

3. Sing, choirs of angels,
   sing in exultation,
   sing, all ye citizens of heav'n above;
   glory to God in the highest:

4. Yea, Lord, we greet thee,
   born this happy morning,
   Jesu, to thee be glory giv'n;
   Word of the Father, now in flesh
   appearing:

395

Frederick William Faber (1814-1863), alt.
© This version 1999 Kevin Mayhew Ltd

1. O come and mourn with me awhile;
   see, Mary calls us to her side;
   O come and let us mourn with her;

   Jesus our love, Jesus our love,
   is crucified.

2. Have we no tears to shed for him
   while soldiers scoff and people sneer?
   Ah, look how patiently he hangs!

3. How fast his feet and hands are
     nailed,
   his blessèd tongue with thirst is tied;
   his failing eyes are blind with blood;

4. Sev'n times he spoke, sev'n words of
     love,
   and all three hours his silence cried
   for mercy on poor human souls.

5. O break, O break, hard heart of
     mine:
   thy weak self-love and guilty pride
   his Pilate and his Judas were:

6. A broken heart, a fount of tears,
   ask, and they will not be denied;
   a broken heart, love's cradle is;

7. O love of God! O mortal sin!
   In this dread act your strength is
     tried;
   and victory remains with love;

396

Michael Forster (b. 1946)
© 2005 Kevin Mayhew Ltd

1. O come, divine renewing Spirit,
   with grace to heal creation's pain,
   and call on Adam's squabbling children
   to give and take, and give again.

2. O come to bless this hurting planet
   with time to care and space to be,
   where countless races, creeds and
     cultures
   may celebrate diversity.

3. O come to turn our words to wisdom,
   our mad stampedes to gracious dance,
   to still the tongues of mindless dogma
   and give the list'ning ear a chance.

Continued overleaf

4. O come, divine renewing Spirit,
   with grace to set our spirits free,
   to recognise in one another
   our shared divine humanity.

397 From the *Great O Antiphons* (12th-13th century) trans. John Mason Neale (1818-1866)

1. O come, O come, Emmanuel,
   and ransom captive Israel,
   that mourns in lonely exile here,
   until the Son of God appear.

   Rejoice, rejoice!
   Emmanuel shall come to thee,
   O Israel.

2. O come, thou rod of Jesse, free
   thine own from Satan's tyranny;
   from depths of hell thy people save,
   and give them vict'ry o'er the grave.

3. O come, thou dayspring, come and
      cheer
   our spirits by thine advent here;
   disperse the gloomy clouds of night,
   and death's dark shadows put to flight.

4. O come, thou key of David, come
   and open wide our heav'nly home;
   make safe the way that leads on high,
   and close the path to misery.

5. O come, O come, thou Lord of might,
   who to thy tribes on Sinai's height
   in ancient times didst give the Law,
   in cloud and majesty and awe.

398 Chrysogonus Waddell (b. 1930), based on Isaiah 40. © *Chrysogonus Waddell*

1. O comfort my people
   and calm all their fear,
   and tell them the time of
   salvation draws near.

O tell them I come
to remove all their shame.
Then they will forever
give praise to my name.

2. Proclaim to the cities
   of Judah my word;
   that 'gentle yet strong
   is the hand of the Lord.
   I rescue the captives,
   my people defend,
   and bring them to justice
   and joy without end.'

3. 'All mountains and hills
   shall become as a plain,
   for vanished are mourning
   and hunger and pain.
   And never again shall
   these war against you.
   Behold I come quickly
   to make all things new.'

399 *O esca viatorum* from *Maintzisch Gesangbuch* (1661), trans. Walter H. Shewring and others

1. O food of trav'llers, angels' bread,
   manna wherewith the blest are fed,
   come nigh, and with thy sweetness fill
   the hungry hearts that seek thee still.

2. O fount of love, O well unpriced,
   outpouring from the heart of Christ,
   give us to drink of very thee,
   and all we pray shall answered be.

3. O Jesus Christ, we pray to thee
   that this thy presence which we see,
   though now in form of bread
      concealed,
   to us may be in heav'n revealed.

400

Michael Perry (1942-1996)
© Mrs B. Perry/Jubilee Hymns. Used by permission

1. O God beyond all praising,
   we worship you today,
   and sing the love amazing
   that songs cannot repay;
   for we can only wonder
   at ev'ry gift you send,
   at blessings without number
   and mercies without end:
   we lift our hearts before you
   and wait upon your word,
   we honour and adore you,
   our great and mighty Lord.

2. Then hear, O gracious Saviour,
   accept the love we bring,
   that we who know your favour
   may serve you as our King;
   and whether our tomorrows
   be filled with good or ill,
   we'll triumph through our sorrows
   and rise to bless you still:
   to marvel at your beauty
   and glory in your ways,
   and make a joyful duty
   our sacrifice of praise.

401

Gilbert Keith Chesterton (1874-1936)

1. O God of earth and altar,
   bow down and hear our cry,
   our earthly rulers falter,
   our people drift and die;
   the walls of gold entomb us,
   the swords of scorn divide,
   take not thy thunder from us,
   but take away our pride.

2. From all that terror teaches,
   from lies of tongue and pen,
   from all the easy speeches
   that comfort cruel men,
   from sale and profanation
   of honour and the sword,
   from sleep and from damnation,
   deliver us, good Lord!

3. Tie in a living tether
   the prince and priest and thrall,
   bind all our lives together,
   smite us and save us all;
   in ire and exultation
   aflame with faith and free,
   lift up a living nation,
   a single sword to thee.

402

Isaac Watts (1674-1748) alt.

1. O God, our help in ages past,
   our hope for years to come,
   our shelter from the stormy blast,
   and our eternal home.

2. Beneath the shadow of thy throne,
   thy saints have dwelt secure;
   sufficient is thine arm alone,
   and our defence is sure.

3. Before the hills in order stood,
   or earth received her frame,
   from everlasting thou art God,
   to endless years the same.

4. A thousand ages in thy sight
   are like an evening gone;
   short as the watch that ends the night
   before the rising sun.

Continued overleaf

5. Time, like an ever-rolling stream,
will bear us all away;
we fade and vanish, as a dream
dies at the op'ning day.

6. O God, our help in ages past,
our hope for years to come,
be thou our guard while troubles last,
and our eternal home.

403 Anthony Nye (b.1932) alt. © *The Trustees for Roman Catholic Purposes Registered*

1. O God, we give ourselves today
with this pure host to thee,
the self-same gift which thy dear Son
gave once on Calvary.

2. Entire and whole, our life and love
with heart and soul and mind,
for all our errors, faults and needs,
thy Church and humankind.

3. With humble and with contrite heart
this bread and wine we give
because thy Son once gave himself
and died that we might live.

4. Though lowly now, soon by thy word
these offered gifts will be
the very body of our Lord,
his soul and deity.

5. His very body, offered up,
a gift beyond all price,
he gives to us, that we may give,
in loving sacrifice.

6. O Lord, who took our human life,
as water mixed with wine,
grant through this sacrifice that we
may share thy life divine.

404 Timothy Dudley-Smith (b. 1926)
© *Timothy Dudley-Smith*

1. O God, who gives the fertile seed,
the life by which the world is fed,
with mercy look on those in need
of hearth and home and daily bread.

2. In flood and famine, drought and
dearth,
a world where want and wars increase,
behold the helpless of the earth
who cry for justice and for peace.

3. Help us to bridge the world's divide,
to share the healing gifts you gave,
for all earth's children stem the tide
of sore disease and infant grave.

4. Teach us to put the past behind
and seek this broken earth restored:
one equal home for humankind,
a better world where Christ is Lord.

405 Bernadette Farrell (b. 1957)
© *1992 Bernadette Farrell/Published by OCP Publications*

1. O God, you search me and you know
me.
All my thoughts lie open to your gaze.
When I walk or lie down you are
before me:
ever the maker and keeper of my days.

2. You know my resting and my rising.
You discern my purpose from afar.
And with love everlasting you besiege
me:
in ev'ry moment of life and death,
you are.

3. Before a word is on my tongue, Lord,
   you have known its meaning through
     and through.
   You are with me, beyond my
     understanding:
   God of my present, my past and
     future too.

4. Although your Spirit is upon me,
   still I search for shelter from your light.
   There is nowhere on earth I can
     escape you:
   even the darkness is radiant in your
     sight.

5. For you created me and shaped me,
   gave me life within my mother's womb.
   For the wonder of who I am, I praise
     you:
   safe in your hands, all creation is
     made new.

406 Anthony Nye (b. 1932). © *The Trustees for Roman Catholic Purposes Registered*

1. O God, your people gather,
   obedient to your word,
   around your holy altar
   to praise your name, O Lord.
   For all your loving kindness
   our grateful hearts we raise;
   but pardon first the blindness
   of all our sinful ways.

2. You are our loving Father,
   you are our holiest Lord,
   but we have sinned against you,
   by thought and deed and word.
   Before the court of heaven
   we stand and humbly pray
   our sins may be forgiven,
   our faults be washed away.

3. Though sinful, we implore you
   to turn and make us live,
   that so we may adore you,
   and our due off'ring give,
   and may the prayers and voices
   of your glad people rise,
   as your whole Church rejoices
   in this great sacrifice.

407 *Adoro te devote*, ascribed to St Thomas Aquinas (1227-1274), trans. Edward Caswall (1814-1878)

1. O Godhead hid, devoutly I
     adore thee,
   who truly art within the forms
     before me;
   to thee my heart I bow with bended
     knee,
   as failing quite in contemplating thee.

*2. Sight, touch and taste in thee are
     each deceived,
   the ear alone most safely is believed:
   I believe all the Son of God
     has spoken;
   than Truth's own word there is not
     truer token.

3. God only on the cross lay hid
     from view;
   but here lies hid at once the
     manhood too;
   and I, in both professing my belief,
   make the same prayer as the
     repentant thief.

4. Thy wounds, as Thomas saw, I do
     not see;
   yet thee confess my Lord and God
     to be;
   make me believe thee ever more and
     more,
   in thee my hope, in thee my love
     to store.

Continued overleaf

5. O thou memorial of our Lord's own
      dying!
   O bread that living art and vivifying!
   Make ever thou my soul on thee
      to live;
   ever a taste of heav'nly sweetness give.

*6. O loving Pelican! O Jesus, Lord!
   Unclean I am, but cleanse me in thy
      blood,
   of which a single drop, for sinners
      spilt,
   is ransom for a world's entire guilt.

7. Jesus, whom for the present veiled
      I see,
   what I so thirst for, O, vouchsafe
      to me;
   that I may see thy countenance
      unfolding,
   and may be blest thy glory
      in beholding.

408 Traditional

O, how good is the Lord! (x3)
*I never will forget what he has done for
me.*

1. He gives us salvation,
   how good is the Lord. *(x3)*
   I never will forget
   what he has done for me.

2. He gives us his Spirit . . . *(x3)*

3. He gives us his healing . . . *(x3)*

4. He gives us his body . . . *(x3)*

5. He gives us his freedom . . . *(x3)*

6. He gives us each other . . . *(x3)*

7. He gives us his glory . . . *(x3)*

409 Edward Caswall (1814-1878)

1. O Jesus Christ, remember,
   when thou shalt come again
   upon the clouds of heaven,
   with all thy shining train;
   when ev'ry eye shall see thee
   in deity revealed,
   who now upon this altar
   in silence art concealed.

2. Remember then, O Saviour,
   I supplicate of thee,
   that here I bowed before thee
   upon my bended knee;
   that here I owned thy presence,
   and did not thee deny,
   and glorified thy greatness
   though hid from human eye.

3. Accept, divine Redeemer,
   the homage of my praise;
   be thou the light and honour
   and glory of my days.
   Be thou my consolation
   when death is drawing nigh;
   be thou my only treasure
   through all eternity.

410 John Ernest Bode (1816-1874)

1. O Jesus, I have promised
   to serve thee to the end;
   be thou for ever near me,
   my Master and my friend:
   I shall not fear the battle
   if thou art by my side,
   nor wander from the pathway
   if thou wilt be my guide.

*2. O let me feel thee near me;
the world is ever near;
I see the sights that dazzle,
the tempting sounds I hear;
my foes are ever near me,
around me and within;
but, Jesus, draw thou nearer,
and shield my soul from sin.

*3. O let me hear thee speaking
in accents clear and still,
above the storms of passion,
the murmurs of self-will;
O speak to reassure me,
to hasten or control;
O speak and make me listen,
thou guardian of my soul.

4. O Jesus, thou hast promised,
to all who follow thee,
that where thou art in glory
there shall thy servant be;
and, Jesus, I have promised
to serve thee to the end:
O give me grace to follow,
my Master and my friend.

5. O let me see thy foot-marks,
and in them plant mine own;
my hope to follow duly
is in thy strength alone:
O guide me, call me, draw me,
uphold me to the end;
and then in heav'n receive me,
my Saviour and my friend.

411 Gregory Murray (1905-1992)
© The estate of Gregory Murray

1. O King of might and splendour,
creator most adored,
this sacrifice we render
to thee as sov'reign Lord.

May these our gifts be pleasing
unto thy majesty,
our hearts from sin releasing
who have offended thee.

2. Thy body thou hast given,
thy blood thou hast outpoured,
that sin might be forgiven,
O Jesus, loving Lord.
As now with love most tender,
thy death we celebrate,
our lives in self-surrender
to thee we consecrate.

412 Estelle White (b. 1925)
© 1976 Kevin Mayhew Ltd

1. O lady, full of God's own grace,
whose caring hands the child
embraced,
who listened to the Spirit's word,
believed and trusted in the Lord.

O Virgin fair, star of the sea,
my dearest mother, pray for me.
(Repeat)

2. O lady, who felt daily joy
in caring for the holy boy,
whose home was plain and shorn of
wealth,
yet was enriched by God's own breath.

3. O lady, who bore living's pain
but still believed that love would reign,
who on a hill watched Jesus die,
as on the cross they raised him high.

4. O lady, who, on Easter day,
had all your sorrow wiped away
as God the Father's will was done
when from death's hold he freed your
Son.

413

John B. Foley (b. 1939), based on Isaiah 55:1-2 and Matthew 11:28-30.
© 1978 John B. Foley, SJ and New Dawn Music

1. O let all who thirst,
   let them come to the water.
   And let all who have nothing,
   let them come to the Lord:
   without money, without price.
   Why should you pay the price,
   except for the Lord?

2. And let all who seek,
   let them come to the water.
   And let all who have nothing,
   let them come to the Lord:
   without money, without strife.
   Why should you spend your life,
   except for the Lord?

3. And let all who toil,
   let them come to the water.
   And let all who are weary,
   let them come to the Lord:
   all who labour, without rest.
   How can your soul find rest,
   except for the Lord?

4. And let all the poor,
   let them come to the water.
   Bring the ones who are laden,
   bring them all to the Lord:
   bring the children without might.
   Easy the load and light:
   oh come to the Lord.

2. O morning stars, together
   proclaim the holy birth,
   and praises sing to God the King,
   and peace to all the earth.
   For Christ is born of Mary;
   and, gathered all above,
   while mortals sleep, the angels keep
   their watch of wond'ring love;

3. How silently, how silently,
   the wondrous gift is giv'n!
   So God imparts to human hearts
   the blessings of his heav'n.
   No ear may hear his coming;
   but in this world of sin,
   where meek souls will receive him, still
   the dear Christ enters in.

4. O holy child of Bethlehem,
   descend to us, we pray;
   cast out our sin, and enter in,
   be born in us today.
   We hear the Christmas angels
   the great glad tidings tell:
   O come to us, abide with us,
   our Lord Emmanuel.

414

Phillips Brooks (1835-1893) alt.

1. O little town of Bethlehem,
   how still we see thee lie!
   Above thy deep and dreamless sleep
   the silent stars go by.
   Yet in thy dark streets shineth
   the everlasting light;
   the hopes and fears of all the years
   are met in thee tonight.

415

Virginia Vissing
© 1974, 1998 Sisters of St Mary of Namur

O living water, refresh my soul.
O living water, refresh my soul.
Spirit of joy, Lord of creation.
Spirit of hope, Spirit of peace.

1. Spirit of God. Spirit of God.

2. O set us free. O set us free.

3. Come, pray in us. Come, pray in us.

416

Patrick Appleford (b. 1925)
© 1965 Josef Weinberger Ltd

1. O Lord, all the world belongs to you,
   and you are always making all things
      new.
   What is wrong you forgive,
   and the new life you give
   is what's turning the world upside
      down.

2. The world's only loving to its friends,
   but you have brought us love that
      never ends;
   loving enemies too,
   and this loving with you
   is what's turning the world upside down.

3. This world lives divided and apart.
   You draw us all together and we start,
   in your body, to see
   that in a fellowship we
   can be turning the world upside down.

4. The world wants the wealth to live
      in state,
   but you show us a new way to be great:
   like a servant you came,
   and if we do the same,
   we'll be turning the world upside down.

5. O Lord, all the world belongs to you,
   and you are always making all things
      new.
   Send your Spirit on all
   in your Church, whom you call
   to be turning the world upside down.

417

Lucien Deiss (b. 1921), based on Psalm 102:17-
18 (Refrain) and Psalm 78:9 (Verses)
© 1965 World Library Publications, a division of
J. S. Paluch Co. Inc.

O Lord, be not mindful
of our guilt and our sins;
O Lord, do not judge us
for our faults and offences.
May your merciful love be upon us.

1. Help your people, Lord,
   O God our Saviour,
   deliver us for the glory of your name!

2. Pardon us, O Lord,
   all our sins,
   deliver us for the glory of your name!

3. Praise to you, O Lord,
   through all ages without end,
   deliver us for the glory of your name!

418

Taizé Community
© Ateliers et Presses de Taizé

O Lord, hear my prayer,
O Lord, hear my prayer:
when I call answer me.
O Lord, hear my prayer,
O Lord, hear my prayer.
Come and listen to me.

419

Stuart K. Hine (1899-1989)
© 1953 Stuart K. Hine/The Stuart Hine Trust
Published by kingswaysongs.com

1. O Lord, my God!
   When I in awesome wonder
   consider all the works
   thy hand has made;
   I see the stars,
   I hear the mighty thunder,
   thy pow'r throughout
   the universe displayed:

   Then sings my soul,
   my Saviour God, to thee,
   how great thou art! How great thou art!
   Then sings my soul,
   my Saviour God, to thee,
   how great thou art! How great thou art!

Continued overleaf

2. When through the woods
   and forest glades I wander
   and hear the birds sing
   sweetly in the trees;
   when I look down
   from lofty mountain grandeur,
   and hear the brook,
   and feel the gentle breeze:

   Then sings my soul,
   my Saviour God, to thee,
   how great thou art! How great thou art!
   Then sings my soul,
   my Saviour God, to thee,
   how great thou art! How great thou art!

3. And when I think that God,
   his Son not sparing,
   sent him to die –
   I scarce can take it in:
   that on the Cross,
   my burden gladly bearing,
   he bled and died
   to take away my sin:

4. When Christ shall come
   with shout of acclamation
   and take me home –
   what joy shall fill my heart!
   Then shall I bow
   in humble adoration,
   and there proclaim,
   my God, how great thou art!

420 Psalm 130
© The Grail/Harper Collins Religious

O Lord, my heart is not proud,
nor haughty my eyes.
I have not gone after things too great,
nor marvels beyond me.
Truly I have set my soul in silence
   and peace;
at rest, as a child in its mother's arms,
so is my soul.

421 Nick Fawcett (b. 1957)
© 2004 Kevin Mayhew Ltd

1. O Lord, we want to praise you,
   your holy name confess,
   your mighty deeds acknowledge,
   your awesome love express.
   We want to give you worship,
   to lift your name on high,
   yet somehow words are lacking
   however hard we try.

2. O Lord, we want to praise you,
   through all we say and do,
   to so live out the gospel
   that all may know it's true.
   We want to bring you glory,
   to help your kingdom grow,
   yet though we strive to serve you,
   it rarely seems to show.

3. O Lord, we want to praise you,
   to celebrate your love,
   to thank you for the blessings
   you pour down from above.
   We want to bring you honour
   respond with all our hearts,
   yet sacrifice is costly –
   we rarely even start.

4. O Lord, we come to praise you,
   poor though our words may be;
   although our faults are many
   we come, still, joyfully.
   For though we often fail you
   and know you but in part,
   you look beneath the surface
   and see what's in the heart.

422 Graham Kendrick (b. 1950)
© 1986 Thankyou Music.
Administered by worshiptogether.com songs

O Lord, your tenderness,
melting all my bitterness,
O Lord, I receive your love.

O Lord, your loveliness,
changing all my ugliness,
O Lord, I receive your love.
O Lord, I receive your love,
O Lord, I receive your love.

423
Damian Lundy (1944-1997)
© 1978 Kevin Mayhew Ltd

1. O Mary, when our God chose you
to bring his only Son to birth,
a new creation made in you
gave joy to all the earth.

2. When he was born on Christmas night
and music made the rafters ring,
the stars were dancing with delight;
now all God's children sing.

3. One winter's night, a heap of straw
becomes a place where ages meet,
when kings come knocking at the door
and kneeling at your feet.

4. In you, our God confounds the strong
and makes the crippled dance with joy;
and to our barren world belong
his mother and her boy.

5. In empty streets and broken hearts
you call to mind what he has done;
where all his loving kindness starts
in sending you a Son.

6. And, Mary, while we stand with you,
may once again his Spirit come,
and all his people follow you
to reach our Father's home.

424
Sei pura, sei pia by St Alphonsus (1696-1787),
trans. Edmund Vaughan (1827-1908)

1. O Mother blest, whom God bestows
on sinners and on just,
what joy, what hope thou givest those
who in thy mercy trust.

Thou art clement, thou art chaste,
Mary, thou art fair;
of all mothers sweetest, best,
none with thee compare.

2. O heav'nly mother, maiden sweet!
It never yet was told
that suppliant sinner left thy feet
unpitied, unconsoled.

3. O mother pitiful and mild,
cease not to pray for me;
for I do love thee as a child
and sigh for love of thee.

4. O mother blest, for me obtain,
ungrateful though I be,
to love that God who first could deign
to show such love for me.

425
Damian Lundy (1944-1997), based on the
Good Friday *Reproaches*
© 1978 Kevin Mayhew Ltd

O my people, what have I done to you?
How have I hurt you? Answer me.

1. I led you out of Egypt;
from slavery I set you free.
I brought you into a land of promise;
you have prepared a cross for me.

2. I led you as a shepherd,
I brought you safely through the sea,
fed you with manna in the desert;
you have prepared a cross for me.

3. I fought for you in battles,
I won you strength and victory,
gave you a royal crown and sceptre;
you have prepared a cross for me.

4. I planted you, my vineyard,
and cared for you most tenderly,
looked for abundant fruit,
    and found none –
only the cross you made for me.

Continued overleaf

5. Then listen to my pleading,
and do not turn away from me.
You are my people: will you reject me?
For you I suffer bitterly.

O my people, what have I done to you?
How have I hurt you? Answer me.

426 Dorothy Francis Gurney (1858-1932)

1. O perfect love,
all human thought transcending,
lowly we kneel
in prayer before thy throne,
that theirs may be
the love which knows no ending,
whom thou for evermore
dost join in one.

2. O perfect life,
be thou their full assurance
of tender charity
and steadfast faith,
of patient hope
and quiet, brave endurance,
with childlike trust that fears
not pain nor death.

3. Grant them the joy
which brightens earthly sorrow,
grant them the peace
which calms all earthly strife;
and to life's day
the glorious unknown morrow
that dawns upon
eternal love and life.

427 Henry Williams Baker (1821-1877) based on Psalms 148 and 150, alt.

1. O praise ye the Lord!
praise him in the height;
rejoice in his word, ye angels of light;
ye heavens, adore him,
by whom ye were made,
and worship before him,
in brightness arrayed.

2. O praise ye the Lord!
praise him upon earth,
in tuneful accord, all you of new birth;
praise him who hath brought you
his grace from above,
praise him who hath taught you
to sing of his love.

3. O praise ye the Lord!
all things that give sound;
each jubilant chord re-echo around;
loud organs his glory
forth tell in deep tone,
and, sweet harp, the story
of what he hath done.

4. O praise ye the Lord!
thanksgiving and song
to him be outpoured all ages along:
for love in creation,
for heaven restored,
for grace of salvation,
O praise ye the Lord!

428 Frederick William Faber (1814-1863)

1. O purest of creatures!
Sweet mother, sweet maid:
the one spotless womb
wherein Jesus was laid.
Dark night hath come down
on us, mother, and we
look out for thy shining,
sweet star of the sea.

2. Earth gave him one lodging;
   'twas deep in thy breast,
   and God found a home where
   the sinner finds rest;
   his home and his hiding-place,
   both were in thee;
   he was won by thy shining,
   sweet star of the sea.

3. O, blissful and calm
   was the wonderful rest
   that thou gavest thy God
   in thy virginal breast;
   for the heaven he left
   he found heaven in thee,
   and he shone in thy shining,
   sweet star of the sea.

429 Traditional

O Sacrament most holy,
O Sacrament divine,
all praise and all thanksgiving
be ev'ry moment thine.

430a
Paul Gerhardt (1607-1676), based on *Salve caput cruentatum*, trans. Ronald Arbuthnott Knox (1888-1957). © *Burns & Oates Ltd/ Continuum Int. Publishing Group*

1. O sacred head ill-usèd,
   by reed and bramble scarred,
   that idle blows have bruisèd,
   and mocking lips have marred,
   how dimmed that eye so tender,
   how wan those cheeks appear,
   how overcast the splendour
   that angels hosts revere!

*2. What marvel if thou languish,
   vigour and virtue fled,
   wasted and spent with anguish,
   and pale as are the dead?

O by the foes' derision,
that death endured for me,
grant that thy open vision
a sinner's eyes may see.

*3. Good Shepherd, spent with loving,
   look on me, who have strayed,
   oft by those lips unmoving
   with milk and honey stayed;
   spurn not a sinner's crying
   nor from thy love outcast,
   but rest thy head in dying
   on these frail arms at last.

4. In this thy sacred passion
   O, that some share had I!
   O, may thy Cross's fashion
   o'erlook me when I die!
   For these dear pains that rack thee
   a sinner's thanks receive;
   O, lest in death I lack thee,
   a sinner's care relieve.

5. Since death must be my ending,
   in that drear hour of need,
   my friendless cause befriending,
   Lord, to my rescue speed;
   thyself, dear Jesus, trace me
   that passage to the grave,
   and from thy cross embrace me
   with arms outstretched to save.

430b
Paul Gerhardt (1607-1676), based on *Salve caput cruentatum*, trans. Robert Bridges (1844-1930)

1. O sacred head sore wounded,
   defiled and put to scorn;
   O kingly head surrounded
   with mocking crown of thorn:
   what sorrow mars thy grandeur?
   Can death thy bloom de-flower?
   O countenance whose splendour
   the hosts of heav'n adore.

Continued overleaf

*2. Thy beauty, long-desirèd,
   hath vanished from our sight;
   thy pow'r is all expirèd,
   and quenched the light of light.
   Ah me, for whom thou diest,
   hide not so far thy grace:
   show me, O love most highest,
   the brightness of thy face.

*3. I pray thee, Jesus, own me,
   me, shepherd good, for thine;
   who to thy fold hast won me,
   and fed with truth divine.
   Me guilty, me refuse not,
   incline thy face to me,
   this comfort that I lose not,
   on earth to comfort thee.

4. In thy most bitter passion
   my heart to share doth cry,
   with thee for my salvation
   upon the cross to die.
   Ah, keep my heart thus movèd,
   to stand thy cross beneath,
   to mourn thee, well-belovèd,
   yet thank thee for thy death.

5. My days are few, O fail not,
   with thine immortal pow'r,
   to hold me that I quail not
   in death's most fearful hour:
   that I may fight befriended,
   and see in my last strife
   to me thine arms extended
   upon the cross of life.

431 Francis Stanfield (1835-1914)

1. O Sacred Heart,
   our home lies deep in thee;
   on earth thou art an exile's rest,
   in heav'n the glory of the blest,
   O Sacred Heart.

2. O Sacred Heart,
   thou fount of contrite tears;
   where'er those living waters flow,
   new life to sinners they bestow,
   O Sacred Heart.

3. O Sacred Heart,
   our trust is all in thee,
   for though earth's night be dark and
      drear,
   thou breathest rest where thou art near,
   O Sacred Heart.

4. O Sacred Heart,
   lead exiled children home,
   where we may ever rest near thee,
   in peace and joy eternally,
   O Sacred Heart.

432 Jean-Paul Lécot (b. 1947), based on Matthew 2:11; Romans 6:8; Wisdom 8:1, trans. W. R. Lawrence. © 1988 Kevin Mayhew Ltd

*O sing a new song
giving praise to the Lord,
alleluia, alleluia, alleluia!*

Advent
1. People of God, be glad and rejoice,
   your Saviour comes: harken his voice!

2. He who will save the world from its
      stain
   comes from the clouds, gentle as rain.

Christmas
3. This is the day the Saviour was born;
   God's love and peace shine in this
      dawn.

Our Lady
4. Mother of God, we honour your
      worth;
   you gave us Christ to ransom earth.

Epiphany

5. This Child you see is Saviour and
   Lord,
   God's Son made Man, by kings
   adored.

Presentation

6. Glory to Christ who brought us his
   light;
   coming from God, he gives us sight.

Ascension

7. As we have died with Christ unto sin,
   so we now share new life with him.

Pentecost

8. God's Spirit fills the earth with his
   love,
   makes all things new, draws them
   above.

9. Spirit of God, come dwell in our
   hearts;
   kindle the fire your love imparts.

Doxology

10. To Father, Son and Spirit be giv'n
    eternal praise, here and in heav'n.

*Verses 1, 6, 7, 8, 9 and 10 can also be for
general use*

433 Estelle White (b. 1925)
    © McCrimmon Publishing Co. Ltd

1. O, the love of my Lord is the essence
   of all that I love here on earth.
   All the beauty I see he has given to me,
   and his giving is gentle as silence.

2. Ev'ry day, ev'ry hour, ev'ry moment
   have been blessed by the strength of
   his love.
   At the turn of each tide he is there at
   my side,
   and his touch is as gentle as silence.

3. There've been times when I've turned
   from his presence,
   and I've walked other paths, other
   ways;
   but I've called on his name in the
   dark of my shame,
   and his mercy was gentle as silence.

434 Damian Lundy (1944-1997), based on
    Jeremiah 1. © *1978 Kevin Mayhew Ltd*

O the word of my Lord,
deep within my being,
O the word of my Lord,
you have filled my mind.

1. Before I formed you in the womb,
   I knew you through and through,
   I chose you to be mine.
   Before you left your mother's side,
   I called to you, my child, to be my sign.

2. I know that you are very young,
   but I will make you strong,
   I'll fill you with my word;
   and you will travel through the land,
   fulfilling my command which you
   have heard.

3. And ev'rywhere you are to go
   my hand will follow you;
   you will not be alone.
   In all the danger that you fear
   you'll find me very near, your words
   my own.

4. With all my strength you will be filled:
   you will destroy and build,
   for that is my design.
   You will create and overthrow,
   reap harvests I will sow, your word is
   mine.

435 William Harry Turton (1856-1938),
based on John 17
© Copyright Control

1. O thou, who at thy Eucharist didst
    pray
  that all thy Church might be for ever
    one,
  grant us at ev'ry eucharist to say,
  with longing heart and soul,
    'Thy will be done.'
  O may we all one bread, one body be,
  through this blest sacrament of unity.

2. For all thy Church, O Lord,
    we intercede;
  make thou our sad divisions soon to
    cease;
  draw us the nearer each to each,
    we plead,
  by drawing all to thee, O Prince of
    Peace:
  thus may we all one bread, one body
    be,
  through this blest sacrament of unity.

3. We pray thee too for wand'rers from
    thy fold;
  O bring them back, good Shepherd
    of the sheep,
  back to the faith which saints
    believed of old,
  back to the Church which still that
    faith doth keep;
  soon may we all one bread, one body
    be,
  through this blest sacrament of unity.

4. So, Lord, at length when sacraments
    shall cease,
  may we be one with all thy Church
    above,
  one with thy saints in one unbroken
    peace,

one with thy saints in one
    unbounded love;
more blessèd still, in peace and love
    to be
one with the Trinity in unity.

436 Traditional

1. O when the saints go marching in,
  O when the saints go marching in,
  I want to be in that number
  when the saints go marching in.

2. O when they crown him Lord of all,
  O when they crown him Lord of all,
  I want to be in that number
  when they crown him Lord of all.

3. O when all knees bow at his name,
  O when all knees bow at his name,
  I want to be in that number
  when all knees bow at his name.

4. O when they sing the Saviour's praise,
  O when they sing the Saviour's praise,
  I want to be in that number
  when they sing the Saviour's praise.

5. O when the saints go marching in,
  O when the saints go marching in,
  I want to be in that number
  when the saints go marching in.

437 Michael Forster (b. 1946)
based on *Creator alme siderum* (7th century)
© 1999 Kevin Mayhew Ltd

1. O Word, in uncreated light,
  who brought to birth the starry height;
  incarnate Saviour of us all,
  hear us, God's people, when we call.

2. Attentive to our helpless cry
  as mortals, so afraid to die,
  you took our flesh in truth and grace
  to save the fallen human race.

3. When earth was in its crisis' hour,
   you came in love's redeeming pow'r,
   with life and grace to burst the tomb,
   unsealing first the Virgin's womb.

4. Now to the glory of your Name
   let praise be sung and due acclaim;
   let all on earth and all above
   declare you Lord of life and love.

5. Prepare us, Lord and Judge, we pray
   to face you on the final day;
   and keep us in this present hour
   from yielding to temptation's pow'r.

6. To God the Father, God the Son,
   and God the Spirit, Three in One,
   all glory, praise and honour be,
   from age to age eternally.

438 Robert Grant (1779-1838), based on Psalm 104

1. O worship the King
   all glorious above;
   O gratefully sing
   his pow'r and his love:
   our shield and defender,
   the Ancient of Days,
   pavilioned in splendour,
   and girded with praise.

2. O tell of his might,
   O sing of his grace,
   whose robe is the light,
   whose canopy space;
   his chariots of wrath
   the deep thunder-clouds form,
   and dark is his path
   on the wings of the storm.

3. This earth, with its store
   of wonders untold,
   almighty, thy pow'r
   hath founded of old:

hath stablished it fast
by a changeless decree,
and round it hath cast,
like a mantle, the sea.

*4. Thy bountiful care
   what tongue can recite?
   It breathes in the air,
   it shines in the light;
   it streams from the hills,
   it descends to the plain,
   and sweetly distils
   in the dew and the rain.

*5. Frail children of dust,
   and feeble as frail,
   in thee do we trust,
   nor find thee to fail;
   thy mercies how tender,
   how firm to the end!
   Our maker, defender,
   redeemer, and friend.

6. O measureless might,
   ineffable love,
   while angels delight
   to hymn thee above,
   thy humbler creation,
   though feeble their lays,
   with true adoration
   shall sing to thy praise.

439 John Samuel Bewley Monsell (1811-1875)

1. O worship the Lord
   in the beauty of holiness;
   bow down before him,
   his glory proclaim;
   with gold of obedience
   and incense of lowliness,
   kneel and adore him:
   the Lord is his name.

Continued overleaf

2. Low at his feet lay
   thy burden of carefulness:
   high on his heart
   he will bear it for thee,
   comfort thy sorrows,
   and answer thy prayerfulness,
   guiding thy steps
   as may best for thee be.

3. Fear not to enter
   his courts in the slenderness
   of the poor wealth
   thou wouldst reckon as thine:
   truth in its beauty,
   and love in its tenderness,
   these are the off'rings
   to lay on his shrine.

4. These, though we bring them
   in trembling and fearfulness,
   he will accept
   for the name that is dear;
   mornings of joy give
   for evenings of tearfulness,
   trust for our trembling
   and hope for our fear.

440 *Corde natus ex parentis* by Aurelius Clemens Prudentius (348-413) trans. John Mason Neale (1818-1866) alt.

1. Of the Father's love begotten,
   ere the worlds began to be,
   he is Alpha and Omega,
   he the source, the ending he,
   of the things that are, and have been,
   and that future years shall see,
   evermore and evermore.

2. At his word they were created;
   he commanded; it was done:
   heav'n and earth and depths of ocean
   in their threefold order one;
   all that grows beneath the shining
   of the light of moon and sun,
   evermore and evermore.

*3. O that birth for ever blessèd,
   when the Virgin, full of grace,
   by the Holy Ghost conceiving,
   bore the Saviour of our race,
   and the babe, the world's Redeemer,
   first revealed his sacred face,
   evermore and evermore.

*4. O ye heights of heav'n, adore him;
   angel hosts, his praises sing;
   pow'rs, dominions, bow before him,
   and extol our God and King:
   let no tongue on earth be silent,
   ev'ry voice in concert ring,
   evermore and evermore.

*5. This is he whom seers and sages
   sang of old with one accord;
   whom the writings of the prophets
   promised in their faithful word;
   now he shines, the long-expected;
   let our songs declare his worth,
   evermore and evermore.

6. Christ, to thee, with God the Father,
   and, O Holy Ghost, to thee,
   hymn and chant and high thanks-
       giving,
   and unwearied praises be;
   honour, glory, and dominion,
   and eternal victory,
   evermore and evermore.

441 St Thomas Aquinas (1227-1274) trans. John Mason Neale (1818-1866), alt.

1. Of the glorious body telling,
   O my tongue, its myst'ries sing,
   and the blood, all price excelling,
   which the world's eternal King,
   in a noble womb once dwelling,
   shed for this world's ransoming.

2. Giv'n for us, for us descending,
   of a virgin to proceed,
   he with us in converse blending,
   scattered he the gospel seed,
   till his sojourn drew to ending,
   which he closed in wondrous deed.

3. At the last great supper lying,
   circled by his brethren's band,
   meekly with the law complying,
   first he finished its command.
   Then, immortal food supplying,
   gave himself with his own hand.

4. Word made flesh, by word is making
   very bread his flesh to be;
   we, in wine, Christ's blood partaking,
   and if senses fail to see,
   faith alone the true heart waking,
   to behold the mystery.

5. Therefore, we before him bending,
   this great sacrament revere;
   types and shadows have their ending,
   for the newer rite is here;
   faith our outward sense befriending,
   makes the inward vision clear.

6. Glory let us give, and blessing,
   to the Father and the Son,
   honour, might and praise addressing,
   while eternal ages run;
   ever too his love confessing,
   who from both, with both is one.

442 George Bennard (1873-1958)
© The Rodeheaver Co.
Administered by CopyCare

1. On a hill far away
   stood an old rugged cross,
   the emblem of suff'ring and shame;
   and I loved that old cross
   where the dearest and best
   for a world of lost sinners was slain.

So I'll cherish the old rugged cross,
till my trophies at last I lay down;
I will cling to the old rugged cross
and exchange it some day for a crown.

2. O that old rugged cross,
   so despised by the world,
   has a wondrous attraction for me:
   for the dear Lamb of God
   left his glory above
   to bear it to dark Calvary.

3. In the old rugged cross,
   stained with blood so divine,
   a wondrous beauty I see.
   For 'twas on that old cross
   Jesus suffered and died
   to pardon and sanctify me.

4. To the old rugged cross
   I will ever be true,
   its shame and reproach gladly bear.
   Then he'll call me some day
   to my home far away;
   there his glory for ever I'll share.

443 Traditional English carol, alt.

1. On Christmas night all Christians sing,
   to hear the news the angels bring,
   on Christmas night all Christians sing,
   to hear the news the angels bring,
   news of great joy, news of great mirth,
   news of our merciful King's birth.

2. Then why should we on earth be so
   sad,
   since our Redeemer made us glad,
   then why should we on earth be so sad,
   since our Redeemer made us glad,
   when from our sin he set us free,
   all for to gain our liberty?

Continued overleaf

3. When sin departs before his grace,
   then life and health come in its place,
   when sin departs before his grace,
   then life and health come in its place,
   angels and earth with joy may sing,
   all for to see the new-born King.

4. All out of darkness we have light,
   which made the angels sing this night:
   all out of darkness we have light,
   which made the angels sing this night:
   'Glory to God and peace to men,
   now and for evermore. Amen.'

445 Traditional

On the holy cross I see
Jesus' hands nailed fast for me;
on the holy cross I see
Jesus' feet nailed fast for me.
Loving Jesus, let me be
still and quiet, close to thee;
learning all thy love for me,
giving all my love to thee.

444 Charles Coffin (1676-1749)
trans. John Chandler (1806-1876) alt.

1. On Jordan's bank the Baptist's cry
   announces that the Lord is nigh;
   awake, and hearken, for he brings
   glad tidings of the King of kings.

2. Then cleansed be ev'ry breast from sin;
   make straight the way for God within;
   prepare we in our hearts a home,
   where such a mighty guest may come.

3. For thou art our salvation, Lord,
   our refuge and our great reward;
   without thy grace we waste away,
   like flow'rs that wither and decay.

4. To heal the sick stretch out thine hand,
   and bid the fallen sinner stand;
   shine forth and let thy light restore
   earth's own true loveliness once more.

5. All praise, eternal Son, to thee
   whose advent doth thy people free,
   whom with the Father we adore
   and Holy Ghost for evermore.

446 Marie Lydia Pereira (b. 1920)
© 1976 Kevin Mayhew Ltd

1. On this church your blessing, Lord,
   on this church your grace bestow.
   On this church your blessing, Lord,
   may it come and never go.
   Bringing peace and joy and happiness,
   bringing love that knows no end.
   On this church your blessing, Lord,
   on this church your blessing send.

2. On this church your loving, Lord,
   may it overflow each day.
   On this church your loving, Lord,
   may it come and with us stay.
   Drawing us in love and unity
   by the love received from you.
   On this church your loving, Lord,
   may it come each day anew.

3. On this church your giving, Lord,
   may it turn and ever flow.
   On this church your giving, Lord,
   on this church your wealth bestow.
   Filling all our hopes and wishes, Lord,
   in the way you know is best.
   On this church your giving, Lord,
   may it come and with us rest.

4. On this church your calling, Lord,
   may it come to us each day.
   On this church your calling, Lord,
   may it come to lead the way.
   Filling us with nobler yearnings, Lord,
   calling us to live in you.
   On this church your calling, Lord,
   may it come each day anew.

*The word 'church' may be replaced
throughout by 'school', 'house', etc.*

447 Marie Lydia Pereira (b. 1920)
© 1999 Kevin Mayhew Ltd

*On this day of joy, on this day of hope,
we come to you in love, O Lord,
on this day of joy, on this day of hope,
we come to you in love.*

1. With this bread and wine we come
   to this eucharistic feast.
   On this day of joy, on this day of hope,
   we come to you in love.

2. Bread to be your body, Lord,
   wine to be your saving blood;
   on this day of joy, on this day of hope,
   we come to you in love.

448 Cecil Frances Alexander (1818-1895) alt.
© This version 1996 Kevin Mayhew Ltd

1. Once in royal David's city
   stood a lowly cattle shed,
   where a mother laid her baby
   in a manger for his bed;
   Mary was that mother mild,
   Jesus Christ her little child.

2. He came down to earth from heaven,
   who is God and Lord of all,
   and his shelter was a stable,
   and his cradle was a stall;
   with the needy, poor and lowly,
   lived on earth our Saviour holy.

3. For he is our childhood's pattern,
   day by day like us he grew;
   he was little, weak and helpless,
   tears and smiles like us he knew;
   and he feeleth for our sadness,
   and he shareth in our gladness.

4. And our eyes at last shall see him
   through his own redeeming love,
   for that child so dear and gentle
   is our Lord in heav'n above;
   and he leads his children on
   to the place where he is gone.

449 John B. Foley (b. 1939), based on 1 Corinthians
10:16-17; 12:4; Galatians 3:28; Didaché 9
© 1978 John B. Foley, SJ and New Dawn Music

*One bread, one body, one Lord of all,
one cup of blessing which we bless:
and we, though many, throughout the
   earth,
we are one body in this one Lord.*

1. Gentile or Jew,
   servant or free,
   woman or man, no more.

2. Many the gifts,
   many the works,
   one in the Lord of all.

3. Grain for the fields,
   scattered and grown,
   gathered to one, for all.

450 Sydney Carter (1915-2004)
© 1971, 1997 Stainer & Bell Ltd

1. One more step along the world I go,
   one more step along the world I go.
   From the old things to the new
   keep me travelling along with you.

Continued overleaf

And it's from the old
I travel to the new,
keep me travelling
along with you.

2. Round the corners of the world I turn,
   more and more about the world I learn.
   All the new things that I see
   you'll be looking at along with me.

3. As I travel through the bad and good,
   keep me travelling the way I should.
   Where I see no way to go,
   you'll be telling me the way, I know.

4. Give me courage when the world is
      rough,
   keep me loving though the world is
      tough.
   Leap and sing in all I do,
   keep me travelling along with you.

5. You are older than the world can be,
   you are younger than the life in me.
   Ever old and ever new,
   keep me travelling along with you.

2. Onward, Christian pilgrims,
   up the rocky way,
   where the dying Saviour
   bids us watch and pray.
   Through the darkened valley
   walk with those who mourn,
   share the pain and anger,
   share the promised dawn!

3. Onward, Christian pilgrims,
   in the early dawn;
   death's great seal is broken,
   life and hope reborn!
   Faith in resurrection
   strengthens pilgrims' hearts,
   ev'ry load is lightened,
   ev'ry fear departs.

4. Onward, Christian pilgrims,
   hearts and voices raise,
   till the whole creation
   echoes perfect praise;
   swords are turned to ploughshares,
   pride and envy cease,
   truth embraces justice,
   hope resolves in peace.

451

Michael Forster (b. 1946)
© 1996 Kevin Mayhew Ltd

1. Onward, Christian pilgrims,
   Christ will be our light;
   see, the heav'nly vision
   breaks upon our sight!
   Out of death's enslavement
   Christ has set us free,
   on then to salvation,
   hope and liberty.

   Onward, Christian pilgrims,
   Christ will be our light;
   see, the heav'nly vision
   breaks upon our sight!

452

Robert Cull (b. 1949)
© 1976 CCCM Music. Administered by CopyCare

Open our eyes, Lord, we want to see
   Jesus,
to reach out and touch him
and say that we love him;
open our ears, Lord, and help us to
   listen;
O, open our eyes, Lord,
we want to see Jesus!

453
Willard F. Jabusch (b.1930)
© 1998 Willard F. Jabusch

1. Open your ears, O Christian people,
   open your ears and hear Good News!
   Open your hearts, O royal priesthood,
   God has come to you!

   God has spoken to his people, alleluia,
   and his words are words of wisdom,
   alleluia.

2. Israel comes to greet the Saviour,
   Judah is glad to see his day.
   From east and west the peoples travel,
   he will show the way.

3. All who have ears to hear his message,
   all who have ears then let them hear.
   All who would learn the way of
   wisdom,
   let them hear God's words.

454
v. 1 unknown
vs. 2-5 Sandra Joan Billington (b. 1946)
© 1976, 1996 Kevin Mayhew Ltd

1. Our God loves us,
   his love will never end.
   He rests within our hearts
   for our God loves us.

2. His gentle hand
   he stretches over us.
   Though storm-clouds threaten the day,
   he will set us free.

3. He comes to us
   in sharing bread and wine.
   He brings us life that will reach
   past the end of time.

4. Our God loves us,
   his faithful love endures,
   and we will live like his child
   held in love secure.

5. The joys of love
   as off'rings now we bring.
   The pains of love will be lost
   in the praise we sing.

455
Damian Lundy (1944-1997)
© 1982 Kevin Mayhew Ltd

1. Our God sent his Son long ago,
   and he came to bring joy to us all.
   For the Lord wants his children to
   know he loves them.

   So sing the good news to the poor and
   the young!
   Praise to the Lord for his Word!
   Sharing the gospel with all those in
   need,
   become the good news you have heard!

2. But how will the good news be heard?
   When we answer the call of our Lord,
   when we live so our faith can be
   shared with others.

3. From the Spirit of God comes our call,
   bringing pow'r to be joyful and free,
   to be brothers and sisters to all: to
   love them.

4. Praise and glory to God for his Word,
   always living in those who believe,
   still made flesh in our lives to be
   shared with others.

456

Aniceto Nazareth, based on Scripture
© 1984 Kevin Mayhew Ltd

Our hearts were made for you, Lord,
our hearts were made for you;
they'll never find, never find, never find
*   rest*
until they find their rest in you.

1. When you call me I will answer,
   when you seek me you will find.
   I will lead you back from exile,
   and reveal to you my mind.

2. I will take you from the nations,
   and will bring you to your land.
   From your idols I will cleanse you
   and you'll cherish my command.

3. I will put my law within you,
   I will write it on your heart;
   I will be your God and Saviour,
   you, my people set apart.

457

Christopher Walker (b. 1947)
© 1989 Christopher Walker. Published by OCP
Publications

Out of darkness God has called us,
claimed by Christ as God's own people.
Holy nation, royal priesthood,
walking in God's marv'llous light.

1. Let us take the words you give,
   strong and faithful words to live,
   words that in our hearts are sown,
   words that bind us as your own.

2. Let us take the Christ you give,
   Broken Body Christ we live,
   Christ, the risen from the tomb,
   Christ, who calls us as your own.

3. Let us take the love you give,
   that the way of love we live,
   love to bring your people home,
   love to make us all your own.

458

St Thomas Aquinas (1227-1274)

1. Pange lingua gloriosi,
   Corporis Mysterium,
   Sanguinisque pretiosi
   quem in mundi pretium,
   fructus ventris generosi
   Rex effudit gentium.

2. Nobis datus, nobis natus
   ex intacta Virgine;
   et in mundo conversatus,
   sparso verbi semine,
   sui moras incolatus
   miro clausit ordine.

3. In supremæ nocte coenæ
   recumbens cum fratribus,
   observata lege plene
   cibis in legalibus:
   cibum turbæ duodenæ
   se dat suis manibus.

4. Verbum caro, panem verum,
   verbo carnem efficit:
   fitque sanguis Christi merum;
   et si sensus deficit,
   ad firmandum cor sincerum
   sola fides sufficit.

5. Tantum ergo Sacramentum
   veneremur cernui:
   et antiquum documentum
   novo cedat ritui;
   præstet fides supplementum
   sensuum defectui.

6. Genitori, genitoque
   laus, et jubilatio,
   salus, honor, virtus quoque
   sit et benedictio;
   procedenti ab utroque
   compar sit laudatio. Amen.

459

Peter Madden
© 1976 Kevin Mayhew Ltd

Peace I leave with you,
peace I give to you;
not as the world gives peace,
do I give.
Take and pass it on,
on to ev'ryone;
thus the world will know,
you are my friends.

460

vs. 1-4 unknown, v. 5 the Editors
v. 5 © 1999 Kevin Mayhew Ltd

1. Peace is flowing like a river,
   flowing out through you and me,
   spreading out into the desert,
   setting all the captives free.

2. Love is flowing like a river,
   flowing out through you and me,
   spreading out into the desert,
   setting all the captives free.

3. Joy is flowing like a river,
   flowing out through you and me,
   spreading out into the desert,
   setting all the captives free.

4. Hope is flowing like a river,
   flowing out through you and me,
   spreading out into the desert,
   setting all the captives free.

5. Christ brings peace to all creation,
   flowing out through you and me,
   love, joy, hope and true salvation,
   setting all the captives free.

461

John Glynn (b. 1948)
© 1976 Kevin Mayhew Ltd

1. Peace is the gift of heaven to earth,
   softly enfolding our fears.
   Peace is the gift of Christ to the world,
   given for us:
   he is the Lamb who bore the pain of
   peace.

2. Peace is the gift of Christ to his
   Church,
   wound of the lance of his love.
   Love is the pain he suffered for all,
   offered to us:
   O, to accept the wound that brings
   us peace!

3. Joy is the gift the Spirit imparts,
   born of the heavens and earth.
   We are his children, children of joy,
   people of God:
   he is our Lord, our peace, our love,
   our joy!

462

Kevin Mayhew (b. 1942)
© 1976 Kevin Mayhew Ltd

1. Peace, perfect peace,
   is the gift of Christ our Lord.
   Peace, perfect peace,
   is the gift of Christ our Lord.
   Thus, says the Lord,
   will the world know my friends.
   Peace, perfect peace,
   is the gift of Christ our Lord.

2. Love, perfect love,
   is the gift of Christ our Lord. *(x2)*
   Thus, says the Lord,
   will the world know my friends.
   Love, perfect love,
   is the gift of Christ our Lord.

Continued overleaf

3. Faith, perfect faith,
   is the gift of Christ our Lord. *(x2)*
   Thus, says the Lord,
   will the world know my friends.
   Faith, perfect faith,
   is the gift of Christ our Lord.

4. Hope, perfect hope,
   is the gift of Christ our Lord. *(x2)*
   Thus, says the Lord,
   will the world know my friends.
   Hope, perfect hope,
   is the gift of Christ our Lord.

5. Joy, perfect joy,
   is the gift of Christ our Lord. *(x2)*
   Thus, says the Lord,
   will the world know my friends.
   Joy, perfect joy,
   is the gift of Christ our Lord.

463 Unknown

1. Praise him, praise him,
   praise him in the morning,
   praise him in the noontime.
   Praise him, praise him,
   praise him when the sun goes down.

2. Love him, love him, . . .

3. Trust him, trust him, . . .

4. Serve him, serve him, . . .

5. Jesus, Jesus, . . .

464 Henry Francis Lyte (1793-1847), based on Psalm 103

1. Praise, my soul, the King of heaven!
   To his feet thy tribute bring;
   ransomed, healed, restored, forgiven,
   who like me his praise should sing?
   Praise him! Praise him!
   Praise him! Praise him!
   Praise the everlasting King!

2. Praise him for his grace and favour
   to our fathers in distress;
   praise him still the same as ever,
   slow to chide and swift to bless.
   Praise him! Praise him!
   Praise him! Praise him!
   Glorious in his faithfulness!

3. Father-like, he tends and spares us;
   well our feeble frame he knows;
   in his hands he gently bears us,
   rescues us from all our foes.
   Praise him! Praise him!
   Praise him! Praise him!
   Widely as his mercy flows!

4. Angels, help us to adore him;
   ye behold him face to face;
   sun and moon, bow down before him,
   dwellers all in time and space.
   Praise him! Praise him!
   Praise him! Praise him!
   Praise with us the God of grace!

465 vs. 1 and 2 from *Foundling Hospital Collection* (1796), v. 3 Edward Osler (1798-1863)

1. Praise the Lord, ye heav'ns, adore him!
   Praise him, angels, in the height;
   sun and moon, rejoice before him,
   praise him, all ye stars and light.
   Praise the Lord, for he hath spoken;
   worlds his mighty voice obeyed:
   laws, which never shall be broken,
   for their guidance he hath made.

2. Praise the Lord, for he is glorious:
   never shall his promise fail.
   God hath made his saints victorious;
   sin and death shall not prevail.
   Praise the God of our salvation,
   hosts on high, his pow'r proclaim;
   heav'n and earth and all creation,
   laud and magnify his name!

3. Worship, honour, glory, blessing,
Lord, we offer to thy name;
young and old, thy praise expressing,
join their Saviour to proclaim.
As the saints in heav'n adore thee,
we would bow before thy throne;
as thine angels serve before thee,
so on earth thy will be done.

4. Praise and honour to the Father,
adoration to the Son,
with the all-embracing Spirit
wholly Three and holy One.
All the universe, united
in complete diversity,
sings as one your endless praises,
ever blessèd Trinity!

466
Michael Forster (b. 1946)
© 1999 Kevin Mayhew Ltd

1. Praise to God for saints and martyrs,
inspiration to us all;
in the presence of our Saviour,
their example we recall:
lives of holy contemplation,
sacrifice or simple love,
witnesses to truth and justice,
honoured here and crowned above.

2. How we long to share their story,
faithful in response to grace,
signs of God's eternal presence
in the realm of time and space.
Now, their pilgrimage completed,
cross of Christ their only boast,
they unite their own rejoicing
with the great angelic host.

3. Saints and martyrs, now in glory,
robed before your Saviour's face,
let us join your intercession
for God's holy human race.
Let us join with you in singing
Mary's liberation song,
till a just and free creation sings,
with the angelic throng:

467
John Henry Newman (1801-1890)

1. Praise to the Holiest in the height,
and in the depth be praise:
in all his words most wonderful,
most sure in all his ways.

2. O loving wisdom of our God!
when all was sin and shame,
a second Adam to the fight,
and to the rescue came.

3. O wisest love! that flesh and blood,
which did in Adam fail,
should strive afresh against the foe,
should strive and should prevail.

4. And that a higher gift than grace
should flesh and blood refine,
God's presence and his very self,
and essence all-divine.

5. And in the garden secretly,
and on the cross on high,
should teach his brethren, and inspire
to suffer and to die.

6. Praise to the Holiest in the height,
and in the depth be praise;
in all his words most wonderful,
most sure in all his ways.

468 Joachim Neander (1650-1680)
trans. Catherine Winkworth, alt. (1827-1878)

1. Praise to the Lord,
   the Almighty, the King of creation!
   O my soul, praise him,
   for he is your health and salvation.
   All you who hear,
   now to his altar draw near;
   join in profound adoration.

2. Praise to the Lord,
   let us offer our gifts at his altar;
   let not our sins and transgressions
   now cause us to falter.
   Christ, the High Priest,
   bids us all join in his feast;
   victims with him on the altar.

3. Praise to the Lord,
   O let all that is in us adore him!
   All that has life and breath,
   come now with praises before him.
   Let the 'Amen'
   sound from his people again,
   now as we worship before him.

For use on ecumenical occasions

469 Joachim Neander (1650-1680)
trans. Catherine Winkworth (1827-1878)

1. Praise to the Lord,
   the Almighty, the King of creation!
   O my soul, praise him,
   for he is thy health and salvation.
   All ye who hear,
   now to his temple draw near;
   joining in glad adoration.

2. Praise to the Lord,
   who o'er all things so wondrously
   reigneth,
   shieldeth thee gently from harm,
   or when fainting sustaineth:

hast thou not seen
how thy heart's wishes have been
granted in what he ordaineth?

3. Praise to the Lord,
   who doth prosper thy work and
   defend thee,
   surely his goodness and mercy
   shall daily attend thee:
   ponder anew
   what the Almighty can do,
   if to the end he befriend thee.

4. Praise to the Lord,
   O let all that is in us adore him!
   All that hath life and breath,
   come now with praises before him.
   Let the 'Amen'
   sound from his people again,
   gladly for ay we adore him.

470 Bernadette Farrell (b. 1957)
© 1986 Bernadette Farrell. Published by OCP
Publications

Praise to you, O Christ, our Saviour,
Word of the Father, calling us to life;
Son of God who leads us to freedom:
glory to you, Lord Jesus Christ!

1. You are the Word
   who calls us out of darkness;
   you are the Word
   who leads us into light;
   you are the Word
   who brings us through the desert:
   glory to you, Lord Jesus Christ!

2. You are the one
   whom prophets hoped and longed for;
   you are the one
   who speaks to us today;
   you are the one
   who leads us to our future;
   glory to you, Lord Jesus Christ!

3. You are the Word
   who calls us to be servants;
   you are the Word
   whose only law is love;
   you are the Word-made-flesh
   who lives among us:
   glory to you, Lord Jesus Christ!

4. You are the Word
   who binds us and unites us;
   you are the Word
   who calls us to be one;
   you are the Word
   who teaches us forgiveness:
   glory to you, Lord Jesus Christ!

471 Frederick Oakley (1802-1880) and others

1. Praise we our God with joy
   and gladness never-ending;
   angels and saints with us
   their grateful voices blending.
   He is our Father dear,
   o'er-filled with parent's love;
   mercies unsought, unknown,
   he showers from above.

2. He is our shepherd true;
   with watchful care unsleeping,
   on us, his erring sheep,
   an eye of pity keeping;
   he with a mighty arm
   the bonds of sin doth break,
   and to our burdened hearts
   in words of peace doth speak.

3. Graces in copious stream
   from that pure fount are welling,
   where, in our heart of hearts,
   our God hath set his dwelling.
   His word our lantern is;
   his peace our comfort still;
   his sweetness all our rest;
   our law, our life, his will.

472 Nick Fawcett (b. 1957) © 1999 Kevin Mayhew Ltd

1. Proclaim, proclaim the story,
   proclaim the one who came that he
      might die!
   Make known to all his glory,
   lift up his name on high!

2. Lift up, lift up your voices,
   for Christ is risen, risen from the tomb!
   All heav'n and earth rejoices:
   his light shines through the gloom.

3. Sing out, sing out hosanna!
   Rejoice and honour Christ the King
      of kings!
   Lift high his royal banner,
   lift up your voice and sing.

4. He reigns, he reigns triumphant –
   come kneel in homage, worship and
      adore.
   Rejoice with hearts exultant:
   he rules for evermore.

473 Edwin le Grice (1911-1992) © 1998 Kevin Mayhew Ltd

1. Proud yet humble, strong and gentle,
   from Iona's holy shore,
   Aidan to King Oswald's princedom
   Christian joy and radiance bore.

*2. Where the ruthless zeal of others
   quenched the smould'ring flax of
      love,
   Aidan warmed the coldest spirits
   with the fire from heav'n above.

3. At the quest of kings and rulers
   seated at the royal right hand,
   Aidan shared both food and silver
   with the poorest of the land.

Continued overleaf

*4. Staff in hand Christ's shepherd
        journeyed
    over northern dale and moor,
    bringing vision, faith and friendship
    to the outcast and the poor.

5. Lindisfarne, his Holy Island,
    wild, yet tranquil, windswept, fair,
    nurtured in severe seclusion
    northern saints and folk of prayer.

6. Cuthbert, Bede and Chad and Hilda,
    folk of courage, faith and fire,
    bright with Aidan's Celtic vision
    still today our lives inspire.

7. In the joy of God the Spirit
    to the Lord of all we bring
    praise for folk of northern England,
    servant saints of Christ the King.

474 Fred Kaan (b. 1929)
© 1989 Stainer & Bell Ltd

1. Put peace into each other's hands
    and like a treasure hold it,
    protect it like a candle-flame,
    with tenderness enfold it.

2. Put peace into each other's hands
    with loving expectation;
    be gentle in your words and ways,
    in touch with God's creation.

3. Put peace into each other's hands
    like bread we break for sharing;
    look people warmly in the eye:
    our life is meant for caring.

4. As at communion, shape your hands
    into a waiting cradle;
    the gift of Christ receive, revere,
    united round the table.

5. Put Christ into each other's hands,
    he is love's deepest measure;
    in love make peace, give peace a
        chance,
    and share it like a treasure.

475 Luke Connaughton (1917-1979)
© McCrimmon Publishing Co. Ltd

1. Reap me the earth as a harvest to God,
    gather and bring it again,
    all that is his, to the Maker of all.
    Lift it and offer it high.

    Bring bread, bring wine,
    give glory to the Lord;
    whose is the earth but God's,
    whose is the praise but his?

2. Go with your song and your music
        with joy,
    go to the altar of God.
    Carry your offerings, fruits of the earth,
    work of your labouring hands.

3. Gladness and pity and passion and
        pain,
    all that is mortal in man,
    lay all before him, return him his gift.
    God, to whom all shall go home.

476 Unknown (12th century)

Regina cæli, lætare, alleluia,
quia quem meruisti portare, alleluia,
resurrexit sicut dixit, alleluia,
Ora pro nobis Deum, alleluia.

477 Unknown
Based on Philippians 4:4

Rejoice in the Lord always and again
I say rejoice. *(Repeat)*
Rejoice, rejoice and again I say rejoice.
    (Repeat)

478 Charles Wesley (1707-1788)

1. Rejoice the Lord is King!
Your Lord and King adore;
mortals, give thanks and sing,
and triumph evermore.

Lift up your heart, lift up your voice;
rejoice, again I say, rejoice.

2. Jesus the Saviour reigns,
the God of truth and love;
when he had purged our stains,
he took his seat above.

3. His kingdom cannot fail;
he rules o'er earth and heav'n;
the keys of death and hell
are to our Jesus giv'n.

4. He sits at God's right hand
till all his foes submit,
and bow to his command,
and fall beneath his feet.

479 Marty Haugen (b. 1952), based on Joel 2:12,
Ezekiel 36:26 and Isaiah 58:9-14
© 1990, 1991 G.I.A. Publications Inc.

Return to God with all your heart,
the source of grace and mercy;
come seek the tender faithfulness of God.
Return to God with all your heart,
the source of grace and mercy;
come seek the tender faithfulness of God.

1. Now the time of grace has come,
the day of salvation;
come and learn now the way of our
God.

2. I will take your heart of stone
and place a heart within you,
a heart of compassion and love.

3. If you break the chains of oppression,
if you set the pris'ner free;
if you share your bread with the
hungry,
give protection to the lost;
give a shelter to the homeless, clothe
the naked in your midst,
then your light shall break forth like
the dawn.

480 Henry Hart Milman (1791-1868) alt.

1. Ride on, ride on in majesty!
Hark, all the tribes hosanna cry;
thy humble beast pursues his road
with palms and scattered garments
strowed.

2. Ride on, ride on in majesty!
In lowly pomp ride on to die;
O Christ, thy triumphs now begin
o'er captive death and conquered sin.

3. Ride on, ride on in majesty!
The wingèd squadrons of the sky
look down with sad and wond'ring eyes
to see th'approaching sacrifice.

4. Ride on, ride on in majesty!
Thy last and fiercest strife is nigh;
the Father, on his sapphire throne,
awaits his own appointed Son.

5. Ride on, ride on in majesty!
In lowly pomp ride on to die;
bow thy meek head to mortal pain,
then take, O God, thy pow'r, and reign.

481 Unknown, based on Genesis 6:4

Rise and shine,
and give God his glory, glory, (x3)
children of the Lord.

1. The Lord said to Noah,
   'There's gonna be a floody, floody.'
   Lord said to Noah,
   'There's gonna be a floody, floody.
   Get those children out of the muddy,
      muddy,
   children of the Lord.'

2. So Noah, he built him,
   he built him an arky, arky,
   Noah, he built him,
   he built him an arky, arky,
   built it out of hickory barky, barky,
   children of the Lord.

3. The animals, they came on,
   they came on, by twosies, twosies,
   animals, they came on, they came on,
   by twosies, twosies,
   elephants and kangaroosies, roosies,
   children of the Lord.

4. It rained and poured
   for forty daysies, daysies,
   rained and poured
   for forty daysies, daysies,
   nearly drove those animals
   crazies, crazies,
   children of the Lord.

5. The sun came out
   and dried up the landy, landy,
   sun came out
   and dried up the landy, landy,
   ev'rything was fine and dandy, dandy,
   children of the Lord.

6. If you get to heaven
   before I do-sies, do-sies,
   you get to heaven
   before I do-sies, do-sies,
   tell those angels I'm comin'
   too-sies, too-sies,
   children of the Lord.

482 Sydney Carter (1915-2004)
© 1964 Stainer & Bell Ltd

1. Said Judas to Mary, 'Now what will
      you do
   with your ointment so rich and so
      rare?'
   'I'll pour it all over the feet of the Lord,
   and I'll wipe it away with my hair,'
      she said,
   'I'll wipe it away with my hair.'

2. 'Oh Mary, oh Mary, oh think of the
      poor,
   this ointment, it could have been sold,
   and think of the blankets and think
      of the bread
   you could buy with the silver and
      gold,' he said,
   'you could buy with the silver and
      gold.'

3. 'Tomorrow, tomorrow, I'll think of
      the poor,
   tomorrow,' she said, 'not today;
   for dearer than all of the poor in the
      world
   is my love who is going away,' she said,
   'my love who is going away.'

4. Said Jesus to Mary, 'Your love is so
      deep,
   today you may do as you will.
   Tomorrow you say I am going away,
   but my body I leave with you still,'
      he said,
   'my body I leave with you still.'

5. 'The poor of the world are my body,'
      he said,
   'to the end of the world they shall be.
   The bread and the blankets you give
      to the poor
   you'll find you have given to me,'
      he said,
   'you'll find you have given to me.'

6. 'My body will hang on the cross of
      the world,
   tomorrow,' he said, 'and today,
   and Martha and Mary will find me
      again
   and wash all my sorrow away,' he said,
   'and wash all my sorrow away.'

483 Hermann the Lame (d. 1054)

Salve, Regina, mater misericordiæ;
vita, dulcedo, et spes nostra, salve.
Ad te clamamus, exules filii Hevæ.
Ad te suspiramus, gementes et fientes
in hac lacrimarum valle.
Eia ergo, advocata nostra,
illos tuos misericordes oculos ad nos
   converte.
Et Jesum, benedictum fructum
   ventris tui,
nobis post hoc exilium ostende.
O clemens, O pia, O dulcis Virgo
   Maria.

484 Traditional

Sanctum nomen Domini magnificat
      anima mea.

Sanctum, sanctum nomen Domini.

*Translation: My soul magnifies the
         holy name of the Lord.*

485 Unknown
© Copyright Control

*Santo, santo, santo, mi corazón te adora!
Mi corazón te sabe decir: santo eres
   Señor.*

Holy, holy, holy, my heart, my heart,
   adores you!
My heart is glad to say the words:
   you are holy, Lord.

486 Robert Dufford (b. 1943)
© 1981 Robert J. Dufford, SJ & New Dawn Music

*Save us, O Lord, carry us back.
Rouse your power and come.
Rescue your people, show us your face.
Bring us back.*

1. O Shepherd of Israel, hear us;
   return and we shall be saved.
   Arise, O Lord; hear our cries, O Lord.
   Bring us back!

2. How long will you hide from your
      people?
   We long to see your face.
   Give ear to us, draw near to us,
   Lord God of hosts!

3. Turn again, care for your vine,
   protect what your right hand has
      planted.
   Your vineyards are trampled,
      uprooted and burned.
   Come to us, Father of might!

487 Edward Caswall (1814-1878)

1. See, amid the winter's snow,
   born for us on earth below,
   see, the tender Lamb appears,
   promised from eternal years.

Continued overleaf

Hail, thou ever-blessèd morn,
hail, redemption's happy dawn!
Sing through all Jerusalem,
Christ is born in Bethlehem.

2. Lo, within a manger lies
   he who built the starry skies;
   he, who, throned in heights sublime,
   sits amid the cherubim.

3. Say, you holy shepherds, say,
   what your joyful news today?
   Wherefore have you left your sheep
   on the lonely mountain steep?

4. 'As we watched at dead of night,
   there appeared a wondrous light;
   angels, singing peace on earth,
   told us of the Saviour's birth.'

5. Sacred infant, all divine,
   what a tender love was thine,
   thus to come from highest bliss,
   down to such a world as this!

6. Virgin mother, Mary, blest,
   by the joys that fill thy breast,
   pray for us, that we may prove
   worthy of the Saviour's love.

488 Brian Foley (1919-2000)
© 1971 Faber Music Ltd

1. See, Christ was wounded for our sake,
   and bruised and beaten for our sin,
   so by his suff'rings we are healed,
   for God has laid our guilt on him.

2. Look on his face, come close to him –
   see, you will find not beauty there;
   despised, rejected, who can tell
   the grief and sorrow he must bear?

3. Like sheep that stray we leave God's path,
   to choose our own and not his will;
   like lamb to slaughter he has gone,
   obedient to his Father's will.

489 Michael Perry (1942-1996)
© 1965 Mrs B. Perry/Jubilate Hymns
Used by permission

1. See him lying on a bed of straw:
   a draughty stable with an open door.
   Mary cradling the babe she bore:
   the Prince of Glory is his name.

O now carry me to Bethlehem
to see the Lord of love again:
just as poor as was the stable then,
the Prince of Glory when he came!

2. Star of silver, sweep across the skies,
   show where Jesus in the manger lies;
   shepherds, swiftly from your stupor
   rise
   to see the Saviour of the world!

3. Angels, sing again the song you sang,
   sing the glory of God's gracious plan;
   sing that Bethlehem's little baby can
   be the Saviour of us all.

4. Mine are riches, from your poverty;
   from your innocence, eternity;
   mine, forgiveness by your death for me,
   child of sorrow for my joy.

490 Michael Forster (b. 1946)
© 1993 Kevin Mayhew Ltd

1. See the holy table,
   spread for our healing;
   hear the invitation
   to share in bread and wine.
   Catch the scent of goodness,
   taste and touch salvation;
   all mortal senses
   tell of love divine!

2. As the bread is broken,
   Christ is remembered;
   as the wine is flowing,
   his passion we recall;
   as redemption's story
   opens up before us,
   hope is triumphant,
   Christ is all in all.

3. Tell again the story,
   wonder of wonders:
   Christ, by grace eternal,
   transforms the simplest food!
   Sign of hope and glory,
   life in all its fullness,
   God's whole creation
   ransomed and renewed!

491 John Greally (b. 1934)
© Trustees for Roman Catholic Purposes Registered

1. See us, Lord, about your altar;
   though so many, we are one;
   many souls by love united
   in the heart of Christ your Son.

2. Hear our prayers, O loving Father,
   hear in them your Son, our Lord;
   hear him speak our love and worship,
   as we sing with one accord.

3. Once were seen the blood and water;
   now he seems but bread and wine;
   then in human form he suffered,
   now his form is but a sign.

4. Wheat and grape contain the meaning;
   food and drink he is to all;
   one in him, we kneel adoring,
   gathered by his loving call.

5. Hear us yet; so much is needful
   in our frail, disordered life;
   stay with us and tend our weakness
   till that day of no more strife.

6. Members of his mystic body,
   now we know our prayer is heard,
   heard by you, because your children
   have received th'eternal Word.

492 v. 1 Karen Lafferty (b. 1948), vs. 2 and 3
unknown, based on Matthew 6:33, 7:7
© 1972 CCCM Music/Maranatha! Music
Administered by CopyCare Ltd

1. Seek ye first the kingdom of God,
   and his righteousness,
   and all these things shall be added
      unto you;
   allelu, alleluia.

   Alleluia, alleluia,
   alleluia, allelu, alleluia.

2. You shall not live by bread alone,
   but by ev'ry word
   that proceeds from the mouth of God;
   allelu, alleluia.

3. Ask and it shall be given unto you,
   seek and ye shall find;
   knock, and it shall be opened unto you;
   allelu, alleluia.

493 Adapted from Psalm 104
by Michael Forster (b. 1946)
© 1997 Kevin Mayhew Ltd

Send forth your Spirit, Lord,
renew the face of the earth. (Repeat)

1. Bless the Lord, O my soul,
   O Lord God, how great you are;
   you are clothed in honour and glory,
   you set the world on its foundations.

2. Lord, how great are your works,
   in wisdom you made them all;
   all the earth is full of your creatures,
   your hand always open to feed them.

3. May your wisdom endure,
   rejoice in your works, O Lord.
   I will sing for ever and ever,
   in praise of my God and my King.

494

Aniceto Nazareth, based on Psalm 104
© 1984 Kevin Mayhew Ltd

Send forth your Spirit, O Lord,
that the face of the earth be renewed.

1. O my soul, arise and bless the Lord
   God.
   Say to him: 'My God, how great you
   are.
   You are clothed with majesty and
   splendour,
   and light is the garment you wear.'

2. 'You have built your palace on the
   waters.
   Like the winds, the angels do your
   word,
   you have set the earth on its
   foundations,
   so firm, to be shaken no more.'

3. 'All your creatures look to you for
   comfort;
   from your open hand they have their
   fill,
   you send forth your Spirit and revive
   them,
   the face of the earth you renew.'

4. While I live, I sing the Lord God's
   praises;
   I will thank the author of these
   marvels.
   Praise to God, the Father, Son and
   Spirit
   both now and for ever. Amen.

495

Sandra Joan Billington (b. 1946)
© 1976, 1999 Kevin Mayhew Ltd

Shalom, my friend, shalom,
my friend, shalom, shalom.
The peace of Christ I give you today,
shalom, shalom.

496

John L. Bell (b. 1949)
Graham Maule (b. 1958)
© 1988 WGRG, Iona Community

1. She sits like a bird, brooding on the
   waters,
   hov'ring on the chaos of the world's
   first day;
   she sighs and she sings, mothering
   creation,
   waiting to give birth to all the Word
   will say.

2. She wings over earth, resting where
   she wishes,
   lighting close at hand or soaring
   through the skies;
   she nests in the womb, welcoming
   each wonder,
   nourishing potential hidden to our
   eyes.

3. She dances in fire, startling her
   spectators,
   waking tongues of ecstasy where
   dumbness reigned;
   she weans and inspires all whose
   hearts are open,
   nor can she be captured, silenced or
   restrained.

4. For she is the Spirit, one with God in
   essence,
   gifted by the Saviour in eternal love;
   she is the key opening the scriptures,
   enemy of apathy and heav'nly dove.

497

Marty Haugen (b. 1952)
© 1986 GIA Publications

Shepherd me, O God,
beyond my wants,
beyond my fears,
from death into life.

1. God is my shepherd, so nothing shall
      I want,
   I rest in the meadows of faithfulness
      and love,
   I walk by the quiet waters of peace.

2. Gently you raise me and heal my
      weary soul,
   you lead me by pathways of
      righteousness and truth,
   my spirit shall sing to the music of
      your name.

3. Though I should wander the valley of
      death,
   I fear no evil, for you are at my side,
   your rod and your staff, my comfort
      and my hope.

4. You have set me a banquet of love
   in the face of hatred,
   crowning me with love beyond my
      pow'r to hold.

5. Surely your kindness and mercy
      follow me
   all the days of my life;
   I will dwell in the house of my God
      for evermore.

498 Joseph Mohr (1792-1848)
     trans. John Freeman Young (1820-1885)

1. Silent night, holy night.
   All is calm, all is bright,
   round yon virgin mother and child;
   holy infant, so tender and mild,
   sleep in heavenly peace,
   sleep in heavenly peace.

2. Silent night, holy night.
   Shepherds quake at the sight,
   glories stream from heaven afar,
   heav'nly hosts sing alleluia:
   Christ, the Saviour is born,
   Christ, the Saviour is born.

3. Silent night, holy night.
   Son of God, love's pure light,
   radiant beams from thy holy face,
   with the dawn of redeeming grace:
   Jesus, Lord, at thy birth,
   Jesus, Lord, at thy birth.

499 v1: Pamela Hayes, v2: Margaret Rizza (b. 1929)
     © 1998 Kevin Mayhew Ltd.

1. Silent, surrendered, calm and still,
   open to the word of God.
   Heart humbled to his will,
   offered is the servant of God.

*2. Come, Holy Spirit, bring us light,
    teach us, heal us, give us life.
    Come, Lord, O let our hearts
    flow with love and all that is true.

    * For use at Pentecost

500 Daniel L. Schutte, based on Psalm 97
     © 1972, 1974 Daniel L. Schutte.
     Administered by New Dawn Music

Sing a new song unto the Lord,
let your song be sung from mountains
   high.
Sing a new song unto the Lord,
singing alleluia.

1. All God's people dance for joy,
   O come before the Lord,
   and play for him on glad tambourines,
   and let your trumpet sound.

2. Rise, O children, from your sleep,
   your Saviour now has come,
   and he has turned your sorrow to joy,
   and filled your soul with song.

3. Glad my soul, for I have seen
   the glory of the Lord.
   The trumpet sounds, the dead shall
      be raised.
   I know my Saviour lives.

501

James Quinn (b. 1919), based on Psalm 99
© 1969 Geoffrey Chapman, an imprint of
Continuum Int. Publishing Group

1. Sing, all creation,
   sing to God in gladness!
   Joyously serve him,
   singing hymns of homage!
   Chanting his praises,
   come before his presence!
   Praise the Almighty!

2. Know that our God
   is Lord of all the ages!
   He is our maker;
   we are all his creatures,
   people he fashioned,
   sheep he leads to pasture!
   Praise the Almighty!

3. Enter his Temple,
   ringing out his praises!
   Sing in thanksgiving
   as you come before him!
   Blessing his bounty,
   glorify his greatness!
   Praise the Almighty!

4. Great in his goodness
   is the Lord we worship;
   steadfast his kindness,
   love that knows no ending!
   Faithful his word is,
   changeless, everlasting!
   Praise the Almighty!

502

Linda Stassen
© 1974 Linda Stassen/New Song Ministries

Sing hallelujah to the Lord.
Sing hallelujah to the Lord.
Sing hallelujah, sing hallelujah,
sing hallelujah to the Lord.

503

Mike Anderson (b. 1956)
© 1999 Kevin Mayhew Ltd

Sing it in the valleys,
shout it from the mountain tops,
Jesus came to save us,
and his saving never stops.
He is King of kings,
and new life he brings,
sing it in the valleys,
shout it from the mountain tops,
oh, shout it from the mountain tops.

1. Jesus, you are by my side,
   you take all my fears.
   If I only come to you,
   you will heal the pain of years.

2. You have not deserted me,
   though I go astray.
   Jesus, take me in your arms,
   help me walk with you today.

3. Jesus, you are living now,
   Jesus, I believe.
   Jesus, take me, heart and soul,
   yours alone I want to be.

504

Michael Cockett (b. 1938)
© 1976 Kevin Mayhew Ltd

Sing, my soul. Sing, my soul.
Sing, my soul of his mercy. (Repeat)

1. The Lord is good to me.
   His light will shine on me.
   When city lights would blind my eyes.
   He hears my silent call.
   His hands help when I fall.
   His gentle voice stills my sighs.

2. The Lord is good to me.
His word will set me free
when men would tie me to the ground.
He mocks my foolish ways
with love that never fails.
When I'm most lost then I'm found.

3. The Lord is good to me.
I hear him speak to me.
His voice is in the rain that falls.
He whispers in the air
of his unending care.
If I will hear, then he calls.

505 *Pange, lingua, gloriosi proelium certaminis* trans. Venantius Fortunatus (c. 530-609) from *The Three Days* (1981)

1. Sing, my tongue, the song of
triumph,
tell the story far and wide;
tell of dread and final battle,
sing of Saviour crucified;
how upon the cross a victim
vanquishing in death he died.

2. He endured the nails, the spitting,
vinegar and spear and reed;
from that holy body broken
blood and water forth proceed;
earth and stars and sky and ocean
by that flood from stain are freed.

3. Faithful Cross, above all other,
one and only noble tree,
none in foliage, none in blossom,
none in fruit your peer may be;
sweet the wood and sweet the iron
and your load, most sweet is he.

4. Bend your boughs, O Tree of glory!
all your rigid branches, bend!
For a while the ancient temper
that your birth bestowed, suspend;
and the King of earth and heaven
gently on your bosom tend.

506 Roland F. Palmer (1891-1985)
© Copyright Control

1. Sing of Mary, pure and lowly,
virgin mother undefiled.
Sing of God's own Son most holy,
who became her little child.
Fairest child of fairest mother,
God, the Lord, who came to earth,
Word made flesh, our very brother,
takes our nature by his birth.

2. Sing of Jesus, son of Mary,
in the home of Nazareth.
Toil and labour cannot weary
love enduring unto death.
Constant was the love he gave her,
though he went forth from her side,
forth to preach and heal and suffer,
till on Calvary he died.

3. Glory be to God the Father,
glory be to God the Son,
glory be to God the Spirit,
glory to the Three in One.
From the heart of blessèd Mary,
from all saints the song ascends,
and the Church the strain re-echoes
unto earth's remotest ends.

507 Ernest Sands © *1981 Ernest Sands*
Published by OCP Publications

1. Sing of the Lord's goodness, Father of
all wisdom,
come to him and bless his name.
Mercy he has shown us, his love is for
ever,
faithful to the end of days.

Come then, all you nations,
sing of your Lord's goodness,
melodies of praise and thanks to God.
Ring out the Lord's glory,
praise him with your music,
worship him and bless his name.

Continued overleaf

2. Power he has wielded, honour is his garment,
risen from the snares of death.
His word he has spoken, one bread he has broken,
new life he now gives to all.

Come then, all you nations,
sing of your Lord's goodness,
melodies of praise and thanks to God.
Ring out the Lord's glory,
praise him with your music,
worship him and bless his name.

3. Courage in our darkness, comfort in our sorrow,
Spirit of our God most high;
solace for the weary, pardon for the sinner,
splendour of the living God.

4. Praise him with your singing, praise him with the trumpet,
praise God with the lute and harp;
praise him with the cymbals, praise him with your dancing,
praise God till the end of days.

508 Robert Dufford (b. 1943), based on Psalm 117
© 1975 Robert J. Dufford and New Dawn Music

Sing to the mountains, sing to the sea,
raise your voices, lift your hearts.
This is the day the Lord has made,
let all the earth rejoice.

1. I will give thanks to you, my Lord,
you have answered my plea;
you have saved my soul from death,
you are my strength and my song.

2. Holy, holy, holy Lord,
heaven and earth are full of your glory.

3. This is the day that the Lord has made,
let us be glad and rejoice.
He has turned all death to life,
sing of the glory of God.

509 George Bourne Timms (1910-1997)
© Oxford University Press, from 'English Praise'.
Used by permission

1. Sing we of the blessèd Mother
who received the angel's word,
and obedient to his summons
bore in love the infant Lord;
sing we of the joys of Mary
at whose breast that child was fed,
who is Son of God eternal
and the everlasting Bread.

2. Sing we, too, of Mary's sorrows,
of the sword that pierced her through,
when beneath the cross of Jesus
she his weight of suff'ring knew,
looked upon her Son and Saviour
reigning high on Calv'ry's tree,
saw the price of our redemption
paid to set the sinner free.

3. Sing again the joys of Mary
when she saw the risen Lord,
and, in prayer with Christ's apostles,
waited on his promised word:
from on high the blazing glory
of the Spirit's presence came,
heav'nly breath of God's own being,
manifest through wind and flame.

4. Sing the greatest joy of Mary
when on earth her work was done,
and the Lord of all creation
brought her to his heav'nly home:
virgin mother, Mary blessèd,
raised on high and crowned with grace,
may your Son, the world's redeemer,
grant us all to see his face.

510 Edward Caswall (1814-1878)

1. Sleep, holy babe,
   upon thy mother's breast;
   great Lord of earth and sea and sky,
   how sweet it is to see thee lie
   in such a place of rest.

2. Sleep, holy babe,
   thine angels watch around,
   all bending low, with folded wings,
   before th'incarnate King of kings,
   in reverent awe profound.

3. Sleep, holy babe,
   while I with Mary gaze
   in joy upon thy face awhile,
   upon the loving infant smile,
   which there divinely plays.

4. Sleep, holy babe,
   ah, take thy brief repose;
   too quickly will thy slumbers break,
   and thou to lengthened pains awake,
   that death alone shall close.

5. O lady blest,
   sweet virgin, hear my cry;
   forgive the wrong that I have done
   to thee, in causing thy dear Son
   upon the cross to die.

511 Christopher Wordsworth (1807-1885)

1. Songs of thankfulness and praise,
   Jesus, Lord, to thee we raise,
   manifested by the star
   to the sages from afar;
   branch of royal David's stem,
   in thy birth at Bethlehem;
   anthems be to thee addressed:
   God in man made manifest.

2. Manifest at Jordan's stream,
   prophet, priest and King supreme,
   and at Cana wedding-guest,
   in thy Godhead manifest,
   manifest in pow'r divine,
   changing water into wine;
   anthems be to thee addressed:
   God in man made manifest.

3. Manifest in making whole,
   palsied limbs and fainting soul,
   manifest in valiant fight,
   quelling all the devil's might,
   manifest in gracious will,
   ever bringing good from ill;
   anthems be to thee addressed:
   God in man made manifest.

4. Sun and moon shall darkened be,
   stars shall fall, the heav'ns shall flee;
   Christ will then like lightning shine,
   all will see his glorious sign.
   All will then the trumpet hear,
   all will see the judge appear;
   thou by all wilt be confessed:
   God in man made manifest.

5. Grant us grace to see thee, Lord,
   mirrored in thy holy word;
   may we imitate thee now,
   and be pure, as pure art thou;
   that we like to thee may be
   at thy great Epiphany,
   and may praise thee, ever blest,
   God in man made manifest.

512 *Anima Christi.* Ascribed to John XXII (1249-1334), trans. unknown

1. Soul of my Saviour,
   sanctify my breast;
   Body of Christ,
   be thou my saving guest;
   Blood of my Saviour,
   bathe me in thy tide,
   wash me with water
   flowing from thy side.

Continued overleaf

2. Strength and protection
   may thy passion be;
   O blessèd Jesus,
   hear and answer me;
   deep in thy wounds, Lord,
   hide and shelter me;
   so shall I never,
   never part from thee.

3. Guard and defend me
   from the foe malign;
   in death's dread moments
   make me only thine;
   call me, and bid me
   come to thee on high,
   when I may praise thee
   with thy saints for aye.

513
Noel Donnelly (b. 1932)
© 2005 Kevin Mayhew Ltd

1. Spirit hov'ring o'er the waters,
   when the world from chaos began,
   living Spirit, re-create us!
   Come, restore our hearts with life.

   Veni, veni, Sancte Spiritus.

2. Spirit speaking through the prophets
   when they cried for justice and peace,
   living Spirit, come renew us,
   fill the earth with peace and love.

3. Spirit hov'ring o'er the virgin,
   Word and flesh are mothered in her,
   living Spirit, breath of Yahweh,
   bring the Word to life in us.

4. Spirit breathed on John and Mary
   as they stood here under the cross,
   living Spirit, strengthen, comfort,
   guide, unite your church today.

5. Spirit hov'ring o'er apostles,
   wind and fire of Pentecost Day,
   living Spirit, now confirm us,
   come inspire us, come, we pray.

514
Helen Kennedy
© St Mungo Music

1. Spirit of God, come dwell within me.
   Open my heart, O come set me free,
   fill me with love for Jesus, my Lord,
   O fill me with living water.

   Jesus is living, Jesus is here.
   Jesus, my Lord, come closer to me.
   Jesus, our Saviour dying for me,
   and rising to save his people.

2. Lord, how I thirst, O Lord, I am weak.
   Lord, come to me, you alone do I seek.
   Lord, you are life, and love and hope,
   O fill me with living water.

3. Lord, I am blind. O Lord, I can't see.
   Stretch out your hand, O Lord,
      comfort me.
   Lead me your way in light and in truth,
   O fill me with living water.

515
Sean Bowman
© 2004 Kevin Mayhew Ltd

1. Spirit of God, our light amid the
      darkness,
   shine on your people, fill our hearts
      anew;
   show us your glory, fill your whole
      creation,
   Light of the world, we bring our lives
      to you.

2. Spirit of hope, our joy and consolation,
   share in our gladness, lift us when we
      fall,
   grant us the strength to be a steadfast
      witness,
   filled with your strength to bring new
      hope to all.

3. Spirit of love, our source of true compassion,
   grant us your peace and fill us with new life,
   come, fill our hearts with your great love unbounded,
   fill all the world with love which ends all strife.

4. Spirit of truth, our shield and our defender,
   be our sure fortress, fill us with your might,
   grant us your wisdom, be our inspiration,
   filled with your truth, your glory and your light.

516 Daniel Iverson (1890-1972)
© 1963 Birdwing Music/EMI Christian Music Publishing. Administered by Kevin Mayhew Ltd

1. Spirit of the living God,
   fall afresh on me.
   Spirit of the living God,
   fall afresh on me.
   Melt me, mould me,
   fill me, use me.
   Spirit of the living God,
   fall afresh on me.

2. Spirit of the living God,
   fall afresh on us.
   Spirit of the living God,
   fall afresh on us.
   Melt us, mould us,
   fill us, use us.
   Spirit of the living God,
   fall afresh on us.

When appropriate, a third verse may be added, singing 'on them', for example, before Confirmation, or at a service for the sick.

517 Ave Maris Stella 9th century,
trans. Ralph Wright (b. 1938)
© 1989 GIA Publications Inc.

1. Star of sea and ocean,
   gateway to God's haven,
   mother of our Maker,
   hear our pray'r, O maiden.

2. Welcoming the Ave
   of God's simple greeting,
   you have borne a Saviour,
   far beyond all dreaming.

3. Loose the bonds that hold us
   bound in sin's own blindness
   that with eyes now opened
   God's own light may guide us.

4. Show yourself our mother;
   he will hear your pleading
   whom your womb has sheltered
   and whose hand brings healing.

5. Gentlest of all virgins,
   that our love be faithful
   keep us from all evil
   gentle, strong and grateful.

6. Guard us through life's dangers,
   never turn and leave us.
   May our hope find harbour
   in the calm of Jesus.

7. Sing to God our Father
   through the Son who saves us,
   joyful in the Spirit,
   everlasting praises.

518 Matthew 26:36-42
© Ateliers et Presses de Taizé

Stay with me, remain here with me, watch and pray, watch and pray.

The following verses may be sung by a Cantor:

1. Stay here and keep watch with me.
   Watch and pray, watch and pray!

Continued overleaf

2. Watch and pray not to give way
   to temptation.

   Stay with me, remain here with me,
   watch and pray, watch and pray.

3. The Spirit is eager,
   but the flesh is weak.

4. My heart is nearly broken with sorrow.
   Remain here with me, stay awake
   and pray.

5. Father, if it is possible let this cup
   pass me by.

6. Father, if this cannot pass me by
   without my drinking it,
   your will be done.

519 Spiritual

Steal away, steal away,
steal away to Jesus.
Steal away, steal away home.
I ain't got long to stay here.

1. My Lord, he calls me,
   he calls me by the thunder.
   The trumpet sounds within my soul;
   I ain't got long to stay here.

2. Green trees are bending,
   the sinner stands a-trembling.
   The trumpet sounds within my soul;
   I ain't got long to stay here.

3. My Lord, he calls me,
   he calls me by the lightning.
   The trumpet sounds within my soul;
   I ain't got long to stay here.

520 From Daniel 3
© *Ateliers et Presses de Taizé*

Surrexit Christus, alleluia!
Cantate Domino, alleluia!
Translation: Christ is risen.
                Sing to the Lord.

The following verses may be sung by a
Cantor:

1. All you heavens, bless the Lord.
   Stars of the heavens, bless the Lord.

2. Sun and moon, bless the Lord.
   And you, night and day, bless the Lord.

3. Frost and cold, bless the Lord.
   Ice and snow, bless the Lord.

4. Fire and heat, bless the Lord.
   And you, light and darkness,
   bless the Lord.

5. Spirits and souls of the just, bless the
   Lord.
   Saints and the humble-hearted, bless
   the Lord.

521 Sister Marie Josephine

1. Sweet heart of Jesus,
   fount of love and mercy,
   today we come,
   thy blessing to implore;
   O touch our hearts,
   so cold and so ungrateful,
   and make them, Lord,
   thine own for evermore.

   Sweet heart of Jesus, we implore,
   O make us love thee more and more.

2. Sweet heart of Jesus,
   make us know and love thee,
   unfold to us
   the treasures of thy grace;
   that so our hearts,
   from things of earth uplifted,
   may long alone
   to gaze upon thy face.

3. Sweet heart of Jesus,
   make us pure and gentle,
   and teach us how
   to do thy blessèd will;
   to follow close
   the print of thy dear footsteps,
   and when we fall –
   sweet heart, O love us still.

4. Sweet heart of Jesus,
   bless all hearts that love thee,
   and may thine own heart
   ever blessèd be;
   bless us, dear Lord,
   and bless the friends we cherish,
   and keep us true
   to Mary and to thee.

522 Francis Stanfield (1835-1914) alt.

1. Sweet sacrament divine,
   hid in thy earthly home,
   lo, round thy lowly shrine,
   with suppliant hearts we come;
   Jesus, to thee our voice we raise,
   in songs of love and heartfelt praise,
   sweet sacrament divine,
   sweet sacrament divine.

2. Sweet sacrament of peace,
   dear home of ev'ry heart,
   where restless yearnings cease,
   and sorrows all depart,

there in thine ear all trustfully
we tell our tale of misery,
sweet sacrament of peace,
sweet sacrament of peace.

3. Sweet sacrament of rest,
   Ark from the ocean's roar,
   within thy shelter blest
   soon may we reach the shore;
   save us, for still the tempest raves;
   save, lest we sink beneath the waves,
   sweet sacrament of rest,
   sweet sacrament of rest.

4. Sweet sacrament divine,
   earth's light and jubilee,
   in thy far depths doth shine
   thy Godhead's majesty;
   sweet light, so shine on us, we pray,
   that earthly joys may fade away,
   sweet sacrament divine,
   sweet sacrament divine.

523 Frederick William Faber (1814-1863)

1. Sweet Saviour, bless us ere we go,
   thy word into our minds instil;
   and make our lukewarm hearts to
      glow
   with lowly love and fervent will.

   *Through life's long day and death's dark
      night,*
   O gentle Jesus, be our light.

2. The day is done; its hours have run,
   and thou hast taken count of all
   the scanty triumphs grace has won,
   the broken vow, the frequent fall.

3. Grant us, dear Lord, from evil ways,
   true absolution and release;
   and bless us more than in past days
   with purity and inward peace.

Continued overleaf

4. Do more than pardon; give us joy,
   sweet fear and sober liberty,
   and loving hearts without alloy,
   that only long to be like thee.

   *Through life's long day and death's dark
   night,*
   O gentle Jesus, be our light.

5. Labour is sweet, for thou hast toiled,
   and care is light, for thou hast cared;
   let not our works with self be soiled,
   nor in unsimple ways ensnared.

6. For all we love – the poor, the sad,
   the sinful – unto thee we call;
   O let thy mercy make us glad,
   thou art our Jesus and our all.

524 Francesca Leftley (b. 1955)
© 1984 Kevin Mayhew Ltd

1. Take me, Lord, use my life
   in the way you wish to do.
   Fill me, Lord, touch my heart
   till it always thinks of you.
   Take me now, as I am,
   this is all I can offer.

   Here today I, the clay,
   will be moulded by my Lord.

2. Lord, I pray that each day
   I will listen to your will.
   Many times I have failed
   but I know you love me still.
   Teach me now, guide me, Lord
   keep me close to you always.

3. I am weak, fill me now
   with your strength and set me free.
   Make me whole, fashion me
   so that you will live in me.
   Hold me now in your hands,
   form me now with your Spirit.

525 Sebastian Temple (1928-1997)
© 1967 Sebastian Temple.
Published by OCP Publications

1. Take my hands and make them as
      your own,
   and use them for your kingdom here
      on earth.
   Consecrate them to your care,
   anoint them for your service where
   you may need your gospel to be sown.

2. Take my hands, they speak now for
      my heart,
   and by their actions they will show
      their love.
   Guard them on their daily course,
   be their strength and guiding force
   to ever serve the Trinity above.

3. Take my hands, I give them to you,
      Lord.
   Prepare them for the service of your
      name.
   Open them to human need
   and by their love they'll sow your seed
   so all may know the love and hope
      you give.

526 vs. 1 and 3 Margaret Rizza (b. 1929),
v. 2 unknown. © 1998 Kevin Mayhew Ltd

1. Take my hands, Lord,
   to share in your labours,
   take my eyes, Lord, to see your needs,
   let me hear the voice of lonely people,
   let my love, Lord, bring riches to
      the poor.

2. Give me someone to feed when
      I'm hungry,
   when I'm thirsty give water for
      their thirst.
   When I stand in need of tenderness,
   give me someone to hold who longs
      for love.

3. Keep my heart ever open to others,
   may my time, Lord, be spent with
       those in need;
   may I tend to those who need
       your care.
   Take my life, Lord, and make it
       truly yours,
   take my life, Lord, and make it truly
       yours.

527 Frances Ridley Havergal (1836-1879)

1. Take my life, and let it be
   consecrated, Lord, to thee;
   take my moments and my days,
   let them flow in ceaseless praise.

2. Take my hands, and let them move
   at the impulse of thy love;
   take my feet, and let them be
   swift and beautiful for thee.

3. Take my voice, and let me sing
   always, only, for my King;
   take my lips, and let them be
   filled with messages from thee.

4. Take my silver and my gold;
   not a mite would I withhold;
   take my intellect, and use
   ev'ry pow'r as thou shalt choose.

5. Take my will, and make it thine:
   it shall be no longer mine;
   take my heart: it is thine own;
   it shall be thy royal throne.

6. Take my love; my Lord, I pour
   at thy feet its treasure-store;
   take myself, and I will be
   ever, only, all for thee.

528 Joe Wise (b. 1939)
© 1966 GIA Publications Inc.

Take our bread, we ask you,
take our hearts, we love you,
take our lives, O Father,
we are yours, we are yours.

1. Yours as we stand at the table you set,
   yours as we eat the bread
   our hearts can't forget.
   We are the signs of your life with us yet;
   we are yours, we are yours.

2. Your holy people stand washed in
       your blood,
   Spirit-filled, yet hungry,
   we await your food.
   Poor though we are, we have brought
   ourselves to you:
   we are yours, we are yours.

529 James Harrison. © *1991 James Harrison.*
Published by OCP Publications

1. Take the word of God with you as
       you go.
   Take the seeds of God's word and
       make them grow.

   Go in peace to serve the world,
   in peace to serve the world.
   Take the love of God, the love of God
   with you as you go.

2. Take the peace of God with you as
       you go.
   Take the seeds of God's peace and
       make them grow.

3. Take the joy of God with you as you
       go.
   Take the seeds of God's joy and make
       them grow.

Continued overleaf

4. Take the love of God with you as you go.
   Take the seeds of God's love and make them grow.

   Go in peace to serve the world,
   in peace to serve the world.
   Take the love of God, the love of God
   with you as you go.

   Add other words if needed, such as
   'faith', 'hope' . . .

530 John L. Bell (b. 1949) and Graham Maule (b. 1958). © 1988 WGRG, Iona Community

1. Take this moment, sign and space;
   take my friends around;
   here among us make the place
   where your love is found.

2. Take the time to call my name,
   take the time to mend
   who I am and what I've been,
   all I've failed to tend.

3. Take the tiredness of my days,
   take my past regret,
   letting your forgiveness touch
   all I can't forget.

4. Take the little child in me,
   scared of growing old;
   help him (her) here to find his (her) worth
   made in Christ's own mould.

5. Take my talents, take my skills,
   take what's yet to be;
   let my life be yours, and yet,
   let it still be me.

531 Martin E. Leckebusch (b. 1962) © 2000 Kevin Mayhew Ltd

1. Teach me, dear Lord, to savour ev'ry moment,
   each precious hour, a gift which is unique;
   for your unhurried guiding hand I cherish
   and the contentment of your ways I seek.
   When date and time demand my full attention,
   from frantic rushing let my heart be free,
   that I may flow within your Spirit's rhythm
   and live each minute just as it was meant to be.

2. But may I also glimpse the broader canvas,
   to all my life, a purpose and a plan;
   and let me hear again that voice which called me
   before this world or time itself began.
   So may your kingdom daily be my watchword
   and may the pulse in all my life be praise,
   across unfolding years and changing seasons,
   until with you I walk through everlasting days.

532 Timothy Dudley-Smith (b. 1926), based on Luke 1:46-55. © 1961 Timothy Dudley-Smith in Europe. Used by permission. Administered by Oxford University Press

1. Tell out, my soul, the greatness of the Lord!
   Unnumbered blessings, give my spirit voice;
   tender to me the promise of his word;
   in God my Saviour shall my heart rejoice.

2. Tell out, my soul, the greatness of
   his Name!
   Make known his might, the deeds his
   arm has done;
   his mercy sure, from age to age
   the same;
   his holy Name, the Lord, the
   Mighty One.

3. Tell out, my soul, the greatness of his
   might!
   Pow'rs and dominions lay their glory
   by.
   Proud hearts and stubborn wills are
   put to flight,
   the hungry fed, the humble lifted high.

4. Tell out, my soul, the glories of
   his word!
   Firm is his promise, and his
   mercy sure.
   Tell out, my soul, the greatness of the
   Lord
   to children's children and for
   evermore!

533 Stephen Dean (b. 1948). © 1994 Stephen Dean
Published by OCP Publications

1. Thanks be to God whose love has
   gathered us today;
   thanks be to God who helps and
   guides us on our way;
   thanks be to God who gives us voice,
   that we may thank him:

   Deo gratias, Deo gratias,
   thanks be to God most high.

2. Thanks be to God for all the gifts of
   life and light;
   thanks be to God whose care protects
   us, day and night;
   thanks be to God who keeps in mind
   us who forget him:

3. Thanks be to God who knows our
   secret joys and fears;
   thanks be to God who when we call
   him, always hears;
   thanks be to God our rock and
   strength, ever sustaining:

4. Thanks be to God who never turns
   his face away;
   thanks be to God who heals and
   pardons all who stray;
   thanks be to God who welcomes us
   into the Kingdom:

5. Thanks be to God who made our
   world and all we see;
   thanks be to God who gave his Son
   to set us free;
   thanks be to God whose Spirit brings
   warmth and rejoicing:

534 Sabine Baring-Gould (1834-1924),
based on *Birjina gaztettobat zegoen*

1. The angel Gabriel from heaven came,
   his wings as drifted snow, his eyes
   as flame.
   'All hail,' said he, 'thou lowly maiden,
   Mary,
   most highly favoured lady.' Gloria!

2. 'For known a blessèd Mother thou
   shalt be.
   All generations laud and honour thee.
   Thy Son shall be Emmanuel, by seers
   foretold,
   most highly favoured lady.' Gloria!

3. Then gentle Mary meekly bowed
   her head.
   'To me be as it pleaseth God,' she said.
   'My soul shall laud and magnify his
   holy name.'
   Most highly favoured lady! Gloria!

Continued overleaf

4. Of her, Emmanuel, the Christ,
      was born
   in Bethlehem, all on a Christmas morn;
   and Christian folk throughout the
      world will ever say:
   'Most highly favoured lady.' Gloria!

535 Carol K. Ikeler (b. 1920)
      © 1963 W. L. Jenkins, Westminster/John Knox Press

1. The Church is wherever God's people
      are praising,
   singing their thanks for his goodness
      this day.
   The Church is wherever disciples of
      Jesus
   remember his story and walk in his
      way.

2. The Church is wherever God's people
      are helping,
   caring for neighbours in sickness and
      need.
   The Church is wherever God's people
      are sharing
   the words of the Bible in gift and in
      deed.

536 Samuel John Stone (1839-1900)

1. The Church's one foundation
   is Jesus Christ, her Lord;
   she is his new creation,
   by water and the word;
   from heav'n he came and sought her
   to be his holy bride,
   with his own blood he bought her,
   and for her life he died.

2. Elect from ev'ry nation,
   yet one o'er all the earth,
   her charter of salvation,
   one Lord, one faith, one birth;
   one holy name she blesses,
   partakes one holy food,
   and to one hope she presses,
   with ev'ry grace endued.

3. 'Mid toil and tribulation,
   and tumult of her war,
   she waits the consummation
   of peace for evermore;
   till with the vision glorious
   her longing eyes are blest,
   and the great Church victorious
   shall be the Church at rest.

4. Yet she on earth hath union
   with God the Three in One,
   and mystic sweet communion
   with those whose rest is won:
   O happy ones and holy!
   Lord, give us grace that we
   like them, the meek and lowly,
   on high may dwell with thee.

537 Instantis adventum Dei by Charles Coffin
      (1676-1749), trans. Robert Campbell
      (1814-1868) and others

1. The coming of our God
   our thoughts must now employ;
   then let us meet him on the road
   with songs of holy joy.

2. The co-eternal Son,
   a maiden's offspring see;
   a servant's form Christ putteth on,
   to set his people free.

3. Daughter of Sion, rise
   to greet thine infant king,
   nor let thy stubborn heart despise
   the pardon he doth bring.

4. In glory from his throne
again will Christ descend,
and summon all that are his own
to joys that never end.

5. Let deeds of darkness fly
before th'approaching morn,
for unto sin 'tis ours to die,
and serve the virgin-born.

6. Our joyful praises sing
to Christ, that set us free;
like tribute to the Father bring
and, Holy Ghost, to thee.

538 St John of Damascus (c. 750)
trans. John Mason Neale (1818-1866)

1. The day of resurrection!
Earth, tell it out abroad;
the passover of gladness,
the passover of God!
From death to life eternal,
from earth unto the sky,
our Christ hath brought us over
with hymns of victory.

2. Our hearts be pure from evil,
that we may see aright
the Lord in rays eternal
of resurrection-light;
and list'ning to his accents,
may hear so calm and plain
his own 'All hail' and, hearing,
may raise the victor strain.

3. Now let the heav'ns be joyful,
and earth her song begin,
the round world keep high triumph,
and all that is therein;
let all things, seen and unseen,
their notes of gladness blend,
for Christ the Lord hath risen,
our joy that hath no end.

539 John Bell (b. 1949) and Graham Maule (b.1958)
© 1987 WGRG, Iona Community

1. The Day of the Lord shall come, as
prophets have told,
when Christ shall make all things
new, no matter how old.
And some at the stars may gaze, and
some at God's word,
in vain to predict the time, the Day
of the Lord.

*The desert shall spring to life, the hills
shall rejoice;*
*the lame of the earth shall leap, the
dumb shall find voice;*
*the lamb with the lion shall lie, and the
last shall be first;*
*and nations for war no more shall
study or thirst.*

2. The Day of the Lord shall come –
a thief in the night,
a curse to those in the wrong who
think themselves right,
a pleasure for those in pain or with
death at the door;
a true liberation for the pris'ners and
poor.

3. The Day of the Lord shall come and
judgement be known,
as nations like sheep and goats come
close to the throne.
Then Christ shall himself reveal,
asking all to draw near
and see in his face all faces once
ignored there.

4. The Day of the Lord shall come, but
now is the time
to subvert earth's wisdom with
Christ's folly sublime,
by loving the loveless, turning the
tide and the cheek,
by walking beneath the cross in step
with the weak.

540
John Ellerton (1826-1893)

1. The day thou gavest, Lord, is ended:
the darkness falls at thy behest;
to thee our morning hymns ascended;
thy praise shall sanctify our rest.

2. We thank thee that thy Church
unsleeping,
while earth rolls onward into light,
through all the world her watch
is keeping,
and rests not now by day or night.

3. As o'er each continent and island
the dawn leads on another day,
the voice of pray'r is never silent,
nor dies the strain of praise away.

4. The sun that bids us rest is waking
our brethren 'neath the western sky,
and hour by hour fresh lips are making
thy wondrous doings heard on high.

5. So be it, Lord; thy throne shall never,
like earth's proud empires, pass away;
thy kingdom stands, and grows
for ever,
till all thy creatures own thy sway.

2. They lookèd up and saw a star,
shining in the east, beyond them far,
and to the earth it gave great light,
and so it continued both day
and night.

3. And by the light of that same star,
three wise men came from
country far;
to seek for a king was their intent,
and to follow the star wherever
it went.

4. This star drew nigh to the north-west,
o'er Bethlehem it took its rest,
and there it did both stop and stay
right over the place where Jesus lay.

5. Then entered in those wise men three,
full rev'rently upon their knee,
and offered there in his presence,
their gold and myrrh and
frankincense.

6. Then let us all with one accord
sing praises to our heav'nly Lord,
who with the Father we adore
and Spirit blest for evermore.

541
From William Sandys' *Christmas Carols, Ancient and Modern* (1833) alt.

1. The first Nowell the angel did say
was to certain poor shepherds in
fields as they lay:
in fields where they lay keeping
their sheep,
on a cold winter's night that was
so deep.

*Nowell, Nowell, Nowell, Nowell,
born is the King of Israel!*

542
John Bell (b. 1949) and Graham Maule (b.1958)
© 1989 WGRG, Iona Community

1. The God of all eternity,
unbound by space yet always near,
is present where his people meet
to celebrate the coming year.

2. What shall we offer God today –
our dreams of what we cannot see,
or, with eyes fastened to the past,
our dread of what is yet to be?

3. God does not share our doubts and
   fears,
   nor shrinks from the unknown or
   strange:
   the one who fashioned heav'n and
   earth
   makes all things new and ushers
   change.

4. Let faith or fortune rise or fall,
   let dreams and dread both have their
   day;
   those whom God loves walk unafraid
   with Christ their guide and Christ
   their way.

5. God grant that we, in this new year,
   may show the world the Kingdom's
   face,
   and let our work and worship thrive
   as signs of hope and means of grace.

543 Thomas Kelly (1769-1855)

1. The head that once was crowned
   with thorns
   is crowned with glory now:
   a royal diadem adorns
   the mighty victor's brow.

2. The highest place that heav'n affords
   is his, is his by right.
   The King of kings and Lord of lords,
   and heav'n's eternal light.

3. The joy of all who dwell above,
   the joy of all below,
   to whom he manifests his love,
   and grants his name to know.

4. To them the cross, with all its shame,
   with all its grace is giv'n;
   their name an everlasting name,
   their joy the joy of heav'n.

5. They suffer with their Lord below,
   they reign with him above,
   their profit and their joy to know
   the myst'ry of his love.

6. The cross he bore is life and health,
   though shame and death to him;
   his people's hope, his people's wealth,
   their everlasting theme.

544 Traditional

1. The holly and the ivy,
   when they are both full grown,
   of all the trees that are in the wood
   the holly bears the crown.

   The rising of the sun
   and the running of the deer,
   the playing of the merry organ,
   sweet singing in the choir.

2. The holly bears a blossom,
   white as the lily flower,
   and Mary bore sweet Jesus Christ
   to be our sweet Saviour.

3. The holly bears a berry,
   as red as any blood,
   and Mary bore sweet Jesus Christ
   to do poor sinners good.

4. The holly bears a prickle,
   as sharp as any thorn,
   and Mary bore sweet Jesus Christ
   on Christmas day in the morn.

5. The holly bears a bark,
   as bitter as any gall,
   and Mary bore sweet Jesus Christ
   for to redeem us all.

6. The holly and the ivy,
   when they are both full grown,
   of all the trees that are in the wood
   the holly bears the crown.

545

Willard F. Jabusch (b.1930)
© 1998 Willard F. Jabusch

The King of glory comes, the nation rejoices,
open the gates before him, lift up your voices.

1. Who is the King of glory,
   how shall we call him?
   He is Emmanuel,
   the promised of ages.

2. In all of Galilee,
   in city and village,
   he goes among his people,
   curing their illness.

3. Sing then of David's Son,
   our Saviour and brother;
   in all of Galilee
   was never another.

4. He gave his life for us,
   the pledge of salvation.
   He took upon himself
   the sins of the nation.

5. He conquered sin and death;
   he truly has risen;
   and he will share with us
   his heavenly vision.

546

Henry Williams Baker (1821-1877),
based on Psalm 23

1. The King of love my shepherd is,
   whose goodness faileth never;
   I nothing lack if I am his
   and he is mine for ever.

2. Where streams of living water flow
   my ransomed soul he leadeth,
   and where the verdant pastures grow
   with food celestial feedeth.

3. Perverse and foolish oft I strayed,
   but yet in love he sought me,
   and on his shoulder gently laid,
   and home, rejoicing, brought me.

4. In death's dark vale I fear no ill
   with thee, dear Lord, beside me;
   thy rod and staff my comfort still,
   thy cross before to guide me.

5. Thou spread'st a table in my sight,
   thy unction grace bestoweth:
   and O what transport of delight
   from thy pure chalice floweth!

6. And so through all the length of days
   thy goodness faileth never;
   good shepherd, may I sing thy praise
   within thy house for ever.

547

Mike Anderson (b. 1956), based on Matthew
5:3-10. © 1999 Kevin Mayhew Ltd

The kingdom of heaven,
the kingdom of heaven is yours.
A new world in Jesus
a new world in Jesus is yours.

1. Blessèd are you in sorrow and grief,
   for you shall all be consoled;
   blessèd are you, the gentle of heart,
   you shall inherit the earth.

2. Blessèd are you who hunger for right,
   for you shall be satisfied;
   blessèd are you the merciful ones,
   for you shall be pardoned too.

3. Blessèd are you whose hearts are pure,
   your eyes shall gaze on the Lord;
   blessèd are you who strive after peace,
   the Lord will call you his own.

4. Blessèd are you who suffer for right,
   the heav'nly kingdom is yours;
   blessèd are you who suffer for me,
   for you shall reap your reward.

548

Donald Fishel (b. 1950)
© 1973 The Word of God Music. Administered by CopyCare Ltd

The light of Christ has come into the
world.
The light of Christ has come into the
world.

1. We must all be born again
   to see the kingdom of God.
   The water and the Spirit bring
   new life in God's love.

2. God gave up his only Son
   out of love for the world,
   so that all who believe in him
   will live for ever.

3. The light of God has come to us
   so that we might have salvation;
   from the darkness of our sins we walk
   into glory with Christ Jesus.

549

John B. Foley (b. 1939), based on Psalm 33
© 1978, 1991 John B. Foley, SJ and New Dawn Music

The Lord hears the cry of the poor.
Blessèd be the Lord.

1. I will bless the Lord at all times,
   his praise ever in my mouth.
   Let my soul glory in the Lord,
   for he hears the cry of the poor.

2. Let the lowly hear and be glad;
   the Lord listens to their pleas;
   and to hearts broken he is near,
   for he hears the cry of the poor.

3. Ev'ry spirit crushed he will save;
   will be ransom for their lives;
   will be safe shelter for their fears,
   for he hears the cry of the poor.

4. We proclaim the greatness of God,
   his praise ever in our mouth;
   ev'ry face brightened in his light,
   for he hears the cry of the poor.

550

Jean-Paul Lécot (b. 1947),
trans. W. R. Lawrence (1925-1997)
© 1988 Kevin Mayhew Ltd

1. The Lord is alive! Alleluia!
   He dwells in our midst! Alleluia!
   Give praise to his name
   throughout all the world!
   Alleluia! Alleluia!

2. He brings us great joy! Alleluia!
   He fills us with hope! Alleluia!
   He comes as our food,
   he gives us our life!
   Alleluia! Alleluia!

3. So let us rejoice! Alleluia!
   Give praise to the Lord! Alleluia!
   He showed us his love,
   by him we are saved!
   Alleluia! Alleluia!

4. The Lord is alive! Alleluia!
   So let us proclaim, alleluia,
   the Good News of Christ
   throughout all the world!
   Alleluia! Alleluia!

5. Christ Jesus had died! Alleluia!
   Christ Jesus is ris'n! Alleluia!
   Christ Jesus will come
   again as the Lord!
   Alleluia! Alleluia!

6. Sing praises to God, alleluia,
   who reigns without end! Alleluia!
   The Father, the Son,
   and Spirit – all one!
   Alleluia! Alleluia!

551

From Psalm 26
© 1998 Kevin Mayhew Ltd

The Lord is my light,
in him I trust. *(Repeat)*
The Lord is my light,
in him I trust,
in him I trust.

552

Taizé Community
© Ateliers et Presses de Taizé

The Lord is my song, the Lord is my
   praise:
all my hope comes from God.
The Lord is my song, the Lord is my
   praise:
God, the well-spring of life.

553

The Scottish Psalter (1650)

1. The Lord's my shepherd, I'll not want.
   He makes me down to lie
   in pastures green.
   He leadeth me the quiet waters by.

2. My soul he doth restore again,
   and me to walk doth make
   within the paths of righteousness,
   e'en for his own name's sake.

3. Yea, though I walk in death's dark vale,
   yet will I fear no ill.
   For thou art with me, and thy rod
   and staff me comfort still.

4. My table thou has furnishèd
   in presence of my foes,
   my head thou dost with oil anoint,
   and my cup overflows.

5. Goodness and mercy all my life
   shall surely follow me.
   And in God's house for evermore
   my dwelling-place shall be.

554

Stuart Townend (b. 1963), based on Psalm 23
© 1996 Thankyou Music.
Administered by worshiptogether.com songs

1. The Lord's my shepherd, I'll not want;
   he makes me lie in pastures green,
   he leads me by the still, still waters,
   his goodness restores my soul.

   And I will trust in you alone,
   and I will trust in you alone,
   for your endless mercy follows me,
   your goodness will lead me home.

2. He guides my ways in righteousness,
   and he anoints my head with oil;
   and my cup – it overflows with joy,
   I feast on his pure delights.

3. And though I walk the darkest path –
   I will not fear the evil one,
   for you are with me, and your rod
      and staff
   are the comfort I need to know.

555

Carey Landry (b. 1944)
© 1971 Carey Landry and North American
Liturgy Resources

1. The love I have for you, my Lord,
   is only a shadow of your love for me;
   only a shadow of your love for me;
   your deep abiding love.

2. My own belief in you, my Lord,
   is only a shadow of your faith in me;
   only a shadow of your faith in me;
   your deep and lasting faith.

3. My life is in your hands;
   my life is in your hands.
   My love for you will grow, my God.
   Your light in me will shine.

4. The dream I have today, my Lord,
is only a shadow of your dreams for me;
only a shadow of all that will be;
if I but follow you.

5. The joy I feel today, my Lord,
is only a shadow of your joys for me;
only a shadow of your joys for me;
when we meet face to face.

6. My life is in your hands;
my life is in your hands.
My love for you will grow, my God.
Your light in me will shine.

556 Susan Sayers (b. 1946)
© 1996 Kevin Mayhew Ltd

1. The love we share, the love we come
to celebrate,
so rich and full, so healing and so
strong,
comes from the love of God our
loving Father
within whose care we all of us belong.
A love which breathed creation into
being,
a love which hears our deepest hopes
and dreams;
a love which now within this
marriage-making
alights on bride and groom to bless
and make them one.

2. Through future years, may they hold
bright the memory
of all the joys on this their wedding
day.
And as their love grows stronger yet
and deeper
their rings express much more than
words can say.

They speak of love that never has an
ending,
of love that shines, encircles in embrace,
of love whose heart is always free and
open;
our human love reflects the beauty of
God's grace.

557 Damian Lundy (1944-1997) alt.
© 1978 Kevin Mayhew Ltd

1. The night before our Saviour died,
he took a loaf of bread.
He blessed it, broke it, passed it round,
and to the friends beside him said:
'Take this and eat it do,
my body now for you.'

2. And taking then a cup of wine,
he offered thanks again,
and gave it to his friends to drink
in mem'ry of his coming pain.
'This is my blood,' he said,
'for you it will be shed.'

3. And so today his people meet,
remembering the night
on which our Saviour gave himself
to be our food, to be our light,
to be our unity,
the bread of charity.

4. Lord, send your Spirit into us
and make us one, we pray.
Make us your body and your blood,
your presence in the world today.
Take us and share us, do,
your body now for you.

5. Lord Jesus, present in our meal,
be with us all the day,
in all the people that we meet,
in ev'rything we do and say.
And our life will be yours,
and your life will be ours.

558

Bernadette Farrell (b. 1957)
© 1995, 1999 Bernadette Farrell.
Published by OCP Publications

The peace of God I leave you,
the peace that knows no ending,
the peace that comes when justice is done:
the peace of God for ev'ryone.

1. Jesus the Lord says, 'I am the Way.'
   Show us the path to follow today.
   Where people need our friendship
      and care,
   give us the courage to love and to share.

2. Jesus the Lord says, 'I am the Light.'
   Keep us awake to see what is right.
   Where there is darkness, fear and
      despair,
   we can bring love and then God will
      be there.

3. Jesus the Lord says, 'I am the Word.'
   Open our lips to speak and be heard.
   Where there is greed and hatred and
      war,
   fill us with courage to live by God's law.

4. Jesus the Lord says, 'I am the Bread.'
   Come to us now and we will be fed.
   Here at your table, hungry no more,
   send us to share out our bread with
      the poor.

559

John Morrison (1750-1798),
based on Isaiah 9:2-7

1. The race that long in darkness pined
   has seen a glorious light:
   the people dwell in day,
   who dwelt in death's surrounding
      night.

2. To hail thy rise, thou better sun,
   the gath'ring nations come,
   joyous as when the reapers bear
   the harvest treasures home.

3. To us a child of hope is born,
   to us a Son is giv'n;
   him shall the tribes of earth obey,
   him all the hosts of heav'n.

4. His name shall be the Prince of Peace
   for evermore adored,
   the Wonderful, the Counsellor,
   the great and mighty Lord.

5. His pow'r increasing still shall spread,
   his reign no end shall know;
   justice shall guard his throne above,
   and peace abound below.

560

Venantius Fortunatus (530-609)
trans. John Mason Neale (1818-1866) and others

1. The royal banners forward go,
   the cross shines forth in mystic glow;
   where he in flesh, our flesh who made,
   our sentence bore, our ransom paid.

2. There whilst he hung, his sacred side
   by soldier's spear was opened wide,
   to cleanse us in the precious flood
   of water mingled with his blood.

3. Fulfilled is now what David told
   in true prophetic song of old,
   how God the sinner's king should be;
   for God is reigning from the tree.

4. O tree of glory, tree most fair,
   ordained those holy limbs to bear,
   how bright in purple robe it stood,
   the purple of a Saviour's blood!

5. To thee, eternal Three in One,
   let homage meet by all be done,
   as by the cross thou dost restore,
   so rule and guide us evermore.
   Amen.

561 Damian Lundy (1944-1997)
© *1978, 1993 Kevin Mayhew Ltd*

1. The Spirit lives to set us free,
   walk, walk in the light.
   He binds us all in unity,
   walk, walk in the light.

   Walk in the light (x3)
   walk in the light of the Lord.

2. Jesus promised life to all,
   walk, walk in the light.
   The dead were wakened by his call,
   walk, walk in the light.

3. He died in pain on Calvary,
   walk, walk in the light,
   to save the lost like you and me,
   walk, walk in the light.

4. We know his death was not the end,
   walk, walk in the light.
   He gave his Spirit to be our friend,
   walk, walk in the light.

5. By Jesus' love our wounds are healed,
   walk, walk in the light.
   The Father's kindness is revealed,
   walk, walk in the light.

6. The Spirit lives in you and me,
   walk, walk in the light.
   His light will shine for all to see,
   walk, walk in the light.

562 Michael Forster (b. 1946)
© *1993 Kevin Mayhew Ltd*

1. The temple of the living God
   is built of living stones,
   a holy people, called to live
   by light of Christ alone.
   With special joy we celebrate
   the word the psalmist said:
   'The stone the builders cast aside
   is now the corner's head!'

2. The temple of the living God
   is set secure above,
   where Christ invites the world to share
   his perfect reign of love.
   And we who seek the Father's face
   are summoned to obey,
   and follow where he goes before,
   the Life, the Truth, the Way.

3. The temple of the living God
   upon the earth must grow,
   and those of ev'ry race and class
   his true compassion know.
   The widow and the fatherless
   receive a special care,
   till all creation, just and free,
   his perfect peace will share.

563 John L. Bell (b. 1949) and Graham Maule
(b.1958). © *1988 WGRG, Iona Community*

1. The time was early evening,
   the place a room upstairs;
   the guests were the disciples,
   few in number and few in prayers.

   Oh, the food comes from the baker,
   the drink comes from the vine,
   the words come from the Saviour,
   'I will meet you in bread and wine.'

2. The company of Jesus
   had met to share a meal,
   but he, who made them welcome,
   had much more to reveal.

3. 'The bread and body broken,
   the wine and blood outpoured,
   the cross and kitchen table
   are one by my sign and word.'

4. On both sides of the table,
   on both sides of the grave,
   the Lord joins those who love him
   to serve them and to save.

Continued overleaf

5. Lord Jesus, now among us,
   confirm our faith's intent,
   as, with your words and actions,
   we unite in this sacrament.

   Oh, the food comes from the baker,
   the drink comes from the vine,
   the words come from the Saviour,
   'I will meet you in bread and wine.'

564 Traditional West Indian

1. The Virgin Mary had a baby boy,
   the Virgin Mary had a baby boy,
   the Virgin Mary had a baby boy,
   and they said that his name was Jesus.

   He came from the glory,
   he came from the glorious kingdom.
   He came from the glory,
   he came from the glorious kingdom.
   O yes, believer. O yes, believer.
   He came from the glory,
   he came from the glorious kingdom.

2. The angels sang when the baby
   was born, *(x3)*
   and proclaimed him the Saviour Jesus.

3. The wise men saw where the baby
   was born, *(x3)*
   and they saw that his name was Jesus.

565 Cecil Frances Alexander (1818-1895) alt.

1. There is a green hill far away,
   outside a city wall,
   where the dear Lord was crucified
   who died to save us all.

2. We may not know, we cannot tell
   what pains he had to bear,
   but we believe it was for us
   he hung and suffered there.

3. He died that we might be forgiv'n,
   he died to make us good;
   that we might go at last to heav'n,
   saved by his precious blood.

4. There was no other good enough
   to pay the price of sin;
   he only could unlock the gate
   of heav'n, and let us in.

5. O, dearly, dearly has he loved,
   and we must love him too,
   and trust in his redeeming blood,
   and try his works to do.

566 Anne Quigley
© 1992 Anne Quigley. Published by GIA Publications Inc.

There is a longing in our hearts,
O Lord, for you to reveal yourself to us.
There is a longing in our hearts for love
we only find in you, our God.

1. For justice, for freedom, for mercy:
   hear our prayer.
   In sorrow, in grief:
   be near, hear our prayer, O God.

2. For wisdom, for courage, for comfort:
   hear our prayer.
   In weakness, in fear:
   be near, hear our prayer, O God.

3. For healing, for wholeness, for new life:
   hear our prayer.
   In sickness, in death:
   be near, hear our prayer, O God.

4. Lord save us, take pity,
   light in our darkness.
   We call you, we wait:
   be near, hear our prayer, O God.

567 Brian A. Wren (b. 1936)
© 1969, 1995 Stainer & Bell Ltd

1. There's a spirit in the air,
   telling Christians ev'rywhere:
   'Praise the love that Christ revealed,
   living, working, in our world!'

*2. Lose your shyness, find your tongue,
   tell the world what God has done:
   God in Christ has come to stay.
   Live tomorrow's life today!

3. When believers break the bread,
   when a hungry child is fed,
   praise the love that Christ revealed,
   living, working, in our world.

*4. Still the Spirit gives us light,
   seeing wrong and setting right:
   God in Christ has come to stay.
   Live tomorrow's life today!

5. When a stranger's not alone,
   where the homeless find a home,
   praise the love that Christ revealed,
   living, working, in our world.

6. May his Spirit fill our praise,
   guide our thoughts and change our
       ways.
   God in Christ has come to stay.
   Live tomorrow's life today!

7. There's a Spirit in the air,
   calling people ev'rywhere:
   praise the love that Christ revealed,
   living, working, in our world.

568 Susan Sayers (b. 1946)
© 2004 Kevin Mayhew Ltd

1. These vows of love are taken,
   as rings of love received,
   we witness here among us a mystery
   believed:

that in God's holy presence a
   marriage has begun
and these your precious children have
   now become as one.
For the things of earth and heaven
   draw closer as we pray,
and in heav'n the angels celebrate
   with us on earth today.

2. For all our many blessings we offer
   thanks and praise,
   for gifts of love and fellowship our
   thankful hearts we raise.
   God's hand has held us safely and
   brought us to this day,
   God has guided and protected and
   taught us on the way.
   For the love we learn on earth is the
   love we'll find in heav'n
   and the human love we celebrate is
   love that God has giv'n.

569 Nick Fawcett (b. 1957)
© 2004 Kevin Mayhew Ltd

1. They had lost the will to live,
   nothing left that they could give –
   spirits bruised and battered,
   seemed like nothing mattered,
   such the grief they wrestled with.

2. Life had brought them to their knees,
   pain like this could never ease –
   dreams seemed lost forever,
   wiped out altogether;
   hope was scattered on the breeze.

3. Then the empty tomb is found,
   life was all at once turned round –
   triumph from disaster,
   tears replacing laughter;
   feet still haven't touched the ground!

Continued overleaf

4. Now with joyful hearts they sing,
   praising God for ev'rything –
   joy just keeps on growing,
   each day overflowing;
   Christ is risen, Lord and King!

5. When you find life hard to bear,
   look to Christ in your despair –
   though your heart feels broken,
   life can be awoken;
   keep believing, if you dare.

3. No more we doubt thee,
   glorious Prince of Life!
   Life is naught without thee:
   aid us in our strife.
   Make us more than conqu'rors
   through thy deathless love.
   Bring us safe through Jordan
   to thy home above.

571 Ascribed to St Patrick (372-466), adapted by James Quinn (b. 1919)
© *1969 Geoffrey Chapman, an imprint of Continuum Int. Publishing Group*

1. This day God gives me strength of
      high heaven,
   sun and moon shining, flame in my
      hearth,
   flashing of lightning, wind in its
      swiftness,
   deeps of the ocean, firmness of earth.

2. This day God sends me strength to
      sustain me,
   might to uphold me, wisdom as guide.
   Your eyes are watchful, your ears are
      list'ning,
   your lips are speaking, friend at my
      side.

3. God's way is my way, God's shield is
      round me,
   God's host defends me, saving from ill.
   Angel of heaven, drive from me always
   all that would harm me, stand by me
      still.

4. Rising, I thank you, mighty and
      strong One,
   King of creation, giver of rest,
   firmly confessing Threeness of persons,
   Oneness of Godhead, Trinity blest.

570 *A toi la gloire* Edmond Louis Budry (1854-1932)
trans. Richard Birch Hoyle (1875-1939)
© *Copyright Control*

1. Thine be the glory,
   risen, conqu'ring Son,
   endless is the vict'ry
   thou o'er death hast won;
   angels in bright raiment
   rolled the stone away,
   kept the folded grave-clothes
   where thy body lay.

   Thine be the glory,
   risen, conqu'ring Son,
   endless is the vict'ry
   thou o'er death hast won.

2. Lo! Jesus meets us,
   risen from the tomb;
   lovingly he greets us,
   scatters fear and gloom.
   Let the Church with gladness
   hymns of triumph sing,
   for her Lord now liveth;
   death hath lost its sting.

vs. 1 and 2 Jimmy Owens (b. 1930),
vs. 3-5 Damian Lundy (1944-1997)
© 1978 Bud John Songs/EMI Christian Music
Publishing. Administered by Kevin Mayhew Ltd

572

1. This is my body, broken for you,
   bringing you wholeness, making you
   free.
   Take it and eat it, and when you do,
   do it in love for me.

2. This is my blood, poured out for you,
   bringing forgiveness, making you free.
   Take it and drink it, and when you do,
   do it in love for me.

3. Back to my Father soon I shall go.
   Do not forget me; then you will see
   I am still with you, and you will know
   you're very close to me.

4. Filled with my Spirit, how you will
   grow!
   You are my branches; I am the tree.
   If you are faithful, others will know
   you are alive in me.

5. Love one another; I have loved you,
   and I have shown you how to be free;
   serve one another, and when you do,
   do it in love for me.

James Quinn (b. 1919)
© Geoffrey Chapman, an imprint of Continuum
Int. Publishing Group

573

1. This is my will, my one command,
   that love should dwell among you all.
   This is my will that you should love
   as I have shown that I love you.

2. No greater love can be than this:
   to choose to die to save one's friends.
   You are my friends if you obey
   all I command that you should do.

3. I call you now no longer slaves;
   no slave knows all his master does.
   I call you friends, for all I hear
   my Father say, you hear from me.

4. You chose not me, but I chose you,
   that you should go and bear much
   fruit.
   I called you out that you in me
   should bear much fruit that will abide.

5. All that you ask my Father dear
   for my name's sake you shall receive.
   This is my will, my one command,
   that love should dwell in each, in all.

Les Garrett (b. 1944)
© 1967 Scripture in Song/Marantha!
Administered by CopyCare

574

1. This is the day, this is the day
   that the Lord has made,
   that the Lord has made;
   we will rejoice, we will rejoice
   and be glad in it, and be glad in it.
   This is the day that the Lord has made;
   we will rejoice and be glad in it.
   This is the day, this is the day
   that the Lord has made.

2. This is the day, this is the day
   when he rose again,
   when he rose again;
   we will rejoice, we will rejoice
   and be glad in it, and be glad in it.
   This is the day when he rose again;
   we will rejoice and be glad in it.
   This is the day, this is the day
   when he rose again.

3. This is the day, this is the day
   when the Spirit came,
   when the Spirit came;
   we will rejoice, we will rejoice
   and be glad in it, and be glad in it.
   This is the day when the Spirit came;
   we will rejoice and be glad in it.
   This is the day, this is the day
   when the Spirit came.

575 Edward Caswall (1814-1878)

1. This is the image of the queen
   who reigns in bliss above;
   of her who is the hope of men,
   whom men and angels love.
   Most holy Mary, at thy feet
   I bend a suppliant knee;
   in this thy own sweet month of May,
   do thou remember me.

2. The homage offered at the feet
   of Mary's image here
   to Mary's self at once ascends
   above the starry sphere.
   Most holy Mary, at thy feet
   I bend a suppliant knee;
   in all my joy, in all my pain,
   do thou remember me.

3. How fair soever be the form
   which here your eyes behold,
   its beauty is by Mary's self
   excelled a thousandfold.
   Most holy Mary, at thy feet
   I bend a suppliant knee;
   in my temptations, each and all,
   do thou remember me.

576 George Ratcliffe Woodward (1848-1934)

1. This joyful Eastertide,
   away with sin and sorrow.
   My love, the Crucified,
   hath sprung to life this morrow.

   Had Christ, that once was slain,
   ne'er burst his three-day prison,
   our faith had been in vain:
   but now hath Christ arisen,
   arisen, arisen, arisen.

2. My flesh in hope shall rest,
   and for a season slumber;
   till trump from east to west
   shall wake the dead in number.

3. Death's flood hath lost its chill,
   since Jesus crossed the river:
   lover of souls, from ill
   my passing soul deliver.

577 Traditional

This little light of mine,
I'm gonna let it shine.
This little light of mine,
I'm gonna let it shine.
This little light of mine,
I'm gonna let it shine,
let it shine, let it shine, let it shine.

1. The light that shines is the light of love,
   lights the darkness from above,
   it shines on me and it shines on you,
   and shows what the power of love
     can do.
   I'm gonna shine my light both far
     and near,
   I'm gonna shine my light both bright
     and clear.
   Where there's a dark corner in this
     land,
   I'm gonna let my little light shine.

2. On Monday he gave me the gift of
     love,
   Tuesday peace came from above.
   On Wednesday he told me to have
     more faith,
   on Thursday he gave me a little
     more grace.
   On Friday he told me to watch and
     pray,
   on Saturday he told me just what to
     say,
   on Sunday he gave me the pow'r
     divine
   to let my little light shine.

578 Damian Lundy (1944-1997),
based on Ephesians 3:14-21
© 1978 Kevin Mayhew Ltd

This, then, is my prayer,
falling on my knees before God
who is Father and source of all life.
May he in his love,
through the Spirit of Christ,
give you pow'r to grow strong
in your innermost self.

1. May Christ live in your hearts
   and may your lives, rooted in love,
   grow strong in him.

2. May you, with all the saints,
   grow in the pow'r to understand
   how he loves you.

3. O how can I explain
   in all its depth and all its scope
   his love, God's love!

   The refrain is not sung after verse 3.

4. For his love is so full,
   it is beyond all we can dream:
   his love, in Christ!

5. And so, glory to him
   working in us, who can do more
   than we can pray!

579 John Marriott (1780-1825) alt.

1. Thou, whose almighty word
   chaos and darkness heard,
   and took their flight;
   hear us, we humbly pray,
   and where the gospel day
   sheds not its glorious ray,
   let there be light.

2. Thou, who didst come to bring
   on thy redeeming wing,
   healing and sight,
   health to the sick in mind,
   sight to the inly blind,
   O now to humankind
   let there be light.

3. Spirit of truth and love,
   life-giving, holy Dove,
   speed forth thy flight;
   move on the water's face,
   bearing the lamp of grace,
   and in earth's darkest place
   let there be light.

4. Holy and blessèd Three,
   glorious Trinity,
   Wisdom, Love, Might;
   boundless as ocean's tide
   rolling in fullest pride,
   through the earth far and wide
   let there be light.

580 Daniel L. Schutte (b. 1947), based on Isaiah
© 1975 Daniel L. Schutte and New Dawn Music

Though the mountains may fall
and the hills turn to dust,
yet the love of the Lord will stand
as a shelter for all who will call on his
name.
Sing the praise and the glory of God.

1. Could the Lord ever leave you?
   Could the Lord forget his love?
   Though the mother forsake her child,
   he will not abandon you.

2. Should you turn and forsake him,
   he will gently call your name.
   Should you wander away from him,
   he will always take you back.

Continued overleaf

3. Go to him when you're weary;
   he will give you eagle's wings.
   You will run, you will never tire,
   for your God will be your strength.

   *Though the mountains may fall
   and the hills turn to dust,
   yet the love of the Lord will stand
   as a shelter for all who will call on his
      name.
   Sing the praise and the glory of God.*

4. As he swore to your fathers,
   when the flood destroyed the land,
   he will never forsake you;
   he will swear to you again.

581 Traditional South African
© *1990 Wild Goose Publications, Iona Community*

1. Thuma mina, thuma mina,
   thuma mina Somandla.

2. Send me, Jesus, send me, Jesus,
   send me, Jesus, send me, Lord.

3. Lead me, Jesus . . .

4. Fill me, Lord . . .

5. Thuma mina . . .

582 Edward Hayes Plumptre (1821-1891) alt.

1. Thy hand, O God, has guided
   thy flock, from age to age;
   the wondrous tale is written,
   full clear, on ev'ry page;
   our forebears owned thy goodness,
   and we their deeds record;
   and both of this bear witness:
   one Church, one Faith, one Lord.

2. Thy heralds brought glad tidings
   to greatest, as to least;
   they bade them rise, and hasten
   to share the great King's feast;
   and this was all their teaching,
   in ev'ry deed and word,
   to all alike proclaiming:
   one Church, one Faith, one Lord.

*3. Through many a day of darkness,
   through many a scene of strife,
   the faithful few fought bravely
   to guard the nation's life.
   Their gospel of redemption,
   sin pardoned, hope restored,
   was all in this enfolded:
   one Church, one Faith, one Lord.

*4. And we, shall we be faithless?
   Shall hearts fail, hands hang down?
   Shall we evade the conflict,
   and cast away our crown?
   Not so: in God's deep counsels
   some better thing is stored:
   we will maintain, unflinching,
   one Church, one Faith, one Lord.

5. Thy mercy will not fail us,
   nor leave thy work undone;
   with thy right hand to help us,
   the vict'ry shall be won;
   and then by all creation,
   thy name shall be adored.
   And this shall be their anthem:
   One Church, one Faith, one Lord.

583 Noel Richards (b. 1955)
© *1991 Thankyou Music.*
Administered by worshiptogether.com songs

1. To be in your presence,
   to sit at your feet,
   where your love surrounds me
   and makes me complete.

This is my desire, O Lord,
this is my desire,
this is my desire, O Lord,
this is my desire.

2. To rest in your presence,
not rushing away,
to cherish each moment,
here I would stay.

584 *Summi parentis filio* from *Catholicum Hymnologium* (1587), trans. Edward Caswall (1814-1878)

1. To Christ, the Prince of Peace,
and Son of God most high,
the Father of the world to come,
sing we with holy joy.

2. Deep in his heart for us
the wound of love he bore;
that love wherewith he still inflames
the hearts that him adore.

3. O Jesu, victim blest,
what else but love divine
could thee constrain to open thus
that sacred heart of thine?

4. O fount of endless life,
O spring of water clear,
O flame celestial, cleansing all
who unto thee draw near!

5. Hide us in thy dear heart,
for thither we do fly;
where seek thy grace through life,
in death
thine immortality.

6. Praise to the Father be,
and sole-begotten Son;
praise, holy Paraclete, to thee,
while endless ages run.

585 *Dem Herzen Jesu singe* by Aloys Schlör (1805-1852), trans. A. J. Christie (1817-1891) alt.

1. To Jesus' heart, all burning
with fervent love for men,
my heart with fondest yearning
shall raise its joyful strain.

While ages course along, blest be with
loudest song
the sacred heart of Jesus by ev'ry heart
and tongue,
the sacred heart of Jesus by ev'ry heart
and tongue.

2. O heart, for me on fire
with love that none can speak,
my yet untold desire
God gives me for thy sake.

3. Too true, I have forsaken
thy love for wilful sin;
yet now let me be taken
back by thy grace again.

4. As thou art meek and lowly,
and ever pure of heart,
so may my heart be wholly
of thine the counterpart.

5. When life away is flying,
and earth's false glare is done,
still, Sacred Heart, in dying,
I'll say I'm all thine own.

586 John B. Foley (b. 1939)
© 1975 John B. Foley, SJ and New Dawn Music

Turn to me, O turn and be saved,
says the Lord, for I am God;
there is no other, none beside me.
I call your name.

1. I am he that comforts you;
who are you to be afraid
of flesh that fades,
is made like the grass of the field,
soon to wither.

Continued overleaf

2. Listen to me, my people,
   give ear to me, my nation:
   a law will go forth from me,
   and my justice for a light
   to the people.

   Turn to me, O turn and be saved,
   says the Lord, for I am God;
   there is no other, none beside me.
   I call your name.

3. Lift up your eyes to the heavens,
   and look at the earth down below.
   The heavens will vanish like smoke,
   and the earth will wear out
   like a garment.

587 Taizé Community
© Ateliers et Presses de Taizé

Ubi caritas et amor.
Ubi caritas Deus ibi est.

Translation: Where there is charity
and love, there is God.

The following verses may be sung by a
Cantor:

1. Your love, O Jesus Christ,
   has gathered us together.

2. May your love, O Jesus Christ,
   be foremost in our lives.

3. Let us love one another
   as God has loved us.

4. Let us be one in love together
   in the one bread of Christ.

5. The love of God in Jesus Christ
   bears eternal joy.

6. The love of God in Jesus Christ
   will never have an end.

588 Bernadette Farrell (b. 1957), based on Scripture
© 1983 Bernadette Farrell.
Published by OCP Publications

Unless a grain of wheat shall fall
upon the ground and die,
it remains but a single grain with no life.

1. If we have died with him,
   then we shall live with him;
   if we hold firm we shall reign with him.

2. If anyone serves me,
   then they must follow me;
   wherever I am my servants will be.

3. Make your home in me
   as I make mine in you;
   those who remain in me bear
       much fruit.

4. If you remain in me
   and my word lives in you;
   then you will be my disciples.

5. Those who love me
   are loved by my Father;
   we shall be with them and dwell in
       them.

6. Peace I leave with you,
   my peace I give to you;
   peace which the world cannot give is
       my gift.

589 *Puer nobis nascitur* (15th century)
trans. Percy Dearmer (1867-1936) alt.

1. Unto us a boy is born!
   King of all creation;
   came he to a world forlorn,
   the Lord of ev'ry nation,
   the Lord of ev'ry nation.

2. Cradled in a stall was he,
   watched by cows and asses;
   but the very beasts could see
   that he the world surpasses,
   that he the world surpasses.

3. Then the fearful Herod cried,
   'Pow'r is mine in Jewry!'
   So the blameless children died
   the victims of his fury,
   the victims of his fury.

4. Now may Mary's Son, who came
   long ago to love us,
   lead us all with hearts aflame
   unto the joys above us,
   unto the joys above us.

5. Omega and Alpha he!
   Let the organ thunder,
   while the choir with peals of glee
   shall rend the air asunder,
   shall rend the air asunder.

590 M. F. C. Wilson (1884-1944), alt.
© Copyright Control

1. Upon thy table, Lord, we place
   these symbols of our work and thine,
   life's food won only by thy grace,
   who giv'st to all the bread and wine.

2. Within these simple things there lie
   the height and depth of human life,
   the thought of all, our tears and toil,
   our hopes and fears, our joy and
       strife.

3. Accept them, Lord; from thee they
       come;
   we take them humbly at thy hand.
   These gifts of thine for higher use
   we offer, as thou dost command.

591 Unknown

1. Vaster far than any ocean,
   deeper than the deepest sea
   is the love of Christ my Saviour,
   reaching through eternity.

2. But my sins are truly many,
   is God's grace so vast, so deep?
   Yes, there's grace o'er sin abounding,
   grace to pardon, grace to keep.

3. Can he quench my thirst for ever?
   Will his Spirit strength impart?
   Yes, he gives me living water,
   springing up within my heart.

592 Ascribed to Rabanus Maurus (776-856)

1. Veni, Creator Spiritus,
   mentes tuorum visita,
   imple superna gratia,
   quæ tu creasti pectora.

2. Qui diceris Paraclitus,
   Altissimi donum Dei,
   fons vivus, ignis, caritas,
   et spiritalis unctio.

3. Tu septiformis munere,
   digitus paternæ dexteræ,
   tu rite promissum Patris,
   sermone ditans guttura.

4. Accende lumen sensibus,
   infunde amorem cordibus,
   infirma nostri corporis
   virtute firmans perpeti.

5. Hostem repellas longius,
   pacemque dones protinus;
   ductore sic te prævio,
   vitemus omne noxium.

6. Per te sciamus da Patrem,
   noscamus atque Filium,
   teque utriusque Spiritum
   credamus omni tempore.

7. Deo Patri sit gloria,
   et Filio, qui, a mortuis
   surrexit, ac Paraclito,
   in sæculorum sæcula. Amen.

593

Stephen Langton (1160-1228)

Veni, lumen cordium.
Veni, Sancte Spiritus.
Veni, lumen cordium.
Veni, Sancte Spiritus.

Translation: Come, light of our hearts.
Come, Holy Spirit, come.

594

Sequence for Pentecost Sunday
Ascribed to Stephen Langton (1160-1228)

1. Veni, Sancte Spiritus,
   et emitte cælitus
   lucis tuæ radium.

2. Veni, pater pauperum,
   veni, dator munerum,
   veni, lumen cordium.

3. Consolator optime,
   dulcis hospes animæ,
   dulce refrigerium.

4. In labore requies,
   in æstu temperies,
   in fletu solatium.

5. O lux beatissima
   reple cordis intima
   tuorum fidelium.

6. Sine tuo numine,
   nihil est in homine,
   nihil est innoxium.

7. Lava quod est sordidum,
   riga quod est aridum,
   sana quod est saucium.

8. Flecte quod est rigidum,
   fove quod est frigidum,
   rege quod est devium.

9. Da tuis fidelibus,
   in te confidentibus,
   sacrum septenarium.

10. Da virtutis meritum,
    da salutis exitum,
    da perenne gaudium. Amen.
    Alleluia.

595

Traditional

Veni, veni, veni, Sancte Spiritus.

Translation: Come, Holy Spirit.

596

Stephen Langton (1160-1228)
trans. Edward Caswall (1814-1878)
alt. Christopher Walker (b. 1947)
© 1981, 1982 Christopher Walker.
Published by OCP Publications

Veni, Sancte Spiritus;
veni Sancte Spiritus;
veni, veni, Sancte Spiritus;
veni, Sancte Spiritus.

1. Holy Spirit, Lord of light,
   radiance give from celestial height.
   Come, thou Father of the poor,
   come now with treasures that endure:
   Light of all who live.

2. Thou, of all consolers, the best.
   Thou the soul's delightful guest;
     refreshing peace bestow.
   Thou, in toil, my comfort sweet;
   thou, coolness in the heat.
   Thou, my solace in time of woe.

3. Light immortal, light divine;
   fire of love, our hearts refine,
     our inmost being fill.
   Take thy grace away and nothing
     pure in us will stay,
   all our good is turned to ill.

4. Heal our wounds, our strength renew,
   on our dryness pour thy dew;
     wash guilt away,
   bend the stubborn heart, melt the
     frozen,
   warm the chill and guide the steps
     that go astray.

5. Sev'nfold gifts on us be pleased to pour,
who thee confess and thee adore;
bring us thy comfort when we die;
give us life with thee on high;
give us joys, give us joys that never end.

597 Attributed to Wipo of Burgundy (c. 1050)

1. Victimae Paschali laudes
immolent Christiani.

2. Agnus redemit oves:
Christus innocens Patri
reconciliavit peccatores.

3. Mors et vita duello conflixere mirando:
dux vitae mortuus, regnat vivus.

4. Dic nobis, Maria, quid vidisti in via?

5. Sepulchrum Christi viventis,
et gloriam vide resurgentis:

6. Angelicos testes, sudarium, et vestes.

7. Surrexit Christus spes mea:
praecedet suos in Galilaeam.

8. Scimus Christum surrexisse
a mortuis vere:
tu nobis, victor Rex, miserere.
Amen. Alleluia.

598 Taizé Community, based on Scripture
© Ateliers et Presses de Taizé

Wait for the Lord, whose day is near.
Wait for the Lord: keep watch, take heart!

1. Prepare the way for the Lord.
Make a straight path for God.
Prepare the way for the Lord.

2. Rejoice in the Lord always:
God is at hand.
Joy and gladness
for all who seek the Lord.

3. The glory of the Lord shall be revealed.
All the earth will see the Lord.

4. I waited for the Lord.
God heard my cry.

5. Our eyes are fixed on the Lord our
God.

6. Seek first the kingdom of God.
Seek and you shall find.

7. O Lord, show us your way.
Guide us in your truth.

599 Michael Forster (b. 1946)
© 1993 Kevin Mayhew Ltd

1. Waken, O sleeper, wake and rise,
salvation's day is near,
and let the dawn of light and truth
dispel the night of fear.

2. Let us prepare to face the day
of judgement and of grace,
to live as people of the light,
and perfect truth embrace.

3. Watch then and pray, we cannot know
the moment or the hour,
when Christ, unheralded, will come
with life-renewing power.

4. Then shall the nations gather round
as futile conflicts cease,
and re-invest the means of war
in justice, truth and peace.

600

Estelle White (b. 1925)
© 1976 Kevin Mayhew Ltd

Walk with me, O my Lord,
through the darkest night and brightest
day.
Be at my side, O Lord,
hold my hand and guide me on my way.

1. Sometimes the road seems long,
my energy is spent.
Then, Lord, I think of you
and I am given strength.

2. Stones often bar my path
and there are times I fall,
but you are always there
to help me when I call.

3. Just as you calmed the wind
and walked upon the sea,
conquer, my living Lord,
the storms that threaten me.

4. Help me to pierce the mists
that cloud my heart and mind,
so that I shall not fear
the steepest mountain-side.

5. As once you healed the lame
and gave sight to the blind,
help me when I'm downcast
to hold my head up high.

601 Unknown

1. We are gathering together unto him.
We are gathering together unto him.
Unto him shall the gath'ring of the
people be,
we are gathering together unto him.

2. We are offering together unto him . . .

3. We are singing together unto him . . .

4. We are praying together unto him . . .

602

Traditional South African. v. 1 trans. Anders
Nyberg (b. 1955); vs. 2 and 3 trans. Andrew Maries
© v. 1 1990 Wild Goose Publications, Iona
Community, vs. 2 and 3 Sovereign Music UK

1. We are marching in the light of God.
(x4)

We are marching,
Oo-ooh! We are marching in the
light of God. *(Repeat)*

2. We are living in the love of God . . .

3. We are moving in the pow'r of
God . . .

603

Bernadette Farrell (b. 1957)
© 2002 Bernadette Farrell.
Published by OCP Publications

During Advent

We are waiting to welcome Jesus.
We are waiting to welcome Jesus.
We are waiting to welcome Jesus:
only Jesus can set us free.

At Christmas

Alleluia! We welcome Jesus.
Aleluia! We welcome Jesus.
Alleluia! We welcome Jesus.
Alleluia! Alleluia!

1. For in Jesus we have a new world. *(x3)*
Come, Lord Jesus, and set your
people free.

2. For in Jesus we have a new hope. (x3)
Come, Lord Jesus, and set your
people free.

3. For in Jesus we have a new joy. *(x3)*
Come, Lord Jesus, and set your
people free.

4. For in Jesus we have a new peace. *(x3)*
Come, Lord Jesus, and set your
people free.

5. For in Jesus life is not ended. *(x3)*
   Come, Lord Jesus, and set your
   people free.

6. For in Jesus we are united. *(x3)*
   Come, Lord Jesus, and set your
   people free.

7. Come, Lord Jesus, and save your
   people. *(x3)*
   Come, Lord Jesus, and set your
   people free!

604 Carey Landry (b. 1944)
© 1976 Carey Landry and North American
Liturgy Resources

We behold the splendour of God
shining on the face of Jesus.
We behold the splendour of God
shining on the face of the Son.

1. And O how his beauty transforms us,
   the wonder of Presence abiding.
   Transparent hearts give reflection
   of Tabor's light within,
   of Tabor's light within.

2. Jesus, Lord of glory,
   Jesus belovèd Son.
   O how good to be with you;
   how good to share your light,
   how good to share your light.

605 The Iona Community
© 1989, 1996 WGRG/Iona Community

1. We cannot measure how you heal
   or answer ev'ry suff'rer's pray'r,
   yet we believe your grace responds
   where faith and doubt unite to care.
   Your hands, though bloodied on the
      cross,
   survive to hold and heal and warn,
   to carry all through death to life
   and cradle children yet unborn.

2. The pain that will not go away,
   the guilt that clings from things long
      past,
   the fear of what the future holds,
   are present as if meant to last.
   But present too is love which tends
   the hurt we never hoped to find,
   the private agonies inside,
   the memories that haunt the mind.

3. So some have come who need your
      help
   and some have come to make amends,
   as hands which shaped and saved the
      world
   are present in the touch of friends.
   Lord, let your Spirit meet us here
   to mend the body, mind and soul,
   to disentangle peace from pain
   and make your broken people whole.

606 Willard F. Jabusch (b. 1930)
© 1998 Willard F. Jabusch

1. We celebrate this festive day
   with pray'r and joyful song.
   Our Father's house is home to us,
   we know that we belong.

   The bread is broken, wine is poured,
   a feast to lift us up!
   Then thank the Lord who gives himself
   as food and saving cup!

2. The door is open, enter in,
   and take your place by right.
   For you've been chosen as his guest
   to share his love and light.

3. We come together as the twelve
   came to the Upper Room.
   Our host is Jesus Christ the Lord,
   now risen from the tomb.

Continued overleaf

4. Who travels needs both food and drink
   to help them on their way.
   Refreshed and strong we'll journey on
   and face another day.

   The bread is broken, wine is poured,
   a feast to lift us up!
   Then thank the Lord who gives himself
   as food and saving cup!

5. Who shares this meal receives the Lord
   who lives, though he was dead.
   So death can hold no terrors now
   for those who eat his bread.

607 David Haas (b.1957)
© 1989 GIA Publications, Inc.

We come to share our story,
we come to break the bread,
we come to know our
rising from the dead.

1. We come as your people,
   we come as your own,
   united with each other,
   love finds a home.

2. We are called to heal the broken,
   to be hope for the poor,
   we are called to feed the hungry
   at our door.

3. Bread of life and cup of promise,
   in this meal we all are one.
   In our dying and our rising
   may your kingdom come.

4. You will lead and we shall follow,
   you will be the breath of life;
   living water, we are thirsting
   for your light.

5. We will live and sing your praises,
   'Alleluia' is our song.
   May we live in love and peace
   our whole life long.

608 Susan Sayers (b. 1946)
© 2004 Kevin Mayhew Ltd

1. We gather here, we gather now,
   drawn by the love we know and share.
   We come to celebrate in our joy
   the union of this bridal pair.
   To them our hearts reach out with love,
   on them the light of heav'n above
   shines down in grace abundant and
       free
   to bless them both eternally.

2. And we who join to wish them well,
   offer them both our love and pray'r
   that they may walk in fullness of life
   the journey they have come to share.
   That they may know if storms come
       near
   that they have friends and fam'ly here
   for we commit ourselves to pray
   and love and cherish them each day.

609 Michael Forster (b. 1946)
based on the speech by Martin Luther King Jr.
© 1995 Kevin Mayhew Ltd

1. We have a dream:
   this nation will arise,
   and truly live
   according to its creed,
   that all are equal
   in their maker's eyes,
   and none shall suffer
   through another's greed.

2. We have a dream
   that one day we shall see
   a world of justice,
   truth and equity,
   where sons of slaves
   and daughters of the free
   will share the banquet
   of community.

*3. We have a dream
of deserts brought to flow'r
once made infertile
by oppression's heat,
when love and truth
shall end oppressive pow'r,
and streams of righteousness
and justice meet.

*4. We have a dream:
our children shall be free
from judgements based on
colour or on race;
free to become
whatever they may be,
of their own choosing
in the light of grace.

5. We have a dream
that truth will overcome
the fear and anger
of our present day;
that black and white
will share a common home,
and hand in hand
will walk the pilgrim way.

6. We have a dream:
each valley will be raised,
and ev'ry mountain,
ev'ry hill brought down;
then shall creation
echo perfect praise,
and share God's glory
under freedom's crown!

610 Edward Joseph Burns (b. 1938)
© The Revd. Edward J. Burns

1. We have a gospel to proclaim,
good news for all throughout the earth;
the gospel of a Saviour's name:
we sing his glory, tell his worth.

2. Tell of his birth at Bethlehem,
not in a royal house or hall,
but in a stable dark and dim,
the Word made flesh, a light for all.

3. Tell of his death at Calvary,
hated by those he came to save;
in lonely suff'ring on the cross:
for all he loved, his life he gave.

4. Tell of that glorious Easter morn,
empty the tomb, for he was free;
he broke the pow'r of death and hell
that we might share his victory.

5. Tell of his reign at God's right hand,
by all creation glorified.
He sends his Spirit on his Church
to live for him, the Lamb who died.

6. Now we rejoice to name him King:
Jesus is Lord of all the earth.
This gospel-message we proclaim:
we sing his glory, tell his worth.

611 Fred Kaan (b. 1929)
© 1968 Stainer & Bell Ltd

1. We have a King who rides a donkey,
(x3)
and his name is Jesus.

*Jesus the King is risen, (x3)
early in the morning.*

2. Trees are waving a royal welcome, *(x3)*
for the King called Jesus.

3. We have a King who cares for people,
(x3)
and his name is Jesus.

4. A loaf and a cup upon the table, *(x3)*
bread-and-wine is Jesus.

5. We have a King with a bowl and
towel, *(x3)*
Servant-King is Jesus.

Continued overleaf

6. What shall we do with our life this
    morning? *(x3)*
   Give it up in service!

   Jesus the King is risen, (x3)
   early in the morning.

612 John B. Foley (b. 1939), based on
2 Corinthians 4 and 1 Corinthians 1
© 1975 John B. Foley, SJ and New Dawn Music

We hold a treasure, not made of gold,
in earthen vessels, wealth untold;
one treasure only: the Lord, the Christ,
in earthen vessels.

1. Light has shone in our darkness;
   God has shone in our heart,
   with the light of the glory
   of Jesus, the Lord.

2. He has chosen the lowly,
   who are small in this world;
   in his weakness is glory,
   in Jesus the Lord.

613 Matthias Claudius (1740-1815), trans. Jane
Montgomery Campbell (1817-1878) alt.

1. We plough the fields and scatter
   the good seed on the land,
   but it is fed and watered
   by God's almighty hand:
   he sends the snow in winter,
   the warmth to swell the grain,
   the breezes and the sunshine,
   and soft, refreshing rain.

   All good gifts around us
   are sent from heav'n above;
   then thank the Lord, O thank the Lord,
   for all his love.

2. He only is the maker
   of all things near and far;
   he paints the wayside flower,
   he lights the ev'ning star;
   he fills the earth with beauty,
   by him the birds are fed;
   much more to us, his children,
   he gives our daily bread.

3. We thank thee then, O Father,
   for all things bright and good:
   the seed-time and the harvest,
   our life, our health, our food.
   Accept the gifts we offer
   for all thy love imparts,
   and, what thou most desirest,
   our humble, thankful hearts.

614 Paul Inwood (b. 1947)
© 1988 Paul Inwood. Administered in England
by the St Thomas More Group.
Published by OCP Publications

We shall draw water joyfully,
singing joyfully, singing joyfully;
we shall draw water joyfully
from the well-springs of salvation.

1. Truly God is our salvation;
   we trust, we shall not fear.
   For the Lord is our strength,
   the Lord is our song;
   he became our Saviour.

2. Give thanks, O give thanks to the Lord;
   give praise to his holy name!
   Make his mighty deeds known
   to all of the nations;
   proclaim his greatness.

3. Sing a psalm, sing a psalm to the Lord
   for he has done glorious deeds.
   Make known his works to all of the
       earth;
   people of Zion, sing for joy,
   for great in your midst, great in your
       midst
   is the Holy One of Israel.

615

June Boyce-Tilman (b. 1943)
© 1993 Stainer & Bell Ltd

1. We shall go out with hope of
resurrection;
we shall go out, from strength to
strength go on;
we shall go out and tell our stories
boldly:
tales of a love that will not let us go.

2. We'll sing our songs of wrongs that
can be righted;
we'll dream our dreams of hurts that
can be healed;
we'll weave a cloth of all the world
united
within the vision of a Christ who
makes us free.

3. We'll give a voice to those who have
not spoken;
we'll find the words for those whose
lips are sealed;
we'll make the tunes for those who
sing no longer,
vibrating love alive in ev'ry heart.

4. We'll share our joy with those who
are still weeping;
chant hymns of strength for hearts
that break in grief;
we'll leap and dance the resurrection
story
including all within the circles of our
love.

616

John Henry Hopkins (1820-1891), alt.

1. We three kings of Orient are;
bearing gifts we traverse afar;
field and fountain, moor and
mountain,
following yonder star.

O star of wonder, star of night,
star with royal beauty bright,
westward leading, still proceeding,
guide us to thy perfect light.

2. Born a King on Bethlehem plain,
gold I bring, to crown him again,
King for ever, ceasing never,
over us all to reign.

3. Frankincense to offer have I,
incense owns a Deity nigh,
pray'r and praising, gladly raising,
worship him, God most high.

4. Myrrh is mine, its bitter perfume
breathes a life of gathering gloom;
sorrowing, sighing, bleeding, dying,
sealed in the stone-cold tomb.

5. Glorious now behold him arise,
King and God and sacrifice;
alleluia, alleluia,
earth to heav'n replies.

617

Robert J. Stamp
© 1972 Dawn Treader Music/ EMI Christian
Music Publishing. Administered by Kevin
Mayhew Ltd

1. Welcome, all you noble saints of old,
as now before your very eyes unfold.
The wonders all so long ago foretold:

In Christ there is a table set for all.
In Christ there is a table set for all.

2. Elders, martyrs, all are falling down;
prophets, patriarchs are gath'ring
'round.
What angels long to see now we have
found.

3. Who is this who spreads the vict'ry
feast?
Who is this who makes our warring
cease?
Jesus, risen Saviour, Prince of Peace.

Continued overleaf

4. Beggars lame, and harlots also here;
   repentant publicans are drawing near;
   wayward sons come home without a
      fear.

   In Christ there is a table set for all.
   In Christ there is a table set for all.

5. Worship in the presence of the Lord
   with joyful songs, and hearts in one
      accord,
   and let our host at table be adored.

6. When at last this earth shall pass away,
   when Jesus and his bride are one to
      stay,
   the feast of love is just begun that day.

618 Spiritual, alt.

1. Were you there
   when they crucified my Lord? *(Repeat)*
   O, sometimes it causes me to
   tremble, tremble, tremble.
   Were you there
   when they crucified my Lord?

2. Were you there
   when they nailed him to a tree? . . .

3. Were you there
   when they pierced him in the side? . . .

4. Were you there
   when they laid him in the tomb? . . .

5. Were you there
   when he rose to glorious life? . . .

619 William Chatterton Dix (1837-1898) alt.

1. What child is this who, laid to rest,
   on Mary's lap is sleeping?
   Whom angels greet with anthems
      sweet,
   while shepherds watch are keeping?

This, this is Christ the King,
whom shepherds guard and angels sing:
come, greet the infant Lord,
the babe, the Son of Mary!

2. Why lies he in such mean estate,
   where ox and ass are feeding?
   Good Christians, fear: for sinners here
   the silent Word is pleading.
   Nails, spear, shall pierce him through,
   the cross be borne for me, for you;
   hail, hail the Word made flesh,
   the babe, the Son of Mary!

3. So bring him incense, gold and myrrh,
   come rich and poor, to own him.
   The King of kings salvation brings,
   let loving hearts enthrone him.
   Raise, raise the song on high,
   the Virgin sings her lullaby:
   joy, joy for Christ is born,
   the babe the Son of Mary!

620 Willard F. Jabusch (b. 1930)
© 1998 Willard F. Jabusch.
Published by OCP Publications

Whatsoever you do
to the least of my people,
that you do unto me.

1. When I was hungry you gave me to
      eat.
   When I was thirsty you gave me to
      drink.
   Now enter into the home of my Father.

2. When I was homeless you opened
      your door.
   When I was naked you gave me your
      coat.
   Now enter into the home of my Father.

3. When I was weary you helped me
   find rest.
   When I was anxious you calmed all
   my fears.
   Now enter into the home of my Father.

4. When in a prison you came to my cell.
   When on a sick-bed you cared for my
   needs.
   Now enter into the home of my Father.

5. When I was agèd you bothered to
   smile.
   When I was restless you listened and
   cared.
   Now enter into the home of my Father.

6. When I was laughed at you stood by
   my side.
   When I was happy you shared in my
   joy.
   Now enter into the home of my Father.

621 E. M. Barrett

1. When Christ our Lord to Andrew
   cried:
   'Come, thou and follow me,'
   the fisher left his net beside
   the Sea of Galilee.
   To teach the truth his Master taught,
   to tread the path he trod was all his will,
   and thus he brought
   un-numbered souls to God.

2. When Andrew's hour had come,
   and he
   was doomed like Christ to die,
   he kissed his cross exultingly,
   and this his loving cry:
   'O noble cross! O precious wood!
   I long have yearned for thee;
   uplift me to my only good
   who died on thee for me.'

3. Saint Andrew, now in bliss above,
   thy fervent prayers renew
   that Scotland yet again may love
   the faith, entire and true;
   that I the cross allotted me
   may bear with patient love!
   'Twill lift me, as it lifted thee,
   to reign with Christ above.

622 Nick Fawcett (b. 1957)
© 2004 Kevin Mayhew Ltd

1. When days are touched with sadness
   and nights are filled with pain;
   when ev'ry waking moment
   your faith is under strain;
   when burdens weigh upon you
   that seem too hard to bear;
   remember then the promise
   of Jesus, 'I'll be there.'

2. When all around forsake you
   and you feel left alone;
   when those you thought most loyal
   have taken wings and flown;
   when dreams lie bruised and broken
   and no one sheds a tear;
   remember then the promise
   of Jesus, 'I am here.'

3. When life is dark with shadows,
   its sparkle long since gone;
   when winter's chill encroaches
   where summer sun once shone;
   when days that gleamed with promise
   are tarnished now with care;
   remember then the promise
   of Jesus, 'I'll be there.'

Continued overleaf

4. When ev'rything you hoped for
lies trampled in the dust;
when there seems nothing solid
in which to put your trust;
when worry holds you captive –
a slave to ev'ry fear;
remember then the promise
of Jesus, 'I am here.'

623 Sydney Carter (1915-2004)
© 1965 Stainer & Bell Ltd

1. When I needed a neighbour,
were you there, were you there?
When I needed a neighbour,
were you there?

*And the creed and the colour
and the name won't matter,
were you there?*

2. I was hungry and thirsty,
were you there, were you there?
I was hungry and thirsty,
were you there?

3. I was cold, I was naked,
were you there, were you there?
I was cold, I was naked,
were you there?

4. When I needed a shelter,
were you there, were you there?
When I needed a shelter,
were you there?

5. When I needed a healer,
were you there, were you there?
When I needed a healer,
were you there?

6. Wherever you travel,
I'll be there, I'll be there,
wherever you travel,
I'll be there.

624 Isaac Watts (1674-1748)

1. When I survey the wondrous cross
on which the Prince of Glory died,
my richest gain I count but loss,
and pour contempt on all my pride.

2. Forbid it, Lord, that I should boast,
save in the death of Christ, my God:
all the vain things that charm me most,
I sacrifice them to his blood.

3. See from his head, his hands, his feet,
sorrow and love flow mingling down:
did e'er such love and sorrow meet,
or thorns compose so rich a crown?

4. Were the whole realm of nature mine,
that were an off'ring far too small;
love so amazing, so divine,
demands my soul, my life, my all.

625 The Benedictines of Stanbrook
© 1974, 1995 Stanbrook Abbey

1. When Jesus comes to be baptised,
he leaves the hidden years behind,
the years of safety and of peace,
to bear the sins of all mankind.

2. The Spirit of the Lord comes down,
anoints the Christ to suffering,
to preach the word, to free the bound,
and to the mourner, comfort bring.

3. He will not quench the dying flame,
and what is bruised he will not break,
and heal the wound injustice dealt,
and out of death his triumph make.

4. Our everlasting Father, praise,
with Christ, his well-belovèd Son,
who with the Spirit reigns serene,
untroubled Trinity in One.

626
Michael Perry (1942-1997)
© *Mrs M Perry/Jubilate Hymns*

1. When the angel came to Mary,
   he said 'Be at peace,
   for the Lord God shall be with you,
   his love will not cease.'

   And Mary bore Jesus Christ,
   our Saviour for to be:
   and the first and the last
   and the greatest is he, is he, is he;
   and the first and the last and the
   greatest is he.

2. When the angel came to Mary,
   he said 'Do not fear,
   for his pow'r shall be upon you,
   a child you will bear.'

3. When the angel came to Mary,
   he said 'Hear his name,
   for his title shall be Jesus
   of kingly acclaim.'

4. When the angel came to Mary,
   she said 'Be it so:
   for the Lord God is my master,
   his will I must do.'

627
Unknown

1. When the Spirit of the Lord
   is within my heart
   I will sing as David sang. *(Repeat)*
   I will sing, I will sing,
   I will sing as David sang. *(Repeat)*

2. When the Spirit of the Lord
   is within my heart
   I will clap as David clapped . . .

3. When the Spirit of the Lord
   is within my heart
   I will dance as David danced . . .

4. When the Spirit of the Lord
   is within my heart
   I will praise as David praised . . .

628
John Glynn (b. 1948)
© *1976 Kevin Mayhew Ltd*

Where are you bound, Mary, Mary,
where are you bound, Mother of God?

1. Beauty is a dove
   sitting on a sunlit bough,
   beauty is a prayer
   without the need of words.
   Words are more than sounds
   falling off an empty tongue:
   let it be according to his word.

2. Mary heard the word
   spoken in her inmost heart.
   Mary bore the Word
   and held him in her arms.
   Sorrow she has known,
   seeing him upon the cross;
   greater joy to see him rise again.

3. Where are we all bound,
   carrying the Word of God?
   Time and place are ours
   to make his glory known.
   Mary bore him first,
   we will tell the whole wide world:
   Let it be according to his word.

629
Michael Forster (b. 1946)
© *1996 Kevin Mayhew Ltd*

1. Where the love of Christ unites us,
   there God is found.
   Where we meet as love invites us,
   there God is found.
   Let us come with jubilation
   to the God of our salvation;
   love enlivens all creation:
   there God is found.

Continued overleaf

2. Where we meet without division,
   there God is found,
   free from anger and derision,
   there God is found.
   Let all bitter feuds be ended,
   strife resolved and foes befriended,
   pride and fear by love transcended:
   there God is found.

3. Where the blessèd live for ever,
   there God is found;
   bonds of love no pain can sever,
   there God is found.
   Christ in glory, we implore you,
   let us with the saints adore you,
   love resplendent flows before you;
   there God is found.

630 Michael Forster (b. 1946), based on *Ubi Caritas*
     © 1998 Kevin Mayhew Ltd

Where true love is found with charity,
God is present there.

1. Christ's own love has called us,
   gathered us together,
   let us come with songs of hope and
   jubilation,
   worship and adore him, God of our
   salvation,
   loving one another, loving one
   another.

2. As his holy people, gathering together,
   let us be united, strife and discord
   ending.
   Christ, our God, among us, ev'ry fear
   transcending,
   known in one another, known in one
   another.

3. With the saints and martyrs, one in
   faith together,
   let us see your glory, Christ our great
   salvation,
   sharing in the great eternal celebration,
   there with one another, there with
   one another.

631 Nahum Tate (1652-1715)

1. While shepherds watched their flocks
   by night,
   all seated on the ground,
   the angel of the Lord came down,
   and glory shone around.

2. 'Fear not,' said he, (for mighty dread
   had seized their troubled mind)
   'glad tidings of great joy I bring
   to you and all mankind.

3. 'To you in David's town this day
   is born of David's line
   a Saviour, who is Christ the Lord;
   and this shall be the sign:

4. 'The heav'nly babe you there shall find
   to human view displayed,
   all meanly wrapped in swathing bands,
   and in a manger laid.'

5. Thus spake the seraph, and forthwith
   appeared a shining throng
   of angels praising God, who thus
   addressed their joyful song:

6. 'All glory be to God on high,
   and on the earth be peace,
   goodwill henceforth from heav'n to all
   begin and never cease.'

632

John L. Bell (b. 1949) & Graham Maule (b. 1958)
© 1987 WGRG, Iona Community

1. Will you come and follow me
   if I but call your name?
   Will you go where you don't know,
   and never be the same?
   Will you let my love be shown,
   will you let my name be known,
   will you let my life be grown
   in you, and you in me?

2. Will you leave yourself behind
   if I but call your name?
   Will you care for cruel and kind,
   and never be the same?
   Will you risk the hostile stare
   should your life attract or scare,
   will you let me answer prayer
   in you, and you in me?

3. Will you let the blinded see
   if I but call your name?
   Will you set the pris'ners free,
   and never be the same?
   Will you kiss the leper clean
   and do such as this unseen,
   and admit to what I mean
   in you, and you in me?

4. Will you love the 'you' you hide
   if I but call your name?
   Will you quell the fear inside,
   and never be the same?
   Will you use the faith you've found
   to reshape the world around
   through my sight and touch and sound
   in you, and you in me?

5. Lord, your summons echoes true
   when you but call my name.
   Let me turn and follow you,
   and never be the same.
   In your company I'll go
   where your love and footsteps show.
   Thus I'll move and live and grow
   in you, and you in me.

633

Taizé Community
© Ateliers et Presses de Taizé

Within our darkest night,
you kindle the fire that never dies away,
that never dies away. *(Repeat)*

634

Michael Forster (b. 1946)
© 1995 Kevin Mayhew Ltd

1. Within this place we gather,
   as people of the Lord;
   a holy, priestly nation,
   by saving grace restored.
   From slav'ry still he bears us
   aloft, on eagles' wings,
   and, in our faithful living,
   a song of freedom sings.

2. Our life is firmly grounded
   in Christ, the living Vine,
   who beautifies creation
   with freedom's heady wine.
   So life in all its fullness
   must be our common aim,
   until a free creation
   sings praises to God's name.

3. A pure and holy temple,
   built up of living stone;
   a precious, royal priesthood
   the Father calls his own;
   from dark to light he calls us,
   his triumphs to proclaim,
   'til all his free creation
   shall glory in his name!

635

Virginia Vissing
© 1974, 1998 Sisters of St Mary of Namur

1. Word made flesh, Son of God.

   Come, Lord Jesus, come again. (x2)

2. Lord and Saviour, Son of God.

3. Prince of Peace, Son of God.

Continued overleaf

4. Alleluia, Son of God.

Come, Lord Jesus, come again. (x2)

5. Bread of Life, Son of God.

6. Light of the World, Son of God.

7. Jesus Christ, Son of God.

636 Daniel L. Schutte (b. 1947), based on Psalm 138
© 1971, 1974 Daniel L. Schutte.
Administered by New Dawn Music

Yahweh, I know you are near,
standing always at my side.
You guard me from the foe
and you lead me in ways everlasting.

1. Lord, you have searched my heart,
   and you know when I sit and when
   I stand,
   for your hand is upon me,
   protecting me from death,
   keeping me from harm.

2. Where can I run from your love?
   If I climb to the heavens you are there.
   If I fly to the sunrise
   or sail beyond the sea,
   still I'd find you there.

3. You know my heart and its ways,
   you who formed me before I was born,
   in the secret of darkness,
   before I saw the sun
   in my mother's womb.

4. Marv'llous to me are your works;
   how profound are your thoughts,
   my Lord!
   Even if I could count them,
   they number as the stars,
   you would still be there.

637 *Chorus novae Jerusalem* St Fulbert of Chartres
(c. 1028), trans. Robert Campbell (1814-1868)

1. Ye choirs of new Jerusalem,
   your sweetest notes employ,
   the Paschal victory to hymn
   in strains of holy joy.

*2. How Judah's Lion burst his chains,
   and crushed the serpent's head;
   and brought with him,
       from death's domain,
   the long-imprisoned dead.

*3. From hell's devouring jaws the prey
   alone our leader bore;
   his ransomed hosts pursue their way
   where he hath gone before.

4. Triumphant in his glory now
   his sceptre ruleth all;
   earth, heav'n and hell before him bow
   and at his footstool fall.

5. While joyful thus his praise we sing,
   his mercy we implore,
   into his palace bright to bring,
   and keep us evermore.

6. All glory to the Father be,
   all glory to the Son,
   all glory, Holy Ghost, to thee,
   while endless ages run.

638 Jean Tisserand (d. 1494),
trans. Edward Caswall (1814-1879)

Alleluia, alleluia, alleluia.

1. Ye sons and daughters of the Lord,
   the King of glory, King adored,
   this day himself from death restored.
   Alleluia.

2. All in the early morning grey
   went holy women on their way
   to see the tomb where Jesus lay.
   Alleluia.

3. Then straightway one in white they see,
who saith, 'Ye seek the Lord; but he
is ris'n, and gone to Galilee.'
Alleluia.

4. That self-same night, while out of fear
the doors were shut, their Lord most
dear
to his apostles did appear.
Alleluia.

5. But Thomas, when of this he heard,
was doubtful of his brethren's word;
wherefore again there comes the Lord.
Alleluia.

6. 'Thomas, behold my side,' saith he;
'my hands, my feet, my body see,
and doubt not, but believe in me.'
Alleluia.

7. When Thomas saw that wounded side,
the truth no longer he denied;
'Thou art my Lord and God!' he cried.
Alleluia.

8. Now let us praise the Lord most high,
and strive his name to magnify
on this great day, through earth and
sky.
Alleluia.

A Cantor may sing the first and third lines
of each verse with everyone joining in the
lines in italics.

639 Marty Haugen (b. 1950)
© 1986 GIA Publications Inc.

1. You are salt for the earth, O people:
salt for the kingdom of God!
Share the flavour of life, O people:
life in the kingdom of God!

Bring forth the kingdom of mercy,
bring forth the kingdom of peace;
bring forth the kingdom of justice,
bring forth the city of God!

2. You are a light on the hill, O people:
light for the city of God!
Shine so holy and bright, O people:
shine for the kingdom of God!

3. You are a seed of the Word, O people:
bring forth the kingdom of God!
Seeds of mercy and seeds of justice,
grow in the kingdom of God!

4. We are a blest and a pilgrim people:
bound for the kingdom of God!
Love our journey and love our
homeland:
love is the kingdom of God!

640 Martin E. Leckebusch (b. 1962)
© 2000 Kevin Mayhew Ltd

1. You are the Bread of Life
which feeds the hungry soul;
your body, broken on the cross,
was torn to make us whole.
Your flesh is food so real,
your blood is drink indeed:
Lord Jesus, in your life we find
the nourishment we need.

2. You are the Prince of Peace,
the one who offers rest
for troubled, weary, aching hearts
by burdens long oppressed.
You will not weigh us down,
our load you humbly bear:
how glad we are to learn your ways,
your easy yoke to share.

Continued overleaf

3. You are the only Way,
   the Truth whom we believe,
   and those who place their trust in you
   eternal life receive.
   You make the Father known,
   his glory lights your face:
   his splendour you reveal to us
   in mercy, truth and grace.

641 Margaret Rizza (b. 1929)
© 1998 Kevin Mayhew Ltd

You are the centre, you are my life,
you are the centre, O Lord, of my life.
Come, Lord, and heal me, Lord of
   my life,
come, Lord, and teach me, Lord, of
   my life.
You are the centre, Lord, of my life.
Give me your Spirit and teach me
   your ways,
give me your peace, Lord, and set me
   free.*
You are the centre, Lord, of my life.

Second time:
You are the centre, you are my life,
you are the centre, O Lord, of my life.

642 Bernadette Farrell (b. 1957)
© 1995, 1999 Bernadette Farrell.
Published by OCP Publications

You have called us by our name.
We belong to you.
You have called us by our name
and we are yours.

1. You have chosen us to be
   members of your family.
   In your love you have created
   us to live in unity.

2. You will lead us to your light,
   walk before us through the night.
   You will guide us on our journey.
   You will keep our vision bright.

3. You will hold us when we fall,
   give new strength to hear your call.
   You will never be beyond us,
   for your love is all in all.

4. You will nourish, you will lead,
   giving ev'ry gift we need,
   for your reign will be established
   from the smallest of all seeds.

5. Through our sharing here today
   may our faith and life convey
   Christ our light and Christ our vision,
   Christ our purpose, Christ our way.

643 David Adam (b. 1936)
© SPCK

1. You, Lord, are in this place.
   Your presence fills it;
   your presence is peace.

2. You, Lord, are in my heart . . .

3. You, Lord, are in my mind . . .

4. You, Lord, are in my life . . .

644 Robert Dufford (b. 1943), based on Isaiah
43:2-4; Luke 6:20. © 1975, 1978 Robert J.
Dufford, SJ and New Dawn Music

1. You shall cross the barren desert,
      but you shall not die of thirst.
   You shall wander far in safety
      though you do not know the way.
   You shall speak your words in foreign
      lands and they will understand.
   You shall see the face of God and live.

Be not afraid.
I go before you always.
Come, follow me, and I will give you rest.

2. If you pass through raging waters in
   the sea, you shall not drown.
   If you walk amid the burning flames,
   you shall not be harmed.
   If you stand before the pow'r of hell
   and death is at your side,
   know that I am with you through it all.

3. Blessèd are the poor, for the kingdom
   shall be theirs.
   Blest are you that weep and mourn,
   for one day you shall laugh.
   And if wicked men insult and hate you
   all because of me,
   blessèd, blessèd are you!

645 Steffi Geiser Rubin and Stuart Dauermann
(b. 1944). © 1975 Lillenas Publishing Co.
Administered by CopyCare

You shall go out with joy
and be led forth with peace,
and the mountains and the hills
shall break forth before you.
There'll be shouts of joy
and the trees of the field shall clap,
shall clap their hands.

And the trees of the field
shall clap their hands,
and the trees of the field
shall clap their hands,
and the trees of the field
shall clap their hands,
and you'll go out with joy.

646 Martin E. Leckebusch (b. 1962)
© 1999 Kevin Mayhew Ltd

1. You stood there on the shoreline
   and waited in the dawn
   to share with your disciples
   the newness of the morn;
   be with us now, Lord Jesus,

and make your presence known:
in resurrection power
declare today your own.

2. When hours of tiring labour
   had brought them scant reward,
   in your immense provision
   they recognised their Lord;
   when drudgery seems endless,
   demeaning all our skill,
   let this be our contentment:
   to know and do your will.

3. On bread and fish they feasted
   around a charcoal fire:
   that resurrection breakfast
   was all they could desire!
   Like them, may we discover
   the joy which never ends
   when you, the King of glory,
   count us among your friends.

4. Where Simon Peter languished
   in guilt and burning shame,
   you spoke of restoration,
   and not of endless blame;
   where sin and failure haunt us,
   remind us what is true:
   that we are now forgiven
   and called to follow you.

647 Michael Joncas (b. 1951), based on Psalm 90
© 1979, 1991 Michael Joncas and New Dawn
Music

1. You who dwell in the shelter of the
   Lord,
   who abide in his shadow for life,
   say to the Lord: 'My refuge,
   my rock in whom I trust!'

And he will raise you up on eagle's wings,
bear you on the breath of dawn,
make you to shine like the sun,
and hold you in the palm of his hand.

Continued overleaf

2. The snare of the fowler will never
     capture you,
   and famine will bring you no fear.
   Under his wings your refuge,
   his faithfulness your shield.

   And he will raise you up on eagle's wings,
   bear you on the breath of dawn,
   make you to shine like the sun,
   and hold you in the palm of his hand.

3. You need not fear the terror of the
     night,
   nor the arrow that flies by day;
   though thousands fall about you,
   near you it shall not come.

4. For to his angels he's given a command
   to guard you in all of your ways;
   upon their hands they will bear you up,
   lest you dash your foot against a stone.

648 Mike Anderson (b. 1956)

648 Mike Anderson (b. 1956)
© 1999 Kevin Mayhew Ltd

Your love's greater (greater),
greater than the greatest mountain,
your love's deeper (deeper),
deeper than the deepest sea;
a love that never dies,
a love that reaches deep inside,
more wondrous than all the universe.

1. You made the heavens,
   the earth and sea;
   your pow'r is awesome,
   and you still love me.

2. Your ways are righteous,
   your laws are just,
   love is your promise,
   and in you I trust.

3. Your love is healing,
   your love endures;
   my life is changed, Lord,
   now I know I'm yours.

Music for the Mass

649 A New People's Mass (Murray)
From the Roman Missal

Penitential Rite

Lord, have mercy.
Lord, have mercy.
Christ, have mercy.
Christ, have mercy.
Lord, have mercy.
Lord, have mercy.

Gloria

Glory to God in the highest,
and peace to his people on earth.
Lord God, heavenly King,
almighty God and Father,
we worship you,
we give you thanks,
we praise you for your glory.
Lord Jesus Christ,
only Son of the Father,
Lord God, Lamb of God,
you take away the sins of the world,
have mercy on us;
you are seated at the right hand of
the Father,
receive our prayer.
For you alone are the Holy One,
you alone are the Lord,
you alone are the Most High,
Jesus Christ, with the Holy Spirit,
in the glory of God the Father.
Amen.

Sanctus

Holy, holy, holy Lord,
God of power and might,
heaven and earth are full of your glory.
Hosanna in the highest.
Blessèd is he who comes in the name
of the Lord.
Hosanna in the highest.

Memorial Acclamation

Christ has died,
Christ is risen,
Christ will come again.

Great Amen

Amen.

Agnus Dei

Lamb of God, you take away the sins
of the world: have mercy on us.
(Repeat)
Lamb of God, you take away the sins
of the world: grant us peace.

650 Mass of the Bread of Life (Rizza)
From the Roman Missal

Penitential Rite

Lord, have mercy.
Lord, have mercy.
Lord, have mercy.
Lord, have mercy.

Christ, have mercy.
Christ, have mercy.
Christ, have mercy.
Christ, have mercy.

Lord, have mercy.
Lord, have mercy.
Lord, have mercy.
Lord, have mercy.

Gloria

Glory, glory to God,
glory to God in the highest;
peace to his people on earth,
peace to his people on earth.
Lord God, heavenly King,
almighty God and Father,
we worship you,
we give you thanks,
we praise you for your glory.

Continued overleaf

Glory, glory to God,
glory to God in the highest;
peace to his people on earth,
peace to his people on earth.

Lord Jesus Christ,
only Son of the Father,
Lord God, Lamb of God,
you take away the sin of the world:
have mercy on us;
you are seated at the right hand of
  the Father:
receive our prayer,
receive our prayer,
receive our prayer.
You alone are the Holy One,
you alone are the Lord,
you alone are the Lord,
you alone are the Most High.
Jesus Christ, with the Holy Spirit,
in the glory, the glory,
the glory of God the Father.
Amen.

Sanctus

Holy, holy, holy Lord,
God of pow'r and God of might,
heaven and earth are full of your glory.
Hosanna in the highest;
hosanna, hosanna,
hosanna in the highest;
hosanna, hosanna,
hosanna in the highest.

Blessèd is he, blessèd is he,
blessèd is he who comes in the name,
he who comes in the name of the Lord.
Hosanna in the highest,
hosanna, hosanna,
hosanna in the highest;
hosanna, hosanna,
hosanna in the highest.

Memorial Acclamation

Christ has died,
Christ is risen,
Christ will come again.
Christ has died,
Christ is risen,
Christ will come again.
Hosanna, hosanna,
hosanna in the highest;
hosanna, hosanna,
hosanna in the highest.

Great Amen

Amen.

Agnus Dei

Jesus, Lamb of God,
Jesus, Lamb of God,
you take away the sins of the world:
have mercy on us.

Jesus, Lamb of God,
Jesus, Lamb of God,
you take away the sins of the world:
have mercy on us.

Jesus, Lamb of God,
Jesus, Lamb of God,
you take away the sins of the world:
grant us your peace,
grant us your peace.

651 Missa de Angelis (Plainsong)
From the Roman Missal

Penitential Rite

Kyrie, eleison.
Christe, eleison.
Kyrie, eleison.
Kyrie, eleison.

Gloria

Gloria in excelsis Deo,
et in terra pax hominibus
bonae voluntatis.
Laudamus te,
benedicimus te,
adoramus te,
glorificamus te,
gratias agimus tibi propter magnam
  gloriam tuam,
Domine Deus, Rex caelestis,
Deus Pater omnipotens.
Domine Fili unigenite, Jesu Christe.
Domine Deus, Agnus Dei,
Filius Patris,
qui tollis peccata mundi,
miserere nobis,
qui tollis peccata mundi,
suscipe deprecationem nostram.
Qui sedes ad dexteram Patris,
miserere nobis.
Quoniam tu solus sanctus,
tu solus Dominus,
tu solus Altissimus,
Jesu Christe, cum Sancto Spiritu,
in gloria Dei Patris. Amen.

Sanctus

Sanctus, sanctus, sanctus
Dominus Deus sabaoth.
Pleni sunt caeli et terra gloria tua.
Hosanna in excelsis.
Benedictus qui venit in nomine
  Domini.
Hosanna in excelsis.

Agnus Dei

Agnus Dei, qui tollis peccata mundi:
miserere nobis.
Agnus Dei, qui tollis peccata mundi:
miserere nobis.
Agnus Dei, qui tollis peccata mundi:
dona nobis pacem.

Dismissal

Ite, missa est.
Deo gratias.

652 The 'American' Eucharist

Adapted from the Liturgy by Sandra Joan
Billington (b. 1946) and Robert B. Kelly (b. 1948)
© McCrimmon Publishing Co. Ltd and
© 1983, 1999 Kevin Mayhew Ltd

Penitential Rite

1. Lord, have mercy; Lord, have mercy;
   on your servants, Lord, have mercy.
   God almighty, just and faithful,
   Lord, have mercy; Lord, have mercy.

2. Christ, have mercy; Christ,
     have mercy;
   gift from heaven, Christ, have mercy.
   Light of truth and light of justice,
   Christ, have mercy; Christ, have mercy.

3. Lord, have mercy; Lord, have mercy;
   on your servants, Lord, have mercy.
   God almighty, just and faithful,
   Lord, have mercy; Lord, have mercy.

Gospel Acclamation

Alleluia, alleluia,
let us praise Christ, our Lord Jesus.
Alleluia, let us praise him,
now among us in his Gospel.

Sanctus

1. Holy, holy, holy, holy,
   Lord of hosts. You fill with glory
   all the earth and all the heavens.
   Sing hosanna, sing hosanna.

2. Blest and holy, blest and holy,
   he who comes now in the Lord's name.
   In the highest sing hosanna,
   in the highest sing hosanna.

Continued overleaf

Memorial Acclamation

When we eat this bread you give us,
and we drink this cup you left us,
we proclaim your death, Lord Jesus,
till you come again in glory.

Agnus Dei

1. Jesus, Lamb of God, have mercy,
bearer of our sins, have mercy.
Jesus, Lamb of God, have mercy,
bearer of our sins, have mercy.

2. Saviour of the world, Lord Jesus,
may your peace be always with us.
Saviour of the world, Lord Jesus,
may your peace be always with us.

653
The 'Hopwood Mass'
Adapted from the Liturgy by Terence Collins
© 1978 Kevin Mayhew Ltd

Penitential Rite

1. Father of all, O Lord, have mercy. *(x 2)*
Father of all, have mercy on us.
Father of all, be ever near us.

2. Saviour of all, O Christ, have mercy.
(x 2)
Saviour of all, have mercy on us.
Saviour of all, be ever near us.

3. Spirit of all, O Lord, have mercy. *(x 2)*
Spirit of all, have mercy on us.
Spirit of all, be ever near us.

Sanctus

1. Holy are you, Lord of creation!
Holy are you, Lord God of angels!
Holy are you, God of all people!
Heaven and earth proclaim your glory.

2. Glory to you! Your name is holy.
Blessèd is he who comes in your name!
Glory to him! We sing his praises.
Heaven and earth proclaim your glory.

Agnus Dei

O Lamb of God, you bore our sinning.
O Lamb of God, you bore our dying.
O Lamb of God, have mercy on us.
O Lamb of God, your peace be with us.

654
The 'Israeli' Mass
Adapted from the Liturgy by Anthony Hamson
© McCrimmon Publishing Co. Ltd

Penitential Rite

1. Lord, have mercy.
Lord, have mercy.
Lord, have mercy on us all,
Lord, have mercy.
Lord, have mercy.
Lord, have mercy on us all.

2. Christ, have mercy . . .

3. Lord, have mercy . . .

Sanctus

1. Holy, holy, holy, holy,
Lord of pow'r, Lord of might.
Heav'n and earth are filled with glory.
Sing hosanna evermore.

2. Blest and holy, blest and holy,
he who comes from God on high.
Raise your voices, sing his glory,
praise his name for evermore.

Agnus Dei

1. Lamb of God, you take away the sin,
the sin of all the world:
give us mercy, give us mercy,
give us mercy, Lamb of God.

2. Lamb of God, you take away the sin,
the sin of all the world:
give us mercy, give us mercy,
give us mercy, Lamb of God.

3. Lamb of God, you take away the sin,
   the sin of all the world:
   grant us peace, Lord; grant us peace,
   Lord;
   grant us peace, Lamb of God.

655 The New Israeli Mass
Adapted from the Liturgy by Kevin Mayhew
(b. 1942)
© 1984 Kevin Mayhew Ltd

Penitential Rite

1. Lord, have mercy on us all.
   Lord, have mercy on us all.
   Lord, have mercy, Lord, have mercy,
   Lord, have mercy on us all.

2. Christ, have mercy on us all.
   Christ, have mercy on us all.
   Christ, have mercy, Christ, have
   mercy,
   Christ, have mercy on us all.

3. Lord, have mercy on us all.
   Lord, have mercy on us all.
   Lord, have mercy, Lord, have mercy,
   Lord, have mercy on us all.

Holy, Holy

1. Holy, holy, holy Lord,
   God of pow'r and God of might,
   all the earth and all the heavens
   sing hosanna to your name.

2. Blessèd is the one who comes,
   comes in peace from God on high.
   Sing his praises, sing his glory,
   sing hosanna to his name.

Memorial Acclamation

Dying you destroyed our death,
rising you restored our life.
Come, Lord Jesus, come in glory,

come, Lord Jesus, come to us.

Lamb of God

1. Lamb of God, you take our sin,
   take the sin of all the world,
   show us mercy, show us mercy,
   show us mercy, Lamb of God.
   (Repeat as necessary)

2. Lamb of God, you take our sin,
   take the sin of all the world,
   grant us peace, Lord,
   grant us peace, Lord,
   grant us peace, O Lamb of God.

656 God of Mercy (Farrell)
© 1995, 1999 Bernadette Farrell.
OCP Publications

Kyrie, kyrie, kyrie, eleison.

1. God of mercy, you are with us.
   Fill our hearts with your kindness.

2. God of patience, strong and gentle,
   fill our hearts with your kindness.

3. Lord, have mercy, Lord, have mercy.
   Lord, have mercy upon us.

657 Kyrie, eleison (Orthodox)
From the Roman Missal

1. Kyrie, eleison.
   Kyrie, eleison.
   Kyrie, eleison.

2. Christe, eleison . . .

3. Kyrie, eleison . . .

   or

1. Lord, have mercy.
   Lord, have mercy.
   Lord, have mercy.

2. Christ, have mercy . . .

658 Kyrie, eleison (Berthier)
From the Roman Missal

Kyrie, Kyrie, eleison.
Kyrie, Kyrie, eleison.

659 Lord, have mercy (Caswall)
Michael Forster (b.1946)
© 1997 Kevin Mayhew Ltd

1. Lord, have mercy on us,
   hear us when we pray;
   Lord, have mercy on us,
   take our sin away.

2. Christ, have mercy on us,
   hear us as we pray;
   Christ, have mercy on us,
   take our sin away.

3. Lord, have mercy on us,
   hear us as we pray;
   Lord, have mercy on us,
   take our sin away.

660 Lord, have mercy (Ghana)
Adapted from the Liturgy

Lord, have mercy. Lord, have mercy.
Lord, have mercy, Lord, have mercy
   on us.

or

Kyrie, eleison. Kyrie, eleison.
Kyrie, eleison. Kyrie, eleison.

661 Lord, have mercy (Mayhew)
Adapted from the Liturgy

Lord, have mercy.
Christ, have mercy.
Lord, have mercy.

662 Lord, have mercy (Quem Pastores)
Adapted by Michael Morgan (b. 1942)
© 2008 Kevin Mayhew Ltd

Lord, have mercy. Lord, have mercy.
Christ, have mercy. Christ, have mercy.
Lord, have mercy. Lord have mercy.
Lord, have mercy on us all.

663 Lord, have mercy (Rock)
Adapted from the Liturgy

1. Lord, have mercy on us all. *(x 2)*
   Lord, have mercy, Lord, have mercy,
   Lord, have mercy on us all.

2. Christ have mercy . . .

3. Lord, have mercy . . .

664 Lord, have mercy (Stabat Mater)
Adapted by Michael Morgan (b. 1942)
© 2008 Kevin Mayhew Ltd

Lord, have mercy. Lord, have mercy.
Christ, have mercy. Christ, have
   mercy.
Lord, have mercy on us all.

665 Lord, have mercy
(Standing in the need of prayer)
Adapted by Michael Morgan (b. 1942)
© 2008, 1999 Kevin Mayhew Ltd

1. O Lord, have mercy on us all.
   Lord, have mercy on us all.
   O Lord, have mercy on us all.
   Lord, have mercy on us all.

2. O Christ, have mercy on us all.
   Christ, have mercy on us all.
   O Christ, have mercy on us all.
   Christ, have mercy on us all.

3. O Lord, have mercy on us all.
   Lord, have mercy on us all.
   O Lord, have mercy on us all.
   Lord, have mercy on us all.

666

Ash Grove Gloria
Michael Forster (b.1946)
© 1995,1999 Kevin Mayhew Ltd

1. Sing glory to God in the height of
   the heavens,
   salvation and peace to his people on
   earth;
   our King and our Saviour, our God
   and our Father,
   we worship and praise you and sing
   of your worth.

   Creation unites in the pow'r of the Spirit,
   in praise of the Father, through Jesus,
   the Son.
   So complex, so simple, so clear,
   so mysterious,
   our God ever three, yet eternally one.

2. Lord Jesus, the Christ, only Son of
   the Father,
   the Lamb who has carried our
   burden of shame,
   now seated on high in the glory of
   heaven,
   have mercy upon us who call on your
   name.

3. For you, only you, we acknowledge
   as holy,
   we name you alone as our Saviour
   and Lord;
   you only, O Christ, with the Spirit
   exalted,
   at one with the Father, for ever adored.

667

Coventry Gloria
From the Roman Missal

If this is sung by the choir and congregation
alternating, the congregation sings the text
in italics. Otherwise sing straight through.

Glory to God, glory in the highest,
peace to his people, peace on earth.
Glory to God, glory in the highest,
peace to his people, peace on earth.

Lord God, heavenly King,
almighty God and Father.
Glory to God, glory in the highest,
peace to his people, peace on earth.
We worship you, *glory in the highest,*
give you thanks, *glory in the highest,*
praise you for your glory.
Glory to God, glory in the highest,
peace to his people, peace on earth.
Lord Jesus Christ, only Son of the
Father,
Lord God, Lamb of God,
you take away the sin of the world:
have mercy on us, *have mercy on us,*
you are seated at the right hand of
the Father:
receive our prayer, *receive our prayer.*
Glory to God, glory in the highest,
peace to his people, peace on earth.
Glory to God, glory in the highest,
peace to his people, peace on earth.
For you alone are the Holy One,
you alone are the Lord,
you alone are the Most High,
Jesus Christ, with the Holy Spirit,
in the glory of God,
the glory of God the Father.
Glory to God, glory in the highest,
peace to his people, peace on earth.
Amen, amen.

668

Cwm Rhondda Gloria
Edwin le Grice (1911-1992)
©1990 Kevin Mayhew Ltd

1. Glory be to God in heaven,
   songs of joy and peace we bring,
   thankful hearts and voices raising,
   to creation's Lord we sing:
   Lord, we thank you, Lord, we bless you,
   glory be to God our King, God our
   King,
   glory be to God our King.

Continued overleaf

2. Lamb of God, who on your shoulders
   bore the load of this world's sin,
   only Son of God the Father,
   you have brought us peace within:
   Lord, have mercy, Christ, have mercy,
   now your glorious reign begin,
   now your glorious reign begin.

669 Clap Hands Gloria (Anderson)
Mike Anderson (b. 1956)
© 1999 Kevin Mayhew Ltd

Gloria, gloria, in excelsis Deo.
Gloria, gloria, in excelsis Deo.

1. Lord God, heavenly King, peace you
   bring to us;
   we worship you, we give you thanks,
   we sing our song of praise.

2. Jesus, Saviour of all, Lord God, Lamb
   of God,
   you take away our sins, O Lord, have
   mercy on us all.

3. At the Father's right hand, Lord,
   receive our prayer,
   for you alone are the Holy One, and
   you alone are Lord.

4. Glory, Father and Son, glory, Holy
   Spirit,
   to you we raise our hands up high,
   we glorify your name.

670 Gloria (Duffy)
From the Roman Missal

Gloria, gloria in excelsis Deo;
gloria, gloria in excelsis Deo.

1. Glory to God in the highest, and
   peace to his people on earth.
   Lord God, heavenly King, almighty
   God and Father,
   we worship you, we give you thanks,
   we praise you for your glory.

2. Lord Jesus Christ, only Son of the
   Father, Lord God, Lamb of God,
   you take away the sin of the world:
   have mercy on us;
   you are seated at the right hand of
   the Father: receive our prayer.

3. For you alone are the Holy One, you
   alone are the Lord,
   you alone are the Most High, Jesus
   Christ,
   with the Holy Spirit, in the glory of
   God the Father.

671 Gloria (Salazar)
George Salazar, trans. Paul Inwood (b. 1947).
© 1984 George Salazar
English translation © 1984, 1993 Paul Inwood

Glory! Glory! Glory to God!
Glory! Glory! Glory to God!

1. Glory to God in the heights of the
   heavens.
   Peace to God's people, all people on
   earth.

2. Son of the Father, all glory and
   worship;
   praise and thanksgiving to you, Lamb
   of God.

3. You take away the sin of the world;
   have mercy on us, receive our prayer.

4. Seated in pow'r at the right of the
   Father,
   Jesus alone is the Lord, the Most High.

5. And with the Spirit of love everlasting,
   reigning in glory for ever. Amen.

672 Gloria (Berthier)
Taizé Community, from the Roman Missal

Gloria, gloria in excelsis Deo!
Gloria, gloria, alleluia, alleluia!

673

Joshua Gloria
Nick Fawcett (b.1957)
© 2008 Kevin Mayhew Ltd

Glory in the highest to the God of gods,
Lord of lords, God of gods,
and to all his people on the earth be
peace,
to his people peace on earth.

1. Heav'nly King, almighty God,
   we worship you,
   for your glory, Lord, we give you praise.
   We worship you with thanks and joy,
   Father God, we give you praise.

2. Lamb of God, Lord Jesus Christ, you
   take away
   all the sins and sorrow of the world.
   You are the Father's only Son,
   Lord, have mercy on us all.

3. You alone are holy Lord, the holy one,
   you alone are Jesus Christ, Most High,
   enthroned beside the Father's hand:
   Jesus Christ, receive our prayer.

4. With the Father you are Lord, yes,
   you alone,
   with the Spirit, you are Christ,
   Most High.
   To you be praise and glory, Lord.
   To your name be praise. Amen.

674

Lourdes Gloria
From the Roman Missal

Gloria, gloria in excelsis Deo.
Gloria, gloria in excelsis Deo.

1. Glory to God in the highest, and
   peace to his people on earth.
   Lord God, heavenly King, almighty
   God and Father,
   we worship you, we give you thanks,
   we praise you for your glory.

2. Lord Jesus Christ, only Son of the
   Father. Lord God, Lamb of God,
   you take away the sin of the world:
   have mercy on us;
   you are seated at the right hand of
   the Father: receive our prayer.

3. For you alone are the Holy One, you
   alone are the Lord.
   You alone are the Most High, Jesus
   Christ,
   with the Holy Spirit, in the glory of
   God the Father. Amen.

675

Maccabaeus Gloria
Edwin le Grice (1911-1992)
© 1990 Kevin Mayhew Ltd

1. Glory to God! Our hearts to you we
   raise!
   Joy and peace on earth, in highest
   heaven praise!
   Songs of adoration, Lord, to you we
   bring,
   praising your great goodness, Father,
   heav'nly King.

   Glory to God! Our hearts to you we raise!
   Joy and peace on earth, in highest
   heaven praise.

2. Son of the Father, bearing this world's
   sin,
   Lamb of God, have mercy, grant us
   peace within.
   You, O Christ, are holy, you alone are
   Lord,
   with the Holy Spirit evermore adored.

676
Peruvian Gloria
© 1976 Kevin Mayhew Ltd

1. Glory to God, glory to God,
   glory to the Father.
   Glory to God, glory to God,
   glory to the Father.
   To him be glory for ever.
   To him be glory for ever.
   Alleluia, amen.
   Alleluia, amen,
   alleluia, amen,
   alleluia, amen.

2. Glory to God, glory to God,
   Son of the Father.
   Glory to God, glory to God,
   Son of the Father.
   To him be glory for ever.
   To him be glory for ever.
   Alleluia, amen.
   Alleluia, amen,
   alleluia, amen,
   alleluia, amen.

3. Glory to God, glory to God,
   glory to the Spirit.
   Glory to God, glory to God,
   glory to the Spirit.
   To him be glory for ever.
   To him be glory for ever.
   Alleluia, amen.
   Alleluia, amen,
   alleluia, amen,
   alleluia, amen.

677
Sing to God Gloria
Francesca Leftley (b. 1955)
© 1978 Kevin Mayhew Ltd

1. Sing to God a song of glory,
   peace he brings to all on earth.
   Worship we the King of heaven;
   praise and bless his holy name.

   Glory, glory, sing his glory.
   Glory to our God on high.

2. Sing to Christ, the Father's loved one,
   Jesus, Lord and Lamb of God:
   hear our prayer, O Lord, have mercy,
   you who bear the sins of all.

3. Sing to Christ, the Lord and Saviour,
   seated there at God's right hand:
   hear our prayer, O Lord, have mercy,
   you alone the Holy One.

4. Glory sing to God the Father,
   glory to his only Son,
   glory to the Holy Spirit,
   glory to the Three in One.

678
Woodlands Gloria
Edwin le Grice (1911-1992)
© 1990 Kevin Mayhew Ltd

1. Glory to God, we give you thanks
      and praise;
   of heav'nly joy and earthly peace we
      sing.
   We worship you, to you our hearts
      we raise,
   Lord God, almighty Father, heav'nly
      King.

2. Lord Jesus Christ, the Father's only
      Son,
   you bore for us the load of this
      world's sin.
   O Lamb of God, your glorious vict'ry
      won,
   receive our pray'r, grant us your peace
      within.

3. Alone, O Christ, you only are the Lord,
   at God's right hand in majesty most
      high:
   who with the Spirit worshipped and
      adored:
   with all the heav'nly host we glorify.

679 Celtic Alleluia
From the Liturgy

Alleluia, alleluia,
alleluia, alleluia.

680 Eightfold Alleluia
From the Liturgy

Alleluia, alleluia, alleluia, alleluia,
alleluia, alleluia, alleluia, alleluia.

681 Plainchant Alleluia
From the Liturgy

Alleluia, alleluia, alleluia.

682 Halle, halle, halle
From the Liturgy

Halle, halle, hallelujah!
Halle, halle, hallelujah!
Halle, halle, hallelujah!
Hallelujah, hallelujah!

683 Easter Alleluia
From the Liturgy

Alleluia, alleluia, alleluia.

684 Alleluia! (Raise the Gospel)
Owen Alstott
© 2002 Owen Alstott. OCP Publications

Alleluia! Alleluia!
Raise the Gospel over the earth!
Alleluia! Alleluia!
Peace and justice bringing to birth!

1. Blessèd those whose hearts are gentle.
   Blessèd those whose spirits are strong.
   Blessèd those who choose to bring
      forth right where there is wrong.

2. Blessèd those who work for justice.
   Blessèd those who answer the call.
   Blessèd those who dare to dream of
      lasting peace for all.

3. Tremble, you who build up riches.
   Tremble, you with opulent lives.
   Tremble, when you meet the poor
      and see Christ in their eyes.

4. Tremble, you who thirst for power.
   Tremble, you who live for acclaim.
   Tremble, when you find no comfort
      in your wealth and fame.

5. Glory like the stars of heaven.
   Glory like the sun in the sky.
   Glory shines upon all people, equal
      in God's eyes.

6. Glory to the Word of Justice.
   Glory to the Spirit of Peace.
   Glory to the God of Love whose
      blessings never cease.

685 Alleluia (Word of God)
Bernadette Farrell (b. 1957)
© 1993 Bernadette Farrell. OCP Publications

Alleluia, alleluia.
Alleluia, alleluia.

1. Word of God, Jesus Christ,
   live within our hearts:
   open our eyes,
   open our minds to you today.

2. Word of God, Jesus Christ,
   show us how to live:
   challenge your Church,
   call us to rise with you today.

3. Word of God, Jesus Christ,
   sharper than a sword:
   enter our lives,
   strike through our comfort and our
      fear.

686 Alleluia (Jesus, risen Lord)
From the Liturgy

Alleluia, alleluia,
Jesus, risen Lord of life!
Alleluia, alleluia, alleluia!

1. Word of the Father: Jesus Christ!
   Hope of the world: Jesus Christ!
   Broken and buried: Jesus Christ!
   Risen to life: Jesus Christ!

2. Light of the nations: Jesus Christ!
   Way, truth and life: Jesus Christ!
   Bearing our sorrow: Jesus Christ!
   With us through time: Jesus Christ!

3. Living among us: Jesus Christ!
   Word in our flesh: Jesus Christ!
   Servant of others: Jesus Christ!
   Friend of the poor: Jesus Christ!

687 Stay awake (Advent Acclamation)
Christopher Walker (b. 1947)
© 1986, 1989, 1990 Christopher Walker.
OCP Publications

1. Stay awake, be ready.
   You do not know the hour when the
      Lord is coming.
   Stay awake, be ready.
   The Lord is coming soon!
   Alleluia, alleluia!
   The Lord is coming soon.

2. Prepare! He's coming!
   The one who will give peace
   to the world is coming!
   Prepare! He's coming!
   The reign of God is near!
   Alleluia, alleluia!
   'The reign of God is near.'

3. Change your lives, he's coming.
   The one who is the light
   of the world is coming.
   Change your lives, he's coming.
   The reign of God is here!
   Alleluia, alleluia!
   'The reign of God is near.'

4. By the pow'r of the Spirit
   Mary will give birth
   to a son called Jesus.
   By the pow'r of the Spirit
   Emmanuel is near.
   Alleluia, alleluia!
   'Emmanuel is near'.

5. Go back, tell John
   all that you have heard
   and seen me doing.
   Go back, tell John
   the wonders that you see!
   Alleluia, alleluia!
   'The wonders that you see.'

6. Change your lives, he's coming,
   the one who is the light
   of the world is coming.
   Change your lives, he's coming,
   the Lord is coming soon!
   Alleluia, alleluia!
   'The Lord is coming soon.'

7. You are blessed among women.
   Mary, you are blessed,
   you believe God's promise.
   You are blessed among women,
   the mother of my Lord.
   Alleluia, alleluia!
   'The Mother of my Lord.'

688

Word of justice alleluia
Bernadette Farrell (b. 1957)
© 1987 Bernadette Farrell. OCP Publications

1. Word of justice, *alleluia,*
   come to dwell here, *maranatha!*

2. Word of mercy, *alleluia,*
   live among us, *maranatha!*

3. Word of power, *alleluia,*
   live within us, *maranatha!*

4. Word of freedom, *alleluia,*
   save your people, *maranatha!*

5. Word of healing, *alleluia,*
   heal our sorrow, *maranatha!*

6. Word of comfort, *alleluia,*
   bring us hope now, *maranatha!*

7. Word of gladness, *alleluia,*
   fill our hearts now, *maranatha!*

8. Word of wisdom, *alleluia,*
   come renew us, *maranatha!*

9. Word we long for, *alleluia,*
   word we thirst for, *maranatha!*

10. Key of David, *alleluia,*
    Son of Mary, *maranatha!*

11. Promised Saviour, *alleluia,*
    true Messiah, *maranatha!*

12. Promised Saviour, *alleluia,*
    hope of ages, *maranatha!*

13. Light of nations, *alleluia,*
    light in darkness, *maranatha!*

14. Risen Saviour, *alleluia,*
    Lord of glory, *maranatha!*

15. You we long for, *alleluia,*
    you we thirst for, *maranatha!*

16. Here among us, *alleluia,*
    living in us, *maranatha!*

689

We shall stay awake
Pierre-Marie Hoog and Robert B. Kelly (b. 1948)
© Rev. Pierre-Marie Hoog S.J.
English translation © 1999 Kevin Mayhew Ltd

Advent 1

We shall stay awake and pray at all
times,
ready to welcome Christ, the Prince
of Justice.
We shall set aside all fears and worries,
ready to welcome Christ, the Prince
of Peace.

Advent 2

We shall set our sights on what is
righteous,
ready to welcome Christ, the Prince
of Justice.
We shall smooth the path, prepare
the Lord's way,
ready to welcome Christ, the Prince
of Peace.

Advent 3

We shall plunge into the saving water,
ready to welcome Christ, the Prince
of Justice.
We shall be reborn and rise to new
life,
ready to welcome Christ, the Prince
of Peace.

Advent 4

We shall hold with faith to what God
promised,
ready to welcome Christ, the Prince
of Justice.
We shall be attentive to his Spirit,
ready to welcome Christ, the Prince
of Peace.

690 Glory and praise to you
(Lent and Holy Week)
From the Liturgy

Glory and praise to you, O Christ!

691 Glory to you, O Christ
(Lent and Holy Week)
From the Liturgy

Glory to you, O Christ,
you are the Word of God!

692 Praise and honour to you
(Lent and Holy Week)
From the Liturgy

Praise and honour to you,
Lord Jesus.

693 Praise to you, O Christ
(Lent and Holy Week)
From the Liturgy

Praise to you, O Christ,
King of eternal glory!

694 Credo 3
From the Roman Missal

Credo in unum Deum,
Patrem omnipotentem,
factorem caeli et terrae,
visibilium omnium,
et invisiblilium.
Et in unum Dominum Jesum
  Christum,
Filium Dei unigenitum,
et ex patre natum ante omnia saecula.
Deum de Deo, lumen de lumine,
Deum verum de Deo vero,
genitum non factum,
consubstantialem Patri:
per quem omnia facta sunt.
Qui propter nos homines,
et propter nostram salutem descendit
  de caelis.
Et incarnatus est de Spiritu Sancto
ex Maria Virgine: et homo factus est.

Crucifixus etiam pro nobis sub
  Pontio Pilato,
passus et sepultus est.
Et resurrexit tertia die,
secundum Scripturas,
et ascendit in caelum:
sedet ad dexteram Patris.
Et iterum venturus est cum gloria,
judicare vivos et mortuos:
cujus regni non erit finis.
Et in Spiritum Sanctum,
Dominum, et vivificantem:
qui ex Patre Filioque procedit.
Qui cum Patre et Filio simul adoratur,
et conglorificatur:
qui locutus est per Prophetas.
Et unam, sanctam catholicam
et apostolicam Ecclesiam.
Confiteor unum baptisma in
  remissionem peccatorum.
Et exspecto resurrectionem
  mortuorum.
Et vitam venturi saeculi. Amen.

695 Lourdes Credo
Jean-Paul Lécot (b. 1947)
© Jean-Paul Lécot

Credo, credo, credo. Amen!

I believe in God the Father,
Creator of heaven and earth.
I believe in Jesus his Son,
who was made man,
who died and rose again.
I believe in the Holy Spirit,
who gives life to the Church.

696 We believe (Fitzpatrick)
From the Roman Missal
© 1986 Kevin Mayhew Ltd

1. Do you believe in God,
   the Father almighty,
   creator of heav'n and earth?
   We believe, we do believe.

2. Do you believe in Jesus Christ,
   his only Son, our Lord,
   who was born of the Virgin Mary,
   was crucified, died and was buried?
   We believe, we do believe.

3. Do you believe in Jesus Christ,
   who rose from the dead,
   and is now seated at the right hand of
      the Father?
   We believe, we do believe.

4. Do you believe in the Holy Spirit,
   the holy Catholic Church,
   the communion of saints?
   We believe, we do believe.

5. Do you believe in the forgiveness of
      sins,
   the resurrection of the body,
   and the life everlasting?
   We believe, we do believe.

697 Ash Grove Sanctus
Michael Forster (b.1946) based on the *Sanctus*
© 1995,1999 Kevin Mayhew Ltd

O holy, most holy, the God of creation,
for ever exalted in pow'r and great
   might.
The earth and the heavens are full of
   your glory.
Hosanna, hosanna and praise in the
   height!

How blessed is he who is sent to redeem
   us,
who puts ev'ry fear and injustice to flight;
who comes in the name of the Lord as
   our Saviour.
Hosanna, hosanna and praise in the
   height!

698 Holy, holy, holy (Argentina)
Adapted from the Liturgy

Sanctus

Holy, holy, holy,
my heart, my heart adores you!
My heart is glad to say the words:
you are holy, Lord.

Benedictus

In God's name is coming
the One whom we call blessèd.
Hosanna in the highest.
Praise and thanks to God.

Acclamation

You alone are holy,
and you alone are Lord,
and you alone are the most high
Jesus Christ our Lord.

699 Holy, holy, holy (Celtic Liturgy)
From the Roman Missal

1. Holy, holy, holy Lord,
   God of power and might,
   heaven and earth are full of your glory.
   Hosanna, hosanna in the highest.

2. Blessèd is he who comes
   in the name of the Lord.
   Hosanna in the highest,
   hosanna in the highest.

700 Holy, holy, holy (Deutsche Messe)
From the Roman Missal

Holy, holy, holy Lord,
God of pow'r and might.
Holy, holy, holy Lord,
God of pow'r and might.
Heaven and earth are full,
full of your glory.
Hosanna in the highest,
hosanna in the highest.

Continued overleaf

Blessèd is he who comes
in the name of the Lord.
Hosanna in the highest,
hosanna in the highest.

701 Holy, holy, holy (Farrell)
From the Liturgy

Holy, holy, holy Lord God of pow'r,
Lord God of might,
Lord God of pow'r and might.
Heav'n and earth are full of your glory.
Hosanna in the highest.
Hosanna, hosanna, hosanna in the
  highest.

Blessèd, blessèd, blessèd, blessèd
is he who comes in the name,
who comes in the Lord's own name.
Hosanna, hosanna, hosanna in the
  highest.
Hosanna, hosanna, hosanna in the
  highest.

702 Holy, holy, holy (Gathering Mass)
From the Liturgy

1. Holy, holy, holy Lord.
   God of pow'r and God of might:
   heaven and earth, heaven and earth
   are full of your glory, your pow'r and
     might.
   Hosanna, hosanna, hosanna in the
     highest heav'ns.
   Hosanna, hosanna, hosanna in the
     highest heav'ns.

2. Blessèd, blessèd is he who comes,
   blessèd, blessèd is he who comes;
   blessèd is he, blessèd is he
   who comes in the name of the Lord.
   Hosanna, hosanna, hosanna in the
     highest heav'ns.
   Hosanna, hosanna, hosanna in the
     highest heav'ns.

703 Holy, holy, holy (MacMillan)
From the Roman Missal

Holy, holy, holy Lord,
God of pow'r and might.
Heav'n and earth are
full of your glory.
Hosanna in the highest.
Blessèd is he,
O blessèd is he who comes
in the name of the Lord.
Hosanna in the highest.
Hosanna in the highest.

704 Holy, holy, holy is the Lord
John Ballantine (b. 1942). Based on the *Sanctus*

1. Holy, holy, holy is the Lord,
   holy is the Lord God almighty!
   Holy, holy, holy is the Lord,
   holy is the Lord God almighty!
   Who was and is, and is to come;
   holy, holy, holy is the Lord.

2. Blessèd, blessèd, blest is he who
     comes,
   blest is he who comes in the Lord's
     name.
   Blessèd, blessèd, blest is he who
     comes,
   blest is he who comes in the Lord's
     name.
   Hosanna in the heights of heav'n.
   Blessèd, blessèd, blessèd is the Lord.

705 Lourdes Sanctus
W. R. Lawrence (1925-1997) based on the *Sanctus*
© 1988 Kevin Mayhew Ltd

Holy, holy, holy Lord,
God of pow'r and might!

1. Full of your glory are heav'n and earth,
   God of pow'r and might.

2. Blessed is he who comes among us
in the name of the Lord.

3. Hosanna in the highest!

706 Sanctus (Taizé)
From the Roman Missal

Sanctus, sanctus, sanctus
Dominus Deus Sabaoth,
Deus Sabaoth.

Holy, holy, holy Lord,
God of pow'r and might.
Heaven and earth are full of your glory.
Hosanna in the highest.
Blest is he who comes in the name of
the Lord.
Hosanna in the highest.

707 Scarborough Fair Sanctus
Michael Forster (b.1946)
© 2008, 1995 Kevin Mayhew Ltd

1. Holy, holy holy the Lord,
God of endless power and might;
the earth, the heav'ns are full of your
love.
Sing hosanna! Glory to God!

2. Blest is he, the one who is sent
in the name of God the Most High.
O holy, holy, holy our Lord!
Sing hosanna! Glory to God!

708 Skye Boat Song Sanctus
Michael Forster (b.1946)
© 1995, 1999 Kevin Mayhew Ltd

Holy, most holy, all holy the Lord,
God of all pow'r and might:
heaven and earth with your glory
abound
wrapped in eternal light.

Blessed is he, he who has come,
come in the Father's name,
Servant and Lord, Saviour and Judge,
making his royal claim.

Holy, most holy, all holy the Lord,
God of all pow'r and might.
Now with hosannas and jubilant
praise,
earth and the heav'ns unite.

709 Slane Sanctus
Michael Forster (b. 1946) based on the *Sanctus*
© 1993, 1995 Kevin Mayhew Ltd

1. Holy, most holy, all holy the Lord,
in power and wisdom for ever adored.
The earth and the heavens are full of
your love;
our joyful hosannas re-echo above.

2. Blessèd, most blessèd, all blessèd is he
whose life makes us whole, and
whose death sets us free;
who comes in the name of the Father
of light,
let endless hosannas resound in the
height.

710 When the Saints Sanctus
Nick Fawcett (b. 1957)
© 2008 Kevin Mayhew Ltd

1. O holy Lord, O holy Lord,
O holy Lord of pow'r and might,
your glory fills the earth and heavens,
O holy Lord of pow'r and might.

2. Hosanna, Lord, hosanna, Lord,
we sing hosanna, Lord, to you,
we sing hosanna in the highest,
we sing hosanna, Lord, to you.

3. Bless'd be the one, bless'd be the one,
who in the Lord's name comes to save,
bless'd be the one who comes among
us,
who in the Lord's name comes to save.

4. Hosanna, Lord, hosanna, Lord,
we sing hosanna, Lord, to you,
we sing hosanna in the highest,
we sing hosanna, Lord, to you.

711 Christ has died (Celtic Liturgy)
From the Roman Missal

Let us proclaim the myst'ry of faith:

Christ has died,
Christ is risen,
Christ will come again,
Christ will come again.

712 Christ has died (Gathering Mass)
From the Roman Missal

Let us proclaim the myst'ry of faith:

Christ has died,
Christ is ris'n,
Jesus Christ will come again.
Hosanna, hosanna,
hosanna in the highest heav'ns!

713 Christ has died (Wise)
From the Roman Missal

Christ has died, alleluia.
Christ is risen, alleluia.
Christ will come again,
alleluia, alleluia.

714 Jesus Christ, our Lord (Monkland)
Michael Forster (b. 1946)
© 1999 Kevin Mayhew Ltd

Jesus Christ, our Lord, has died,
Jesus Christ, our Lord, has ris'n,
Jesus Christ will come again.
Alleluia! Come, Lord, come.

715 Dying you destroyed our death
(Gathering Mass)
From the Roman Missal

Let us proclaim the myst'ry of faith:

Dying you destroyed our death,
rising you restored our life.
Lord Jesus, come.
Lord Jesus, come;
Lord Jesus, come in glory.

Hosanna, hosanna, hosanna in the
highest heav'ns.
Hosanna, hosanna, hosanna in the
highest heav'ns.

716 Dying you destroyed our death
(Aus der Tiefe)
Adapted from the Roman Missal
by John Ballantine (b. 1942)
This adaptation © 2007 Kevin Mayhew Ltd

Dying you destroyed our death;
rising you restored our life.
Lord Jesus, come in glory.
Lord Jesus, come in glory.

717 When we eat this living bread
(Gathering Mass)
From the Roman Missal

Let us proclaim the myst'ry of faith:

When we eat this living bread,
when we drink this saving cup,
we proclaim your death,
Lord Jesus, until you come in glory.
Hosanna, hosanna,
hosanna in the highest heav'ns.
Hosanna, hosanna,
hosanna in the highest heav'ns!

718 When we eat this bread (Irish melody)
From the Liturgy

When we eat this bread and drink
this cup,
we proclaim your death, Lord Jesus,
until you come in glory,
until you come in glory.

719 When we eat this bread
(Peace is flowing)
From the Roman Missal
This adaptation © 1999 Kevin Mayhew Ltd

When we eat this bread and drink
this cup,
we proclaim your death, Lord Jesus,
until you come in glory,
until you come in glory.

720

Lord, by your cross and resurrection
(Gathering Mass)
From the Roman Missal

Let us proclaim the myst'ry of faith:

Lord, by your cross,
Lord, by your cross,
Lord, by your cross and resurrection,
you have set your people free.
You are the Saviour of the world.
Hosanna, hosanna,
hosanna in the highest heav'ns.
Hosanna, hosanna,
hosanna in the highest heav'ns!

721

Lord, by your cross and resurrection
(St Clement)
Adapted from the Roman Missal
This adaptation © 2007 Kevin Mayhew Ltd

Lord, by your cross and resurrection
you have set us free from sin.
You are the Saviour of the world,
you are the Saviour of the world.

722

Doxology and Great Amen
(Gathering Mass)
From the Roman Missal

Through him, with him and in him,
in the unity of the Holy Spirit,
all glory and honour is yours,
almighty Father, almighty Father,
for ever and ever, for ever and ever.
Amen, amen.

723

Doxology and Great Amen (Lourdes)
From the Roman Missal

Through him, with him, in him,
 Amen
in the unity of the Holy Spirit, *Amen*
all glory and honour is yours,
 almighty Father,
for ever and ever, *Amen.*

Per ipsum, et cum ipso, et in ipso,
 Amen
est tibi, Deo Patri omnipotenti, in
 unitate Spiritus Sancti, Amen
omnis honor et gloria, per omnia
 saecula saeculorum, Amen.

724

Doxology and Great Amen (Plainsong)
From the Roman Missal

Through him, with him, in him,
in the unity of the Holy Spirit,
all glory and honour is yours,
 almighty Father,
for ever and ever. Amen.

725

Doxology and Great Amen
(Tallis' Canon)
Michael Forster (b.1946)
© 1999 Kevin Mayhew Ltd

Then through him, with him and in him,
and in the Spirit's unity,
all glory, honour, praise to you,
eternal Father, ever be.

Amen! We praise the Father's name!
Amen! We glorify the Son!
Amen! The Spirit we acclaim!
Amen! The Three for ever One!

726

Great Amen (Deutsche Messe)
From the Liturgy

Amen, amen,
amen, amen,
amen.

727

Great Amen (South African)
Robert B. Kelly (b. 1948)
© 1999 Kevin Mayhew Ltd

Honour and glory, amen!
Honour and glory, amen!
Amen! Amen! Amen! Amen!
Honour and glory, amen!

728 Our Father (Caribbean)
Traditional Caribbean
Based on Matthew 6:9-13; Luke 11:2-4

1. Our Father, who art in heaven,
   hallowèd be thy name.
   Thy kingdom come, thy will be
      done,
   hallowèd be thy name,
   hallowèd be thy name.

2. On earth as it is in heaven,
   Give us this day our daily bread.

3. Forgive us our trespasses,
   as we forgive those who trespass
      against us.

4. Lead us not into temptation,
   but deliver us from all that is evil.

5. For thine is the kingdom, the power
      and the glory,
   for ever, and for ever and ever.

6. Amen, amen, it shall be so.
   Amen, amen, it shall be so.

729 Our Father (Celtic Mass)
From the Liturgy

Our Father, who art in heaven,
hallowed be thy name,
thy kingdom come,
thy will be done on earth
as it is in heaven.
Give us this day our daily bread,
and forgive us our trespasses,
as we forgive those who trespass
   against us;
and lead us not into temptation,
but deliver us from evil.

Deliver us, Lord, from ev'ry evil,
and grant us peace in our day.

In your mercy keep us free from sin
and protect us from all anxiety
as we wait in joyful hope
for the coming of our Saviour,
   Jesus Christ.

Doxology

For the kingdom, the power,
and the glory are yours,
now and for ever.

730 Our Father (Rimsky-Korsakov)
Traditional, based on Matthew 6:9-13; Luke 11:2-4

Our Father, who art in heaven,
hallowed be thy name;
thy kingdom come;
thy will be done on earth
as it is in heaven.
Give us this day our daily bread;
and forgive us our trespasses
as we forgive those who trespass
   against us;
and lead us not into temptation,
but deliver us from evil.

Doxology

For the kingdom, the pow'r,
and the glory are yours,
now and for ever. Amen.

731 Our Father (White)
Matthew 6:9-13; Luke 11:2-4

Our Father, who art in heaven,
hallowed be thy name;
thy kingdom come;
thy will be done on earth
as it is in heaven.
Give us this day our daily bread;
and forgive us our trespasses
as we forgive those who trespass
   against us;
and lead us not into temptation,
but deliver us from evil.

Doxology

For the kingdom, the pow'r,
and the glory are yours,
now and for ever.

732 Our Father (Wiener)
Matthew 6:9-13; Luke 11:2-4

Our Father, who art in heaven,
hallowed be thy name;
thy kingdom come;
thy will be done on earth
as it is in heaven.
Give us this day our daily bread;
and forgive us our trespasses
as we forgive those who trespass
    against us;
and lead us not into temptation,
but deliver us from all that is evil.

Doxology

For the kingdom, the pow'r
and the glory are yours,
now and for ever. Amen.

733 Jesus, Lamb of God (Farrell)
© 1991 Bernadette Farrell. OCP Publications

1. Jesus, Lamb of God, bearer of our sin;
Jesus, Saviour:

Hear our prayer, hear our prayer:
through this bread and wine we share,
may we be your sign of peace ev'rywhere.

2. Jesus, Lamb of God, bearer of our
    pain;
Jesus, healer:

3. Jesus, Lamb of God, broken as our
    bread,
here among us:

4. Jesus, Lamb of God, poured out as
    our wine,
shared in gladness:

5. Jesus, Word of God, dwelling with
    the poor,
Jesus, prophet:

6. Jesus, Word of God, dwelling in our
    midst;
Jesus with us:

7. Jesus, Word of God, speaking in our
    hearts,
God's compassion:

8. Jesus, Word made flesh, touching
    each one's need;
Jesus, lover:

9. Kneeling by your friends, washing
    each one's feet:
Jesus, servant:

10. Hope beyond despair, dawn of
    fragile light;
Jesus, risen:

11. Tomb of secret hope, open to the
    dawn;
Jesus, living:

734 Jesus, Lamb of God (Inwood)
Adapted from the Liturgy by Paul Inwood
© 1982, 1989 Paul Inwood

1. Jesus, Lamb of God, have mercy on us.
Jesus, Lamb of God, have mercy on us.
Jesus, Word made flesh, bearer of our
    sins:
Jesus, Lamb of God, have mercy on us.

2. Jesus, Bread of Life, have mercy on us.
Jesus, Bread of Life, have mercy on us.
Jesus, Morning Star; Jesus, Prince of
    Peace:
Jesus, Bread of Life, have mercy on us.

3. Jesus, Lamb of God, have mercy on us.
Jesus, Lamb of God, have mercy on us.
Jesus, King of kings; Jesus, Lord of all:
Jesus, Lamb of God, give us your peace.

735 Jesus, Lamb of God and source of life
Adapted from the Liturgy by Paul Inwood
© 1982,1989 Paul Inwood. OCP Publications

1. Jesus, Lamb of God and source of
   life,
   Jesus, loving bearer of our sins:

   Hear our prayer, have mercy;
   hear our prayer, have mercy;
   give us your peace.

2. Jesus, Lamb of God and Son of
   Man;
   Jesus, true Redeemer of the world:

3. Jesus, Christ, our Way, our Truth,
   our life;
   Jesus Christ, our living Cornerstone:

4. Jesus, Lord of life and Lord of light;
   Jesus, here in form of bread and
   wine:

Advent

5. Jesus, Lamb of God and source of
   life;
   Jesus, loving bearer of our sins:

6. Jesus, coming near to bring us joy;
   Jesus, Son of God, Emmanuel:

7. Jesus, bringing hope to all who fear;
   Jesus, bringing strength to all who
   mourn:

8. Jesus, Saviour, heralded by John;
   Jesus, Son of David's house and line:

9. Jesus, Lamb of God and source of
   life;
   Jesus, loving bearer of our sins:

Christmas

10. Jesus, Lamb of God the Word made
    flesh;
    Jesus, Son of God come down to
    earth:

11. Jesus, King of glory, Prince of Peace;
    Jesus, shining in our darkened world:

12. Jesus, King of angels, Lord of joy;
    Jesus, born to save the world from
    sin:

13. Jesus, Lord of life and Lord of light;
    Jesus, here in form of bread and
    wine:

Eucharistic
(Maundy Thursday, Corpus Christi)

17. Jesus, Lamb of God and Bread of
    Life;
    Jesus, blood that cleanses us from sin;

18. Jesus, showing how we ought to serve;
    Jesus, teaching how we ought to be:

19. Jesus Christ, our true, eternal priest;
    Jesus, food and drink that makes us
    one:

20. Jesus, Lord of life and Lord of light;
    Jesus, here in form of bread and wine:

Easter

21. Jesus, risen Lord, triumphant King;
    Jesus, true Redeemer of the world:

22. Jesus, Morning Star which never sets;
    Jesus, Paschal Lamb and sacrifice:

23. Jesus, bursting from the shattered
    tomb;
    Jesus, mighty Victor over death:

24. Jesus, Lord of life and Lord of light;
    Jesus, here in form of bread and wine:

Pentecost (Spirit, healing)

25. Jesus, glorious brightness, flame of
    love;
    Jesus, filling hearts and minds with
    life:

26. Jesus, healing strength, redeeming power;
Jesus, burning out the mark of sin:

27. Jesus, by whose truth we are inspired;
Jesus, present here among us now:

28. Jesus, Lord of life and Lord of light;
Jesus, here in form of bread and wine:

736 Lamb of God (Ar hyd y nos)
Nick Fawcett (b.1957)
© 2008, 1996 Kevin Mayhew Ltd

Lamb of God, you take away the sins of the world.
In your mercy, come and heal us;
Lord, hear our prayer.
Take away our sins, forgive us,
Lamb of God, restore, redeem us,
grant us peace, Lord, in your mercy,
Lord, hear our prayer.

737 Lamb of God (Fitzpatrick)
From the Roman Missal

Lamb of God, you take away the sins of the world;
have mercy on us, have mercy on us.
(Repeat)
Lamb of God, you take away the sins of the world;
grant us peace, grant us peace.

738 Lamb of God (Michael, row the boat)
Nick Fawcett (b.1957)
© 1996, 2008 Kevin Mayhew Ltd

1. Lamb of God, you bear our sin,
Lord, have mercy,
Lamb of God, you bear our sin,
Lord, forgive us all.

2. Lamb of God, you bear our sin,
Lord, have mercy,
this world's sin you take away,
Lord, forgive us all.

3. Lamb of God, you bear our sin,
grant us peace, Lord,
Lamb of God, you bear our sin,
grant us peace, O Lord.

739 O Lamb of God (Our God loves us)
Adapted by John Ballentine (b. 1942)
This adaptation © 1976, 1996 Kevin Mayhew Ltd

1. O Lamb of God,
you take away our sins;
have mercy, Lamb of God,
have mercy.

2. O Lamb of God,
you take away our sins;
have mercy, Lamb of God,
have mercy.

3. O Lamb of God,
you take away our sins;
have mercy, Lamb of God,
and grant us peace.

740 O Lamb of God (Repton)
Michael Forster (b. 1946) based on the *Agnus Dei*
© 1997, 1999 Kevin Mayhew Ltd

1. O Lamb of God, come cleanse our hearts
and take our sin away.
O Lamb of God, your grace impart,
and let our guilty fear depart,
have mercy, Lord, we pray,
have mercy, Lord, we pray.

2. O Lamb of God, our lives restore,
our guilty souls release.
Into our lives your Spirit pour
and let us live for evermore
in perfect heav'nly peace,
in perfect heav'nly peace.

741

Lord, I am not worthy
Mike Anderson (b.1956)
© 1999 Kevin Mayhew Ltd

This is the Lamb of God who takes
   our sins.
Happy are those who are called to his
   supper.

Lord, I am not worthy, Lord, I am
   not worthy,
Lord, I am not worthy to receive you.
But only say the word and I'll be
   healed,
but only say the word and I'll be
   healed.

Eucharistic Adoration with Benediction

742-745 O salutaris
St Thomas Aquinas (1227-1274), trans. John Mason Neale (1818-1866)

Latin text

1. O salutaris hostia,
   quae caeli pandis ostium,
   bella premunt hostilia,
   da robur, fer auxilium.

2. Uni trinoque Domino sit
   sempiterna gloria,
   qui vitam sine termino
   nobis donet in patria. Amen.

English text

1. O saving victim, op'ning wide
   the gate of heav'n to man below;
   our foes press on from ev'ry side;
   thine aid supply, thy strength bestow.

2. To thy great name be endless praise,
   immortal Godhead, One in Three;
   O grant us endless length of days
   in our true native land with thee.
   Amen.

746-748 Tantum ergo
St Thomas Aquinas (1227-1274), trans. James Quinn (b. 1919)

Latin text

1. Tantum ergo Sacramentum
   veneremur cernui:
   et antiquum documentum novo
   cedat ritui;
   praestet fides supplementum
   sensuum defectui.

2. Genitori, genitoque laus et jubilatio,
   salus, honor, virtus, quoque
   sit et benedictio;
   procedenti ab utroque compar sit
   laudatio. Amen.

English text

1. Come, adore this wondrous presence,
   bow to Christ, the source of grace.
   Here is kept the ancient promise
   of God's earthly dwelling-place.
   Sight is blind before God's glory,
   faith alone may see his face.

2. Glory be to God the Father,
   praise to his co-equal Son,
   adoration to the Spirit,
   bond of love, in Godhead one.
   Blest be God by all creation
   joyously while ages run.

749 Adoremus in aeternum
Psalm 116

*Adoremus in aeternum
sanctissimum sacramentum.*

1. Laudate Dominum, omnes gentes;
   laudate eum, omnes populi.

2. Quoniam confirmata est super nos
   misericordia ejus;
   et veritas Domini manet in
   aeternum.

3. Gloria Patri et Filio;
   et Spiritui Sancto.

4. Sicut erat in principio et nunc et
   semper;
   et in saecula saeculorum. Amen.

Psalms

750 1st Sunday of Advent (A)
Psalm 121:1-2, 4-5, 6-9. R℣ cf. v1

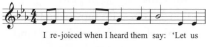

I re-joiced when I heard them say: 'Let us go to God's house.'

1. I rejoiced when I <u>heard</u> them say:
   'Let us go <u>to</u> God's house.'
   And now our <u>feet</u> are standing
   within your gates, <u>O</u> Jerusalem.

2. It is there that the <u>tribes</u> go up,
   the tribes <u>of</u> the Lord.
   For Israel's <u>law</u> it is,
   there to praise <u>the</u> Lord's name.

3. For the peace of Jeru<u>sa</u>lem pray:
   'Peace be <u>to</u> your homes!
   May peace reign <u>in</u> your walls,
   in your pa<u>la</u>ces, peace!'

4. For love of my bre<u>thren</u> and friends
   I say: 'Peace <u>upon</u> you!'
   For love of the house <u>of</u> the Lord
   I will ask <u>for</u> your good.

Gospel Acclamation Psalm 84:8
   Let us see, O <u>Lord</u>, your mercy,
   and give us your <u>saving</u> help.

751 1st Sunday of Advent (B)
Psalm 79:2-3, 15-16, 18-19. R℣ v.4

God of hosts, bring us back; let your face shine on us and we shall be saved.

1. O Shepherd of Is<u>ra</u>el, hear us,
   shine forth from your che<u>ru</u>bim
      throne.

O Lord, rouse <u>up</u> your might,
O Lord, come <u>to</u> our help.

2. God of hosts, turn again, <u>we</u> implore,
   look down from hea<u>ven</u> and see.
   Visit this vine <u>and</u> protect it,
   the vine your right <u>hand</u> has planted.

3. May your hand be on the one <u>you</u>
      have chosen,
   the one you have <u>given</u> your strength.
   And we shall never forsake <u>you</u> again:
   give us life that we may call up<u>on</u>
      your name.

Gospel Acclamation Psalm 84:8
   Let us see, O <u>Lord</u>, your mercy,
   and give us your <u>saving</u> help.

752 1st Sunday of Advent (C)
Psalm 24:4-5, 8-9, 10, 14. R℣ v.1

To you, O Lord, I lift up my soul.

1. Lord, make me <u>know</u> your ways.
   Lord, teach <u>me</u> your paths.
   Make me walk in your <u>truth</u>, and
      teach me:
   for you are <u>God</u> my Saviour.

2. The Lord is <u>good</u> and upright.
   He shows the path to <u>those</u> who stray,
   he guides the humble <u>in</u> the right path;
   he teaches his way <u>to</u> the poor.

3. His ways are faithful<u>ness</u> and love
   for those who keep his cove<u>nant</u> and
      will.
   The Lord's friendship is for those
      <u>who</u> revere him;
   to them he re<u>veals</u> his covenant.

Gospel Acclamation Psalm 84:8
   Let us see, O <u>Lord</u>, your mercy,
   and give us your <u>saving</u> help.

753 2nd Sunday of Advent (A)
Psalm 71:1-2, 7-8, 12-13, 17. R℞ cf. v.7

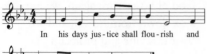

In his days jus-tice shall flou-rish and

peace till the moon fails.

1. O God, give your judgement to the
   king,
   to a king's son your justice,
   that he may judge your people in
   justice
   and your poor in right judgement.

2. In his days justice shall flourish
   and peace till the moon fails.
   He shall rule from sea to sea,
   from the Great River to earth's bounds.

3. For he shall save the poor when they cry
   and the needy who are helpless.
   He will have pity on the weak
   and save the lives of the poor.

4. May his name be blest for ever
   and endure like the sun.
   Ev'ry tribe shall be blest in him,
   all nations bless his name.

Gospel Acclamation Luke 3:4, 6
   Prepare a way for the Lord and make
   his paths straight,
   and all mankind shall see the
   salvation of our God.

754 2nd Sunday of Advent (B)
Psalm 84:9-14. R℞ v.8

Let us see, O Lord, your mer-cy and

give us your sav-ing help.

1. I will hear what the Lord God has to
   say,
   a voice that speaks of peace.
   His help is near for those who fear him
   and his glory will dwell in our land.

2. Mercy and faithfulness have met;
   justice and peace have embraced.
   Faithfulness shall spring from the earth
   and justice look down from heaven.

3. The Lord will make us prosper
   and our earth shall yield its fruit.
   Justice shall march before him
   and peace shall follow his steps.

Gospel Acclamation Luke 3:4, 6
   Prepare a way for the Lord and make
   his paths straight,
   and all mankind shall see the
   salvation of our God.

755 2nd Sunday of Advent (C)
Psalm 125. R℞ v.3

What mar-vels the Lord worked for us!

In-deed we were glad.

1. When the Lord delivered Zion from
   bondage,
   it seemed like a dream.
   Then was our mouth filled with
   laughter,
   on our lips there were songs.

2. The heathens themselves said:
   'What marvels the Lord worked for
   them!'
   What marvels the Lord worked for us!
   Indeed we were glad.

3. Deliver us, O Lord, <u>from</u> our bondage
   as streams <u>in</u> dry land.
   Those who are sow<u>ing</u> in tears
   will sing <u>when</u> they reap.

4. They go out, they go out, <u>full</u> of tears
   carrying seed <u>for</u> the sowing:
   they come back, they come back,
       <u>full</u> of song,
   carry<u>ing</u> their sheaves.

Gospel Acclamation Luke 3:4, 6
   Prepare a way for the Lord and make
       <u>his</u> paths straight,
   and all mankind shall see the
       salvation <u>of</u> our God.

756 3rd Sunday of Advent (A)
Psalm 145:6-10. R℟ cf. Isaiah 35:4

Come, Lord, and save   us,   come, Lord, and

save   us.

1. It is the Lord who keeps <u>faith</u> for ever,
   who is just to those who <u>are</u> oppressed.
   It is he who gives bread <u>to</u> the hungry,
   the Lord, who sets pri<u>so</u>ners free.

2. It is the Lord who gives sight <u>to</u> the
       blind,
   who raises up those who <u>are</u> bowed
       down,
   the Lord, who pro<u>tects</u> the stranger
   and upholds the wi<u>dow</u> and orphan.

3. It is the Lord who <u>loves</u> the just
   but thwarts the path <u>of</u> the wicked.
   The Lord will <u>reign</u> for ever,
   Zion's God, from <u>age</u> to age.

Gospel Acclamation Isaiah 61:1 (Luke 4:18)
   The spirit of the Lord has been <u>given</u>
       to me.
   He has sent me to bring good news
       <u>to</u> the poor.

757 3rd Sunday of Advent (B)
Psalm Luke 1:46-50, 53-54.
R℟ Isaiah 61:10

My   soul   re - joi-ces in my God.

1. My soul glori<u>fies</u> the Lord,
   my spirit rejoices in <u>God</u>, my Saviour.
   He looks on his servant <u>in</u> her
       nothingness;
   henceforth all ages will <u>call</u> me blessed.

2. The Almighty works mar<u>vels</u> for me.
   Holy <u>is</u> his name!
   His mercy is from <u>age</u> to age,
   on <u>those</u> who fear him.

3. He fills the starving <u>with</u> good things,
   sends the rich <u>away</u> empty.
   He protects Isra<u>el</u>, his servant,
   remember<u>ing</u> his mercy.

Gospel Acclamation Isaiah 61:1 (Luke 4:18)
   The spirit of the Lord has been <u>given</u>
       to me.
   He has sent me to bring good news
       <u>to</u> the poor.

758 3rd Sunday of Advent (C)
Psalm Isaiah 12:2-6. R℟ cf. v.6

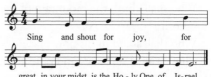

Sing   and shout for   joy,   for

great in your midst is the Ho - ly One of   Is-rael.

Continued overleaf

1. Truly, God is my salvation,
   I trust, I shall not fear.
   For the Lord is my strength, my song,
   he became my Saviour.

2. Give thanks to the Lord,
   give praise to his name!
   Make his mighty deeds known to
      the peoples!
   Declare the greatness of his name.

3. Sing a psalm to the Lord for he has
      done glorious deeds,
   make them known to all the earth!
   People of Zion, sing and shout for joy
   for great in your midst is the Holy
      One of Israel.

Gospel Acclamation Isaiah 61:1 (Luke 4:18)
   The spirit of the Lord has been given
      to me.
   He has sent me to bring good news
      to the poor.

759 4th Sunday of Advent (A)
Psalm 23:1-6. R7 cf. vv.7, 10

Let the Lord en - ter, let the Lord en - ter!

He is the King of glo - ry.

1. The Lord's is the earth and its fullness,
   the world and all its peoples.
   It is he who set it on the seas;
   on the waters he made it firm.

2. Who shall climb the mountain of the
      Lord?
   Who shall stand in his holy place?
   Those with clean hands and pure heart,
   who desire not worthless things.

3. They shall receive blessings from the
      Lord
   and reward from the God who saves
      them.
   Such are the ones who see him,
   seek the face of the God of Jacob.

Gospel Acclamation Matthew 1:23
   The virgin will conceive and give
      birth to a son
   and they will call him Emmanuel, a
      name which means 'God-is-with-us'.

760 4th Sunday of Advent (B)
Psalm 88:2-5, 27, 29. R7 cf. v.2

I will sing for e-ver of your love, O Lord.

1. I will sing for ever of your love, O Lord;
   through all ages my mouth will
      proclaim your truth.
   Of this I am sure, that your love lasts
      for ever,
   that your truth is firmly established as
      the heavens.

2. 'I have made a covenant with my
      chosen one;
   I have sworn to David my servant:
   I will establish your dynasty for ever
   and set up your throne through all ages.'

3. He will say to me 'You are my father,
   my God, the rock who saves me.'
   I will keep my love for him always;
   for him my covenant shall endure.

Gospel Acclamation Luke 1:38
   I am the handmaid of the Lord:
   let what you have said be done to me.

761 4th Sunday of Advent (C)
Psalm 79:2-3, 15-16, 18-19. R℣ v.4

God of hosts, bring us back; let your

face shine on us and we shall be saved.

1. O Shepherd of Israel, hear us,
   shine forth from your cherubim throne.
   O Lord, rouse up your might,
   O Lord, come to our help.

2. God of hosts, turn again, we implore,
   look down from heaven and see.
   Visit this vine and protect it,
   the vine your right hand has planted.

3. May your hand be on the one you have chosen,
   the one you have given your strength.
   And we shall never forsake you again:
   give us life that we may call upon your name.

Gospel Acclamation Luke 1:38
   I am the handmaid of the Lord:
   let what you have said be done to me.

762 Nativity of Our Lord – Midnight Mass (A, B, C)
Psalm 95:1-3, 11-13. R℣ Luke 2:11

To-day a Sa-viour has been born to us;

he is Christ the Lord.

1. O sing a new song to the Lord,
   sing to the Lord all the earth.
   O sing to the Lord, bless his name.

2. Proclaim his help day by day,
   tell among the nations his glory
   and his wonders among all the nations.

3. Let the heavens rejoice and earth be glad,
   let the sea and all within it thunder praise,
   let the land and all it bears rejoice.

4. All the trees of the wood shout for joy
   at the presence of the Lord for he comes,
   he comes to rule the earth.

Gospel Acclamation Luke 2:10-11
   I bring you news of great joy:
   today a Saviour has been born to us,
   Christ the Lord.

763 Nativity of Our Lord – Mass During the Day (A, B, C)
Psalm 97:1-6. R℣ v.3

All the ends of the earth have seen the sal-

va - tion of our God.

1. Sing a new song to the Lord
   for he has worked wonders.
   His right hand and his holy arm
   have brought salvation.

2. The Lord has made known his salvation;
   has shown his justice to the nations.
   He has remembered his truth and love
   for the house of Israel.

3. All the ends of the earth have seen
   the salvation of our God.
   Shout to the Lord all the earth,
   ring out your joy.

Continued overleaf

4. Sing psalms to the Lord <u>with</u> the harp,
with the <u>sound</u> of music.
With trumpets and the sound <u>of</u> the horn
acclaim the <u>King</u>, the Lord.

Gospel Acclamation
Come, you nations, wor<u>ship</u> the Lord,
for today a great light has shone
down up<u>on</u> the earth.

764 Holy Family (A, B, C)
Psalm 127:1-5. R℟ v.1

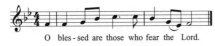
O bles - sed are those who fear the Lord.

1. O blessed are those who <u>fear</u> the Lord
and walk <u>in</u> his ways!
By the labour of your hands <u>you</u> shall eat.
You will be hap<u>py</u> and prosper.

2. Your wife like a <u>fruitful</u> vine
in the heart <u>of</u> your house;
your children like shoots <u>of</u> the olive,
a<u>round</u> your table.

3. Indeed thus <u>shall</u> be blessed
those who <u>fear</u> the Lord.
May the Lord bless <u>you</u> from Zion
all the days <u>of</u> your life!

Gospel Acclamation Colossians 3:15, 16
May the peace of Christ reign <u>in</u> your hearts;
let the message of Christ find a <u>home</u> within you.

765 Holy Family (B Ad Lib)
Psalm 104:1-6, 8-9. R℟ vv.7, 8

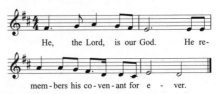
He, the Lord, is our God. He re-
mem - bers his co - ven - ant for e - ver.

1. Give thanks to the Lord, <u>tell</u> his name,
make known his deeds a<u>mong</u> the peoples.
O sing to him, <u>sing</u> his praise;
tell all his won<u>derful</u> works!

2. Be proud of his <u>holy</u> name,
let the hearts that seek the <u>Lord</u> rejoice.
Consider the Lord <u>and</u> his strength;
constantly <u>seek</u> his face.

3. Remember the wonders <u>he</u> has done,
his miracles, the judge<u>ments</u> he spoke.
O children of Abra<u>ham</u>, his servant,
O sons of the Ja<u>cob</u> he chose.

4. He remembers his cove<u>nant</u> for ever,
his promise for a thousand <u>generations</u>,
the covenant he <u>made</u> with Abraham,
the oath he <u>swore</u> to Isaac.

Gospel Acclamation Hebrews 1:1-2
At various times in the past and in
various dif<u>ferent</u> ways,
God spoke to our ancestors <u>through</u>
the prophets;
but in our own <u>time</u>, the last days,
he has spoken to us <u>through</u> his Son.

766 Holy Family (C Ad Lib)
Psalm 83:2-3, 5-6, 9-10. R℟ v.5

They are hap-py who dwell in your house, O Lord.

1. How lovely is your dwelling-place,
   Lord God of hosts.
   My soul is longing and yearning,
   is yearning for the courts of the Lord.

2. They are happy, who dwell in your
      house,
   for ever singing your praise.
   They are happy, whose strength is in
      you;
   they walk with ever-growing strength.

3. O Lord, God of hosts, hear my prayer,
   give ear, O God of Jacob.
   Turn your eyes, O God, our shield,
   look on the face of your anointed.

Gospel Acclamation cf. Acts 16:14
   Open our heart, O Lord,
   to accept the words of your Son.

Gospel Acclamation Hebrews 1:1-2
   At various times in the past and in
      various different ways,
   God spoke to our ancestors through
      the prophets;
   but in our own time, the last days,
   he has spoken to us through his Son.

768 2nd Sunday after Christmas
         (A, B, C)
         Psalm 147:12-15, 19-20. R℣ John 1:14

The Word was made flesh, and lived a-mong us.

1. O praise the Lord, Jerusalem!
   Zion, praise your God!
   He has strengthened the bars of your
      gates,
   he has blessed the children within you.

2. He established peace on your borders,
   he feeds you with finest wheat.
   He sends out his word to the earth
   and swiftly runs his command.

3. He makes his word known to Jacob,
   to Israel his laws and decrees.
   He has not dealt thus with other
      nations;
   he has not taught them his decrees.

Gospel Acclamation cf. 1 Timothy 3:16
   Glory be to you, O Christ,
      proclaimed to the pagans;
   glory be to you, O Christ, believed in
      by the world.

767 Solemnity of Mary,
         Mother of God (A, B, C)
         Psalm 66:2-3, 5, 6, 8. R℣ v.2

O God, be gra-cious and bless us.

1. God, be gracious and bless us
   and let your face shed its light upon us.
   So will your ways be known upon
      earth
   and all nations learn your saving help.

2. Let the nations be glad and exult
   for you rule the world with justice.
   With fairness you rule the peoples,
   you guide the nations on earth.

3. Let the peoples praise you, O God;
   let all the peoples praise you.
   May God still give us his blessing
   till the ends of the earth revere him.

769
Epiphany of the Lord (A, B, C)
Psalm 71:1-2, 7-8, 10-13. R℟ cf. v.11

All na-tions shall fall pros-trate be -
fore you, O Lord.

1. O God, give your judgement to the
   king,
   to a king's son your justice,
   that he may judge your people in justice
   and your poor in right judgement.

2. In his days justice shall flourish
   and peace till the moon fails.
   He shall rule from sea to sea,
   from the Great River to earth's bounds.

3. The kings of Tarshish and the sea
      coasts shall pay him tribute.
   The kings of Sheba and Seba shall
      bring him gifts.
   Before him all kings shall fall prostrate,
   all nations shall serve him.

4. For he shall save the poor when
      they cry
   and the needy who are helpless.
   He will have pity on the weak
   and save the lives of the poor.

Gospel Acclamation Matthew 2:2
   We saw his star as it rose
   and we have come to pay homage to
      the Lord.

770
Baptism of the Lord (A, B, C)
Psalm 28:1-4, 9-10. R℟ v.11

The Lord will bless his peo - ple with
peace, with peace.

1. O give the Lord you children of God,
   give the Lord glory and power;
   give the Lord the glory of his name.
   Adore the Lord in his holy court.

2. The Lord's voice resounding on the
      waters,
   the Lord on the immensity of waters;
   the voice of the Lord, full of power,
   the voice of the Lord, full of
      splendour.

3. The God of glory thunders.
   In his temple they all cry: 'Glory!'
   The Lord sat enthroned over the flood;
   the Lord sits as king for ever.

Gospel Acclamation cf. Mark 9:8
   The heavens opened and the Father's
      voice resounded:
   'This is my Son, the Beloved. Listen
      to him.'

771
Baptism of the Lord (B Ad Lib)
Psalm Isaiah 12:2-6. R℟ v.6

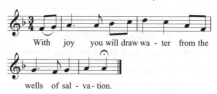

With joy you will draw wa - ter from the
wells of sal - va - tion.

1. Truly, God is my salvation,
   I trust, I shall not fear.
   For the Lord is my strength, my song,
   he became my Saviour.

2. Give thanks to the Lord,
   give praise to his name!
   Make his mighty deeds known to the
      peoples!
   Declare the greatness of his name.

3. Sing a psalm to the Lord for he has
   done glorious deeds,
   make them known to all the earth!
   People of Zion, sing and shout for joy
   for great in your midst is the Holy
   One of Israel.

Gospel Acclamation cf. John 1:29
   John saw Jesus coming towards him,
   and said:
   'This is the Lamb of God who takes
   away the sin of the world.'

772 Baptism of the Lord (C Ad Lib)
Psalm 103:1-2, 3-4, 24-25, 27-30.
R℣ v.1

Bless the Lord, my soul! Lord

God, how great you are.

1. Lord God, how great you are,
   clothed in majesty and glory,
   wrapped in light as in a robe!
   You stretch out the heavens like a tent.

2. The earth is full of your riches.
   There is the sea, vast and wide,
   with its moving swarms past counting,
   living things great and small.

3. All of these look to you
   to give them their food in due season.
   You give it, they gather it up:
   you open your hand, they have their
   fill.

4. You take back your spirit, they die,
   returning to the dust from which
   they came.
   You send forth your spirit, they are
   created;
   and you renew the face of the earth.

Gospel Acclamation cf. Luke 3:16
   Someone is coming, said John,
   someone greater than I.
   He will baptise you with the Holy
   Spirit and with fire.

773 Ash Wednesday (A, B, C)
Psalm 50:3-6, 12-14, 17. R℣ v.3

Have mer-cy on us, Lord, for we have sinned.

1. Have mercy on me, God, in your
   kindness.
   In your compassion blot out my
   offence.
   O wash me more and more from my
   guilt
   and cleanse me from my sin.

2. My offences truly I know them;
   my sin is always before me.
   Against you, you alone, have I sinned;
   what is evil in your sight I have done.

3. A pure heart create for me, O God,
   put a steadfast spirit within me.
   Do not cast me away from your
   presence,
   nor deprive me of your holy spirit.

4. Give me again the joy of your help;
   with a spirit of fervour sustain me.
   O Lord, open my lips
   and my mouth shall declare your
   praise.

Gospel Acclamation Psalm 50:12, 14
   A pure heart create for me, O God,
   and give me again the joy of your help.

774 1st Sunday of Lent (A)
Psalm 50:3-6, 12-14, 17. R/ v.3

Have mer-cy on us, Lord, for we have sinned.

1. Have mercy on me, God, in your
   kindness.
   In your compassion blot out my
   offence.
   O wash me more and more from my
   guilt
   and cleanse me from my sin.

2. My offences truly I know them;
   my sin is always before me.
   Against you, you alone, have I sinned;
   what is evil in your sight I have done.

3. A pure heart create for me, O God,
   put a steadfast spirit within me.
   Do not cast me away from your
   presence,
   nor deprive me of your holy spirit.

4. Give me again the joy of your help;
   with a spirit of fervour sustain me.
   O Lord, open my lips
   and my mouth shall declare your
   praise.

Gospel Acclamation Matthew 4:4
   Man does not live on bread alone,
   but on every word that comes from
   the mouth of God.

775 1st Sunday of Lent (B)
Psalm 24:4-9. R/ cf. v.10

Your ways, Lord, are faith-ful-ness and love, for

those who keep your co - ve-nant.

1. Lord, make me know your ways.
   Lord, teach me your paths.
   Make me walk in your truth, and
   teach me:
   for you are God my Saviour.

2. Remember your mercy, Lord,
   and the love you have shown from of
   old.
   In your love remember me,
   because of your goodness, O Lord.

3. The Lord is good and upright.
   He shows the path to those who stray,
   he guides the humble in the right path;
   he teaches his way to the poor.

Gospel Acclamation Matthew 4:4
   Man does not live on bread alone,
   but on every word that comes from
   the mouth of God.

776 1st Sunday of Lent (C)
Psalm 90:1-2, 10-15. R/ v.15

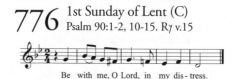

Be with me, O Lord, in my dis- tress.

1. He who dwells in the shelter of the
   Most High
   and abides in the shade of the
   Almighty,
   says to the Lord: 'My refuge,
   my stronghold, my God in whom I
   trust!'

2. Upon you no evil shall fall,
   no plague approach where you dwell.
   For you has he commanded his angels,
   to keep you in all your ways.

3. They shall bear you up<u>on</u> their hands
lest you strike your foot a<u>gainst</u> a stone.
On the lion and the viper <u>you</u> will tread
and trample the young lion <u>and</u> the dragon.

4. His love he set on me, so <u>I</u> will rescue him;
protect him for he <u>knows</u> my name.
When he calls I shall answer: '<u>I</u> am with you.'
I will save him in distress and <u>give</u> him glory.

Gospel Acclamation Matthew 4:4
Man does not live on <u>bread</u> alone,
but on every word that comes from the <u>mouth</u> of God.

777 2nd Sunday of Lent (A)
Psalm 32:4-5, 18-20, 22. R℣ v.22

May your love be up-on us, O Lord,
as we place all our hope in you.

1. The word of the <u>Lord</u> is faithful
and all his works <u>to</u> be trusted.
The Lord loves jus<u>tice</u> and right
and fills the earth <u>with</u> his love.

2. The Lord looks on those <u>who</u> revere him,
on those who hope <u>in</u> his love,
to rescue their <u>souls</u> from death,
to keep them a<u>live</u> in famine.

3. Our soul is waiting <u>for</u> the Lord.
The Lord is our help <u>and</u> our shield.
May your love be upon <u>us</u>, O Lord,
as we place all our <u>hope</u> in you.

Gospel Acclamation Matthew 17:5
From the bright cloud the Father's <u>voice</u> was heard:
'This is my Son, the Beloved. <u>Lis</u>ten to him.'

778 2nd Sunday of Lent (B)
Psalm 115:10, 15-19. R℣ Psalm 114:9

I will walk in the pre-sence of the Lord in the
land of the liv - ing.

1. I trusted, even <u>when</u> I said:
'I am sore<u>ly</u> afflicted.'
O precious in the eyes <u>of</u> the Lord
is the death <u>of</u> his faithful.

2. Your servant, Lord, your ser<u>vant</u> am I;
you have loos<u>ened</u> my bonds.
A thanksgiving sacri<u>fice</u> I make;
I will call <u>on</u> the Lord's name.

3. My vows to the Lord I <u>will</u> fulfil
before <u>all</u> his people,
in the courts of the house <u>of</u> the Lord,
in your midst, <u>O</u> Jerusalem.

Gospel Acclamation Matthew 17:5
From the bright cloud the Father's <u>voice</u> was heard:
'This is my Son, the Beloved. <u>Lis</u>ten to him.'

779 2nd Sunday of Lent (C)
Psalm 26:1, 7-9, 13-14. R℣ v.1

The Lord is my light and my help.

Continued overleaf

1. The Lord is my light <u>and</u> my help;
   whom <u>shall</u> I fear?
   The Lord is the stronghold <u>of</u> my life;
   before whom <u>shall</u> I shrink?

2. O Lord, hear my voice <u>when</u> I call;
   have mer<u>cy</u> and answer.
   Of you my <u>heart</u> has spoken:
   'Seek, <u>seek</u> his face.'

3. It is your face O Lord, <u>that</u> I seek;
   hide <u>not</u> your face.
   Dismiss not your ser<u>vant</u> in anger;
   you have <u>been</u> my help.

4. I am sure I shall see <u>the</u> Lord's goodness
   in the land <u>of</u> the living.
   Hope in him, hold firm <u>and</u> take heart.
   Hope <u>in</u> the Lord!

Gospel Acclamation Matthew 17:5
   From the bright cloud the Father's
      <u>voice</u> was heard:
   'This is my Son, the Beloved.
      Lis<u>ten</u> to him.'

780 3rd Sunday of Lent (A)
Psalm 94:1-2, 6-9. R℞ v.8

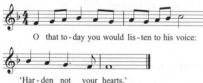

O that to-day you would lis-ten to his voice:

'Har-den not   your hearts.'

1. Come, ring out our joy <u>to</u> the Lord;
   hail the <u>rock</u> who saves us.
   Let us come before him, <u>giving</u> thanks,
   with songs let us <u>hail</u> the Lord.

2. Come in; let us bow <u>and</u> bend low;
   let us kneel before the <u>God</u> who
      made us
   for he is our God, and we the people
      who belong <u>to</u> his pasture,
   the flock that is led <u>by</u> his hand.

3. O that today you would listen <u>to</u> his
   voice!
   'Harden not your hearts <u>as</u> at Meribah,
   as on that day at Massah in the desert,
      when your fathers put me <u>to</u> the test;
   when they tried me, though they <u>saw</u>
   my work.'

Gospel Acclamation cf. John 4:42, 15
   Lord, you really are the Saviour <u>of</u> the
      world;
   give me the living water, so that I
      may ne<u>ver</u> get thirsty.

781 3rd Sunday of Lent (B)
Psalm 18:8-11. R℞ John 6:68

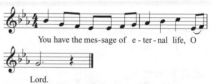

You have the mes-sage of e-ter-nal life, O

Lord.

1. The law of the <u>Lord</u> is perfect,
   it re<u>vives</u> the soul.
   The rule of the Lord is <u>to</u> be trusted,
   it gives wisdom <u>to</u> the simple.

2. The precepts of the <u>Lord</u> are right,
   they glad<u>den</u> the heart.
   The command of the <u>Lord</u> is clear,
   it gives light <u>to</u> the eyes.

3. The fear of the <u>Lord</u> is holy,
   abi<u>ding</u> for ever.
   The decrees of the <u>Lord</u> are truth
   and all <u>of</u> them just.

4. They are more to be de<u>sired</u> than gold,
   than the pur<u>est</u> of gold
   and sweeter are <u>they</u> than honey,
   than honey <u>from</u> the comb.

Gospel Acclamation John 11:25-26
I am the resurrection and the life,
 <u>says</u> the Lord,
whoever believes in me will <u>never</u> die.

782 3rd Sunday of Lent (C)
Psalm102:1-4, 6-8, 11. R℣ v.8

The Lord is com-pas-sion and love.

1. My soul, give thanks <u>to</u> the Lord,
   all my being, bless his <u>holy</u> name.
   My soul, give thanks <u>to</u> the Lord
   and never forget <u>all</u> his blessings.

2. It is he who forgives <u>all</u> your guilt,
   who heals every one <u>of</u> your ills,
   who redeems your life <u>from</u> the grave,
   who crowns you with love <u>and</u>
   compassion.

3. The Lord does <u>deeds</u> of justice,
   gives judgement for all who <u>are</u>
   oppressed.
   He made known his <u>ways</u> to Moses
   and his deeds to Is<u>rael</u>'s sons.

4. The Lord is compas<u>sion</u> and love,
   slow to anger and <u>rich</u> in mercy.
   For as the heavens are high a<u>bove</u> the
   earth
   so strong is his love for <u>those</u> who
   fear him.

Gospel Acclamation Matthew 4:17
Repent, <u>says</u> the Lord,
for the kingdom of heaven is <u>close</u> at
hand.

783 4th Sunday of Lent (A)
Psalm 22. R℣ v.1

The Lord is my shep-herd; there is
no-thing I shall want.

1. The Lord <u>is</u> my shepherd;
   there is nothing <u>I</u> shall want.
   Fresh and green <u>are</u> the pastures
   where he gives <u>me</u> repose.

2. Near restful wa<u>ters</u> he leads me,
   to revive my <u>drooping</u> spirit.
   He guides me along <u>the</u> right path;
   he is true <u>to</u> his name.

3. If I should walk in the val<u>ley</u> of
   darkness
   no evil <u>would</u> I fear.
   You are there with your crook <u>and</u>
   your staff;
   with these you <u>give</u> me comfort.

4. You have prepared a ban<u>quet</u> for me
   in the sight <u>of</u> my foes.
   My head you have anoin<u>ted</u> with oil;
   my cup is <u>overflowing</u>.

5. Surely goodness and kind<u>ness</u> shall
   follow me
   all the days <u>of</u> my life.
   In the Lord's own house <u>shall</u> I dwell
   for <u>ever</u> and ever.

Gospel Acclamation John 8:12
I am the light of the world, <u>says</u> the
Lord;
anyone who follows me will have the
<u>light</u> of life.

784 4th Sunday of Lent (B)
Psalm 136. R⁊ v.6

O let my tongue cleave to my
mouth if I re-mem-ber you not!

1. By the rivers of Babylon there we sat
   and wept,
   remembering Zion;
   on the poplars that grew there
   we hung up our harps.

2. For it was there that they asked us,
   our captors, for songs,
   our oppressors, for joy.
   'Sing to us,' they said,
   'one of Zion's songs.'

3. O how could we sing the song of the
   Lord
   on alien soil?
   If I forget you, Jerusalem,
   let my right hand wither!

4. O let my tongue cleave to my mouth
   if I remember you not,
   if I prize not Jerusalem,
   above all my joys!

Gospel Acclamation John 3:16
   God loved the world so much that he
   gave his only Son;
   everyone who believes in him has
   eternal life.

785 4th Sunday of Lent (C)
Psalm 33:1-6. R⁊ v.8

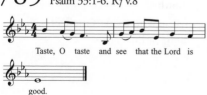

Taste, O taste and see that the Lord is
good.

1. I will bless the Lord at all times,
   his praise always on my lips;
   in the Lord my soul shall make its
   boast.
   The humble shall hear and be glad.

2. Glorify the Lord with me.
   Together let us praise his name.
   I sought the Lord and he answered me;
   from all my terrors he set me free.

3. Look towards him and be radiant;
   let your faces not be abashed.
   This poor man called; the Lord heard
   him
   and rescued him from all his distress.

Gospel Acclamation Luke 15:18
   I will leave this place and go to my
   father and say:
   'Father, I have sinned against heaven
   and against you.'

786 5th Sunday of Lent (A)
Psalm 129. R⁊ v.7

With the Lord there is mer - cy and
full - ness of re-demp- tion.

1. Out of the depths I cry to you, O Lord,
   Lord, hear my voice!
   O let your ears be attentive
   to the voice of my pleading.

2. If you, O Lord, should mark our guilt,
   Lord, who would survive?
   But with you is found forgiveness:
   for this we revere you.

3. My soul is waiting for the Lord,
   I count on his word.
   My soul is longing for the Lord
   more than watchman for daybreak.

4. Because with the Lord there is mercy
   and fullness of redemption,
   Israel indeed he will redeem
   from all its iniquity.

Gospel Acclamation John 11:25, 26
   I am the resurrection and the life,
      says the Lord;
   whoever believes in me will never die.

787 5th Sunday of Lent (B)
Psalm 50:3-4, 12-15. Ry v.12

A pure heart cre - ate for me, O God.

1. Have mercy on me, God, in your
   kindness.
   In your compassion blot out my
   offence.
   O wash me more and more from my
   guilt
   and cleanse me from my sin.

2. A pure heart create for me, O God,
   put a steadfast spirit within me.
   Do not cast me away from your
   presence,
   nor deprive me of your Holy Spirit.

3. Give me again the joy of your help;
   with a spirit of fervour sustain me,
   that I may teach transgressors your
   ways
   and sinners may return to you.

Gospel Acclamation John 12:26
   If a man serves me, says the Lord, he
      must follow me,
   wherever I am, my servant will be
   there too.

788 5th Sunday of Lent (C)
Psalm 125. Ry v.3

What mar - vels the Lord worked for us!

In - deed we were glad.

1. When the Lord delivered Zion from
   bondage,
   it seemed like a dream.
   Then was our mouth filled with
   laughter,
   on our lips there were songs.

2. The heathens themselves said:
   'What marvels the Lord worked for
   them!'
   What marvels the Lord worked for us!
   Indeed we were glad.

3. Deliver us, O Lord, from our bondage
   as streams in dry land.
   Those who are sowing in tears
   will sing when they reap.

4. They go out, they go out, full of tears
   carrying seed for the sowing:
   they come back, they come back, full
   of song,
   carrying their sheaves.

Gospel Acclamation Amos 5:14
   Seek good and not evil so that you
      may live,
   and that the Lord God of hosts may
      really be with you.

789 Passion Sunday (A, B, C)
Psalm 21:8-9, 17-20, 23-24. R℣ v.2

My God, my God, why have you for-sak-en me?

1. All who see _me_ deride me.
   They curl their lips, they _toss_ their
   heads.
   'He trusted in the Lord, _let_ him save
   him;
   let him release him if this _is_ his friend.'

2. Many dogs _have_ surrounded me,
   a band of the wic_ked_ beset me.
   They tear holes in my hands _and_ my
   feet;
   I can count every one _of_ my bones.

3. They divided my cloth_ing_ among
   them.
   They cast lots _for_ my robe.
   O Lord, do not leave _me_ alone,
   my strength, make _haste_ to help me!

4. I will tell of your name _to_ my brethren
   and praise you where they _are_
   assembled.
   'You who fear the Lord _give_ him
   praise;
   all sons of Jacob, _give_ him glory.'

Gospel Acclamation Philippians 2:8-9
   Christ was humbler yet, even to
   ac_cept_ing death, death _on_ a cross.
   But God _raised_ him high and gave
   him the name which is a_bove_ all
   names.

790 Holy Thursday – Evening Mass of the Lord's Supper (A, B, C)
Psalm 115:12-13, 15-18.
R℣ cf. 1 Corinthians 10:16

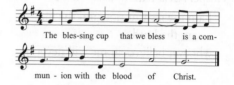

The bles-sing cup that we bless is a com-mun - ion with the blood of Christ.

1. How can I re_pay_ the Lord
   for his good_ness_ to me?
   The cup of salvation _I_ will raise;
   I will call _on_ the Lord's name.

2. O precious in the eyes _of_ the Lord
   is the death _of_ his faithful.
   Your ser_vant_, Lord, your servant am I;
   you have loos_ened_ my bonds.

3. A thanksgiving sacri_fice_ I make:
   I will call _on_ the Lord's name.
   My vows to the Lord I _will_ fulfil
   before _all_ his people.

Gospel Acclamation John 13:34
   I give you a _new_ commandment:
   love one another just as I _have_ loved
   you.

791 Good Friday – Celebration of the Lord's Passion (A, B, C)
Psalm 30:2, 6, 12-13, 15-17, 25.
R℣ Luke 23:46

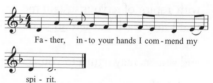

Fa - ther, in - to your hands I com - mend my spi - rit.

1. In you, O Lord, _I_ take refuge,
   let me never be _put_ to shame.
   In your justice, _set_ me free.
   It is you who will re_deem_ me, Lord.

2. In the face of <u>all</u> my foes
   I am <u>a</u> reproach,
   an object of scorn <u>to</u> my neighbours
   and of fear <u>to</u> my friends.

3. Those who see me <u>in</u> the street
   run <u>far</u> away from me.
   I am like the dead, forgo<u>tten</u> by all,
   like a thing <u>thrown</u> away.

4. But as for me, I trust <u>in</u> you, Lord,
   I say: 'You <u>are</u> my God.'
   My life is in your <u>hands</u>, deliver me
   from the hands of <u>those</u> who hate me.

5. Let your face shine <u>on</u> your servant.
   Save me <u>in</u> your love.
   Be strong, let your <u>heart</u> take courage,
   all who hope <u>in</u> the Lord.

Gospel Acclamation Philippians 2:8-9
   Christ was humbler yet, even to
      acce<u>pting</u> death, death <u>on</u> a cross.
   But God <u>raised</u> him high and gave
      him the name which is a<u>bove</u> all
      names.

792 Easter Sunday –
The Easter Vigil (A, B, C)

After the first Reading

Psalm 103:1-2, 5-6, 10, 12-14, 24, 35. R̸ cf. v.30

Send forth your Spi-rit, O Lord, and re-new the face of the earth.

1. Bless the <u>Lord</u>, my soul!
   Lord God, how <u>great</u> you are,
   clothed in majes<u>ty</u> and glory,
   wrapped in light as <u>in</u> a robe!

2. You founded the earth <u>on</u> its base,
   to stand firm from <u>age</u> to age.
   You wrapped it with the ocean <u>like</u> a
      cloak:
   the waters stood higher <u>than</u> the
      mountains.

3. You make springs gush forth <u>in</u> the
      valleys:
   they flow in be<u>tween</u> the hills.
   On their banks dwell the <u>birds</u> of
      heaven;
   from the branches they <u>sing</u> their song.

4. From your dwelling you wa<u>ter</u> the hills;
   earth drinks its fill <u>of</u> your gift.
   You make the grass grow <u>for</u> the cattle
   and the plants to <u>serve</u> our needs.

5. How many are your <u>works</u>, O Lord!
   In wisdom you have <u>made</u> them all.
   The earth is full <u>of</u> your riches.
   Bless the <u>Lord</u>, my soul!

After the second Reading

Psalm 15:5, 8-11. R̸ v.1

Pre-serve me, God, I take ref-uge in you.

1. O Lord, it is you who are my por<u>tion</u>
      and cup;
   it is you yourself who <u>are</u> my prize.
   I keep the Lord ever <u>in</u> my sight:
   since he is at my right hand, I <u>shall</u>
      stand firm.

2. And so my heart rejoices, my <u>soul</u> is
      glad;
   even my body shall <u>rest</u> in safety.
   For you will not leave my soul a<u>mong</u>
      the dead,
   nor let your beloved <u>know</u> decay.

Continued overleaf

3. O Lord, <u>you</u> will show me
   the <u>path</u> of life,
   the fullness of joy <u>in</u> your presence,
   at your right hand happ<u>iness</u> for ever.

After the third Reading

Psalm Exodus 15:1-6, 17-18. R℣ v.1

I will sing   to the Lord,   glo - rious his

tri - umph!

1. I will sing to the Lord, glor<u>ious</u> his
   triumph!
   Horse and rider he has thrown in<u>to</u>
   the sea!
   The Lord is my strength, my song,
   <u>my</u> salvation.

2. This is my God and <u>I</u> extol him,
   my father's God and I <u>give</u> him praise.
   The Lord is a warrior! The Lord <u>is</u> his
   name.

3. The chariots of Pharaoh he hurled
   in<u>to</u> the sea,
   the flower of his army is drowned <u>in</u>
   the sea.
   The deeps hide them; they sank <u>like</u> a
   stone.

4. Your right hand, Lord, glorious <u>in</u> its
   power,
   your right hand, Lord, has sha<u>ttered</u>
   the enemy.
   In the greatness of your glory you
   <u>crushed</u> the foe.

5. You will lead your people and plant
   them <u>on</u> your mountain,
   the sanctuary, Lord, which your
   <u>hands</u> have made.
   The Lord will reign for e<u>ver</u> and ever.

After the fourth Reading

Psalm 29:2, 4-6, 11-13. R℣ v.2

I   will praise you,   Lord,

you have res - cued   me.

1. I will praise you, Lord, <u>you</u> have
   rescued me
   and have not let my enemies rejoice
   <u>over</u> me.
   O Lord, you have raised my soul
   <u>from</u> the dead,
   restored me to life from those who
   sink in<u>to</u> the grave.

2. Sing psalms to the Lord, <u>you</u> who
   love him,
   give thanks to his <u>holy</u> name.
   His anger lasts but a moment; his
   fa<u>vour</u> through life.
   At night there are tears, but joy
   <u>comes</u> with dawn.

3. The Lord listened <u>and</u> had pity.
   The Lord came <u>to</u> my help.
   For me you have changed my
   mourning <u>into</u> dancing,
   O Lord, my God, I will thank <u>you</u>
   for ever.

After the fifth Reading

Psalm Isaiah 12:2-6. R℣ v.3

With   joy   you will draw wa - ter   from the

wells   of sal - va - tion.

1. Truly God is <u>my</u> salvation,
   I trust, I <u>shall</u> not fear.
   For the Lord is my <u>strength</u>, my song,
   he be<u>came</u> my Saviour.

2. Give thanks <u>to</u> the Lord,
   give praise <u>to</u> his name!
   Make his mighty deeds known <u>to</u> the
      peoples,
   declare the greatness <u>of</u> his name.

3. Sing a psalm to the Lord for he has
      done glo<u>ri</u>ous deeds,
   make them known to <u>all</u> the earth!
   People of Zion, sing and <u>shout</u> for joy
   for great in your midst is the Holy
      <u>One</u> of Israel.

After the sixth Reading

Psalm 18:8-11. R℟ John 6:69

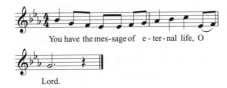

You have the mes-sage of e - ter - nal life, O

Lord.

1. The law of the <u>Lord</u> is perfect,
   it re<u>vives</u> the soul.
   The rule of the Lord is <u>to</u> be trusted,
   it gives wisdom <u>to</u> the simple.

2. The precepts of the <u>Lord</u> are right,
   they glad<u>den</u> the heart.
   The command of the <u>Lord</u> is clear,
   it gives light <u>to</u> the eyes.

3. The fear of the <u>Lord</u> is holy,
   abi<u>ding</u> for ever.
   The decrees of the <u>Lord</u> are truth
   and all <u>of</u> them just.

4. They are more to be de<u>sired</u> than gold,
   than the pur<u>est</u> of gold
   and sweeter are <u>they</u> than honey,
   than honey <u>from</u> the comb.

After the seventh Reading

Psalm 41:3, 5, 42:3, 4. R℟ 41:2

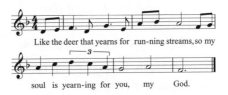

Like the deer that yearns for run-ning streams, so my

soul is yearn-ing for you,   my   God.

1. My soul is thirs<u>ting</u> for God,
   the God <u>of</u> my life;
   when can I en<u>ter</u> and and see
   the <u>face</u> of God?

2. These things will I remember as I
      pour <u>out</u> my soul:
   how I would lead the rejoicing crowd
      into the <u>house</u> of God,
   amid cries of gladness <u>and</u>
      thanksgiving,
   the throng <u>wild</u> with joy.

3. O send forth your light <u>and</u> your
      truth;
   let these <u>be</u> my guide.
   Let them bring me to your <u>holy</u>
      mountain
   to the place <u>where</u> you dwell.

4. And I will come to the al<u>tar</u> of God,
   the God <u>of</u> my joy.
   My Redeemer, I will thank you <u>on</u>
      the harp,
   O <u>God</u>, my God.

*If a Baptism takes place, the Psalm which
follows the fifth Reading is used, or the one
that follows here.*

Psalm 50:12-15, 18, 19. R℟ v.12

A pure   heart cre - ate for me, O God.

Continued overleaf

1. A pure heart create for <u>me</u>, O God,
   put a steadfast sp<u>irit</u> within me.
   Do not cast me away <u>from</u> your
       presence,
   nor deprive me of your <u>Ho</u>ly Spirit.

2. Give me again the joy <u>of</u> your help;
   with a spirit of fer<u>vour</u> sustain me,
   that I may teach transgr<u>ess</u>ors your
       ways
   and sinners may re<u>turn</u> to you.

3. For in sacrifice you take <u>no</u> delight,
   burnt offering from me you <u>would</u>
       refuse,
   my sacrifice, a <u>con</u>trite spirit.
   A humbled, contrite heart you <u>will</u>
       not spurn.

793 Easter Sunday – The Mass of Easter Night (A, B, C)
Psalm 117:1-2, 16-17, 22-23

Al - le - lu - ia, al - le - lu - ia, al - le - lu - ia.

1. Give thanks to the Lord for <u>he</u> is good,
   for his love <u>has</u> no end.
   Let the family of Is<u>ra</u>el say:
   'His love <u>has</u> no end.'

2. The Lord's right <u>hand</u> has triumphed;
   his right hand <u>raised</u> me up.
   I shall not die, <u>I</u> shall live
   and re<u>count</u> his deeds.

3. The stone which the bui<u>lders</u> rejected
   has become the <u>cor</u>nerstone.
   This is the work <u>of</u> the Lord,
   a marvel <u>in</u> our eyes.

794 Easter Sunday – Mass of the Day (A, B, C)
Psalm 117:1-2, 16-17, 22-23. R℣ v.24

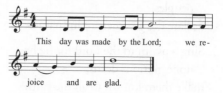

This day was made by the Lord; we rejoice and are glad.

1. Give thanks to the Lord for <u>he</u> is good,
   for his love <u>has</u> no end.
   Let the family of Is<u>ra</u>el say:
   'His love <u>has</u> no end.'

2. The Lord's right <u>hand</u> has triumphed;
   his right hand <u>raised</u> me up.
   I shall not die, <u>I</u> shall live
   and re<u>count</u> his deeds.

3. The stone which the bui<u>lders</u> rejected
   has become the <u>cor</u>nerstone.
   This is the work <u>of</u> the Lord,
   a marvel <u>in</u> our eyes.

Gospel Acclamation 1 Corinthians 5:7-8
   Christ, our passover, <u>has</u> been
       sacrificed;
   let us celebrate the feast, then, <u>in</u> the
       Lord.

795 2nd Sunday of Easter (A)
Psalm 117:2-4, 13-15, 22-24. R℣ v.1

Give thanks to the Lord for he is good, for his
love has no end.

OR

Plainsong

Al - le - lu - ia, al - le - lu - ia,
al - le - lu - ia.

1. Let the sons of Israel say: 'His love
    has no end.'
   Let the sons of Aaron say: 'His love
    has no end.'
   Let those who fear the Lord say:
   'His love has no end.'

2. I was thrust down and falling but the
    Lord was my helper.
   The Lord is my strength and my
    song: he was my Saviour.
   There are shouts of joy and victory
   in the tents of the just.

3. The stone which the builders rejected
    has become the cornerstone.
   This is the work of the Lord,
    a marvel in our eyes.
   This day was made by the Lord;
   we rejoice and are glad.

Gospel Acclamation John 20:29
   Jesus said: 'You believe because you
    can see me.
   Happy are those who have not seen
    and yet believe.'

1. Let the sons of Israel say: 'His love
    has no end.'
   Let the sons of Aaron say: 'His love
    has no end.'
   Let those who fear the Lord say:
   'His love has no end.'

2. The Lord's right hand has
    triumphed; his right hand raised
    me up.
   I shall not die, I shall live and recount
    his deeds.
   I was punished, I was punished by
    the Lord,
   but not doomed to die.

3. The stone which the builders rejected
    has become the cornerstone.
   This is the work of the Lord,
    a marvel in our eyes.
   This day was made by the Lord;
   we rejoice and are glad.

Gospel Acclamation John 20:29
   Jesus said: 'You believe because you
    can see me.
   Happy are those who have not seen
    and yet believe.'

796 2nd Sunday of Easter (B)
Psalm 117:2-4, 15-18, 22-24. R℣ v.1

Give thanks to the Lord for he   is good, for his

love has no end.

OR   Plainsong

Al - le - lu - ia,   al - le - lu - ia,

al - le - lu - ia.

797 2nd Sunday of Easter (C)
Psalm 117:2-4, 22-27. R℣ v.1

Give thanks to the Lord for he   is good, for his

love has no end.

OR   Plainsong

Al - le - lu - ia,   al - le - lu - ia,

al - le - lu - ia.

Continued overleaf

1. Let the sons of Israel say: 'His love
   has no end.'
   Let the sons of Aaron say: 'His love
   has no end.'
   Let those who fear the Lord say:
   'His love has no end.'

2. The stone which the builders rejected
   has become the cornerstone.
   This is the work of the Lord,
   a marvel in our eyes.
   This day was made by the Lord;
   we rejoice and are glad.

3. O Lord, grant us salvation; O Lord,
   grant success.
   Blessed in the name of the Lord is he
   who comes.
   We bless you from the house of the
   Lord;
   the Lord God is our light.

Gospel Acclamation John 20:29
   Jesus said: 'You believe because you
   can see me.
   Happy are those who have not seen
   and yet believe.'

2. I will bless the Lord who gives me
   counsel,
   who even at night directs my heart.
   I keep the Lord ever in my sight:
   since he is at my right hand, I shall
   stand firm.

3. And so my heart rejoices, my soul is
   glad;
   even my body shall rest in safety.
   For you will not leave my soul among
   the dead,
   not let your beloved know decay.

4. O Lord, you will show me
   the path of life.
   The fullness of joy in your presence,
   at your right hand happiness for ever.

Gospel Acclamation cf. Luke 24:32
   Lord Jesus, explain the scriptures to us.
   Make our hearts burn within us as
   you talk to us.

798 3rd Sunday of Easter (A)
Psalm 15:1-2, 5, 7-11. R℣ v.11

Show us, Lord, the path   of life.

1. Preserve me, God, I take refuge in you.
   I say to the Lord: 'You are my God.
   O Lord, it is you who are my portion
   and cup;
   it is you yourself who are my prize.'

799 3rd Sunday of Easter (B)
Psalm 4:2, 4, 7, 9. R℣ v.7

Lift up the light of your face on us, O Lord.

1. When I call, answer me, O God of
   justice;
   from anguish you release me, have
   mercy and hear me!
   It is the Lord who grants favours to
   those whom he loves;
   the Lord hears me whenever I call him.

2. 'What can bring us happiness?' <u>many</u>
   say.
  Lift up the light of your face on <u>us</u>,
   O Lord.
  I will lie down in peace and sleep
   <u>comes</u> at once,
  for you alone, Lord, make me <u>dwell</u>
   in safety.

Gospel Acclamation cf. Luke 24:32
  Lord Jesus, explain the scrip<u>tures</u> to us.
  Make our hearts burn within us as
   you <u>talk</u> to us.

3. The Lord listened <u>and</u> had pity.
  The Lord came <u>to</u> my help.
  For me you have changed my
   mourning <u>into</u> dancing,
  O Lord, my God, I will thank <u>you</u>
   for ever.

Gospel Acclamation cf. Luke 24:32
  Lord Jesus, explain the scrip<u>tures</u> to us.
  Make our hearts burn within us as
   you <u>talk</u> to us.

800 3rd Sunday of Easter (C)
Psalm 29:2, 4-6, 11-13. R℣ v.2

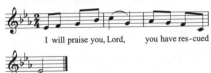

I will praise you, Lord,   you have res-cued
me.

1. I will praise you, Lord, <u>you</u> have
   rescued me
  and have not let my enemies rejoice
   <u>over</u> me.
  O Lord, you have raised my soul
   <u>from</u> the dead,
  restored me to life from those who
   sink in<u>to</u> the grave.

2. Sing psalms to the Lord, <u>you</u> who
   love him,
  give thanks to his <u>holy</u> name.
  His anger lasts but a moment; his
   fa<u>vour</u> through life.
  At night there are tears, but joy
   <u>comes</u> with dawn.

801 4th Sunday of Easter (A)
Psalm 22:1-6. R℣ v.1

The Lord is my shep-herd; there is
no-thing I shall want.

1. The Lord <u>is</u> my shepherd;
   there is nothing <u>I</u> shall want.
  Fresh and green <u>are</u> the pastures
  where he gives <u>me</u> repose.

2. Near restful wa<u>ters</u> he leads me,
  to revive my <u>drooping</u> spirit.
  He guides me along <u>the</u> right path;
  he is true <u>to</u> his name.

3. If I should walk in the val<u>ley</u> of
   darkness
  no evil <u>would</u> I fear.
  You are there with your crook <u>and</u>
   your staff;
  with these you <u>give</u> me comfort.

4. You have prepared a ban<u>quet</u> for me
  in the sight <u>of</u> my foes.
  My head you have anoin<u>ted</u> with oil;
  my cup is <u>overflowing</u>.

Continued overleaf

5. Surely goodness and kind<u>ness</u> shall
    follow me
 all the days <u>of</u> my life.
 In the Lord's own house <u>shall</u> I dwell
 for e<u>ver</u> and ever.

Gospel Acclamation John 10:14

 I am the good shepherd, <u>says</u> the
    Lord;
 I know my own sheep and my <u>own</u>
    know me.

802 4th Sunday of Easter (B)
Psalm 117:1, 8-9, 21-23, 26, 28-29.
R⁊ v.22

1. Give thanks to the Lord for he is
    good, for his love <u>has</u> no end.
 It is better to take refuge in the Lord
    than to <u>trust</u> in mortals;
 it is better to take refuge <u>in</u> the Lord
    than to <u>trust</u> in rulers.

2. I will thank you for you have given
    answer and you <u>are</u> my Saviour.
 The stone which the builders rejected
    has be<u>come</u> the cornerstone.
 This is the work <u>of</u> the Lord,
    a marvel <u>in</u> our eyes.

3. Blessed in the name of the Lord is <u>he</u>
    who comes.
 We bless you from the house <u>of</u> the
    Lord;
 I will thank you for you have given
    answer and you <u>are</u> my Saviour.
 Give thanks to the Lord for he is
    good; for his love <u>has</u> no end.

Gospel Acclamation John 10:14

 I am the good shepherd, <u>says</u> the
    Lord;
 I know my own sheep and my <u>own</u>
    know me.

803 4th Sunday of Easter (C)
Psalm 99:1-3, 5. R⁊ v.3

1. Cry out with joy to the Lord, <u>all</u> the
    earth.
 Serve the <u>Lord</u> with gladness.
 Come before him, sing<u>ing</u> for joy.

2. Know that he, the <u>Lord</u>, is God.
 He made us, we be<u>long</u> to him,
 we are his people, the sheep <u>of</u> his
    flock.

3. Indeed, how good <u>is</u> the Lord,
 eternal his mer<u>ci</u>ful love.
 He is faithful from <u>age</u> to age.

Gospel Acclamation John 10:14

 I am the good shepherd, <u>says</u> the
    Lord;
 I know my own sheep and my <u>own</u>
    know me.

804 5th Sunday of Easter (A)
Psalm 32:1-2, 4-5, 18-19. R⁊ v.22

1. Ring out your joy to the Lord,
   O you just;
   for praise is fitting for loyal hearts.
   Give thanks to the Lord upon the harp,
   with a ten-stringed lute sing him songs.

2. For the word of the Lord is faithful
   and all his works to be trusted.
   The Lord loves justice and right
   and fills the earth with his love.

3. The Lord looks on those who revere
   him,
   on those who hope in his love,
   to rescue their souls from death,
   to keep them alive in famine.

Gospel Acclamation John 14:6
   Jesus said: 'I am the Way, the Truth
   and the Life.'
   No one can come to the Father
   except through me.'

2. All the earth shall remember and
   return to the Lord,
   all families of the nations worship
   before him.
   They shall worship him, all the
   mighty of the earth;
   before him shall bow all who go
   down to the dust.

3. And my soul shall live for him, my
   children serve him.
   They shall tell of the Lord to
   generations yet to come,
   declare his faithfulness to peoples yet
   unborn:
   'These things the Lord has done.'

Gospel Acclamation John 15:4-5
   Make your home in me, as I make
   mine in you.
   Whoever remains in me bears fruit in
   plenty.

806 5th Sunday of Easter (C)
Psalm 144:8-13. R℣ cf. v.1

I will bless your name for e - ver, O
God my King.

1. The Lord is kind and full of
   compassion,
   slow to anger, abounding in love.
   How good is the Lord to all,
   compassionate to all his creatures.

2. All your creatures shall thank you,
   O Lord,
   and your friends shall repeat their
   blessing.
   They shall speak of the glory of your
   reign
   and declare your might, O God.

805 5th Sunday of Easter (B)
Psalm 21:26-28, 30-32. R℣ v.26

You are my praise, O Lord, in the
great as - sem - bly.

1. My vows I will pay before those who
   fear him.
   The poor shall eat and shall have
   their fill.
   They shall praise the Lord, those who
   seek him.
   May their hearts live for ever and ever!

Continued overleaf

3. They will make known to all your
   mighty deeds
   and the glorious splendour of your
   reign.
   Yours is an everlasting kingdom;
   your rule lasts from age to age.

Gospel Acclamation John 13:34
   Jesus said: 'I give you a new
   commandment:
   love one another, just as I have loved
   you.'

807 6th Sunday of Easter (A)
Psalm 65:1-7, 16, 20. R⁊ v.1

Cry out with joy to God all the earth.

1. Cry out with joy to God all the earth,
   O sing to the glory of his name.
   O render him glorious praise,
   say to God: 'How tremendous your
   deeds!'

2. 'Before you all the earth shall bow;
   shall sing to you, sing to your name!'
   Come and see the works of God,
   tremendous his deeds among men.

3. He turned the sea into dry land,
   they passed through the river dry-shod.
   Let our joy then be in him;
   he rules for ever by his might.

4. Come and hear, all who fear God.
   I will tell what he did for my soul:
   blessed be God who did not reject
      my prayer
   nor withhold his love from me.

Gospel Acclamation John 14:23
   Jesus said: 'If anyone loves me they
      will keep my word,
   and my Father will love them and we
      shall come to them.'

808 6th Sunday of Easter (B)
Psalm 97:1-4. R⁊ cf. v.2

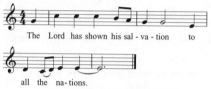

The Lord has shown his sal - va - tion to

all the na- tions.

1. Sing a new song to the Lord
   for he has worked wonders.
   His right hand and his holy arm
   have brought salvation.

2. The Lord has made known his
      salvation;
   has shown his justice to the nations.
   He has remembered his truth and love
   for the house of Israel.

3. All the ends of the earth have seen
   the salvation of our God.
   Shout to the Lord all the earth,
   ring out your joy.

Gospel Acclamation John 14:23
   Jesus said: 'If anyone loves me they
      will keep my word,
   and my Father will love them and we
      shall come to them.'

809 6th Sunday of Easter (C)
Psalm 66:2-3, 5-6, 8. R⁊ v.4

Let   the peo - ples praise you, O God, let

all the peo - ples   praise you.

1. O God, be gracious and bless us
   and let your face shed its light upon us.
   So will your ways be known upon
       earth,
   and all nations learn your saving help.

2. Let the nations be glad and exult
   for you rule the world with justice.
   With fairness you rule the peoples,
   you guide the nations on earth.

3. Let the peoples praise you, O God;
   let all the peoples praise you.
   May God still give us his blessing
   till the ends of the earth revere him.

Gospel Acclamation John 14:23
   Jesus said: 'If anyone loves me they
       will keep my word,
   and my Father will love them and we
       shall come to them.'

810 The Ascension of the Lord
     (A, B, C)
     Psalm 46:2-3, 6-9. R℣ v.6

God goes up with shouts of joy; the
Lord goes up with trum - pet blast.

1. All peoples, clap your hands,
   cry to God with shouts of joy!
   For the Lord, the Most High,
       we must fear,
   great King over all the earth.

2. God goes up with shouts of joy;
   the Lord goes up with trumpet blast.
   Sing praise for God, sing praise,
   sing praise to our King, sing praise.

3. God is King of all the earth.
   Sing praise with all your skill.
   God is King over the nations;
   God reigns on his holy throne.

Gospel Acclamation Matthew 28:19, 20
   Go, make disciples of all the nations;
   I am with you always; yes, to the end
       of time.

811 7th Sunday of Easter (A)
     Psalm 26:1, 4, 7-8. R℣ v.13

I am sure I shall see the Lord's
good - ness in the land of the liv - ing.

1. The Lord is my light and my help;
   whom shall I fear?
   The Lord is the stronghold of my life;
   before whom shall I shrink?

2. There is one thing I ask of the Lord,
   for this I long,
   to live in the house of the Lord,
   all the days of my life.

3. O Lord, hear my voice when I call;
   have mercy and answer.
   Of you my heart has spoken:
   'Seek, seek his face.'

Gospel Acclamation cf. John 14:18
   I will not leave you orphans,
       says the Lord;
   I will come back to you, and your
       hearts will be full of joy.

812 7th Sunday of Easter (B)
Psalm 102:1-2, 11-12, 19-20. R℔ v.19

The Lord has set his sway in heav'n.

1. My soul, give thanks <u>to</u> the Lord;
   all my being, bless his <u>holy</u> name.
   My soul, give thanks <u>to</u> the Lord
   and never forget <u>all</u> his blessings.

2. For as the heavens are high a<u>bove</u> the
      earth
   so strong is his love for <u>those</u> who
      fear him.
   As far as the east is <u>from</u> the west
   so far does he re<u>move</u> our sins.

3. The Lord has set his <u>sway</u> in heaven
   and his kingdom is ruling <u>over</u> all.
   Give thanks to the Lord, <u>all</u> his angels,
   mighty in power, ful<u>filling</u> his word.

Gospel Acclamation cf. John 14:18
   I will not leave you orphans,
      <u>says</u> the Lord;
   I will come back to you, and your
      hearts will be <u>full</u> of joy.

813 7th Sunday of Easter (C)
Psalm 96:1-2, 6-7, 9. R℔ vv.1, 9

The Lord is King, most

high a-bove all the earth.

1. The Lord is King, let <u>earth</u> rejoice,
   the many coast<u>lands</u> be glad.
   His throne is jus<u>tice</u> and right.

2. The skies pro<u>claim</u> his justice;
   all peoples <u>see</u> his glory.
   All you spirits, <u>wor</u>ship him.

3. For you indeed <u>are</u> the Lord
   most high above <u>all</u> the earth
   exalted far a<u>bove</u> all spirits.

Gospel Acclamation cf. John 14:18
   I will not leave you orphans,
      <u>says</u> the Lord;
   I will come back to you, and your
      hearts will be <u>full</u> of joy.

814 Pentecost Sunday (A, B, C)
Psalm 103:1, 24, 29-31, 34. R℔ cf. v.30

Send forth your Spi-rit, O Lord, and re-

new the face of the earth.

1. Bless the <u>Lord</u>, my soul!
   Lord God, how <u>great</u> you are.
   How many are your <u>works</u>, O Lord!
   The earth is full <u>of</u> your riches.

2. You take back your Spi<u>rit</u>, they die,
   returning to the dust from <u>which</u>
      they came.
   You send forth your Spirit, they <u>are</u>
      created;
   and you renew the face <u>of</u> the earth.

3. May the glory of the Lord <u>last</u> for ever!
   May the Lord rejoice <u>in</u> his works!
   May my thoughts be pleas<u>ing</u> to him.
   I find my joy <u>in</u> the Lord.

Gospel Acclamation
   Come, Holy Spirit, fill the hearts <u>of</u>
      your faithful
   and kindle in them the fire <u>of</u> your
      love.

815 The Most Holy Trinity (A)
Psalm Daniel 3:52-56. R7 v.52

To you glo - ry and praise for
e - ver - more.

1. You are blest, Lord God of our fathers.
   Blest your glorious holy name.

2. You are blest in the temple of your
   glory.
   You are blest on the throne of your
   kingdom.

3. You are blest who gaze into the depths.
   You are blest in the firmament of
   heaven.

Gospel Acclamation cf. Revelation 1:8
   Glory be to the Father, and to the
      Son, and to the Holy Spirit,
   the God who is, who was, and who is
   to come.

816 The Most Holy Trinity (B)
Psalm 32:4-6, 9, 18-20, 22. R7 v.12

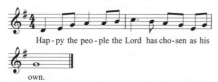

Hap - py the peo - ple the Lord has cho - sen as his
own.

1. The word of the Lord is faithful
   and all his works to be trusted.
   The Lord loves justice and right
   and fills the earth with his love.

2. By his word the heavens were made,
   by the breath of his mouth all the stars.
   He spoke; and they came to be.
   He commanded; they sprang into
   being.

3. The Lord looks on those who revere
   him,
   on those who hope in his love,
   to rescue their souls from death,
   to keep them alive in famine.

4. Our soul is waiting for the Lord.
   The Lord is our help and our shield.
   May your love be upon us, O Lord,
   as we place all our hope in you.

Gospel Acclamation cf. Revelation 1:8
   Glory be to the Father, and to the
      Son, and to the Holy Spirit,
   the God who is, who was, and who is
   to come.

817 The Most Holy Trinity (C)
Psalm 8:4-9. R7 v.2

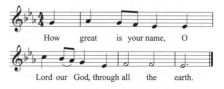

How great is your name, O
Lord our God, through all the earth.

1. When I see the heavens, the work of
   your hands,
   the moon and the stars which you
   arranged,
   what are we that you should keep us
   in mind,
   mortals that you care for us?

2. Yet you have made us little less than
   gods;
   with glory and honour you crowned us,
   gave us power over the works of your
   hand,
   put all things under our feet.

3. All of them, sheep and cattle,
   yes, even the savage beasts,
   birds of the air, and fish
   that make their way through the waters.

Continued overleaf

Gospel Acclamation cf. Revelation 1:8

Glory be to the Father, and to the
  Son, and to the <u>Ho</u>ly Spirit,
the God who is, who was, and who <u>is</u>
  to come.

818 Corpus Christi, The Body and
Blood of Christ (A)
Psalm 147:12-15, 19-20. R℣ v.12

O praise the Lord, Je - ru - sa- lem!

1. O praise the <u>Lord</u>, Jerusalem!
   Zion, <u>praise</u> your God!
   He has strengthened the bars <u>of</u> your
     gates,
   he has blessed the chil<u>dren</u> within you.

2. He established peace <u>on</u> your borders,
   he feeds you with <u>fin</u>est wheat.
   He sends out his word <u>to</u> the earth
   and swiftly runs <u>his</u> command.

3. He makes his word <u>known</u> to Jacob,
   to Israel his laws <u>and</u> decrees.
   He has not dealt thus with <u>oth</u>er
     nations;
   he has not taught them <u>his</u> decrees.

Gospel Acclamation John 6:51-52

I am the living bread which has come
  down from heaven, <u>says</u> the Lord.
Anyone who eats this bread will <u>live</u>
  for ever.

819 Corpus Christi, The Body and
Blood of Christ (B)
Psalm 115:12-13, 15-18. R℣ v.13

The cup of sal-va-tion I will raise; I will

call on the Lord's name.

1. How can I re<u>pay</u> the Lord
   for his good<u>ness</u> to me?
   The cup of salvation <u>I</u> will raise;
   I will call <u>on</u> the Lord's name.

2. O precious in the eyes <u>of</u> the Lord
   is the death <u>of</u> his faithful.
   Your servant, Lord, your ser<u>vant</u> am I;
   you have loos<u>ened</u> my bonds.

3. A thanksgiving sacri<u>fice</u> I make:
   I will call <u>on</u> the Lord's name.
   My vows to the Lord I <u>will</u> fulfil
   before <u>all</u> his people.

Gospel Acclamation John 6:51-52

I am the living bread which has come
  down from heaven, <u>says</u> the Lord.
Anyone who eats this bread will <u>live</u>
  for ever.

820 Corpus Christi, The Body and
Blood of Christ (C)
Psalm 109:1-4. R℣ v.4

You are a priest for e - ver,

like Mel - chi - ze - dek of old.

1. The Lord's revelation <u>to</u> my Master:
   'Sit <u>on</u> my right:
   I will put your foes be<u>neath</u> your feet.

2. The Lord will <u>send</u> from Zion
   your scep<u>tre</u> of power:
   rule in the midst of <u>all</u> your foes.

3. A prince from the day <u>of</u> your birth
   on the <u>ho</u>ly mountains;
   from the womb before the daybreak <u>I</u>
     begot you.

4. The Lord has sworn an oath he <u>will</u>
   not change.
   'You are a <u>priest</u> for ever,
   a priest like Melchize<u>dek</u> of old.'

Gospel Acclamation John 6:51-52
   I am the living bread which has come
   down from heaven, <u>says</u> the Lord.
   Anyone who eats this bread will <u>live</u>
   for ever.

Gospel Acclamation
   Blessings on the King who comes, in
   the name <u>of</u> the Lord!
   Peace in heaven and glory in the
   <u>high</u>est heavens!

822 3rd Sunday in Ordinary Time (A)
Psalm 26:1, 4, 13-14. R℣ v.1

The Lord is my light and my help.

1. The Lord is my light <u>and</u> my help;
   whom <u>shall</u> I fear?
   The Lord is the stronghold <u>of</u> my life;
   before whom <u>shall</u> I shrink?

2. There is one thing I ask <u>of</u> the Lord,
   for <u>this</u> I long,
   to live in the house <u>of</u> the Lord,
   all the days <u>of</u> my life.

3. I am sure I shall see <u>the</u> Lord's goodness
   in the land <u>of</u> the living.
   Hope in him, hold firm <u>and</u> take heart.
   Hope <u>in</u> the Lord!

Gospel Acclamation Matthew 4:23
   Jesus proclaimed the Good News <u>of</u>
   the kingdom,
   and cured all kinds of sickness <u>among</u>
   the people.

821 2nd Sunday in Ordinary Time (A)
Psalm 39:2, 4, 7-10. R℣ vv.8-9

Here I am, Lord! I come to do your will.

1. I waited, I waited for the Lord and <u>he</u>
   stooped down to me;
   he <u>heard</u> my cry.
   He put a new song in<u>to</u> my mouth,
   praise <u>of</u> our God.

2. You do not ask for sacri<u>fice</u> and
   offerings,
   but an <u>open</u> ear.
   You do not ask for holo<u>caust</u> and
   victim.
   Instead, <u>here</u> am I.

3. In the scroll of the book <u>it</u> stands
   written
   that I should <u>do</u> your will.
   My God, I delight <u>in</u> your law
   in the depth <u>of</u> my heart.

4. Your justice I <u>have</u> proclaimed
   in the <u>great</u> assembly.
   My lips I <u>have</u> not sealed;
   you know <u>it</u>, O Lord.

823 4th Sunday in Ordinary Time (A)
Psalm 145:7-10. R℣ Matthew 5:3

How happy are the poor in spirit;
for theirs is the kingdom of heav'n.

Continued overleaf

1. It is the Lord who keeps <u>faith</u> for ever,
   who is just to those who <u>are</u> oppressed.
   It is he who gives bread <u>to</u> the hungry,
   the Lord, who sets pri<u>so</u>ners free.

2. It is the Lord who gives sight <u>to</u> the
   blind,
   who raises up those who <u>are</u> bowed
   down,
   the Lord, who pro<u>tects</u> the stranger
   and upholds the wi<u>dow</u> and orphan.

3. It is the Lord who <u>loves</u> the just
   but thwarts the path <u>of</u> the wicked.
   The Lord will <u>reign</u> for ever,
   Zion's God, from <u>age</u> to age.

Gospel Acclamation Matthew 11:25
   Blessed are you, Father, Lord of
   hea<u>ven</u> and earth,
   for revealing the mysteries of the
   kingdom <u>to</u> mere children.

3. With a steadfast heart they <u>will</u> not fear;
   open-handed, they give <u>to</u> the poor;
   their justice stands <u>firm</u> for ever.
   Their heads will be <u>raised</u> in glory.

Gospel Acclamation John 8:12
   I am the light of the world,
   <u>says</u> the Lord,
   anyone who follows me will have the
   <u>light</u> of life.

824 5th Sunday
in Ordinary Time (A)
Psalm 111:4-9. R℣ v.4

The good will be   a light   in the
dark - ness.

1. They are a light in the darkness <u>for</u>
   the upright:
   they are generous, merci<u>ful</u> and just.
   The good take pi<u>ty</u> and lend,
   they conduct their af<u>fairs</u> with honour.

2. The just will <u>never</u> waver:
   they will be remem<u>bered</u> for ever.
   They have no fear of <u>evil</u> news;
   with a firm heart they trust <u>in</u> the Lord.

825 6th Sunday
in Ordinary Time (A)
Psalm 118:1-2, 4-5, 17-18, 33-34.
R℣ v.1

They are hap - py who fol - low God's   law.

1. They are happy whose <u>life</u> is blameless,
   who fol<u>low</u> God's law!
   They are happy those who <u>do</u> his will,
   seeking him with <u>all</u> their hearts.

2. You have laid <u>down</u> your precepts
   to be o<u>beyed</u> with care.
   May my foot<u>steps</u> be firm
   to o<u>bey</u> your statutes.

3. Bless your servant and <u>I</u> shall live
   and o<u>bey</u> your word.
   Open my eyes that I <u>may</u> consider
   the wonders <u>of</u> your law.

4. Teach me the demands <u>of</u> your statutes
   and I will keep them <u>to</u> the end.
   Train me to ob<u>serve</u> your law,
   to keep it <u>with</u> my heart.

Gospel Acclamation 1 Samuel 3:9; John 6:68
   Speak, Lord, your ser<u>vant</u> is listening;
   you have the message of e<u>ternal</u> life.

826

7th Sunday in Ordinary Time (A)
Psalm 102:1-4, 8, 10, 12-13. R℟ v.8

The Lord is com-pas-sion, com-pas-sion and love.

1. My soul, give thanks <u>to</u> the Lord,
   all my being, bless his <u>holy</u> name.
   My soul, give thanks <u>to</u> the Lord
   and never forget <u>all</u> his blessings.

2. It is he who forgives <u>all</u> your guilt,
   who heals every one <u>of</u> your ills,
   who redeems your life <u>from</u> the grave,
   who crowns you with love <u>and</u>
   compassion.

3. The Lord is compas<u>sion</u> and love,
   slow to anger and <u>rich</u> in mercy.
   He does not treat us according <u>to</u> our
   sins
   nor repay us according <u>to</u> our faults.

4. As far as the east is <u>from</u> the west
   so far does he re<u>move</u> our sins.
   As a father has compassion <u>on</u> his sons,
   the Lord has pity on <u>those</u> who fear
   him.

Gospel Acclamation John 14:23
   If anyone loves me they will <u>keep</u> my
   word,
   and my Father will love them and <u>we</u>
   shall come to them.

827

8th Sunday in Ordinary Time (A)
Psalm 61:2-3, 6-9. R℟ v.6

In God a-lone is my soul at rest.

1. In God alone is my <u>soul</u> at rest;
   my help <u>comes</u> from him.
   He alone is my <u>rock</u>, my stronghold,
   my fortress: <u>I</u> stand firm.

2. In God alone be at <u>rest</u>, my soul;
   for my hope <u>comes</u> from him.
   He alone is my <u>rock</u>, my stronghold,
   my fortress: <u>I</u> stand firm.

3. In God is my safe<u>ty</u> and glory,
   the rock <u>of</u> my strength.
   Take refuge in God <u>all</u> you people.
   Trust him <u>at</u> all times.

Gospel Acclamation John 17:17
   You word is <u>truth</u>, O Lord,
   consecrate us <u>in</u> the truth.

828

9th Sunday in Ordinary Time (A)
Psalm 30:2-4, 17, 25. R℟ v.3

Be a rock of ref-uge for me,

O Lord.

1. In you, O Lord, <u>I</u> take refuge.
   Let me never be <u>put</u> to shame.
   In your justice, <u>set</u> me free,
   hear me and spee<u>dily</u> rescue me.

2. Be a rock of re<u>fuge</u> to me,
   a mighty strong<u>hold</u> to save me,
   for you are my <u>rock</u>, my stronghold.
   For your name's sake, lead <u>me</u> and
   guide me.

3. Let your face shine <u>on</u> your servant.
   Save me <u>in</u> your love.
   Be strong, let your <u>heart</u> take courage,
   all who hope <u>in</u> the Lord.

Continued overleaf

Gospel Acclamation John 14:23

Ifanyone loves me they will <u>keep</u> my
word,

and my Father will love them and <u>we</u>
shall come to them.

829 10th Sunday
in Ordinary Time (A)
Psalm 49:1, 8, 12-15. R℣ v.23

I will show God's sal-va-tion to the up-right.

1. The God of gods, the Lord, has
spoken and sum<u>moned</u> the earth,
from the rising of the sun <u>to</u> its setting.
'I find no fault <u>with</u> your sacrifices,
your offerings are al<u>ways</u> before me.'

2. 'Were I hungry, I <u>would</u> not tell you,
for I own the world and <u>all</u> it holds.
Do you think I eat the <u>flesh</u> of bulls,
or drink the <u>blood</u> of goats?'

3. 'Pay your sacrifice of thanksgiv<u>ing</u> to
God
and render him your <u>votive</u> off'rings.
Call on me in the day <u>of</u> distress.
I will free you and <u>you</u> shall honour
me.'

Gospel Acclamation cf. Acts 16:14

Open our <u>heart</u>, O Lord,
to accept the words <u>of</u> your Son.

830 11th Sunday
in Ordinary Time (A)
Psalm 99:2-3, 5. R℣ v.3

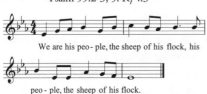

We are his peo- ple, the sheep of his flock, his

peo - ple, the sheep of his flock.

1. Cry out with joy to the Lord, <u>all</u> the
earth.
Serve the <u>Lord</u> with gladness.
Come before him, sing<u>ing</u> for joy.

2. Know that he, the <u>Lord</u>, is God.
He made us, we be<u>long</u> to him,
we are his people, the sheep <u>of</u> his
flock.

3. Indeed, how good <u>is</u> the Lord,
eternal his mer<u>ciful</u> love.
He is faithful from <u>age</u> to age.

Gospel Acclamation John 10:27

The sheep that belong to me listen to
my voice, <u>says</u> the Lord,
I know them <u>and</u> they follow me.

831 12th Sunday
in Ordinary Time (A)
Psalm 68:8-10, 14, 17, 33-35. R℣ v.14

In your great love,   in your great love,

ans - wer me, O   God.

1. It is for you that I <u>suffer</u> taunts,
that shame co<u>vers</u> my face,
that I have become a stranger <u>to</u> my
brothers,
an alien to my own <u>mother's</u> sons.

2. I burn with zeal <u>for</u> your house
and taunts against you <u>fall</u> on me.
This is my <u>prayer</u> to you,
my prayer <u>for</u> your favour.

3. In your great love, answer <u>me</u>, O God,
with your help that <u>never</u> fails:
Lord, answer, for your <u>love</u> is kind;
in your compassion, <u>turn</u> towards me.

4. The poor when they see it <u>will</u> be glad
   and God-seeking hearts <u>will</u> revive;
   for the Lord listens <u>to</u> the needy
   and does not spurn his servants <u>in</u>
     their chains.

5. Let the heavens and the earth <u>give</u>
     him praise,
   the sea and all its <u>living</u> creatures.
   Let the heavens and the earth <u>give</u>
     him praise,
   the sea and all its <u>living</u> creatures.

Gospel Acclamation John 1:14, 12
   The Word was made flesh and <u>lived</u>
     among us;
   to all who did accept him he gave
     power to become chil<u>dren</u> of God.

3. For it is you, O Lord, who are the
     glory <u>of</u> their strength;
   it is by your favour that our might <u>is</u>
     exalted;
   for our ruler is in the keeping <u>of</u> the
     Lord;
   our king in the keeping of the Holy
     <u>One</u> of Israel.

Gospel Acclamation cf. Acts 16:14
   Open our <u>heart</u>, O Lord,
   to accept the words <u>of</u> your Son.

832 13th Sunday in Ordinary Time (A)
Psalm 88:2-3, 16-19. R℣ v.2

I will sing for e-ver of your love, O Lord.

1. I will sing for ever of your <u>love</u>, O Lord;
   through all ages my mouth will
     pro<u>claim</u> your truth.
   Of this I am sure, that your love <u>lasts</u>
     for ever,
   that your truth is firmly established <u>as</u>
     the heavens.

2. Happy the people who acclaim <u>such</u>
     a king,
   who walk, O Lord, in the light <u>of</u>
     your face,
   who find their joy every day <u>in</u> your
     name,
   who make your justice the source <u>of</u>
     their bliss.

833 14th Sunday in Ordinary Time (A)
Psalm 144:1-2, 8-11, 13-14. R℣ v.1

I will bless your name for e-ver, O
God my King.

1. I will give you glory, O <u>God</u> my King,
   I will bless your <u>name</u> for ever.
   I will bless you day <u>after</u> day
   and praise your <u>name</u> for ever.

2. The Lord is kind and full <u>of</u>
     compassion,
   slow to anger, abound<u>ing</u> in love.
   How good is the <u>Lord</u> to all,
   compassionate to <u>all</u> his creatures.

3. All your creatures shall thank <u>you</u>,
     O Lord,
   and your friends shall re<u>peat</u> their
     blessing.
   They shall speak of the glory <u>of</u> your
     reign
   and declare your <u>might</u>, O God.

Continued overleaf

4. The Lord is faithful in <u>all</u> his words
    and loving in <u>all</u> his deeds.
    The Lord supports <u>all</u> who fall
    and raises all who <u>are</u> bowed down.

Gospel Acclamation cf. Matthew 11:25
    Blessed are you, Father, Lord of
        hea<u>ven</u> and earth,
    for revealing the mysteries of the
        kingdom <u>to</u> mere children.

834 15th Sunday
in Ordinary Time (A)
Psalm 64:10-14. R℞ Luke 8:8

Some seed fell in-to rich soil and yield-ed a rich har - vest.

1. You care for the earth, <u>give</u> it water,
    you fill <u>it</u> with riches.
    Your river in hea<u>ven</u> brims over
    to pro<u>vide</u> its grain.

2. And thus you provide <u>for</u> the earth;
    you <u>drench</u> its furrows,
    you level it, soften <u>it</u> with showers,
    you <u>bless</u> its growth.

3. You crown the year <u>with</u> your
        goodness.
    Abundance flows <u>in</u> your steps,
    in the pastures <u>of</u> the wilderness
    your a<u>bun</u>dance flows.

4. The hills are gir<u>ded</u> with joy,
    the meadows co<u>vered</u> with flocks,
    the valleys are <u>decked</u> with wheat.
    They shout for joy, <u>yes</u>, they sing.

Gospel Acclamation 1 Samuel 3:9; John 6:68
    Speak, Lord, your ser<u>vant</u> is listening;
    you have the message of e<u>ter</u>nal life.

835 16th Sunday
in Ordinary Time (A)
Psalm 85:5-6, 9-10, 15-16. R℞ v.5

O Lord, you are good and for - giv - ing.

1. O Lord, you are good <u>and</u> forgiving,
    full of love to <u>all</u> who call.
    Give heed, O Lord, <u>to</u> my prayer
    and attend to the sound <u>of</u> my voice.

2. All the nations shall come <u>to</u> adore you
    and glorify your <u>name</u>, O Lord:
    for you are great and do mar<u>vel</u>lous
        deeds,
    you who a<u>lone</u> are God.

3. But you, God of mercy <u>and</u>
        compassion,
    slow to ang<u>er</u>, O Lord,
    abounding in <u>love</u> and truth,
    turn and take pi<u>ty</u> on me.

Gospel Acclamation cf. Ephesians 1:17-18
    May the Father of our Lord Jesus
        Christ enlighten the eyes <u>of</u> our
        mind,
    so that we can see what hope his call
        <u>holds</u> for us.

836 17th Sunday
in Ordinary Time (A)
Psalm 118:57, 72, 76-77, 127-130.
R℞ v.97

Lord, Lord, how I love your law!

1. My part, I have re<u>solved</u>, O Lord,
   is to o<u>bey</u> your word.
   The law from your mouth means
      <u>more</u> to me
   than sil<u>ver</u> and gold.

2. Let your love be ready <u>to</u> console me
   by your promise <u>to</u> your servant.
   Let your love come to me and <u>I</u> shall
      live
   for your law is <u>my</u> delight.

3. That is why I love <u>your</u> commands
   more than <u>fin</u>est gold.
   That is why I rule my life <u>by</u> your
      precepts;
   I <u>hate</u> false ways.

4. Your will is wonder<u>ful</u> indeed;
   therefore <u>I</u> obey it.
   The unfolding of your <u>word</u> gives light
   and teach<u>es</u> the simple.

Gospel Acclamation John 15:15
   I call you friends, <u>says</u> the Lord,
   because I have made known to you
      everything I have learnt <u>from</u> my
   Father.

837 18th Sunday
   in Ordinary Time (A)
   Psalm 144:8-9, 15-18. R℞ v.16

You o - pen wide your hand, O Lord, you
grant our   de - sires.

1. The Lord is kind and full <u>of</u>
      compassion,
   slow to anger, abound<u>ing</u> in love.
   How good is the <u>Lord</u> to all,
   compassionate to <u>all</u> his creatures.

2. The eyes of all creatures <u>look</u> to you
   and you give them their food <u>in</u> due
      time.
   You open <u>wide</u> your hand,
   grant the desires of <u>all</u> who live.

3. The Lord is just in <u>all</u> his ways
   and loving in <u>all</u> his deeds.
   He is close to <u>all</u> who call him,
   call on him <u>from</u> their hearts.

Gospel Acclamation Luke 19:38
   Blessings on the King who comes in
      the name <u>of</u> the Lord!
   Peace in heaven and glory in the
      <u>high</u>est heavens!

838 19th Sunday
   in Ordinary Time (A)
   Psalm 84:9-14. R℞ v.8

Let us see, O Lord, your mer - cy and
give   us your sav - ing help.

1. I will hear what the Lord God <u>has</u> to
      say,
   a voice that <u>speaks</u> of peace.
   His help is near for <u>those</u> who fear him
   and his glory will dwell <u>in</u> our land.

2. Mercy and faithful<u>ness</u> have met;
   justice and peace <u>have</u> embraced.
   Faithfulness shall spring <u>from</u> the earth
   and justice look <u>down</u> from heaven.

3. The Lord will <u>make</u> us prosper
   and our earth shall <u>yield</u> its fruit.
   Justice shall <u>march</u> before him
   and peace shall fol<u>low</u> his steps.

Continued overleaf

Gospel Acclamation Luke 19:38

Blessings on the King who comes in
the name of the Lord!
Peace in heaven and glory in the
highest heavens!

839 20th Sunday
in Ordinary Time (A)
Psalm 66:2-3, 5-6, 8. R℞ v.4

Let the peo - ples praise you, O God, let

all the peo-ples praise you.

1. O God, be gracious and bless us
   and let your face shed its light upon us.
   So will your ways be known upon earth,
   and all nations learn your saving help.

2. Let the nations be glad and exult
   for you rule the world with justice.
   With fairness you rule the peoples,
   you guide the nations on earth.

3. Let the peoples praise you, O God;
   let all the peoples praise you.
   May God still give us his blessing
   till the ends of the earth revere him.

Gospel Acclamation John 10:27

The sheep that belong to me listen to
my voice, says the Lord,
I know them and they follow me.

840 21st Sunday
in Ordinary Time (A)
Psalm 137:1-3, 6, 8. R℞ v.8

Your love, O Lord, is e - ter - nal; dis -

card not the work of your hands.

1. I thank you, Lord, with all my heart,
   you have heard the words of my
   mouth.
   Before the angels I will bless you.
   I will adore before your holy temple.

2. I thank you for your faithfulness and
   love
   which excel all we ever knew of you.
   On the day I called, you answered;
   you increased the strength of my soul.

3. The Lord is high yet he looks on the
   lowly
   and the haughty he knows from afar.
   Your love, O Lord, is eternal,
   discard not the work of your hands.

Gospel Acclamation 2 Corinthians 5:19

God in Christ was reconciling the
world to himself,
and he has entrusted to us the news
that they are reconciled.

841 22nd Sunday
in Ordinary Time (A)
Psalm 62:2-6, 8-9. R℞ v.2

For you my soul is thirst - ing,

O Lord, my God.

1. O God, you are my God, for you I
   long:
   for you my soul is thirsting.
   My body pines for you
   like a dry, weary land without water.

2. So I gaze on you in the sanctuary
   to see your strength and your glory.
   For your love is better than life,
   my lips will speak your praise.

3. So I will bless you <u>all</u> my life,
   in your name I will lift <u>up</u> my hands.
   My soul shall be filled as <u>with</u> a
     banquet,
   my mouth shall praise <u>you</u> with joy.

4. For you have <u>been</u> my help;
   in the shadow of your wings <u>I</u> rejoice.
   My soul <u>clings</u> to you:
   your right hand <u>holds</u> me fast.

Gospel Acclamation cf. Ephesians 1:17-18
   May the Father of our Lord Jesus Christ
     enlighten the eyes <u>of</u> our mind,
   so that we can see what hope his call
     <u>holds</u> for us.

842 23rd Sunday in Ordinary Time (A)
Psalm 94:1-2, 6-9. R℟ v.8

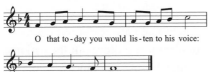

O that to-day you would lis-ten to his voice:

'Har-den not your hearts.'

1. Come, ring out our joy <u>to</u> the Lord;
   hail the <u>rock</u> who saves us.
   Let us come before him, <u>giving</u> thanks,
   with songs let us <u>hail</u> the Lord.

2. Come in; let us bow <u>and</u> bend low;
   let us kneel before the <u>God</u> who
     made us
   for he is our God, and we the people
     who belong <u>to</u> his pasture,
   the flock that is led <u>by</u> his hand.

3. O that today you would listen <u>to</u> his
     voice!
   'Harden not your hearts <u>as</u> at Meribah,
   as on that day at Massah in the desert,
     when your fathers put me <u>to</u> the test;
   when they tried me, though they <u>saw</u>
     my work.

Gospel Acclamation John 17:17
   Your word is <u>truth</u>, O Lord,
   consecrate us <u>in</u> the truth.

843 24th Sunday in Ordinary Time (A)
Psalm 102:1-4, 9-12. R℟ v.8

The Lord   is com-pas-sion   and love.

1. My soul, give thanks <u>to</u> the Lord,
   all my being, bless his <u>holy</u> name.
   My soul, give thanks <u>to</u> the Lord
   and never forget <u>all</u> his blessings.

2. It is he who forgives <u>all</u> your guilt,
   who heals every one <u>of</u> your ills,
   who redeems your life <u>from</u> the grave,
   who crowns you with love <u>and</u>
     compassion.

3. His wrath will come <u>to</u> an end;
   he will not be <u>angry</u> for ever.
   He does not treat us according <u>to</u> our
     sins
   nor repay us according <u>to</u> our faults.

4. For as the heavens are high a<u>bove</u> the
     earth
   so strong is his love for <u>those</u> who
     fear him.
   As far as the east is <u>from</u> the west
   so far does he re<u>move</u> our sins.

Gospel Acclamation 1 Samuel 3:9, John 6:68
   Speak, Lord, your ser<u>vant</u> is listening:
   you have the message of e<u>ternal</u> life.

844 25th Sunday in Ordinary Time (A)
Psalm 144:2-3, 8-9, 17-18. R℣ v.18

The Lord is close to all who call him.

1. I will bless you day after day
   and praise your name for ever.
   The Lord is great, highly to be praised,
   his greatness cannot be measured.

2. The Lord is kind and full of
      compassion,
   slow to anger, abounding in love.
   How good is the Lord to all,
   compassionate to all his creatures.

3. The Lord is just in all his ways
   and loving in all his deeds.
   He is close to all who call him,
   who call on him from their hearts.

Gospel Acclamation Luke 19:38
   Blessings on the King who comes, in
      the name of the Lord!
   Peace in heaven and glory in the
      highest heavens!

845 26th Sunday in Ordinary Time (A)
Psalm 24:4-9. R℣ v.6

Re - mem - ber, re - mem - ber your

mer - cy, O Lord.

1. Lord, make me know your ways.
   Lord, teach me your paths.
   Make me walk in your truth, and
      teach me;
   for you are God my Saviour.

2. Remember your mercy, Lord,
   and the love you have shown from of
      old.
   Do not remember the sins of my
      youth.
   In your love remember me.

3. The Lord is good and upright.
   He shows the path to those who stray,
   he guides the humble in the right path;
   he teaches his way to the poor.

Gospel Acclamation John 14:23
   If anyone loves me they will keep my
      word.
   And my Father will love them and we
      shall come to them.

846 27th Sunday in Ordinary Time (A)
Psalm 79:9, 12-16, 19-20. R℣ Isaiah 5:7

The vine-yard of the Lord is the

house of Is - ra - el.

1. You brought a vine out of Egypt;
   to plant it you drove out the nations.
   It stretches out its branches to the sea,
   to the Great River it stretched out its
      shoots.

2. Then why have you broken down its
      walls?
   It is plucked by all who pass by.
   It is ravaged by the boar of the forest,
   devoured by the beasts of the field.

3. God of hosts, turn again, we implore,
   look down from heaven and see.
   Visit this vine and protect it,
   the vine your right hand has planted.

4. And we shall never forsake <u>you</u> again:
   give us life that we may call up<u>on</u>
      your name.
   God of hosts, <u>bring</u> us back;
   let your face shine on us and we <u>shall</u>
      be saved.

Gospel Acclamation John 15:15
   I call you friends, <u>says</u> the Lord,
   because I have made known to you
      everything I have learnt <u>from</u> my
      Father.

5. Surely goodness and kind<u>ness</u> shall
      follow me
   all the days <u>of</u> my life.
   In the Lord's own house <u>shall</u> I dwell
   for ev<u>er</u> and ever.

Verse 3 may be omitted

Gospel Acclamation John 1:14, 12
   The Word was made flesh and <u>lived</u>
      among us;
   to all who did accept him he gave
      power to become child<u>ren</u> of God.

847 28th Sunday in Ordinary Time (A)
Psalm 22. R℣ v.1

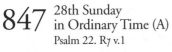

The Lord is my shep-herd; there is

no-thing I shall want.

1. The Lord <u>is</u> my shepherd;
   there is nothing <u>I</u> shall want.
   Fresh and green <u>are</u> the pastures
   where he gives <u>me</u> repose.

2. Near restful wa<u>ters</u> he leads me,
   to revive my <u>drooping</u> spirit.
   He guides me along <u>the</u> right path;
   he is true <u>to</u> his name.

3. If I should walk in the val<u>ley</u> of
      darkness
   no evil <u>would</u> I fear.
   You are there with your crook <u>and</u>
      your staff;
   with these you <u>give</u> me comfort.

4. You have prepared a ban<u>quet</u> for me
   in the sight <u>of</u> my foes.
   My head you have anoin<u>ted</u> with oil;
   my cup is <u>o</u>verflowing.

848 29th Sunday in Ordinary Time (A)
Psalm 95:1, 3-5, 7-10. R℣ v.7

Give the Lord glo - ry, glo - ry and pow'r.

1. O sing a new song <u>to</u> the Lord,
   sing to the Lord <u>all</u> the earth.
   Tell among the na<u>tions</u> his glory
   and his wonders among <u>all</u> the peoples.

2. The Lord is great and wor<u>thy</u> of praise,
   to be feared <u>above</u> all gods;
   the gods of the hea<u>thens</u> are naught.
   It was the Lord who <u>made</u> the heavens.

3. Give the Lord, you famil<u>ies</u> of peoples,
   give the Lord glo<u>ry</u> and power,
   give the Lord the glory <u>of</u> his name.
   Bring an offering and en<u>ter</u> his courts.

4. Worship the Lord <u>in</u> his temple.
   O earth, trem<u>ble</u> before him.
   Proclaim to the nations; '<u>God</u> is King.'
   He will judge the peo<u>ples</u> in fairness.

Gospel Acclamation John 17:17
   Your word is <u>truth</u>, O Lord,
   consecrate us <u>in</u> the truth.

849

30th Sunday
in Ordinary Time (A)
Psalm 17:2-4, 47, 51. R̷ v.2

I love you, Lord, O God, my strength.

1. I love you, <u>Lord</u>, my strength,
   my rock, my for<u>tress</u>, my Saviour.
   My God is the rock where <u>I</u> take refuge;
   my shield, my mighty <u>help</u>,
      my stronghold.

2. The Lord is worthy <u>of</u> all praise:
   when I call I am saved <u>from</u> my foes.
   Long life to the <u>Lord</u>, my rock!
   Praised be the <u>God</u> who saves me.

3. He has given great victories <u>to</u> his king
   and shown his love for <u>his</u> anointed.
   I love you, <u>Lord</u>, my strength,
   my rock, my for<u>tress</u>, my Saviour.

Gospel Acclamation cf. Acts 16:14
   Open our <u>heart</u>, O Lord,
   to accept the words <u>of</u> your Son.

850

31st Sunday
in Ordinary Time (A)
Psalm 130

Keep my soul in peace be-fore you, Lord.

1. O Lord, my heart <u>is</u> not proud
   nor haugh<u>ty</u> my eyes.
   I have not gone after <u>things</u> too great
   nor mar<u>vels</u> beyond me.

2. Truly I have set my soul in si<u>lence</u>
      and peace.
   A weaned child on its mother's
      breast, even so <u>is</u> my soul.
   O Israel, hope <u>in</u> the Lord
   both now <u>and</u> for ever.

Gospel Acclamation 1 Samuel 3:9, John 6:68
   Speak, Lord, your ser<u>vant</u> is listening;
   you have the message of e<u>ter</u>nal life.

851

32nd Sunday
in Ordinary Time (A)
Psalm 62:2-8. R̷ v.2

For you my soul is thirst - ing,

O Lord, my God.

1. O God, you are my God, for <u>you</u>
      I long:
   for you my <u>soul</u> is thirsting.
   My body <u>pines</u> for you
   like a dry, weary land <u>without</u> water.

2. So I gaze on you <u>in</u> the sanctuary
   to see your strength <u>and</u> your glory.
   For your love is bet<u>ter</u> than life,
   my lips will <u>speak</u> your praise.

3. So I will bless you <u>all</u> my life,
   in your name I will lift <u>up</u> my hands.
   My soul shall be filled as <u>with</u> a
      banquet,
   my mouth shall praise <u>you</u> with joy.

4. On my bed I re<u>member</u> you.
   On you I muse <u>through</u> the night
   for you have <u>been</u> my help;
   in the shadow of your wings <u>I</u> rejoice.

Gospel Acclamation Matthew 24:42, 44
   Stay awake <u>and</u> stand ready,
   because you do not know the hour
      when the Son of <u>Man</u> is coming.

852

33rd Sunday
in Ordinary Time (A)
Psalm 127:1-5. R℟ v.1

O bles-sed are those who fear the Lord.

1. O blessèd are those who <u>fear</u> the Lord
   and walk <u>in</u> his ways!
   By the labour of your hands <u>you</u> shall
   eat.
   You will be hap<u>py</u> and prosper.

2. Your wife like a <u>fruit</u>ful vine
   in the heart <u>of</u> your house;
   your children like shoots <u>of</u> the olive,
   a<u>round</u> your table.

3. Indeed thus <u>shall</u> be blessed
   those who <u>fear</u> the Lord.
   May the Lord bless <u>you</u> from Zion
   all the days <u>of</u> your life.

Gospel Acclamation Apoc. 2:10
   Even if you have to die, <u>says</u> the Lord,
   keep faithful, and I will give you the
   <u>crown</u> of life.

2. Near restful wa<u>ters</u> he leads me,
   to revive my <u>droop</u>ing spirit.
   He guides me along <u>the</u> right path;
   he is true <u>to</u> his name.

3. If I should walk in the val<u>ley</u> of
   darkness
   no evil <u>would</u> I fear.
   You are there with your crook <u>and</u>
   your staff;
   with these you <u>give</u> me comfort.

4. You have prepared a ban<u>quet</u> for me
   in the sight <u>of</u> my foes.
   My head you have anoin<u>ted</u> with oil;
   my cup is <u>over</u>flowing.

5. Surely goodness and kind<u>ness</u> shall
   follow me
   all the days <u>of</u> my life.
   In the Lord's own house <u>shall</u> I dwell
   for e<u>ver</u> and ever.

Verse 3 may be omitted

Gospel Acclamation Mark 11:9-10
   Blessings on him who comes in the
   name <u>of</u> the Lord!
   Blessings on the coming kingdom of
   our <u>father</u> David!

853

Our Lord Jesus Christ,
Universal King (A)
Psalm 22. R℟ v.1

The Lord is my shep-herd; there is
no-thing I shall want.

1. The Lord <u>is</u> my shepherd;
   there is nothing <u>I</u> shall want.
   Fresh and green <u>are</u> the pastures
   where he gives <u>me</u> repose.

854

2nd Sunday
in Ordinary Time (B)
Psalm 39:2, 4, 7-10. R℟ vv. 8-9

Here I am, Lord! I come to do your will.

1. I waited, I waited for the Lord and <u>he</u>
   stooped down to me;
   he <u>heard</u> my cry.
   He put a new song in<u>to</u> my mouth,
   praise <u>of</u> our God.

Continued overleaf

2. You do not ask for sacrifice and
   offerings,
   but an open ear.
   You do not ask for holocaust and
   victim.
   Instead, here am I.

3. In the scroll of the book it stands
   written
   that I should do your will.
   My God, I delight in your law
   in the depth of my heart.

4. Your justice I have proclaimed
   in the great assembly.
   My lips I have not sealed;
   you know it, O Lord.

Gospel Acclamation 1 Samuel 3:9 John 6:68
   Speak, Lord, your servant is listening:
   you have the message of eternal life.

855 3rd Sunday in Ordinary Time (B)
Psalm 24:4-9. R℣ v.4

Lord, make me know your ways.

1. Lord, make me know your ways.
   Lord, teach me your paths.
   Make me walk in your truth, and
   teach me:
   for you are God my Saviour.

2. Remember your mercy Lord,
   and the love you have shown from of
   old.
   In your love remember me,
   because of your goodness, O Lord.

3. The Lord is good and upright.
   He shows the path to those who stray,
   he guides the humble in the right path;
   he teaches his way to the poor.

Gospel Acclamation Mark 1:15
   The kingdom of God is close at hand;
   believe the Good News.

856 4th Sunday in Ordinary Time (B)
Psalm 94:1-2, 6-9. R℣ v.9

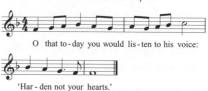

O that to-day you would lis-ten to his voice:

'Har-den not your hearts.'

1. Come, ring out our joy to the Lord;
   hail the rock who saves us.
   Let us come before him, giving thanks,
   with songs let us hail the Lord.

2. Come in; let us kneel and bend low;
   let us kneel before the God who
   made us
   for he is our God, and we the people
   who belong to his pasture,
   the flock that is led by his hand.

3. O that today you would listen to his
   voice!
   'Harden not your hearts as at Meribah,
   as on that day at Massah in the
   desert, when your fathers put me to
   the test;
   when they tried me, though they saw
   my work.'

Gospel Acclamation cf. Matthew 11:25
   Blessed are you, Father, Lord of
   heaven and earth,
   for revealing the mysteries of the
   kingdom to mere children.

857 5th Sunday in Ordinary Time (B)
Psalm 146:1-6. R℣ v.3

Praise the Lord who heals the bro-ken-heart-ed.

1. Praise, O praise the Lord
   for he is good;
   sing to the Lord for he is loving:
   to him our praise is due.

2. The Lord builds up Jerusalem and
      brings back Israel's exiles,
   he heals the broken-hearted, he binds
      up all their wounds.
   He fixes the number of the stars;
   he calls each one by its name.

3. Our God is great and almighty;
   his wisdom can never be measured.
   The Lord raises the lowly;
   he humbles the wicked to the dust.

Gospel Acclamation John 8:12
   I am the light of the world, says the
      Lord,
   anyone who follows me will have the
      light of life.

858 6th Sunday in Ordinary Time (B)
Psalm 31:1-2, 5, 11. R℣ v.7

You are my re - fuge, O Lord; you
fill me with the joy of sal - va - tion.

1. Happy are those whose offence is
      forgiven,
   whose sin is remitted.
   O happy are those to whom the Lord
   imputes no guilt.

2. But now I have acknowledged my sins;
   my guilt I did not hide,
   and you, Lord, have forgiven
   the guilt of my sin.

3. Rejoice, rejoice in the Lord,
   exult, you just!
   O come, ring out your joy,
   all you upright of heart.

Gospel Acclamation cf. Ephesians 1:17-18
   May the Father of our Lord Jesus
      Christ enlighten the eyes of our
      mind,
   so that we can see what hope his call
      holds for us.

859 7th Sunday in Ordinary Time (B)
Psalm 40:2-5, 13-14. R℣ v.5

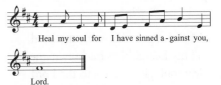

Heal my soul for I have sinned a-gainst you,
Lord.

1. Happy are those who consider the
      poor and the weak.
   The Lord will save them in the day of
      evil,
   will guard them, give them life, make
      them happy in the land
   and will not give them up to the will
      of their foes.

2. The Lord will give them strength in
      their pain,
   he will bring them back from
      sickness to health.
   As for me, I said: 'Lord, have mercy
      on me,
   heal my soul for I have sinned against
      you.'

Continued overleaf

3. If you uphold me I shall <u>be</u>
   unharmed
   and set in your presence for <u>e</u>vermore.
   Blessed be the Lord, the <u>God</u> of Israel
   from age to age. A<u>men</u>. Amen.

Gospel Acclamation John 1:14, 12
   The Word was made flesh and <u>lived</u>
   among us;
   to all who did accept him he gave
   power to become chil<u>dren</u> of God.

860 8th Sunday in Ordinary Time (B)
Psalm 102:1-4, 8, 10, 12-13. Ry v.8

The Lord   is com - pas - sion,   com -

pas - sion and   love.

1. My soul, give thanks <u>to</u> the Lord,
   all my being, bless his <u>holy</u> name.
   My soul, give thanks <u>to</u> the Lord
   and never forget <u>all</u> his blessings.

2. It is he who forgives <u>all</u> your guilt,
   who heals every one <u>of</u> your ills,
   who redeems your life <u>from</u> the grave,
   who crowns you with love <u>and</u>
   compassion.

3. The Lord is compas<u>sion</u> and love,
   slow to anger and <u>rich</u> in mercy.
   He does not treat us according <u>to</u> our
   sins
   nor repay us according <u>to</u> our faults.

4. As far as the east is <u>from</u> the west
   so far does he re<u>move</u> our sins.
   As a father has compassion <u>on</u> his sons,
   the Lord has pity on <u>those</u> who fear
   him.

Gospel Acclamation John 10:27
   The sheep that belong to me listen to
   my voice, <u>says</u> the Lord,
   I know them <u>and</u> they follow me.

861 9th Sunday in Ordinary Time (B)
Psalm 80:3-8, 10-11. Ry v.2

Ring out your joy   to God our strength.

1. Raise a song and <u>sound</u> the timbrel,
   the sweet-sounding harp <u>and</u> the lute,
   blow the trumpet <u>at</u> the new moon,
   when the moon is full, <u>on</u> our feast.

2. For this is Is<u>rae</u>l's law,
   a command of the <u>God</u> of Jacob.
   He imposed it as a <u>rule</u> on Joseph,
   when he went out against the <u>land</u> of
   Egypt.

3. A voice I did not know <u>said</u> to me:
   'I freed your shoulder <u>from</u> the burden;
   your hands were freed <u>from</u> the load.
   You called in distress <u>and</u> I saved you.

4. 'Let there be no foreign <u>god</u> among
   you,
   no worship of an a<u>lien</u> god.
   I am the <u>Lord</u> your God,
   who brought you from the <u>land</u> of
   Egypt.'

Gospel Acclamation cf. John 6:63, 68
   Your words are spirit, Lord, and <u>they</u>
   are life:
   you have the message of e<u>ternal</u> life.

862 10th Sunday in Ordinary Time (B)
Psalm 129. R℣ v.7

With the Lord there is mer - cy and full - ness of re - demp - tion.

1. Out of the depths I cry to you, O Lord,
   Lord, hear my voice!
   O let your ears be attentive
   to the voice of my pleading.

2. If you, O Lord, should mark our guilt,
   Lord, who would survive?
   But with you is found forgiveness:
   for this we revere you.

3. My soul is waiting for the Lord,
   I count on his word.
   My soul is longing for the Lord
   more than watchman for daybreak.

4. Because with the Lord there is mercy
   and fullness of redemption,
   Israel indeed he will redeem
   from all its iniquity.

Gospel Acclamation John 14:23
   If anyone loves me they will keep my
      word,
   and my Father will love them and we
      shall come to them.

863 11th Sunday in Ordinary Time (B)
Psalm 91:2-3, 13-16. R℣ cf. v.2

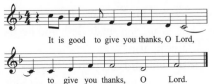

It is good to give you thanks, O Lord, to give you thanks, O Lord.

1. It is good to give thanks to the Lord
   to make music to your name,
      O Most High,
   to proclaim your love in the morning
   and your truth in the watches of the
      night.

2. The just will flourish like the palm-tree
   and grow like a Lebanon cedar.
   Planted in the house of the Lord
   they will flourish in the courts of our
      God.

3. Still bearing fruit when they are old,
   still full of sap, still green,
   they will proclaim that the Lord is just.
   In him, my rock, there is no wrong.

Gospel Acclamation John 15:15
   I call you friends, says the Lord,
   because I have made known to you
      everything I have learnt from my
      Father.

864 12th Sunday in Ordinary Time (B)
Psalm 106:23-26, 28-31. R℣ v.1

O give thanks to the Lord, for his love en-dures for e - ver.

1. Some sailed to the sea in ships
   to trade on the mighty waters.
   These have seen the Lord's deeds,
   the wonders he does in the deep.

2. For he spoke; he summoned the gale,
   tossing the waves of the sea
   up to heaven and back into the deep;
   their soul melted away in their distress.

Continued overleaf

3. Then they cried to the Lord <u>in</u> their
     need
   and he rescued them from <u>their</u>
     distress.
   He stilled the storm <u>to</u> a whisper:
   all the waves of the <u>sea</u> were hushed.

4. They rejoiced because <u>of</u> the calm
   and he led them to the haven <u>they</u>
     desired.
   Let them thank the Lord <u>for</u> his love,
   the wonders he does <u>for</u> his people.

Gospel Acclamation cf. Ephesians 1:17-18
   May the Father of our Lord Jesus Christ
     enlighten the eyes <u>of</u> our mind,
   so that we can see what hope his call
     <u>holds</u> for us.

865 13th Sunday
in Ordinary Time (B)
Psalm 29:2, 4-6, 11-13. R℣ v.2

I will praise you, Lord,

you have res - cued me.

1. I will praise you, Lord, <u>you</u> have
     rescued me
   and have not let my enemies rejoice
     <u>over</u> me.
   O Lord, you have raised my soul
     <u>from</u> the dead,
   restored me to life from those who
     sink in<u>to</u> the grave.

2. Sing psalms to the Lord, <u>you</u> who
     love him,
   give thanks to his <u>holy</u> name.
   His anger lasts but a moment; his
     fav<u>our</u> through life.
   At night there are tears, but joy
     <u>comes</u> with dawn.

3. The Lord listened <u>and</u> had pity.
   The Lord came <u>to</u> my help.
   For me you have changed my
     mourning <u>into</u> dancing,
   O Lord, my God, I will thank <u>you</u>
     for ever.

Gospel Acclamation cf. John 6:63, 68
   Your words are spirit, Lord, and <u>they</u>
     are life:
   you have the message of e<u>ter</u>nal life.

866 14th Sunday
in Ordinary Time (B)
Psalm 122. R℣ v.2

Our eyes are on the Lord till he

show us his mer - cy.

1. To you I have lifted <u>up</u> my eyes,
   you who dwell <u>in</u> the heavens:
   my eyes, like the <u>eyes</u> of slaves
   on the hand <u>of</u> their lords.

2. Like the eyes <u>of</u> a servant
   on the hand <u>of</u> his mistress,
   so our eyes are on the <u>Lord</u> our God
   till he show <u>us</u> his mercy.

3. Have mercy on us, <u>Lord</u>, have mercy.
   We are filled <u>with</u> contempt.
   Indeed all too full <u>is</u> our soul
   with the scorn <u>of</u> the rich.

Gospel Acclamation John 1:14, 12
   The Word was made flesh and <u>lived</u>
     among us;
   to all who did accept him he gave
     power to become chil<u>dren</u> of God.

867 15th Sunday in Ordinary Time (B)
Psalm 84:9-14. R℣ v.8

Let us see, O Lord, your mer-cy and give us your sav - ing help.

1. I will hear what the Lord God <u>has</u> to say,
   a voice that <u>speaks</u> of peace.
   His help is near for <u>those</u> who fear him
   and his glory shall dwell <u>in</u> our land.

2. Mercy and faithful<u>ness</u> have met;
   justice and peace <u>have</u> embraced.
   Faithfulness shall spring <u>from</u> the earth
   and justice look <u>down</u> from heaven.

3. The Lord will <u>make</u> us prosper
   and our earth shall <u>yield</u> its fruit.
   Justice shall <u>march</u> before him
   and peace shall fol<u>low</u> his steps.

Gospel Acclamation cf. John 6:63, 68
   Your words are spirit, Lord, and <u>they</u> are life:
   you have the message of e<u>ternal</u> life.

868 16th Sunday in Ordinary Time (B)
Psalm 22. R℣ v.1

The Lord is my shep - herd; there is no-thing I shall want.

1. The Lord <u>is</u> my shepherd;
   there is nothing <u>I</u> shall want.
   Fresh and green <u>are</u> the pastures
   where he gives <u>me</u> repose.

2. Near restful wa<u>ters</u> he leads me,
   to revive my <u>drooping</u> spirit.
   He guides me along <u>the</u> right path;
   he is true <u>to</u> his name.

3. If I should walk in the val<u>ley</u> of darkness
   no evil <u>would</u> I fear.
   You are there with your crook <u>and</u> your staff;
   with these you <u>give</u> me comfort.

4. You have prepared a ban<u>quet</u> for me
   in the sight <u>of</u> my foes.
   My head you have anoin<u>ted</u> with oil;
   my cup is <u>over</u>flowing.

5. Surely goodness and kind<u>ness</u> shall follow me
   all the days <u>of</u> my life.
   In the Lord's own house <u>shall</u> I dwell
   for e<u>ver</u> and ever.

Verse 3 may be omitted

Gospel Acclamation John 10:27
   The sheep that belong to me listen to my voice, <u>says</u> the Lord,
   I know them <u>and</u> they follow me.

869 17th Sunday in Ordinary Time (B)
Psalm 144:10-11, 15-18. R℣ v.16

You o - pen wide your hand, O Lord, you grant our de - sires.

1. All your creatures shall thank <u>you</u>, O Lord,
   and your friends shall re<u>peat</u> their blessing.
   They shall speak of the glory <u>of</u> your reign
   and declare your <u>might</u>, O God.

Continued overleaf

2. The eyes of all creatures <u>look</u> to you
   and you give them their food <u>in</u> due
   time.
   You open <u>wide</u> your hand,
   grant the desires of <u>all</u> who live.

3. The Lord is just in <u>all</u> his ways
   and loving in <u>all</u> his deeds.
   He is close to <u>all</u> who call him,
   call on him <u>from</u> their hearts.

Gospel Acclamation cf. John 6:63, 68
   Your words are spirit, Lord, and <u>they</u>
   are life:
   you have the message of e<u>ter</u>nal life.

870 18th Sunday
in Ordinary Time (B)
Psalm 77:3-4, 23-25, 54. R⁷ v.24

The Lord gave them bread from hea - ven.

1. The things we have heard and
   <u>un</u>derstood,
   the things our fore<u>bears</u> have told us,
   we will tell to the next <u>gen</u>eration:
   the glories of the Lord <u>and</u> his might.

2. He commanded the <u>clouds</u> above
   and opened the <u>gates</u> of heaven.
   He rained down manna <u>for</u> their food,
   and gave them <u>bread</u> from heaven.

3. Mere mortals ate the <u>bread</u> of angels.
   He sent them abun<u>dance</u> of food.
   He brought them to his <u>holy</u> land,
   to the mountain which his right <u>hand</u>
   had won.

Gospel Acclamation John 14:6
   I am the Way, the Truth <u>and</u> the Life,
   says the Lord;
   no one can come to the Father ex<u>cept</u>
   through me.

871 19th Sunday
in Ordinary Time (B)
Psalm 33:1-8. R⁷ v.8

Taste, O taste and see that the Lord is good.

1. I will bless the Lord <u>at</u> all times,
   his praise always <u>on</u> my lips;
   in the Lord my soul shall <u>make</u> its
   boast.
   The humble shall hear <u>and</u> be glad.

2. Glorify the <u>Lord</u> with me.
   Together let us <u>praise</u> his name.
   I sought the Lord <u>and</u> he answered me;
   from all my terrors he <u>set</u> me free.

3. Look towards him <u>and</u> be radiant;
   let your faces not <u>be</u> abashed.
   When the poor cry out <u>the</u> Lord
   hears them
   and rescues them from all <u>their</u> distress.

4. The angel of the Lord <u>is</u> encamped
   around those who revere <u>him</u>, to
   rescue them.
   Taste and see the <u>Lord</u> is good.
   They are happy who seek re<u>fuge</u> in him.

Gospel Acclamation John 14:23
   If anyone loves me they will <u>keep</u> my
   word,
   and my Father will love them and <u>we</u>
   shall come to them.

872 20th Sunday
in Ordinary Time (B)
Psalm 33:1-2, 11-14. R⁷ v.8

Taste, O taste and see that the Lord is good.

1. I will bless the Lord <u>at</u> all times,
   his praise always <u>on</u> my lips;
   in the Lord my soul shall <u>make</u> its
      boast.
   The humble shall hear <u>and</u> be glad.

2. Revere the Lord, <u>you</u> his saints.
   They lack nothing, those <u>who</u> revere
      him.
   Strong lions suffer want <u>and</u> go hungry
   but those who seek the Lord <u>lack</u> no
      blessing.

3. Come, chil<u>dren</u>, and hear me
   that I may teach you the fear <u>of</u> the
      Lord.
   Who are they who <u>long</u> for life
   and many days, to enjoy <u>their</u>
      prosperity?

4. Then keep your <u>tongue</u> from evil
   and your lips from speak<u>ing</u> deceit.
   Turn aside from evil <u>and</u> do good;
   seek and strive <u>after</u> peace.

Gospel Acclamation John 1:14, 12
   The Word was made flesh and <u>lived</u>
      among us;
   to all who did accept him he gave
      power to become chil<u>dren</u> of God.

2. The Lord turns his face a<u>gainst</u> the
      wicked
   to destroy their remembrance <u>from</u>
      the earth.
   The Lord turns his eyes <u>to</u> the just
   and his ears to <u>their</u> appeal.

3. They call and <u>the</u> Lord hears
   and rescues them in all <u>their</u> distress.
   The Lord is close to the <u>broken</u>-hearted;
   those whose spirit is crushed <u>he</u> will
      save.

4. Many are the trials of <u>the</u> just man
   but from them all the <u>Lord</u> will
      rescue him.
   He will keep guard over <u>all</u> his bones,
   not one of his bones <u>shall</u> be broken.

5. Evil brings death <u>to</u> the wicked;
   those who hate the <u>good</u> are doomed.
   The Lord ransoms the souls <u>of</u> his
      servants.
   Those who hide in him shall not <u>be</u>
      condemned.

Gospel Acclamation cf. John 6:63, 68
   Your words are spirit, Lord, and <u>they</u>
      are life:
   you have the message of e<u>ternal</u> life.

874 22nd Sunday in Ordinary Time (B)
Psalm 14:2-5. R⁷ v.1

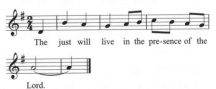

The just will live in the pre-sence of the

Lord.

1. Lord, who shall dwell on your <u>holy</u>
      mountain?
   Those who walk <u>without</u> fault;
   those who <u>act</u> with justice
   and speak the truth <u>from</u> their hearts.

873 21st Sunday in Ordinary Time (B)
Psalm 33:1-2, 15-22. R⁷ v.8

Taste, O taste and see that the Lord is good.

1. I will bless the Lord <u>at</u> all times,
   his praise always <u>on</u> my lips;
   in the Lord my soul shall <u>make</u> its
      boast.
   The humble shall hear <u>and</u> be glad.

Continued overleaf

2. Those who do no wrong <u>to</u> their
  kindred,
  who cast no slur <u>on</u> their neighbours,
  who hold the godless <u>in</u> disdain,
  but honour those who <u>fear</u> the Lord.

3. Those who keep their pledge, <u>come</u>
  what may;
  who take no interest <u>on</u> a loan
  and accept no bribes <u>against</u> the
  innocent.
  Such people will stand <u>firm</u> for ever.

Gospel Acclamation cf. John 6:63, 68
  Your words are spirit, Lord, and <u>they</u>
  are life:
  you have the message of <u>eternal</u> life.

875 23rd Sunday
  in Ordinary Time (B)
  Psalm 145:7-10. R̷ v.1

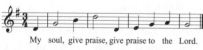

My soul, give praise, give praise to the Lord.

1. It is the Lord who keeps <u>faith</u> for ever,
  who is just to those who <u>are</u> oppressed.
  It is he who gives bread <u>to</u> the hungry,
  the Lord, who sets pri<u>son</u>ers free.

2. It is the Lord who gives sight <u>to</u> the
  blind,
  who raises up those who <u>are</u> bowed
  down,
  the Lord who <u>loves</u> the just,
  the Lord, who pro<u>tects</u> the stranger.

3. The Lord upholds the wi<u>dow</u> and
  orphan,
  but thwarts the path <u>of</u> the wicked.
  The Lord will <u>reign</u> for ever,
  Zion's God, from <u>age</u> to age.

Gospel Acclamation 1 Samuel 3:9; John 6:68
  Speak, Lord, your ser<u>vant</u> is listening:
  you have the message of <u>eternal</u> life.

876 24th Sunday
  in Ordinary Time (B)
  Psalm 114:1-6, 8-9. R̷ v.9

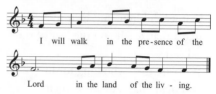

I will walk   in the pre-sence of the
Lord   in the land   of the liv - ing.

1. I love the Lord for <u>he</u> has heard
  the cry of <u>my</u> appeal;
  for he turned his <u>ear</u> to me
  in the day <u>when</u> I called him.

2. They surrounded me, the <u>snares</u> of
  death,
  with the anguish <u>of</u> the tomb;
  they caught me, sorrow <u>and</u> distress.
  O Lord my <u>God</u>, deliver me!

3. How gracious is the <u>Lord</u>, and just;
  our God <u>has</u> compassion.
  The Lord protects the <u>simple</u> hearts;
  I was helpless <u>so</u> he saved me.

4. He has kept my soul from death, my
  <u>eyes</u> from tears
  and my <u>feet</u> from stumbling.
  I will walk in the presence <u>of</u> the Lord
  in the land <u>of</u> the living.

Gospel Acclamation John 14:6
  I am the Way, the Truth <u>and</u> the Life,
  says the Lord;
  no one can come to the Father ex<u>cept</u>
  through me.

877 — 25th Sunday in Ordinary Time (B)

Psalm 53:3-6, 8. R℟ v.6

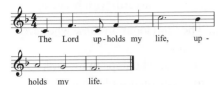

The Lord up-holds my life, up-holds my life.

1. O God, save me by your name;
   by your power, uphold my cause.
   O God, hear my prayer;
   listen to the words of my mouth.

2. For the proud have risen against me,
   ruthless foes seek my life.
   They have no regard for God,
   no regard for God.

3. But I have God for my help.
   The Lord upholds my life.
   I will sacrifice to you with willing heart
   and praise your name for it is good.

Gospel Acclamation John 8:12
   I am the light of the world, says the Lord,
   anyone who follows me will have the light of life.

878 — 26th Sunday in Ordinary Time (B)

Psalm 18:8, 10, 12-14. R℟ v.9

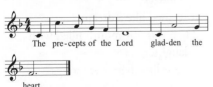

The pre-cepts of the Lord glad-den the heart.

1. The law of the Lord is perfect,
   it revives the soul.
   The rule of the Lord is to be trusted,
   it gives wisdom to the simple.

2. The fear of the Lord is holy,
   abiding for ever.
   The decrees of the Lord are truth
   and all of them just.

3. So in them your servant finds instruction;
   great reward is in their keeping.
   But who can detect all their errors?
   From hidden faults acquit me.

4. From presumption restrain your servant
   and let it not rule me.
   Then shall I be blameless,
   clean from grave sin.

Gospel Acclamation cf. John 17:17
   Your word is truth, O Lord,
   consecrate us in the truth.

879 — 27th Sunday in Ordinary Time (B)

Psalm 127. R℟ v.5

May the Lord bless us all the days of our life.

1. O blessed are those who fear the Lord
   and walk in his ways!
   By the labour of your hands you shall eat.
   You will be happy and prosper.

2. Your wife will be like a fruitful vine
   in the heart of your house;
   your children like shoots of the olive,
   around your table.

3. Indeed thus shall be blessed
   those who fear the Lord.
   May the Lord bless you from Zion
   in a happy Jerusalem.

Continued overleaf

Gospel Acclamation cf. John 17:17
Your word is truth, O Lord,
consecrate us in the truth.

880 28th Sunday
in Ordinary Time (B)
Psalm 89:12-17. R℣ v.14

Fill us with your love that we may re-joice.

1. Make us know the shortness of our life
that we may gain wisdom of heart.
Lord, relent! Is your anger for ever?
Show pity to your servants.

2. In the morning, fill us with your love;
we shall exult and rejoice all our days.
Give us joy to balance our affliction
for the years when we knew
misfortune.

3. Show forth your work to your servants;
let your glory shine on their children.
Let the favour of the Lord be upon us:
give success to the work of our hands.

Gospel Acclamation cf. Matthew 11:25
Blessed are you, Father, Lord of
heaven and earth,
for revealing the mysteries of the
kingdom to mere children.

881 29th Sunday
in Ordinary Time (B)
Psalm 32:4-5, 18-20, 22. R℣ v.22

May your love be up-on us, O Lord,

as we place all our hope in you.

1. The word of the Lord is faithful
and all his works to be trusted.
The Lord loves justice and right
and fills the earth with his love.

2. The Lord looks on those who revere
him,
on those who hope in his love,
to rescue their souls from death,
to keep them alive in famine.

3. Our soul is waiting for the Lord.
The Lord is our help and our shield.
May your love be upon us, O Lord,
as we place all our hope in you.

Gospel Acclamation John 14:6
I am the Way, the Truth and the Life,
says the Lord;
no one can come to the Father except
through me.

882 30th Sunday
in Ordinary Time (B)
Psalm 125. R℣ v.3

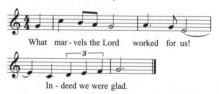

What mar-vels the Lord worked for us!

In - deed we were glad.

1. When the Lord delivered Zion from
bondage,
it seemed like a dream.
Then was our mouth filled with
laughter,
on our lips there were songs.

2. The heathens themselves said:
'What marvels the Lord worked for
them!'
What marvels the Lord worked for us!
Indeed we were glad.

3. Deliver us, O Lord, <u>from</u> our bondage
   as streams <u>in</u> dry land.
   Those who are sow<u>ing</u> in tears
   will sing <u>when</u> they reap.

4. They go out, they go out, <u>full</u> of tears
   carrying seed <u>for</u> the sowing:
   they come back, they come back,
   <u>full</u> of song,
   carry<u>ing</u> their sheaves.

Gospel Acclamation John 8:12
   I am the light of the world, <u>says</u> the
   Lord,
   anyone who follows me will have the
   <u>light</u> of life.

883 31st Sunday
in Ordinary Time (B)
Psalm 17:2-4, 47, 51. R7 v.2

I love you, Lord, O God, my strength.

1. I love you, <u>Lord</u>, my strength,
   my rock, my fort<u>ress</u>, my Saviour.
   My God is the rock where <u>I</u> take refuge;
   my shield, my mighty <u>help</u>, my
   stronghold.

2. The Lord is worthy <u>of</u> all praise:
   when I call I am saved <u>from</u> my foes.
   Long life to the <u>Lord</u>, my rock!
   Praise be the <u>God</u> who saves me.

3. He has given great victories <u>to</u> his
   king
   and shown his love for <u>his</u> anointed.
   I love you, <u>Lord</u>, my strength,
   my rock, my fort<u>ress</u>, my Saviour.

Gospel Acclamation cf. John 6:63, 68
   Your words are spirit, Lord, and <u>they</u>
   are life:
   you have the message of e<u>ter</u>nal life.

884 32nd Sunday
in Ordinary Time (B)
Psalm 145:7-10. R7 v.2

My soul, give praise, give praise to the Lord.

1. It is the Lord who keeps <u>faith</u> for ever,
   who is just to those who <u>are</u> oppressed.
   It is he who gives bread <u>to</u> the hungry,
   the Lord, who sets pri<u>son</u>ers free.

2. It is the Lord who gives sight <u>to</u> the
   blind,
   who raises up those who <u>are</u> bowed
   down,
   it is the Lord who <u>loves</u> the just,
   the Lord, who pro<u>tects</u> the stranger.

3. The Lord upholds the wi<u>dow</u> and
   orphan,
   but thwarts the path <u>of</u> the wicked.
   The Lord will <u>reign</u> for ever,
   Zion's God, from <u>age</u> to age.

Gospel Acclamation Revelation 2:10
   Even if you have to die, <u>says</u> the Lord,
   keep faithful, and I will give you the
   <u>crown</u> of life.

885 33rd Sunday
in Ordinary Time (B)
Psalm 15:5, 8-11. R7 v.1

Pre-serve me, God, I take ref-uge in you.

1. O Lord, it is you who are my por<u>tion</u>
   and cup;
   it is you yourself who <u>are</u> my prize.
   I keep the Lord ever <u>in</u> my sight:
   since he is at my right hand, I <u>shall</u>
   stand firm.

Continued overleaf

2. And so my heart rejoices, my <u>soul</u> is
    glad;
    even my body shall <u>rest</u> in safety.
    For you will not leave my soul <u>among</u>
        the dead,
    nor let your beloved <u>know</u> decay.

3. O Lord, <u>you</u> will show me
    the <u>path</u> of life,
    the fullness of joy <u>in</u> your presence,
    at your right hand happ<u>iness</u> for ever.

Gospel Acclamation Matthew 24:42, 44
    Stay awake <u>and</u> stand ready,
    because you do not know the hour
        when the Son of <u>Man</u> is coming.

886 Our Lord Jesus Christ,
Universal King (B)
Psalm 92:1-2, 5. R℣ v.1

The Lord is King, with ma-jes-ty en-robed.

1. The Lord is King, with majes<u>ty</u>
    enrobed;
    the Lord has robed him<u>self</u> with might,
    he has girded him<u>self</u> with power.

2. The world you made firm, not <u>to</u> be
    moved;
    your throne has stood firm <u>from</u> of old.
    From all eternity, O <u>Lord</u>, you are

3. Truly your decrees are <u>to</u> be trusted.
    Holiness is fitting <u>to</u> your house,
    O Lord, until the <u>end</u> of time.

Gospel Acclamation Mark 11:9-10
    Blessings on him who comes in the
        name <u>of</u> the Lord!
    Blessings on the coming kingdom of
        our <u>father</u> David!

887 2nd Sunday
in Ordinary Time (C)
Psalm 95:1-3, 7-10. R℣ v.3

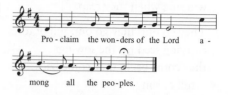

Pro - claim the won-ders of the Lord   a -

mong   all   the peo-ples.

1. O sing a new song <u>to</u> the Lord,
    sing to the Lord <u>all</u> the earth.
    O sing to the Lord, <u>bless</u> his name.

2. Proclaim his help <u>day</u> by day,
    tell among the na<u>tions</u> his glory
    and his wonders among <u>all</u> the peoples.

3. Give the Lord, you fam<u>ilies</u> of peoples,
    give the Lord glo<u>ry</u> and power,
    give the Lord the glory <u>of</u> his name.

4. Worship the Lord <u>in</u> his temple.
    O earth, trem<u>ble</u> before him.
    Proclaim to the nations: '<u>God</u> is King.'

Gospel Acclamation cf. John 6:63, 68
    Your words are spirit, Lord, and <u>they</u>
        are life:
    you have the message of e<u>ternal</u> life.

888 3rd Sunday
in Ordinary Time (C)
Psalm 18:8-10, 15. R℣ John 6:63

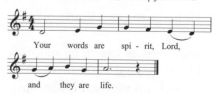

Your   words are   spi - rit, Lord,

and   they are life.

1. The law of the <u>Lord</u> is perfect,
    it re<u>vives</u> the soul.
    The rule of the Lord is <u>to</u> be trusted,
    it gives wisdom <u>to</u> the simple.

2. The precepts of the <u>Lord</u> are right,
   they gla<u>dd</u>en the heart.
   The command of the <u>Lord</u> is clear,
   it gives light <u>to</u> the eyes.

3. The fear of the <u>Lord</u> is holy,
   abi<u>ding</u> for ever.
   The decrees of the <u>Lord</u> are truth
   and all <u>of</u> them just.

4. May the spoken words <u>of</u> my mouth,
   the thoughts <u>of</u> my heart,
   win favour in your <u>sight</u>, O Lord,
   my rescu<u>er</u>, my rock!

Gospel Acclamation Luke 4:18
   The Lord has sent me to bring the
      good news <u>to</u> the poor,
   to proclaim liber<u>ty</u> to captives.

4. My lips will tell <u>of</u> your justice
   and day by day <u>of</u> your help.
   O God, you have taught me <u>from</u> my
      youth
   and I proclaim your <u>won</u>ders still.

Gospel Acclamation John 14:6
   I am the Way, the Truth <u>and</u> the Life,
      says the Lord;
   no one can come to the Father ex<u>cept</u>
      through me.

890 5th Sunday
in Ordinary Time (C)
Psalm 137:1-5, 7-8. R℣ v.1

Be-fore the an-gels I will bless you, O
Lord.

1. I thank you, Lord, with <u>all</u> my heart,
   you have heard the words <u>of</u> my
      mouth.
   Before the angels <u>I</u> will bless you.
   I will adore before your <u>holy</u> temple.

2. I thank you for your faithful<u>ness</u> and
      love
   which excel all we <u>ever</u> knew of you.
   On the day I <u>called</u>, you answered;
   you increased the strength <u>of</u> my soul.

3. All earth's <u>kings</u> shall thank you
   when they hear the words <u>of</u> your
      mouth.
   They shall sing of <u>the</u> Lord's ways:
   'How great is the glory <u>of</u> the Lord!'

4. You stretch out your <u>hand</u> and save
      me,
   your hand will do all <u>things</u> for me.
   Your love, O Lord, <u>is</u> eternal,
   discard not the work <u>of</u> your hand.

889 4th Sunday
in Ordinary Time (C)
Psalm 70:1-6, 15, 17. R℣ v.15

My   lips   will   tell   of your help.

1. In you, O Lord, <u>I</u> take refuge;
   let me never be <u>put</u> to shame.
   In your justice res<u>cue</u> me, free me:
   pay heed to <u>me</u> and save me.

2. Be a rock where I <u>can</u> take refuge,
   a mighty strong<u>hold</u> to save me;
   for you are my <u>rock</u>, my stronghold.
   Free me from the hand <u>of</u> the wicked.

3. It is you, O Lord, who <u>are</u> my hope,
   my trust, O Lord, <u>since</u> my youth.
   On you I have leaned <u>from</u> my birth,
   from my mother's womb you have
      <u>been</u> my help.

Continued overleaf

Gospel Acclamation John 15:15
I call you friends, <u>says</u> the Lord,
because I have made known to you
everything I have learnt <u>from</u> my
Father.

892 7th Sunday
in Ordinary Time (C)
Psalm 102:1-4, 8, 10, 12-13. R℣ v.8

The Lord is com-pas-sion, com-
pas - sion and love.

1. My soul, give thanks <u>to</u> the Lord,
   all my being, bless his <u>holy</u> name.
   My soul, give thanks <u>to</u> the Lord
   and never forget <u>all</u> his blessings.

2. It is he who forgives <u>all</u> your guilt,
   who heals every one <u>of</u> your ills,
   who redeems your life <u>from</u> the grave,
   who crowns you with love <u>and</u>
   compassion.

3. The Lord is compa<u>ssion</u> and love,
   slow to anger and <u>rich</u> in mercy.
   He does not treat us according <u>to</u> our
   sins
   nor repay us according <u>to</u> our faults.

4. As far as the east is <u>from</u> the west
   so far does he re<u>move</u> our sins.
   As a father has compassion <u>on</u> his sons,
   the Lord has pity on <u>those</u> who fear
   him.

Gospel Acclamation cf. Acts 16:14
Open our <u>hearts</u>, O Lord,
to accept the words <u>of</u> your Son.

891 6th Sunday
in Ordinary Time (C)
Psalm 1:1-4, 6. R℣ Psalm 39:5

Hap-py are those, hap-py are those who have
placed their trust in the Lord.

1. Happy indeed are those who follow
   not the counsel <u>of</u> the wicked;
   nor linger in the way of sinners nor
   sit in the compa<u>ny</u> of scorners,
   but whose delight is the law <u>of</u> the Lord
   and who ponder his law <u>day</u> and night.

2. They are like a tree that is planted
   beside the <u>flowing</u> waters,
   that yields its fruit <u>in</u> due season
   and whose leaves shall <u>never</u> fade;
   and all that they <u>do</u> shall prosper.

3. Not so are the wic<u>ked</u>, not so!
   For they like winnowed chaff shall be
   driven away <u>by</u> the wind.
   For the Lord guards the way <u>of</u> the just
   but the way of the wicked <u>leads</u> to
   doom.

Gospel Acclamation cf. Matthew 11:25
Blessed are you, Father, Lord of
   hea<u>ven</u> and earth,
for revealing the mysteries of the
   kingdom <u>to</u> mere children.

893 8th Sunday
in Ordinary Time (C)
Psalm 91:2-3, 13-16. R℣ cf. v.2

It is good to give you thanks, O Lord,
to give you thanks, O Lord.

1. It is good to give thanks <u>to</u> the Lord
   to make music to your name,
   <u>O</u> Most High,
   to proclaim your love <u>in</u> the morning
   and your truth in the watches <u>of</u> the
   night.

2. The just will flourish <u>like</u> the palm-tree
   and grow like a Le<u>ba</u>non cedar.
   Planted in the house <u>of</u> the Lord
   they will flourish in the courts <u>of</u> our
   God.

3. Still bearing fruit when <u>they</u> are old,
   still full of <u>sap</u>, still green,
   they will proclaim that the <u>Lord</u> is just.
   In him, my rock, there <u>is</u> no wrong.

Gospel Acclamation cf. Acts 16:14
   Open our <u>hearts</u>, O Lord,
   to accept the words <u>of</u> your Son.

894 9th Sunday
in Ordinary Time (C)
Psalm 116:1-2. R℣ Mark 16:15

Go out to the whole world and proclaim the Good News.

1. O praise the Lord, <u>all</u> you nations,
   acclaim him <u>all</u> you peoples!

2. Strong is his <u>love</u> for us;
   he is faith<u>ful</u> for ever.

Gospel Acclamation John 1:14, 12
   The Word was made flesh and <u>lived</u>
   among us;
   to all who did accept him he gave
   power to become child<u>ren</u> of God.

895 10th Sunday
in Ordinary Time (C)
Psalm 29:2, 4-6, 11-13. R℣ v.2

I will praise you, Lord,
you have res - cued me.

1. I will praise you, Lord, <u>you</u> have
   rescued me
   and have not let my enemies rejoice
   <u>over</u> me.
   O Lord, you have raised my soul
   <u>from</u> the dead,
   restored me to life from those who
   sink in<u>to</u> the grave.

2. Sing psalms to the Lord, <u>you</u> who
   love him,
   give thanks to his <u>holy</u> name.
   His anger lasts but a moment; his
   fa<u>vour</u> through life.
   At night there are tears, but joy
   <u>comes</u> with dawn.

3. The Lord listened <u>and</u> had pity.
   The Lord came <u>to</u> my help.
   For me you have changed my
   mourning <u>into</u> dancing;
   O Lord, my God, I will thank <u>you</u>
   for ever.

Gospel Acclamation cf. Ephesians 1:17-18
   May the Father of our Lord Jesus
   Christ enlighten the eyes <u>of</u> our
   mind,
   so that we can see what hope his call
   <u>holds</u> for us.

896
11th Sunday in Ordinary Time (C)
Psalm 31:1-2, 5, 7, 11. R℣ cf. v.5

For - give, Lord, the guilt of my sin.

1. Happy are those whose offence is forgiven,
   whose sin is remitted.
   O happy are those whom the Lord imputes no guilt.

2. But now I have acknowledged my sins:
   my guilt I did not hide.
   And you, Lord, have forgiven
   the guilt of my sin.

3. Rejoice, rejoice in the Lord,
   exult, you just!
   O come, ring out your joy,
   all you upright of heart.

Gospel Acclamation John 14:6
   I am the Way, the Truth and the Life,
   says the Lord;
   no one can come to the Father except
   through me.

897
12th Sunday in Ordinary Time (C)
Psalm 62:2-6, 8-9. R℣ v.2

For you my soul is thirst - ing,

O   Lord, my God.

1. O God, you are my God, for you I long:
   for you my soul is thirsting.
   My body pines for you
   like a dry, weary land without water.

2. So I gaze on you in the sanctuary
   to see your strength and your glory.
   For your love is better than life,
   my lips will speak your praise.

3. So I will bless you all my life,
   in your name I will lift up my hands.
   My soul shall be filled as with a
      banquet,
   my mouth shall praise you with joy.

4. For you have been my help;
   in the shadow of your wings I rejoice.
   My soul clings to you:
   your right hand holds me fast.

Gospel Acclamation John 8:12
   I am the light of the world, says the
   Lord,
   anyone who follows me will have the
   light of life.

898
13th Sunday in Ordinary Time (C)
Psalm 15:1-2, 5, 7-11. R℣ v.1

Pre-serve me, God, I take ref-uge in you.

1. Preserve me, God, I take refuge in you.
   I say to the Lord: 'You are my God.'
   O Lord, it is you who are my portion
      and cup;
   it is you yourself who are my prize.

2. I will bless the Lord who gives me
      counsel,
   who even at night directs my heart.
   I keep the Lord ever in my sight:
   since he is at my right hand, I shall
      stand firm.

3. And so my heart rejoices, my <u>soul</u> is glad;
   even my body shall <u>rest</u> in safety.
   For you will not leave my soul <u>among</u> the dead,
   nor let your beloved <u>know</u> decay.

4. O Lord, <u>you</u> will show me
   the <u>path</u> of life,
   the fullness of joy <u>in</u> your presence,
   at your right hand happ<u>iness</u> for ever.

Gospel Acclamation 1 Samuel 3:9, John 6:68
   Speak, Lord, your ser<u>vant</u> is listening:
   you have the message of e<u>ternal</u> life.

899 14th Sunday in Ordinary Time (C)
Psalm 65:1-7, 16, 20. R℟ v.1

Cry out with joy to God, all the earth.

1. Cry out with joy to God, <u>all</u> the earth,
   O sing to the glory <u>of</u> his name.
   O render him glo<u>rious</u> praise.
   Say to God 'How tremen<u>dous</u> your deeds!'

2. 'Before you all the <u>earth</u> shall bow;
   shall sing to you, sing <u>to</u> your name!'
   Come and see the <u>works</u> of God,
   tremendous his deeds <u>among</u> men.

3. He turned the sea in<u>to</u> dry land,
   they passed through the ri<u>ver</u> dry-shod.
   Let our joy then <u>be</u> in him;
   he rules for ever <u>by</u> his might.

4. Come and hear, all <u>who</u> fear God.
   I will tell what he did <u>for</u> my soul.
   Blessed be God who did not re<u>ject</u> my prayer
   nor with<u>hold</u> his love from me.

Gospel Acclamation John 15:15
   I call you friends, <u>says</u> the Lord,
   because I have made known to you
     everything I have learnt <u>from</u> my Father.

900 15th Sunday in Ordinary Time (C)
Psalm 68:14, 17, 30-31, 34-35,
36-37. R℟ cf. v.33

Seek the Lord, you who are poor, and your hearts will re - vive.

1. This is my prayer to you, my prayer
     <u>for</u> your favour.
   In your great love, answer <u>me</u>,
     O God,
   with your help that <u>never</u> fails:
   Lord, answer, for your <u>love</u> is kind.

2. As for me in my pover<u>ty</u> and pain
   let your help, O God, <u>lift</u> me up.
   I will praise God's name <u>with</u> a song;
   I will glorify him <u>with</u> thanksgiving.

3. The poor when they see it <u>will</u> be glad
   and God-seeking hearts <u>will</u> revive;
   for the Lord listens <u>to</u> the needy
   and does not spurn his servants <u>in</u> their chains.

4. For God will bring <u>help</u> to Zion
   and rebuild the ci<u>ties</u> of Judah.
   The sons of his servants <u>shall</u> inherit it;
   those who love his <u>name</u> shall dwell there.

Continued overleaf

Gospel Acclamation John 10:27
> The sheep that belong to me listen to
> my voice, <u>says</u> the Lord,
> I know them <u>and</u> they follow me.

901 16th Sunday in Ordinary Time (C)
Psalm 14:2-5. R℣ v.1

The just will live in the pre-sence of the

Lord.

1. Lord, who shall dwell on your <u>ho</u>ly
   mountain?
   Those who walk <u>with</u>out fault;
   those who <u>act</u> with justice
   and speak the truth <u>from</u> their hearts.

2. Those who do no wrong <u>to</u> their
   kindred,
   who cast no slur <u>on</u> their neighbour,
   who hold the godless <u>in</u> disdain,
   but honour those who <u>fear</u> the Lord.

3. Those who keep their pledge,
   <u>come</u> what may;
   who take no interest <u>on</u> a loan
   and accept no bribes <u>against</u> the
   innocent.
   Such people will stand <u>firm</u> for ever.

Gospel Acclamation cf. Acts 16:14
> Open our <u>hearts</u>, O Lord,
> to accept the words <u>of</u> your Son.

902 17th Sunday in Ordinary Time (C)
Psalm 137:1-3, 6-8. R℣ v.3

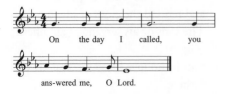

On the day I called, you

ans-wered me, O Lord.

1. I thank you, Lord with <u>all</u> my heart,
   you have heard the words <u>of</u> my mouth.
   Before the angels <u>I</u> will bless you.
   I will adore before your <u>ho</u>ly temple.

2. I thank you for your faithful<u>ness</u> and
   love
   which excel all we <u>ev</u>er knew of you.
   On the day I <u>called</u>, you answered;
   you increased the strength <u>of</u> my
   soul.

3. The Lord is high yet he looks <u>on</u> the
   lowly
   and the haughty he knows <u>from</u> afar.
   Though I walk in the midst <u>of</u>
   affliction
   you give me life and frus<u>trate</u> my foes.

4. You stretch out your <u>hand</u> and save me,
   your hand will do all <u>things</u> for me.
   Your love, O Lord, <u>is</u> eternal,
   discard not the work <u>of</u> your hands.

Gospel Acclamation John 1:14, 12
> The Word was made flesh and <u>lived</u>
> among us;
> to all who did accept him he gave
> power to become child<u>ren</u> of God.

903 18th Sunday in Ordinary Time (C)
Psalm 89:3-6, 12-14, 17. R℣ v.1

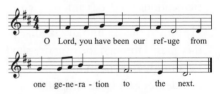

O Lord, you have been our ref-uge from

one ge-ne-ra - tion to the next.

1. You turn us back <u>into</u> dust
   and say: 'Go back children <u>of</u> the earth.'
   To your eyes a thousand years are like
   yesterday, <u>come</u> and gone,
   no more than a watch <u>in</u> the night.

2. You sweep us away <u>like</u> a dream,
   like grass which springs up <u>in</u> the
      morning.
   In the morning it springs <u>up</u> and
      flowers:
   by evening it wi<u>thers</u> and fades.

3. Make us know the shortness <u>of</u> our
      life
   that we may gain wis<u>dom</u> of heart.
   Lord, relent! Is your <u>anger</u> for ever?
   Show pity <u>to</u> your servants.

4. In the morning, fill us <u>with</u> your love;
   we shall exult and rejoice <u>all</u> our days.
   Let the favour of the Lord <u>be</u> upon us:
   give success to the work <u>of</u> our hands.

Gospel Acclamation cf. John 17:17
   Your word is <u>truth</u>, O Lord,
   consecrate us <u>in</u> the truth.

904 19th Sunday
     in Ordinary Time (C)
     Psalm 32:1, 12, 18-20, 22. R℞ v.12

Hap-py the peo-ple the Lord has cho-sen as his
own.

1. Ring out your joy to the Lord,
      <u>O</u> you just;
   for praise is fitting for <u>loyal</u> hearts.
   They are happy, whose God <u>is</u> the
      Lord,
   the people he has chosen <u>as</u> his own.

2. The Lord looks down on those <u>who</u>
      revere him,
   on those who hope <u>in</u> his love,
   to rescue their <u>souls</u> from death,
   to keep them a<u>live</u> in famine.

3. Our soul is waiting <u>for</u> the Lord.
   The Lord is our help <u>and</u> our shield.
   May your love be upon <u>us</u>, O Lord,
   as we place all our <u>hope</u> in you.

Gospel Acclamation cf. Matthew 11:25
   Blessed are you, Father, Lord of
      hea<u>ven</u> and earth,
   for revealing the mysteries of the
      kingdom <u>to</u> mere children.

905 20th Sunday
     in Ordinary Time (C)
     Psalm 39:2-4, 18. R℞ v.14

Lord, come to my aid, Lord, come to my
aid!

1. I waited, I waited <u>for</u> the Lord
   and <u>he</u> stooped down to me;
   he <u>heard</u> my cry,
   he <u>heard</u> my cry.

2. He drew me from the <u>deadly</u> pit,
   from the <u>miry</u> clay.
   He set my feet up<u>on</u> a rock
   and made my <u>foot</u>steps firm.

3. He put a new song in<u>to</u> my mouth,
   praise <u>of</u> our God.
   Many shall <u>see</u> and fear
   and shall trust <u>in</u> the Lord.

4. As for me, wret<u>ched</u> and poor,
   the Lord <u>thinks</u> of me.
   You are my rescu<u>er</u>, my help,
   O God, do <u>not</u> delay.

Gospel Acclamation cf. Acts 16:14
   Open our <u>heart</u>, O Lord,
   to accept the words <u>of</u> your Son.

906

21st Sunday
in Ordinary Time (C)
Psalm 116:1-2. R℣ Mark 16:15

Go out to the whole world and pro-claim the Good News.

1. O praise the Lord, all you nations,
   acclaim him, all you peoples!

2. Strong is his love for us;
   he is faithful for ever.

Gospel Acclamation John 14:23
   If anyone loves me they will keep my
   word,
   and my Father will love them and we
   shall come to them.

907

22nd Sunday
in Ordinary Time (C)
Psalm 67:4-7, 10-11. R℣ cf. v.11

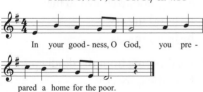

In your good-ness, O God, you pre-pared a home for the poor.

1. The just shall rejoice at the presence
   of God,
   they shall exult and dance for joy.
   O sing to the Lord, make music to
   his name;
   rejoice in the Lord, exult at his
   presence.

2. Father of the orphan, defender of the
   widow,
   such is God in his holy place.
   God gives the lonely a home to live in;
   he leads the prisoners forth into
   freedom.

3. You poured down, O God, a
   generous rain:
   when your people were starved you
   gave them new life.
   It was there that your people found a
   home,
   prepared in your goodness, O God,
   for the poor.

Gospel Acclamation John 14:23
   If anyone loves me they will keep my
   word,
   and my Father will love them and we
   shall come to them.

908

23rd Sunday
in Ordinary Time (C)
Psalm 89:3-6, 12-14, 17. R℣ v.1

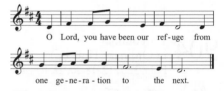

O Lord, you have been our ref-uge from one ge-ne-ra-tion to the next.

1. You turn us back into dust
   and say: 'Go back children of the earth.'
   To your eyes a thousand years are like
   yesterday, come and gone,
   no more than a watch in the night.

2. You sweep us away like a dream,
   like grass which springs up in the
   morning.
   In the morning it springs up and
   flowers:
   by evening it withers and fades.

3. Make us know the shortness of our life
   that we may gain wisdom of heart.
   Lord, relent! Is your anger for ever?
   Show pity to your servants.

4. In the morning, fill us <u>with</u> your love;
   we shall exult and rejoice <u>all</u> our days.
   Let the favour of the Lord <u>be</u> upon us:
   give success to the work <u>of</u> our hands.

Gospel Acclamation John 15:15
   I call you friends, <u>says</u> the Lord,
   because I have made known to you
      everything I have learnt <u>from</u> my
      Father.

909 24th Sunday in Ordinary Time (C)
Psalm 50:3-4, 12-13, 17, 19.
R℣ Luke 15:18

I will leave this place and
go to my Fa - ther.

1. Have mercy on me, God, <u>in</u> your
      kindness.
   In your compassion, blot out <u>my</u>
      offence.
   O wash me more and more <u>from</u> my
      guilt
   and cleanse me <u>from</u> my sin.

2. A pure heart create for <u>me</u>, O God,
   put a steadfast sp<u>ir</u>it within me.
   Do not cast me away <u>from</u> your
      presence,
   nor deprive me of your <u>Ho</u>ly Spirit.

3. O Lord, o<u>pen</u> my lips
   and my mouth shall de<u>clare</u> your
      praise.
   My sacrifice is a <u>con</u>trite spirit;
   a humbled, contrite heart you <u>will</u>
      not spurn.

Gospel Acclamation cf. Ephesians 1:17-18
   May the Father of our Lord Jesus
      Christ enlighten the eyes <u>of</u> our
      mind,
   so that we can see what hope his call
      <u>holds</u> for us.

910 25th Sunday in Ordinary Time (C)
Psalm 112:1-2, 4-8. R℣ cf. vv.1, 7

Praise the Lord, who rai - ses the poor.

1. Praise, O servants <u>of</u> the Lord,
   praise the name <u>of</u> the Lord!
   May the name of the <u>Lord</u> be blessed
   both now and for <u>ever</u>more.

2. Who is like the <u>Lord</u>, our God,
   who has risen on high <u>to</u> his throne
   yet stoops from the heights <u>to</u> look
      down,
   to look down upon hea<u>ven</u> and earth?

3. From the dust he lifts <u>up</u> the lowly,
   from the dungheap he rai<u>ses</u> the poor
   to set them in the compa<u>ny</u> of rulers,
   yes, with the rulers <u>of</u> his people.

Gospel Acclamation cf. Acts 16:14
   Open our <u>hearts</u>, O Lord,
   to accept the words <u>of</u> your Son.

911 26th Sunday in Ordinary Time (C)
Psalm 145:6-10. R℣ v.2

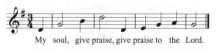

My soul, give praise, give praise to the Lord.

1. It is the Lord who keeps <u>faith</u> for ever,
   who is just to those who <u>are</u> oppressed.
   It is he who gives bread <u>to</u> the hungry,
   the Lord, who sets pri<u>so</u>ners free.

Continued overleaf

2. It is the Lord who gives sight <u>to</u> the blind,
who raises up those who <u>are</u> bowed down.
It is the Lord who <u>loves</u> the just,
the Lord, who pro<u>tects</u> the stranger.

3. He upholds the wi<u>dow</u> and orphan,
but thwarts the path <u>of</u> the wicked.
The Lord will <u>reign</u> for ever,
Zion's God, from <u>age</u> to age.

Gospel Acclamation John 10:27
The sheep that belong to me listen to my voice, <u>says</u> the Lord,
I know them <u>and</u> they follow me.

3. O that today you would listen <u>to</u> his voice!
'Harden not your hearts <u>as</u> at Meribah,
as on that day at Massah in the desert, when your fathers put me <u>to</u> the test;
when they tried me, though they <u>saw</u> my work.'

Gospel Acclamation 1 Samuel 3:9; John 6:68
Speak, Lord, your ser<u>vant</u> is listening:
you have the message of e<u>ter</u>nal life.

913 28th Sunday in Ordinary Time (C)
Psalm 97:1-4. R℣ cf. v.2

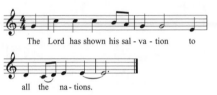

The Lord has shown his sal - va - tion to all the na - tions.

1. Sing a new song <u>to</u> the Lord
for he <u>has</u> worked wonders.
His right hand and his <u>holy</u> arm
have <u>brought</u> salvation.

2. The Lord has made known <u>his</u> salvation;
has shown his justice <u>to</u> the nations.
He has remembered his <u>truth</u> and love
for the <u>house</u> of Israel.

3. All the ends of the <u>earth</u> have seen
the salvation <u>of</u> our God.
Shout to the Lord <u>all</u> the earth,
ring <u>out</u> your joy.

Gospel Acclamation cf. John 6:63, 68
Your words are spirit, Lord, and <u>they</u> are life:
you have the message of e<u>ter</u>nal life.

912 27th Sunday in Ordinary Time (C)
Psalm 94:1-2, 6-9. R℣ v.9

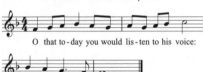

O that to - day you would lis - ten to his voice:
'Har - den not your hearts.'

1. Come, ring out our joy <u>to</u> the Lord;
hail the <u>rock</u> who saves us.
Let us come before him, <u>giving</u> thanks,
with songs let us <u>hail</u> the Lord.

2. Come in; let us bow <u>and</u> bend low;
let us kneel before the <u>God</u> who made us
for he is our God, and we the people
who belong <u>to</u> his pasture,
the flock that is led <u>by</u> his hand.

914 — 29th Sunday in Ordinary Time (C)
Psalm 120. R℣ cf. v.2

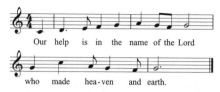

Our help is in the name of the Lord
who made hea-ven and earth.

1. I lift up my eyes <u>to</u> the mountains:
   from where shall <u>come</u> my help?
   My help shall come <u>from</u> the Lord
   who made hea<u>ven</u> and earth.

2. May he never allow <u>you</u> to stumble!
   Let him sleep <u>not</u>, your guard.
   No, he sleeps <u>not</u> nor slumbers,
   Is<u>ra</u>el's guard.

3. The Lord is your guard <u>and</u> your shade;
   at your right <u>side</u> he stands.
   By day the sun <u>shall</u> not smite you
   nor the moon <u>in</u> the night.

4. The Lord will guard <u>you</u> from evil,
   he will <u>guard</u> your soul.
   The Lord will guard your <u>go</u>ing and
       coming
   both now <u>and</u> for ever.

Gospel Acclamation cf. Ephesians 1:17-18
   May the Father of our Lord Jesus
       Christ enlighten the eyes <u>of</u> our
       mind,
   so that we can see what hope his call
       <u>holds</u> for us.

915 — 30th Sunday in Ordinary Time (C)
Psalm 33:2-3, 17-19, 23. R℣ v.7

The Lord hears the cry, the
cry of the poor.

1. I will bless the Lord <u>at</u> all times,
   his praise always <u>on</u> my lips;
   in the Lord my soul shall <u>make</u> its
       boast.
   The humble shall hear <u>and</u> be glad.

2. The Lord turns his face a<u>gainst</u> the
       wicked
   to destroy their remembrance <u>from</u>
       the earth.
   The just call and <u>the</u> Lord hears
   and rescues them in all <u>their</u> distress.

3. The Lord is close to the <u>bro</u>ken-
       hearted;
   those whose spirit is crushed <u>he</u> will
       save.
   The Lord ransoms the souls <u>of</u> his
       servants.
   Those who hide in him shall not <u>be</u>
       condemned.

Gospel Acclamation cf. Matthew 11:25
   Blessed are you, Father, Lord of
       hea<u>ven</u> and earth,
   for revealing the mysteries of the
       kingdom <u>to</u> mere children.

916 — 31st Sunday in Ordinary Time (C)
Psalm 144:1-2, 8-11, 13-14. R℣ v.1

I will bless your name for e - ver, O
God my King.

1. I will give you glory, O <u>God</u> my King,
   I will bless your <u>name</u> for ever.
   I will bless you day <u>after</u> day
   and praise your <u>name</u> for ever.

Continued overleaf

2. The Lord is kind and full of
     compassion,
   slow to anger, abounding in love.
   How good is the Lord to all,
   compassionate to all his creatures.

3. All your creatures shall thank you,
     O Lord,
   and your friends shall repeat their
     blessing.
   They shall speak of the glory of your
     reign
   and declare your might, O God.

4. The Lord is faithful in all his words
   and loving in all his deeds.
   The Lord supports all who fall
   and raises all who are bowed down.

Gospel Acclamation Luke 19:38
   Blessings on the King who comes in
     the name of the Lord!
   Peace in heaven and glory in the
     highest heavens!

917 32nd Sunday
in Ordinary Time (C)
Psalm 16:1, 5-6, 8, 15. R℣ v.15

I shall be filled when I   a - wake with the

sight of your glo - ry, O Lord.

1. Lord, hear a cause that is just,
   pay heed to my cry.
   Turn your ear to my prayer:
   no deceit is on my lips.

2. I kept my feet firmly in your paths;
   there was no faltering in my steps.
   I am here and I call you, you will
     hear me, O God.
   Turn your ear to me; hear my words.

3. Guard me as the apple of your eye.
   Hide me in the shadow of your wings.
   As for me, in my justice I shall see
     your face
   and be filled, when I awake, with the
     sight of your glory.

Gospel Acclamation Luke 21:36
   Stay awake, praying at all times
   for the strength to stand with
     confidence before the Son of Man.

918 33rd Sunday
in Ordinary Time (C)
Psalm 97:5-9. R℣ cf. v.9

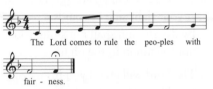

The Lord comes to rule the peo-ples with

fair - ness.

1. Sing psalms to the Lord with the harp
   with the sound of music.
   With trumpets and the sound of the
     horn
   acclaim the King, the Lord.

2. Let the sea and all within it, thunder;
   the world, and all its peoples.
   Let the rivers clap their hands
   and the hills ring out their joy.

3. Rejoice at the presence of the Lord,
   for he comes to rule the earth.
   He will rule the world with justice
   and the peoples with fairness.

Gospel Acclamation Luke 21:36
   Stay awake, praying at all times
   for the strength to stand with
     confidence before the Son of Man.

919 Our Lord Jesus Christ,
Universal King (C)
Psalm 121:1-5. R℞ v.1

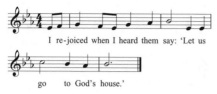

I re-joiced when I heard them say: 'Let us

go to God's house.'

1. I rejoiced when I <u>heard</u> them say:
'Let us go <u>to</u> God's house.'
And now our <u>feet</u> are standing
within your gates, <u>O</u> Jerusalem.

2. Jerusalem is built <u>as</u> a city
strong<u>ly</u> compact.
It is there that the <u>tribes</u> go up,
the tribes <u>of</u> the Lord.

3. For Israel's <u>law</u> it is,
there to praise <u>the</u> Lord's name.
There were set the <u>thrones</u> of
judgement
of the <u>house</u> of David.

Gospel Acclamation Mark 11:9, 10
Blessings on him who comes in the
name <u>of</u> the Lord!
Blessings on the coming kingdom of
our <u>father</u> David!

920 The Presentation of the Lord
(A, B, C)
Psalm 23:7-10. R℞ v.8

Who is this King of Glo - ry? It

is the Lord.

1. O gates, lift <u>up</u> your heads;
grow higher, <u>ancient</u> doors.
Let him enter, the <u>King</u> of Glory!

2. Who is the <u>King</u> of Glory?
The Lord, the migh<u>ty</u>, the valiant,
the Lord, the vali<u>ant</u> in war.

3. O gates, lift <u>high</u> your heads;
grow higher, <u>ancient</u> doors.
Let him enter, the <u>King</u> of Glory!

4. Who is he, the <u>King</u> of Glory?
He, the <u>Lord</u> of armies,
he is the <u>King</u> of Glory!

Gospel Acclamation Luke 2:32
The light to enligh<u>ten</u> the Gentiles
and give glory to Isra<u>el</u>, your people.

921 The Birth of St John the
Baptist (A, B, C)
Psalm 138:1-3, 13-15. R℞ v.14

I thank you, Lord, for the won - der of my

be - ing.

1. O Lord, you search me and you
know me, you know my resting
<u>and</u> my rising,
you discern my purpose <u>from</u> afar.
You mark when I walk <u>or</u> lie down,
all my ways lie o<u>pen</u> to you.

2. For it was you who crea<u>ted</u> my being,
knit me together in my <u>mother's</u>
womb.
I thank you for the wonder <u>of</u> my
being,
for the wonders of all <u>your</u> creation.

3. Already you <u>knew</u> my soul,
my body held no sec<u>ret</u> from you
when I was being <u>fashioned</u> in secret
and moulded in the depths <u>of</u> the
earth.

Continued overleaf

Gospel Acclamation cf. Luke 1:76
As for you, little child, you shall be
called a prophet of God, <u>the</u> Most
High.
You shall go ahead of the Lord to
prepare his <u>ways</u> before him.

922 SS Peter and Paul, Apostles
(A, B, C)
Psalm 33:2-9. R̶℣ v.5

From all my ter-rors the Lord has set me

free.

1. I will bless the Lord <u>at</u> all times,
his praise always <u>on</u> my lips;
in the Lord my soul shall <u>make</u> its
boast.
The humble shall hear <u>and</u> be glad.

2. Glorify the <u>Lord</u> with me.
Together let us <u>praise</u> his name.
I sought the Lord <u>and</u> he answered me;
from all my terrors he <u>set</u> me free.

3. Look towards him <u>and</u> be radiant;
let your faces not <u>be</u> abashed.
When the poor cry out <u>the</u> Lord
hears them,
and rescues them from all <u>their</u> distress.

4. The angel of the Lord <u>is</u> encamped
around those who revere <u>him</u>, to
rescue them.
Taste and see that the <u>Lord</u> is good.
They are happy who seek re<u>fuge</u> in
him.

Gospel Acclamation Matthew 16:18
You are Peter and on this rock I will
<u>build</u> my church.
And the gates of the underworld can
never hold <u>out</u> against it.

923 The Transfiguration of the
Lord (A, B, C)
Psalm 96:1-2, 5-6, 9. R̶℣ vv.1, 9

The Lord is King, most

high a-bove all the earth.

1. The Lord is King, let <u>earth</u> rejoice,
let all the coast<u>lands</u> be glad.
Cloud and darkness <u>are</u> his raiment;
his throne, jus<u>tice</u> and right.

2. The mountains <u>melt</u> like wax
before the Lord of <u>all</u> the earth.
The skies pro<u>claim</u> his justice;
all peoples <u>see</u> his glory.

3. For you indeed <u>are</u> the Lord
most high above <u>all</u> the earth,
exalted far a<u>bove</u> all spirits,
exalted far a<u>bove</u> all spirits.

Gospel Acclamation Matthew 17:5
This is my Son, <u>the</u> Beloved,
he enjoys my favour; <u>listen</u> to him.

924 The Assumption of the
Blessed Virgin Mary (A, B, C)
Psalm 44:10-12, 16. R̶℣ v.10

On your right hand stands the queen, in

gar - ments of gold.

1. The daughters of kings are a<u>mong</u>
   your loved ones.
   On your right stands the queen in
   <u>gold</u> of Ophir.
   Listen, O daughter, give ear <u>to</u> my
   words:
   forget your own people and your
   <u>fa</u>ther's house.

2. So will the king de<u>sire</u> your beauty.
   He is your lord, pay hom<u>age</u> to him.
   They are escorted amid glad<u>ness</u> and
   joy;
   they pass within the palace <u>of</u> the king.

Gospel Acclamation
   Mary has been taken up <u>into</u> heaven;
   all the choirs of angels <u>are</u> rejoicing.

925 The Triumph of the Cross
(A, B, C)
Psalm 77:1-2, 34-38. R℣ v.7

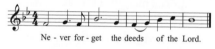
Ne - ver for - get   the deeds   of the Lord.

1. Give heed, my people, <u>to</u> my teaching;
   turn your ear to the words <u>of</u> my
   mouth.
   I will open my mouth <u>in</u> a parable
   and reveal hidden lessons <u>of</u> the past.

2. When he slew them then <u>they</u> would
   seek him,
   return and seek <u>him</u> in earnest.
   They would remember that God <u>was</u>
   their rock,
   God the Most High <u>their</u> Redeemer.

3. But the words they spoke <u>were</u> mere
   flattery;
   they lied to him <u>with</u> their lips.
   For their hearts were not <u>truly</u> with
   him;
   they were not faithful <u>to</u> his covenant.

4. Yet he who is full <u>of</u> compassion
   forgave their <u>sin</u> and spared them.
   So often he held <u>back</u> his anger
   when he might have stirred <u>up</u> his rage.

Gospel Acclamation
   We adore you, O Christ, <u>and</u> we
   bless you;
   because by your cross you have
   re<u>deemed</u> the world.

926 All Saints (A, B, C)
Psalm 23:1-6. R℣ cf. v.6

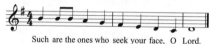
Such are the ones who seek your face, O Lord.

1. The Lord's is the earth <u>and</u> its fullness,
   the world and <u>all</u> its peoples.
   It is he who set it <u>on</u> the seas;
   on the waters he <u>made</u> it firm.

2. Who shall climb the mountain <u>of</u> the
   Lord?
   Who shall stand in his <u>holy</u> place?
   Those with clean hands <u>and</u> pure heart,
   who desire not <u>worthless</u> things.

3. They shall receive blessings <u>from</u> the
   Lord
   and reward from the <u>God</u> who saves
   them.
   Such are the <u>ones</u> who seek him,
   seek the face of the <u>God</u> of Jacob.

Gospel Acclamation Matthew 11:28
   Come to me, all you who labour and
   are <u>overburdened</u>,
   and I will give you rest, <u>says</u> the Lord.

927 The Commemoration of all the Faithful Departed (A, B, C)

Psalm 26:1, 4, 7-9, 13-14. R℔ v.1

I am sure I shall see the Lord's
good-ness in the land of the liv-ing.

1. The Lord is my light <u>and</u> my help;
   whom <u>shall</u> I fear?
   The Lord is the stronghold <u>of</u> my life;
   before whom <u>shall</u> I shrink?

2. There is one thing I ask <u>of</u> the Lord,
   for <u>this</u> I long,
   to live in the house <u>of</u> the Lord,
   all the days <u>of</u> my life.

3. O Lord, hear my voice <u>when</u> I call;
   have mer<u>cy</u> and answer.
   It is your face, O Lord, <u>that</u> I seek;
   hide <u>not</u> your face.

4. I am sure I shall see <u>the</u> Lord's goodness
   in the land <u>of</u> the living.
   Hope in him, hold firm <u>and</u> take heart.
   Hope <u>in</u> the Lord!

Gospel Acclamation John 6:39
   It is my Father's will, says the Lord,
      that I should lose nothing of all
      that <u>he</u> has given me,
   and that I should raise it up <u>on</u> the
      last day.

928 The Dedication of a Church (A, B, C)

Psalm 45:2-3, 5-6, 8-9. R℔ v.5

The wa-ters of the ri-ver give joy, give
joy to God's ci-ty.

1. God is for us a re<u>fuge</u> and strength,
   a helper close at hand, in time <u>of</u>
      distress:
   so we shall not fear though the <u>earth</u>
      should rock,
   though the mountains fall into the
      depths <u>of</u> the sea.

2. The waters of a river give joy <u>to</u> God's
      city,
   the holy place where the <u>Most</u> High
      dwells.
   God is within, it can<u>not</u> be shaken;
   God will help it at the dawning <u>of</u>
      the day.

3. The Lord of <u>hosts</u> is with us:
   the God of Jacob <u>is</u> our stronghold.
   Come, consider the works <u>of</u> the Lord
   the redoubtable deeds he has done <u>on</u>
      the earth.

Gospel Acclamation 2 Chronicles 7:16
   I have chosen and consecrated this
      house, <u>says</u> the Lord,
   for my name to be <u>there</u> for ever.

929 Alleluia for use throughout the year

Al-le-lu-ia, al - le-lu-ia, al-le - lu - ia.

930 Alleluia for use throughout the year

Al - le - lu - ia, al - le -
lu - ia, al - le - lu - ia,
al - le - lu - ia.

931 Alleluia for use throughout the year

Al‑le‑lu‑ia, al‑le‑lu‑ia, al‑le‑lu‑ia, al‑le‑lu‑ia, al‑le‑lu‑ia, al‑le‑lu‑ia, al‑le‑lu‑ia, al‑le‑lu‑ia, al‑le‑lu‑ia.

932 Alleluia for use throughout the year

Hal‑le, hal‑le, hal‑le‑lu‑jah! Hal‑le, hal‑le, hal‑le‑lu‑jah! Hal‑le, hal‑le, hal‑le‑lu‑jah! Hal‑le‑lu‑jah, hal‑le‑lu‑jah!

933 Acclamation for use during Lent and Holy Week

Praise to you, O Christ, King of e‑ter‑nal glo‑ry!

934 Acclamation for use during Lent and Holy Week

Glo‑ry and praise to you, O Christ!

935 Acclamation for use during Lent and Holy Week

Praise and hon‑our to you, Lord Je‑sus.

936 Acclamation for use during Lent and Holy Week

Glo‑ry to you, O Christ, you are the Word of God!

Full liturgy planning indexes will be found in the Melody and Organ editions of *Catholic Hymns Old & New* and are also available separately from the publisher. Contact details will be found on the second page of this book.

Index of First Lines and Titles

This index gives the first line of each hymn. If a hymn is known also by a title (e.g. Jerusalem) this is given as well, but indented and in italics.

A

A butterfly, an Easter egg	1
A new commandment	2
A blessing	366
A touching place	91
Abba, Abba, Father	3
Abba, Father, from your hands	4
Abba, Father, send your Spirit	5
Abide with me	6
Across the years there echoes still	7
Adeste fideles	8
Adoramus te, Domine	9
Adoramus te, Domine Deus	10
Advent Ring	90
Advent song	103
All are welcome	319
All creation, bless the Lord	11
All creatures of our God and King	12
All glory, laud and honour	13
All glory, laud and honour	14
All God's people, here together	15
All hail the power of Jesus' name	16
All heaven declares	17
All my hope on God is founded	18
All over the world	19
All people that on earth do dwell	20
All that I am	21
All the earth proclaim the Lord	22
All the nations of the earth	23
All things bright and beautiful	24
All who would valiant be	25
All you who seek a comfort sure	26
Alleluia, alleluia, give thanks to the risen Lord	27
Alleluia, alleluia! I will praise the Father	28
Alleluia, sing to Jesus	29
Alma redemptoris mater	30
Almighty Father, Lord most high	31
Amazing grace	32
An upper room did our Lord prepare	33
And did those feet	34
Angels from the realms of glory	35
Angels we have heard on high	36
Arise, come to your God	37
As earth that is dry	38
As gentle as silence	433
As I kneel before you	39
As the deer longs	40
As the deer pants for the water	41
As with gladness men of old	42

At the cross she keeps her station	43
At the Lamb's high feast we sing	44
At the name of Jesus	45
At your feet	46
Ave Maria	47
Ave Maria, O maiden, O mother	48
Ave, Regina caelorum!	49
Ave verum corpus	50
Awake, awake: fling off the night!	51
Awake from your slumber!	52
Away in a manger	53

B

Battle is o'er, hell's armies flee	54
Be humble of heart	112
Be not afraid	644
Be still and know	55
Be still and know I am with you	56
Be still and know that I am God	57
Be still, for the presence of the Lord	58
Be still, my soul	59
Be thou my vision	60
Because the Lord is my shepherd	61
Behold, the Lamb of God	62
Benedictus qui venit	63
Bethlehem, of noblest cities	64
Bind us together, Lord	65
Bless the Lord, my soul	66
Bless the Lord, O my soul	67
Blessed be God	69
Blest are the pure in heart	68
Blest are you, Lord	69
Blest be the Lord	70
Breathe on me, breath of God	71
Bridegroom and bride	183
Bring, all ye dear-bought nations	72
Bring flowers of the rarest	73
Bring forth the kingdom	639
Broken for me	74
Brother, sister, let me serve you	75
By the blood that flowed from thee	76
By the waters of Babylon	77

C

Called to shed light	78
Calm me, Lord	79
Centre of my life	298
Child in the manger	80
Children of Jerusalem	81
Christ be beside me	82
Christ be with me	83
Christ, be our light	329
Christ is King of earth and heaven!	84
Christ is made the sure foundation	85
Christ is our King	86
Christ the Lord is risen today	87

Christ triumphant	88
City of God	52
Christ, be our light	329
Christians, awake!	89
Christmas is coming	90
Christ's is the world	91
Christus vincit	92
City of God	52
Close to you	248
Colours of day	93
Come and celebrate	94
Come and find the quiet centre	95
Come and join the celebration	96
Come and praise him	97
Come back to me	98
Come, come, come to the manger	99
Come down, O Love divine	100
Come, Holy Ghost, Creator, come	101
Come into his presence	102
Come, Lord Jesus	103
Come, Lord Jesus, come	104
Come, my Way, my Truth, my Life	105
Come now, the table's spread	106
Come, O divine Messiah!	107
Come on and celebrate	108
Come, praise the Lord	109
Come, they told me	110
Come, thou long-expected Jesus	111
Come to me, come, my people	112
Come to set us free	113
Come to the table of the Lord	114
Come to the water	413
Come, ye thankful people, come	115
Confitemini Domino	116
Creator of the day	117
Creator of the stars of night	118
Crown him with many crowns	119

D

Daily, daily, sing to Mary	120
Dance in your Spirit	121
Day is done, but love unfailing	122
Dear Lord and Father of mankind	123
Ding dong, merrily on high!	124
Do not be afraid	125
Dona nobis pacem	126
Don't build your house on the sandy land	127

E

Earthen vessels	612
Eat this bread	128
Embrace the universe with love	129
Enemy of apathy	496
Eternal Father, strong to save	130
Exaudi nos, Domine	131